ROCKIN' IN TIME

SECOND EDITION

ROCKIN' IN TIME

A Social History
of
Rock-and-Roll

David P. Szatmary

PRENTICE HALL, Englewood Cliffs, New Jersey 07632

Library of Congress Cataloging-in-Publication Data

Szatmary, David P., 1951-
   Rockin' in time : a social history of rock-and-roll / David P.
Szatmary. -- 2nd ed.
     p.   cm.
   Includes index.
   ISBN 0-13-775339-X
   1. Rock music--United States--History and criticism.   I. Title.
II. Title: Rocking in time.
ML3534.S94 1991
781.66'0973--dc20   91-2317
                                                               CIP
                                                                MN

Acquisition editor: Bud Therien
Editorial/production supervision and
   interior design: Mary McKinley
Cover design: Bruce Kenselaar
Prepress buyer: Herb Klein
Manufacturing buyer: Patrice Fraccio

 © 1991, 1987 by Prentice-Hall, Inc.
A Simon & Schuster Company
Englewood Cliffs, New Jersey 07632

Printed in the United States of America

10 9 8 7

ISBN 0-13-775339-X

Prentice-Hall International (UK) Limited, *London*
Prentice-Hall of Australia Pty. Limited, *Sydney*
Prentice-Hall of Canada Inc., *Toronto*
Prentice-Hall Hispanoamericana, S.A., *Mexico*
Prentice-Hall of India Private Limited, *New Delhi*
Prentice-Hall of Japan, Inc., *Tokyo*
Simon & Schuster Asia Pte. Ltd., *Singapore*
Editora Prentice-Hall do Brasil, Ltda., *Rio de Janeiro*

To My Father and Mother

CONTENTS

PREFACE

This book intends to be a social history of rock-and-roll. It will place an ever-changing rock music in the context of American and, to some extent, British history from roughly 1950 to 1990. *Rockin' In Time* will try to explain how rock-and-roll both influenced and was affected by major social transformations of the last forty years.

Rockin' In Time concentrates on a number of main themes. It shows the importance of African-American culture in the stylistic development of rock music. The blues, originating in the work songs of American slaves, provided the foundation for rock. During the early 1950s, southern blacks who had migrated to Chicago created an urbanized, electric rhythm and blues that was the immediate precursor of rock-and-roll and served as the testing ground for pioneer rock and rollers such as Little Richard and Chuck Berry. Blacks continued to create such new styles as the Motown sound and the soul explosion of the 1960s, the disco beat of the next decade, and, most recently, rap music.

The new rock styles many times coincided with and reflected the struggle of African-Americans for equality. The rhythm and blues of Muddy Waters gained popularity amid the beginnings of the civil rights movement during the 1950s. In the early 1960s as the movement for civil rights gained momentum, folk protesters such as Bob Dylan and Joan Baez sang paeans about the cause. In 1964 and 1965 as Congress passed the most sweeping civil rights legislation since the Civil War, Motown artists topped the popular charts. When disgruntled, frustrated blacks took to the streets later in the decade, soul musicians such as Aretha Franklin shouted for respect. During the late eighties and into the nineties, hip hoppers such as Public Enemy rapped about inequality and called for a new black identity.

As the civil rights struggle began to foster an awareness and acceptance of African-American culture, rock-and-roll became accessible to white teenagers. Teens such as Elvis Presley listened to late-night, rhythm-and-blues radio shows that started to challenge and break down racial barriers. During the 1960s, black performers such as the Ronettes, the Crystals, the Temptations, and the Supremes achieved mass popularity among both blacks and whites. By the 1980s, black entertainers such as Michael Jackson achieved superstar status. Throughout the last forty years, rock music has helped integrate white and black America.

A dramatic population growth during the postwar era provided the audience for a black-inspired rock-and-roll. After World War II, both the United States and Great Britain experienced a tremendous baby boom. By the mid-1950s, the baby boomers had become an army of youngsters who demanded their own music. Along with their older brothers and sisters who had been born during the war, they latched onto the new rock-and-roll, idolizing Little Richard and Chuck Berry. Blacks continued to create such new styles as the Motown sound and the soul explosion of the 1960s, the disco beat of the next decade, and, most recently, rap music.

Rock music appealed to and reflected the interests of the baby-boom generation until the end of the seventies. The music of the Dick Clark era, the Brill Building songwriters, the Beach Boys, the Motown artists, and the early Beatles was preoccupied with dating, cars, high school, and teen love. As the generation matured and entered college or the work force, the music scene was dominated by the protest music of Bob Dylan and psychedelic bands which questioned the basic tenets of American society. The music became harsh and violent when college-age baby boomers were threatened by the Vietnam-era military draft and National Guardsmen. During the 1970s after the war ended and when many of the college rebels landed lucrative jobs, glitter rock and disco exemplified the excessive behavior of the boomers. The yearning for lost youth crept into the music during the 1980s, with such artists as Bruce Springsteen who matured with his audience and celebrated his fortieth birthday by the end of the decade. Rock-and-roll, especially punk rock and MTV, became the music of a new generation only during the late 1970s and 1980s.

A favorable economic climate allowed rock to flourish among the baby-boom generation. Compared to the preceding generation, which had been raised during the most severe economic depression of the twentieth century, the baby boomers in America lived in relative affluence. In the 1950s and early 1960s, many youths had allowances that enabled them to purchase the latest rock records. During the next fifteen years, unparalleled prosperity allowed youths to consider the alternatives of hippiedom and led to the excesses and unmatched record sales of the late 1970s. The economic scene first changed significantly during the late 1970s in Britain, where a new generation of youths created the sneering protest of punk which reflected harsh economic realities.

Certain technological advances have been essential to the development of rock and have enhanced the popularity of the music by delivering it easily and inexpensively. The electric guitar, developed by Leo Fender and popularized during the 1950s, gave rock its distinctive sound. Television brought and still brings rock to teens in their homes — Elvis Presley and the Beatles on the "Ed Sullivan Show," Dick Clark's "American Bandstand," and, currently, MTV. The portable transistor radio, and later the portable cassette tape player-recorder, provided teens the opportunity to listen to their favorite songs in the privacy of their rooms, at school, or on the streets. The inexpensive 45-rpm record allowed youths to purchase the latest hits and dominated rock sales until the 1960s, when the baby-boom generation grew older and could afford the price of an LP. Advances in the quality of sound such as hi fidelity, stereo, component stereo systems, and recently the compact disc have made the music more immediate and more accessible.

The increasing popularity of rock music has been entwined with the development of the music industry. Rock-and-roll has always been a business. At first, rock records were pressed by small, independent companies such as Chess, Sun, Modern, and King. As it became more popular among teens, rock-and-roll began to interest major record companies such as RCA, Decca, and Capitol, which by the 1960s dominated the field. By the 1970s, the major companies aggressively marketed their product and consolidated ranks to increase profits and successfully create a business more profitable than network television and professional sports. In 1978 as the majors experienced a decline, independent labels again arose to produce new rock styles such as punk, rap, and speed metal. By the end of the 1980s, the major companies reasserted their dominance of the record industry, bouyed by the signing of new acts that had been tested by the independents and by the introduction of the compact disc, which forced many record consumers to purchase their favorite music in a different, more expensive format.

Though a business, rock music has been rebellious. Fueled by uncontrolled hormones, teenage rockers in the 1950s and early 1960s rebelled against their parents by wearing sideburns and long hair, driving fast cars, and screaming for the gyrations of Elvis Presley. In the 1960s, college-age rockers directed their frustration and anger at racial and social injustice, taking freedom rides to the South, demanding social change, and protesting the war in Vietnam. Entering the work force during the 1970s, many baby boomers submerged their anger in material excess as rock became theatrical and extravagant. A new generation of rockers and the older baby boomers still interested in rock reintroduced rebellion during the late 1970s and 1980s. Sneering British punks, growing spiked hair, wearing ripped T-shirts and spitting at their audiences, lashed out against economic and racial inequalities. Trying to foster a pride among black Americans, rappers unabashedly condemned racial prejudice and its effects on African-Americans in the inner cities. Legions of male, adolescent heavy metalers rebelled by wearing leather jackets and shoulder-length hair. Older rock-and-rollers such as Bruce Springsteen committed themselves to specific causes such as aid to African famine victims and the crusade against apartheid. Throughout much of its forty-year existence, rebellion defined rock-and-roll.

This book places the rebellion of rock in larger racial, demographic, technological, and economic frameworks. Rather than present an encyclopaedic compilation of the thousands of well-known and obscure bands that have played throughout the years, it deals with rock-and-rollers who reflected and sometimes changed the social fabric. It does not deal with many artists and some of my favorites, who never gained general popularity and remained outside the mainstream of rock.

Rockin' In Time also deals with musicians when they helped define an era. Though some creative rock musicians have changed with the times to create new styles of music that encapsulate several eras, most continue to record the music developed during their youth. This book deals with artists when they reflected the world around them.

The social forces of history seldom separate into neat packages. Many of the different types of rock overlapped with one another. For example, from 1961 to the advent of the British invasion, the Brill Building songwriters, surf music, and Bob Dylan existed side by side on the charts. Though sometimes intersecting and cross-pollinating, the different periods in rock history have been divided into chapters to clearly distinguish the motivating factors behind each type of music.

Rockin' In Time tries to be as impartial as possible. Even though a book cannot be wrenched from the biases of its social setting, I have attempted to present the music in a social rather than a personal context and have tried to avoid any effusive praise or disparaging remarks about any type of rock. As Sting of The Police once said, "There is no bad music, only bad musicians."

These pages explore the social history of rock-and-roll. During the forty years that it has been an important part of American culture, rock-and-roll has reflected the frustrations, hopes, joys, fears, ambitions, and desires of two generations. The different forms rock music had assumed, some of them intensely defiant and others tame, have been influenced by and have themselves affected the social climate of the United States and Great Britain.

ACKNOWLEDGMENTS

I wish to thank several people who helped me with this book. Bill Flanagan, Timothy Leary, Michael Batt, Jamie Steiwer, Peter Blecha, Chris Waterman, Charles Cross, Gene Stout, Jeff Taylor and Sonny Masso provided perceptive comments on various drafts of the text. I want to thank Robert Palmer, Bob Guiccione, Jr., Alan Douglas, Mike Farrace, Gregg Vershay and Bob Jeniker for their encouragement. My colleagues at University of Washington Extension provided understanding and support during the writing of the book. I would especially like to thank Stewart Stern, Richard Hell, and Ed "Sugar Bear" Wells for their insights. Obviously, none of those who provided assistance can be held responsible for the contents of this book.

As in the first edition, I have others to thank for this volume. Jerry Kwiatkowski (Kaye) introduced me to the world of rock and prodded me to listen to everyone from Captain Beefheart to Eric Clapton. Mike Miller helped me explore the summer concert scene in Milwaukee. Ramona Wright, Neil Fligstein, Eileen Mortenson, Gail Fligstein, and Tom Speer did the same for me in Tucson and

Seattle. On the East Coast, Dave Sharp fearlessly accompanied me on journeys to see Sid Vicious and Root Boy Slim.

I would like to acknowledge former coworkers at Second Time Around Records in Seattle — owners Wes and Barbara Geesman, Dan Johnson, Mike Schwartz, Michael Wellman, Howie Whalen, Jim Rifleman, and Dave Wolters — for adding to my understanding of rock music and the rock business. At the University of Arizona in Tucson, Donald Weinstein graciously allowed me to teach a class on the social history of rock-and-roll, the beginnings of this book; Rick Venneri did the same at the University of Washington. Students in those classes added to my knowledge of rock music. Thanks to Dudley Johnson at the University of Washington for putting me in contact with Prentice Hall.

I owe a special debt to Bob "Wildman" Campbell, who spent many hours with me analyzing the lyrics of Larry Fischer, the nuances of Tibetan Buddhist chants, Bonzo Dog Band album covers, and the hidden meaning behind the grunts of Furious Pig. Besides reading and commenting on this manuscript, he expanded my musical horizons with a series of demented tapes, which twisted this book into shape. Such a debt can never be repaid.

I wish to thank my parents, Peter and Eunice, for instilling in me a love of music and the written word. Thanks go to my mother for commenting on the manuscript and giving suggestions for a title. My daughter, Sara, brought me back to reality when I became overly absorbed in the manuscript and showed me that energy can be boundless. Most of all, I would like to thank my wife, Mary, for her love and companionship, her musical prowess, her editorial comments, and her indulgence of my vinyl addiction during both editions of this book.

CREDITS

I wish to thank the following for use of photos and help in finding them: Alligator Records, especially Bruce Iglauer; Peter Asher Management with special help from Ira Koslow; Atlantic Records; Roberta Bayley; David Bowie; Bill Graham Presents (BGP) Archives; Capitol Records; Chrysalis Records; Columbia Records; Delmark Records and Bob Koester; Brian O'Neal at D.M.B.B. Entertainment; Alan Douglas and the staff at Are You Experienced?; Elektra Records; the Estate of Elvis Presley, especially Marc Magaliff; Don Everly; Cam Garrett; Richard Hell; Isolar Enterprises; Marilyn Laverty at Shore Fire; the Library of Congress; Living Blues Archival Collection, University of Mississippi Blues Archive; MCA Records; RCA Records, especially J. Matthew Van Ryn; *Rush* Artist Management; the Seattle Times; Sire Records; Beverly Rupe at Specialty Records; Chris Stamp; Sun Records; and Warner Brothers Records.

I wish to pay special thanks to Barbara Krohn of the Daily of the University of Washington for her help in locating photos.

Every effort has been made to locate, identify, and properly credit photographers, songwriters, and song publishers. Any inadvertent omissions or errors will be corrected in future editions.

ROCKIN' IN TIME

1

The Blues, Rock-and-Roll, and Racism

"It used to be called boogie-woogie, it used to be called blues, used to be called rhythm and blues. . . . It's called rock now."

Chuck Berry

A smoke-filled club, the Macomba Lounge, on the South Side of Chicago, late on a Saturday night in 1950. On a small, dimly lit stage behind the bar in the long, narrow club stood an intense, black man dressed in a bright blue suit with baggy pants, a white shirt, and a wide, striped tie. He gripped an oversized electric guitar—the revolutionary new instrument born in the postwar, urban environment—caressing, pulling, pushing, and bending the strings until they produced a sorrowful, razor-sharp cry that cut through the souls of his listeners, who hollered and shrieked a loud, carnal sound in response. With half-closed eyes, the guitarist peered through the smoke. The bar was jammed with patrons and littered with half-empty beer bottles. Growling out the lyrics of "Rollin' Stone," the man's face was contorted in a painful expression that told of cotton fields in Mississippi and of being black in middle America at mid-century. The singer's name was Muddy Waters, and he was playing a new, electrified music called rhythm and blues.

The rhythm and blues of Muddy Waters and other urban blues artists served as the foundation for Elvis, the Beatles, the Rolling

1

Stones, Jimi Hendrix, Led Zeppelin, the Sex Pistols, and most other rock-and-rollers. A subtle blend of African and European traditions, this strain provided the necessary ingredients and inspiration for the birth of rock and the success of Chuck Berry and Little Richard. Despite their innovative roles, R & B artists seldom received the recognition or the money they deserved. Established crooners, disc jockeys, and record company executives, watching their share of the market shrink with the increasing popularity of R & B and its rock-and-roll offspring, torpedoed the new music by offering toned-down, white copies of black originals that left many black trailblazers bitter and, sometimes, broken.

THE BIRTH OF THE BLUES

The blues were an indigenous creation of black slaves who adapted their African musical heritage to the new, American environment. Though taking many forms and undergoing many permutations through the years, the blues formed the basis of rock-and-roll.

African blacks, torn from their kin, enduring an often fatal journey from their homes in West Africa to the American South, and forced into a brutally servile way of life, still retained continuity with their past through music. Their voices glided between the lines of the more rigid European musical scale to create a distinctive new sound. To the plantation owners and overseers, the music seemed to be "rising and falling" and sounded off-key.

The music involved calculated repetitions. In this call-and-response, used often to decrease the monotony of work, one worker would call or play a lead part, and his fellow slaves would follow suit with the same phrase or an embellishment of it until another took the lead. As one observer wrote in 1845, "Our black oarsmen made the woods echo to their song. One of them, taking the lead, first improvised a verse, paying compliments to his master's family, and to a celebrated black beauty of the neighborhood, who was compared to the 'red bird.' The other five then joined in the chorus, always repeating the same words." Some slaves, especially those from the Bantu tribe, whooped, or jumped octaves, during the call-and-response. This whooping became an important aspect of field hollers.

Probably most important, the slaves, accustomed to dancing and singing to the beat of drums in Africa, emphasized rhythm over harmony. In a single song, they clapped, danced, and slapped their bodies in several different rhythms, compensating for the absence of drums, which were outlawed by plantation owners, who feared that the instrument would be used to coordinate slave insurrections. One ex-slave, writing in 1853, called the polyrhythmic practice "patting juba." It was performed by "striking the right shoulder with one hand, the left with the other—all the while keeping time with the feet and singing." In contrast, noted President John Adams, whites "droned out [Protestant hymns] . . . like the braying of asses in one steady beat."

These African musical traits, nurtured by American slaves, extended to American black religion. One writer in the *Nation* described a "praise-meeting" held in 1867: "At regular intervals one hears the elder 'deaconing' a hymn-book hymn, which is sung two lines at a time, and whose wailing cadences, borne on the night air, are indescribably melancholy." The subsequent response from the congregation to the bluesy call of the minister, along with the accompanying instruments, created the rhythmic complexity so common in African music.

Such African-inspired church music, later known as gospel, became the basis of the blues style, which incorporated it and applied it to secular themes. Bluesman Big Bill Broonzy, who recorded nearly two hundred songs from 1925 to 1952, started as "a preacher—preached in the church. One day I quit and went to music." Broonzy maintained that "the blues won't die because spirituals won't die. Blues—a steal from spirituals. And rock is a steal from the blues. . . . Blues singers start out singing spirituals."

FROM THE RURAL SOUTH TO THE URBAN NORTH

During and after World War I, many southern blacks brought the blues to northern cities, especially Chicago, the end of the Illinois Central railroad line, where the black population mushroomed from 40,000 in 1910 to 234,000 twenty years later. Many blacks left to escape the boll weevil, a parasitic worm that ravaged the Mississippi Delta cottonfields in 1915 and 1916. Some migrated to break loose from the crippling racial discrimination in the South. As Delta-born pianist Eddie Boyd told *Living Blues*, "I thought of coming to Chicago where I could get away from some of that racism and where I would have an opportunity to, well, do something with my talent. . . . It wasn't peaches and cream [in Chicago], man, but it was a hell of a lot better than down there where I was born." Once in Chicago, blacks found jobs in steel mills, food-processing plants, and stockyards needing extra hands because of the wartime draft and a sudden cutoff of European immigration. They settled in Chicago's South and West Side neighborhoods.

Among the migrants to the Windy City was Tampa Red, who migrated from Florida to Chicago in 1925. Pianist Eurreal Wilford ("Little Brother") Montgomery, born in 1907 on the grounds of a Louisiana lumber company, performed around logging camps until he ended up in Chicago. Big Bill Broonzy, an ex-slave's son who worked as a plowhand in Mississippi and laid railroad track in Arkansas, headed for the same destination in 1916, when drought

On the cotton plantation, 1937

destroyed the crops on his farm. In 1929, pianist Roosevelt Sykes, "The Honeydripper," took the same route. A few years later, harmonica wizard John Lee ("Sonny Boy") Williamson (the first Sonny Boy) migrated from Jackson, Tennessee. And about the same time, guitarist Sleepy John Estes, the son of a Tennessee sharecropper, moved to the Windy City. All told, remembered George Leaner, who began selling blues discs in Chicago during the 1930s, "The Illinois Central Railroad brought the blues to Chicago. With the thousands of laborers who came to work in the meat-packing plants and the steel mills came Peetie Wheatstraw, Ollie Shepard, Blind Boy Fuller, Washboard Sam, Little Brother Montgomery, Blind Lemon [Jefferson], Memphis Minnie, and Rosetta Howard."

These migrants played a stylistic mixture. At first, they delivered straight country blues. By the early 1940s, when the influence of the city began to seep into their music, they recorded a hybrid of blues, vaudeville styles, and newer swing rhythms, which included the boogie-woogie, rolling-bass piano, a sound that had been associated with the jump blues band of Louis Jordan. Some dubbed the early Chicago blues the "Bluebird Beat" because many of the blues artists recorded for RCA Victor's Bluebird label, started in 1933.

Lester Melrose, a white music talent-scout producer, coordinated the Chicago blues scene during the 1930s and 1940s. As Willie Dixon, bassist, songwriter, and talent scout told *Living Blues*, "I started goin' up to Tampa Red's house where a lot of the other blues artists was, on 35th and State Street. He had a place up over a pawnshop. And a lotta the musicians used to go up there and write songs, lay around in there, and sleep. Lester Melrose always came there when he was in town. That was his kind of headquarters, like. And whenever he was in town, and different people had different songs that they wanted him to hear, they came by Tampa's house . . . Big Bill Broonzy and a bunch of 'em would hang around there. And we get to singing it and seein' how it sounds. If it sounded like it was alright, then Melrose would say, 'Well, looky here, we'll try it out and see what happens.'" Melrose himself boasted that "from March 1934 to February 1951 I recorded at least 90 percent of all rhythm-and-blues talent for RCA and Columbia records." He included on his roster Big Bill Broonzy, Tampa Red, Sleepy John Estes, Roosevelt Sykes, Sonny Boy Williamson, and many others. By using the artists interchangeably, Melrose helped to create the Chicago blues, which featured vocals, a guitar, and a piano. The latter enlivened and added a sophisticated touch to the more sullen country blues.

The blues became even more entrenched in northern urban areas during and after World War II, when thousands of Southerners in search of work streamed into the cities. "World War I started bluesmen up North and No. II made it a mass migration," pointed out Atlantic record executive Jerry Wexler. From 1940 to 1944, estimated *Time* magazine, over fifty thousand blacks from Mississippi alone headed for Chicago. They paid around fifteen dollars for the trip on the Illinois Central Railroad and ended in the Windy City, the home of *The Defender*, the widely read, black-owned newspaper that encouraged southern sharecroppers to migrate to the North. From 1940 to 1950, 214,000 southern blacks arrived in Chicago, an increase of 77 percent in just one decade. About half the migrants came from the Mississippi Delta region, which stretched two hundred miles from Memphis to Vicksburg.

Many of the Delta migrants had heard a propulsive, acoustic, personalized style of blues on their plantations. On Saturdays at parties, at picnics, and in juke joints, they listened to the moans, the heavy bass beat, and the bottleneck slide guitar of local musicians. Their favorites included Charley Patton, the king of the Delta blues, who played around Will Dockery's plantation during the 1920s and in 1929 recorded his classics "Pony Blues," "Pea Vine Blues," and "Tom Rushen Blues." He played with Eddie ("Son")

Listening to the blues. The South, early 1940s

House, a Baptist preacher who taught himself guitar at the age of twenty-five and in the 1930s cut such discs as "Preachin' the Blues." Robert Johnson, one of the most celebrated and legendary of the Delta blues artists, learned guitar technique from the Patton disciple Willie Brown and picked up Delta stylizings from Son House. During his two-year recording career, which began in 1936, he released such gems as "Dust My Broom," "Sweet Home Chicago," "Crossroads," "Love in Vain," and "Rambling on My Mind."

MUDDY WATERS AND CHICAGO R & B

Muddy Waters (a.k.a. McKinley Morganfield), who grew up in Clarksdale, Mississippi, listening to Johnson, Patton, and Son House, merged his Delta influences with a new urban environment

The Muddy Waters band, early 1950s. From left to right. Muddy Waters (guitar); unknown; Otis Spann (piano); Henry Strong (harmonica); Elgin Evans (drums); and Jimmy Rogers (guitar)

in Chicago. Muddy bought his first guitar when he was thirteen. "The first one I got," he told writer Robert Palmer, "I sold the last horse we had. Made about fifteen dollars for him, gave my grandmother seven dollars and fifty cents, I kept seven-fifty and paid about two-fifty for that guitar. It was a Stella. The peoples ordered them from Sears-Roebuck in Chicago." A young Muddy played locally around his home base, a plantation owned by Colonel William Howard Stovall. In 1941, on a trip to the Mississippi Delta in search of American folk music, musicologists Alan Lomax and John Work discovered Waters, then a tenant farmer, and recorded him for the Library of Congress.

Two years later, Muddy moved to Chicago "with a suitcase, a suit of clothes, and a guitar," hoping to "get into the big record field." "I wanted to get out of Mississippi in the worst way," Waters told a journalist. "They had such as my mother and the older people brainwashed that people can't make it too good in the city. But I figured if anyone else was living in the city, I could make it there, too." Waters worked in a paper container factory and then as a truck driver by day, playing at parties in the evenings.

In 1944 Muddy bought his first electric guitar and two years later formed his first electric combo. Muddy Waters, possibly the archetype of Chicago R & B artists, combined his Delta upbringing with the electrified guitar and amplifier, which blasted forth the tension, volume, and confusion of the big-city streets.

The resulting marriage of city and country, a nitty-gritty, low-down, jumpy sound, reflected the optimism of postwar American blacks, who had escaped from the seemingly inescapable southern cotton fields. The urban music contrasted sharply with the more subdued country blues, born in slavery. Remembered Willie Dixon— a bassist from Vicksburg, Mississippi, and composer of such blues-rock classics as "Hoochie Coochie Man," "I'm a Man," and "Just Want to Make Love to You,"—"there was quite a few people around singin' the blues but most of 'em was singing all *sad* blues. Muddy was giving his blues a little pep." The peppy blues of artists such as Muddy Waters became known as rhythm and blues.

After four years of perfecting his electric sound in Chicago clubs, Muddy signed with Aristocrat Records, owned by Polish immigrants Leonard and Phil Chess, who operated several South Side bars, including the Macomba Lounge. At first, as Muddy told journalist Pete Welding, Leonard Chess "didn't like my style of singing; he wondered who was going to buy that. The lady [Evelyn, a partner of the Chess brothers] said 'You'd be surprised.' . . . Everybody's records came out before mine, [Macomba house vocalist] Andrew Tibbs had two records before me. . . . But when they released mine, it hit the ceiling." "I had a hot blues out, man," Muddy remembered about his first disc, "I Can't Be Satisfied," backed with "Feel Like Going Home." "I'd be driving my truck and whenever I'd see a neon beer sign, I'd stop, go in, look at the jukebox, and see my record on there. . . . Pretty soon I'd hear it walking along the street. I'd hear it *driving* along the street."

Buoyed by success and the abandonment of the blues market by RCA and Columbia, in 1950 the brothers bought out their partner, Evelyn, changed the name of the company to Chess, and began to release a series of Muddy Waters sides that became hits on the "race" charts: They first cut "Rolling Stone" backed by "Walkin' Blues," then later a Robert Johnson tune. They followed the next year with "Long Distance Call" and "Honey Bee." By the mid-1950s, Waters had defined the raucous, urbanized, electric Delta blues, recording "Got My Mojo Working," the Delta standard "Rollin' and Tumblin'," "Mad Love," "(I'm Your) Hoochie Coochie Man," "I Just Wanna Make Love To You," and "I'm Ready" among many others. His group of the early fifties, which included Otis Spann on piano, Little Walter on harmonica, Jimmy Rogers on guitar, and Leroy ("Baby-Face") Foster on drums, stands out as one of the most explosive R & B units ever formed.

THE WOLF

Chester ("Howlin' Wolf") Burnett, Waters's musical rival at Chess, also delivered an electric version of the Delta blues. A teenaged Burnett, living on Young and Morrow's plantation near Ruleville, Mississippi, in 1926, met Charley Patton who lived nearby on Will Dockery's plantation. As he told writer Pete Welding, "Charley Patton started me off playing. He took a liking to me, and I asked him would he learn me, and at night, after I'd get off work, I'd go and hang around." A few years later, he listened to the country yodeling of another Mississippian, Jimmie Rodgers, and decided to emulate the singer. But Burnett's harsh, raspy voice never mastered the yodel technique and the blues singer earned a series of nicknames for his distinctive style, which included "Bull Cow," "Foot," and "The Wolf." "I just stuck to Wolf. I could do no yodelin' so I turned to Howlin'," remembered Burnett. To perfect his raspy blues, Howlin' Wolf traveled across the Delta during the next two decades and played with legendary blues artists of the area such as Robert Johnson and Rice Miller (also known as Sonny Boy Williamson II).

In 1948, at the age of thirty-eight, the Wolf plugged his Delta blues into an electric amplifier and in West Memphis formed an electric band, which at times included harp players James Cotton and Little Junior Parker. The Wolf landed a regular spot on station KWEM and began to attract attention.

Four years later, the Wolf joined the exodus to Chicago. At first, remembered Wolf's guitarist Hubert Sumlin, "he stayed at Muddy [Waters's] house for about two months. And Muddy introduced him around. Muddy was on the road a good bit in those days, so he took Wolf and introduced him to Sylvio, Bobby and Mutt at the Zanzibar, and Ray and Ben Gold at the 708 Club. When Muddy went on the road, Wolf just stepped in his shoes in [those] three places."

A rivalry began to develop between Waters and the Wolf, who quickly established himself among the Chicago R & B crowd. Sumlin pointed out that "ever since the Wolf came to Chicago and started taking over, Muddy didn't like him too well. A kind of rivalry started up between them about who was the boss of the blues." "Every once in a while [the Wolf] would mention the fact, 'Hey man, you wrote that [song] for Muddy. How come you won't write me one like that?' But when you write one for him he wouldn't like it," recalled Willie Dixon who the Chess Brothers hired in 1950 as a songwriter and talent scout. Dixon "found out that all I could do was use backward psychology and tell him, 'Now here's one I wrote for Muddy, man.' 'Yeah, man, let me hear it. Yeah, that's the one for me.' And so, I'd just let him have it."

The Wolf scored a series of hits with Dixon's songs and traditional blues standards that would influence the course of rock-and-roll. He recorded his calling card, "Moanin' at Midnight," "Killing Ground," later recorded by Jimi Hendrix, "How Many More Years," which became Led Zeppelin's "How Many More Times," "I Ain't Superstitious" covered by Jeff Beck, and "Smokestack Lightnin'," later popularized by the Yardbirds.

Wolf's stage performances presaged later rock-and-roll hysteria. At the end of one performance, he raced toward the wings of the stage, took a flying leap, and grabbed onto the stage curtain, still singing into his microphone. As the song built to a climax, the Wolf scaled the curtain and, as the song drew to a close, slid down the drapery. He hit the floor just as the song ended, to the screams of the audience. Recalled Sam Phillips, the genius behind Sun Records who recorded a few Howlin' Wolf songs and sold them to Chess, "God, what it would be worth on film to see the fervor in that man's face when he sang. His eyes would light up, you'd see the veins come out on his neck and, buddy, there was *nothing* on his mind but that song. He sang with his damn soul."

OTHER CHESS DISCOVERIES

The Chess brothers recorded other hard-driving rhythm and blues performers from the Delta. Born Ellas McDaniel in McComb, Mississippi, Bo Diddley moved to the Windy City with his family. "Oh, I played street corners until I was 19 or 20, from about 15 on," he told rock critic and musician Lenny Kaye. "Then I walked the streets around Chicago for about 12 years, before I got somebody to listen to me." Eventually, he landed a job at the 708 Club and in 1955 signed with Chess, where Leonard Chess gave him his stage name, Bo Diddley, "because it meant 'funny storyteller.' " That year, Diddley hit the charts with "Bo Diddley" and "I'm a Man" and subsequently with "Mona," "You Can't Judge a Book by Its Cover," and "Say Man." Though sometimes appealing to rock-and-roll fans, Diddley stood firmly rooted in the electrified Delta sound. The striking similarity between his "I'm a Man" and Muddy Waters's "Mannish Boy," both recorded in 1955, attests to Bo Diddley's Delta foundation.

Chess also recorded two pioneers of the amplified harmonica. Marion Walter Jacobs, otherwise known as Little Walter, grew up in the cotton fields of Louisiana. He learned to play the harmonica (the harp, as he called it) during his teens, patterning himself after Rice Miller, whom he discovered on the "King Biscuit Time," a daily, fifteen-minute radio show on station KFFA broadcast from Helena, Arkansas. Two years after World War II, Little Walter left home for Chicago, where he joined the Muddy Waters band. After impressing the Chess Brothers with his talent, Little Walter re-

Little Walter Jacobs at the Chess Studios

corded his own compositions. In 1952, backed by the Muddy Waters group, he hit the charts with "Juke," which remained in the R & B Top 10 for fourteen weeks. Little Walter quickly formed his own band, the Night Cats, and followed with "Sad Hours," "Blues with a Feeling," "You're So Fine," and in 1955 his biggest commercial success, "My Babe," a Willie Dixon composition based on the gospel song "This Train."

Leonard Chess snagged Rice Miller (Sonny Boy Williamson II), the idol of Little Walter and the undisputed king of the R & B harmonica, when Miller moved to Milwaukee in 1955. His band included the Muddy Waters outfit and, sometimes, Robert Jr. Lockwood, who had learned guitar from Robert Johnson and for two years had played with Williamson on "King Biscuit Time." Though already a popular artist when he signed with Chess in 1955, Sonny

Boy cut a number of now-classic singles for the Chicago label, including "One Way Out" covered by the Allman Brothers and "Eyesight for the Blind," later recorded by The Who.

THE MODERN "BLUES BOY"

Modern Records and its various subsidiaries, owned by Saul and Jules Bihari of Los Angeles, gave Chess its stiffest competition in the search for R & B talent. During the late forties and early fifties, the Bihari brothers made numerous scouting trips to the Mississippi Delta. They also commissioned as talent scout pianist Ike Turner, who was then the leader of the Rhythm Kings and later gained fame as half of the Ike and Tina Turner duo.

The Biharis' efforts resulted in the signing of one of the most successful rhythm and blues artists, Riley "Blues Boy" King. Born on a cotton plantation near Indianola, Mississippi, the heart of the Delta, King was forced into the fields at the age of nine, working for fifteen dollars a month. "I guess the earliest sound of blues that I can remember was in the fields while people would be pickin' cotton or choppin' or somethin'," King told *Living Blues*. "Usually one guy would be plowin' by himself or maybe one guy would take his hoe and chop way out in front of everybody else and usually you would hear this guy sing most of the time. No special lyrics or anything. Just what he felt at the time." "When I sing and play now I can hear those same sounds that I used to hear as a kid," he added.

As with most R & B performers, King began his musical career in the church. "Singing was the thing I enjoyed doing, and when I started in school, I sang with a group: a quartet singing spirituals," B. B. told *Downbeat*. From his father, fifteen-year-old B. B. received an eight-dollar guitar, which became the boy's constant companion. King continued to "sing gospel music, using the guitar to tune up the group I played with," he related. "When I was introduced into the army at the age of 18, I started playing around little towns, just standing on the corner. People asked me to play gospel tunes and complimented me real nicely: 'Son, if you keep it up, you're going to be real good someday.' But the people who asked me to play the blues tunes normally tipped me, many times getting me beer. So that motivated me to play the blues, you might say."

In 1949, after being discharged from the army, King hitch-hiked to Memphis, Tennessee, and moved in with a cousin, Booker T. ("Bukka") White, a renowned Delta blues figure. He found a job at the Newberry Equipment Company and by 1949 began singing Peptikon commercials on the black-owned radio station WDIA. Remembered the guitarist: "This Peptikon was supposed to be good for whatever ails you, y'know, like a toothache. Anyway, they put me on from 3:30 to 3:40 and my popularity began to grow. I sang and I

B. B. "Blues Boy" King

played by myself and I later got two men with me . . . Earl Forrest
playing drums and Johnny Ace playing piano."

After a year on WDIA, King, by now called Blues Boy, B. B.
for short, signed a contract with Modern Records and its subsidiaries, RPM, Kent, and Crown. His music, now almost fully developed, fused his Delta influences with a piercing falsetto vocal style
and a jazzy, single-note guitar attack picked up from jazz guitarist
Django Reinhardt and Texas bluesman Aaron (T-Bone) Walker, who
in turn had electrified the technique he had learned from country
bluesman Blind Lemon Jefferson. In a few years, King's new syn-
thesis produced dozens of R & B classics that subsequent rock guitarists have either copied or stolen including "Everyday I Have the
Blues," "I Woke Up This Morning," and "You Upset Me Baby."

The Blues, Rock-and-Roll, and Racism **13**

Elmore James eventually joined B. B. King at Modern Records. Born on a farm near Richland, Mississippi, James taught himself guitar by stringing a broom wire to a wall of his cabin and plunking on it. He listened to such Delta giants as Robert Johnson and Charley Patton, and by the late 1940s, he had become a master of the slide guitar. Lillian McMurry, who set up Trumpet Records in Jackson, Mississippi, first recorded James. In 1952, Trumpet released his gut-wrenching, slashing version of Robert Johnson's "Dust My Broom." The next year, the Bihari brothers lured Elmore to Chicago, and he began to record for the Meteor label, another subsidiary of Modern. His output included a number of now classic R & B tunes such as "Shake Your Moneymaker," "It Hurts Me Too," "The Sky Is Crying," and "Hawaiian Boogie." As with his fellow Delta performers, Elmore James captured in his music the pain and anguish of three centuries of slavery and tenant farming. As black producer Bobby Robinson suggested, listen "to the raw-nerved, spine-tingling picking of the guitar and the agonized screams and the soul-stirring of Elmore James. Close your eyes, you'll see the slave ships, the auction blocks, the cotton fields, the bare backs straining, totin' that barge and liftin' that bale. You will smell the sweat, feel the lash, taste the tears and see the blood, and relive 300 years of the Blues."

The Biharis also recorded John Lee Hooker, the Delta-born guitarist who traveled north to Detroit during the postwar era. Hooker learned guitar from his stepfather, Will Moore, who had performed with Charley Patton on Dockery's plantation. He sang with various gospel groups in the Delta, left home by the age of fourteen, and in 1943 moved to Detroit. "At that time jobs weren't hard to get, it was during the war," recalled Hooker. "Good money, too. You could go anywhere any day and get a job, nothing to worry about too much." In the Motor City, Hooker worked by day as an orderly, as a janitor at the Dodge automobile factory and at Comco Steel and at night played in various Detroit nightclubs. After a few years, he boasted, "I became the talk of the town around at the house parties. Finally, I met this very, very great musician, who I loved so much, I treasured him like I would a piece of gold, the great T-Bone Walker. He was the first person to get me my electric guitar."

In 1948, John Lee was spotted by Lee Sensation, a talent scout for Modern Records who signed Hooker. As his first single, he recorded "Boogie Chillin," an electric, chantlike, dark, superstitious-sounding stomp that vividly described black Detroit's main thoroughfare, Hastings Street. According to Hooker, the single "caught fire. It was ringin' all around the country. When it come out, every juke box you went to, everyplace you went to, every drug store you went, everywhere you went, department stores, they were playin' it in there." Hooker followed with such rhythm and blues chart climbers as "Hobo Blues," "Crawling Kingsnake Blues," "Sally Mae" and "I'm in the Mood."

Chicago disc jockey Vivian Carter and her husband, founding Vee Jay Records of Chicago in 1953, noticed the success that Chess and Modern had achieved with the electrified Delta blues and jumped into the R & B field with Jimmy Reed. Born on a plantation near Dunleith, Mississippi, Reed discovered the guitar with friend and later backup musician Eddie Taylor, whose style derived from Charley Patton and Robert Johnson. He learned harmonica by "listening to Sonny Boy Williams [Rice Miller]. . . . I'd slip out of the fields and go up to the house to listen to them do the 15 minutes he had to do over the radio show. He was broadcastin' for King Biscuit flour out of Helena, Arkansas." In 1941, Reed headed toward Chicago, where he worked at various steel mills and foundries. During his breaks and lunch hours, he practiced one-chord, Delta guitar shuffles and a laid-back vocal style that masked the biting lyrics of such songs as "Big Boss Man." In 1953, after being rejected by Leonard Chess, who "was too tied up with Little Walter and Muddy Waters and Wolf and them, till he didn't have no time for me," Reed signed with the newly organized Vee Jay Records. He first topped the R & B charts in 1955 with "You Don't Have to Go" and followed with a series of hits that included "Ain't That Loving You Baby," "Hush-Hush," "Honest I Do," and "Take Out Some Insurance on Me, Baby," the last covered by the Beatles in their early years.

R & B OUTSIDE CHICAGO

Small, independent record companies in cities other than Chicago specialized in different styles of the new R & B sound. Los Angeles had two such companies. Aladdin, owned by the Mesner brothers, recorded a postwar Texas sound that spanned the relaxed vocal stylings of Charles Brown and the more jumpy blues of Amos Milburn, who hit the charts in the early 1950s with songs about alcohol: "Bad, Bad Whiskey," "One Scotch, One Bourbon, One Beer," "Let Me Go Home, Whiskey," and "Thinking and Drinking." In 1956, the company also released Shirley and Lee's "Let the Good Times Roll," which became a rallying cry for rock and rollers.

Lew Chudd established Imperial Records in 1945 and achieved success with the barrelhouse, rolling piano of Antoine "Fats" Domino. Born in New Orleans, Domino learned to play piano at the age of nine and as a teenager worked in a bedspring factory by day and in local bars at night. He quickly mastered the New Orleans piano style and in 1949 signed with Imperial. He debuted with the single "Fat Man," which sold a million copies. Domino followed with a string of hits: "Ain't That A Shame," "Blueberry Hill," "Blue Monday," and "I'm Walking." From 1949 to 1962, Fats had forty-three records that made *Billboard's* charts, twenty-three gold records, and record sales of 65 million units.

In Cincinnati, Syd Nathan set up King Records in an abandoned ice house and recorded the velvety, big-band sound of Ivory Joe Hunter, Lonnie Johnson, and Wynonie ("Mr. Blues") Harris. Black entrepreneur Don Robey established Peacock Records in Houston. In 1952, he bought the Memphis-based Duke Records and scored hits with the smooth-voiced, gospel-influenced Bobby Blue Bland and teen star Johnny Ace, a former member of the B. B. King band. Ace lost his life in a game of Russian roulette on Christmas Eve, 1954, at the age of twenty-five.

In New York City, the bustling hub of urban America, independent labels such as Herald, Regal, Old Town, and Deluxe delivered the distinctive, gospel-based doo-wop sound. Ghetto youths, too poor to afford a guitar, banded together on street corners and sang their way through Harlem, using each voice as a different instrument. The names of many of the groups reflected their urban dreams: the Edsels, the Fiestas, the Impalas, the Imperials, the Cadillacs, the Belvederes, and the Fleetwoods—the automobiles that glided down the city streets.

The Ravens led the way for subsequent doo-wop groups. Formed in 1945, the six-man choir featured the deep bass tone of Jimmy Ricks. They signed with King Records and released their first hit, "Bye Bye Baby Blues." The song inspired a spate of other R & B singing combinations: the Chords, who hit the charts with "Sh-Boom"; the Heartbeats; the Charts; the Penguins, of "Earth Angel" fame; Otis Williams and the Charms; the Jive Five; the Monotones from nearby New Jersey, who scored a hit with "The Book of Love"; the Jesters, who faced off with another New York doo-wop group in the now-sought-after album *The Paragons Meet the Jesters;* the Crows, who prompted George Goldner to start Gee Records with their 1954 song of the same name; and Harlem's favorite, the Harptones.

The most well-known New York doo-wop combinations centered around Clyde McPhatter and Frankie Lymon. McPhatter first joined the Dominoes, a gospel group ruled by the iron hand of Billy Ward. Soon after their television debut on "The Arthur Godfrey Show," the group began to record blues numbers and in May 1951 released the classic "Sixty Minute Man." Within two years, leader McPhatter bolted from the Dominoes and formed probably the most famous of the R & B vocal groups, the Drifters, settling on that name because the members "drifted" from one group to another. The Drifters signed with Atlantic Records, the company founded in 1947 by Ahmet and Nesuhi Ertegun, sons of the Turkish ambassador to the United States. Avid jazz and blues record collectors, they auctioned off 15,000 78-rpm discs to start Atlantic with Herb Abramson. In 1953, the Drifters scaled the *Billboard* charts with "Money Honey."

A string of hits followed ("Such a Night," "Honey Love," and "Bip Bam") before McPhatter left the group in 1954 for the army.

The Teenagers, fronted by thirteen-year-old Frankie Lymon, practiced on street corners, in a junk-filled backyard, or on the top of a Harlem tenement house. One day, Richard Barrett, the lead singer of the Valentines, overheard the Teenagers as he passed by a street corner. Excitedly, he brought the boys, all in their teens, to the offices of his label, Gee Records, where they sang "Why Do Fools Fall in Love." Company executives George Goldner and Joe Kilsky asked Lymon if he had the sheet music for the song. "Nope," replied Frankie, "we don't know anything about written-down music." The next day, the Teenagers recorded "Why Do Fools Fall in Love" for Gee. It was released in January 1956, and within a few months became a national hit. Though more pop-oriented and gospel-flavored than the electrified guitar sound of Chicago—"devil's music" in the words of B. B. King—New York doo-wop mirrored the cityscape of America in the 1950s and became a popular form of R & B.

FROM R & B TO ROCK AND ROLL: LITTLE RICHARD AND CHUCK BERRY

A few young R & B showmen completed the transition from an acoustic, more slow-moving country blues to the jumpy, electric, urban sound that became known as rock and roll. The term *rock-and-roll*, originally a black euphemism for sexual intercourse, at first generically referred to all R & B artists. By the middle of the 1950s, it began to be applied to the most frenetic, hard-driving version of an already spirited rhythm and blues. As Howlin' Wolf suggested, with "a twelve-bar and a four-bar intro, you're playing the blues. You step the stuff up and you're playing rock and roll."

Little Richard and Chuck Berry stood in the vanguard of the rock-and-roll pioneers. Little Richard, born Richard Penniman in Macon, Georgia, in late 1932, sang in a Baptist church choir as a youth and traveled with his family gospel troupe, the Penniman Family. He joined various circuses and traveling shows and in the Broadway Follies met gospel R & B shouter Billy Wright, who secured a recording contract from Camden Records for the eighteen-year-old Little Richard. In 1951, Richard cut eight sides for Camden, which featured boogie-woogie and urban blues numbers in the style of Billy Wright.

The next year, a local tough shot and killed Little Richard's father, the owner of the Tip In Inn. To support the family, Richard washed dishes in the Macon Greyhound Bus station by day and at night sang with his group, the Upsetters, at local theaters for fifteen dollars a show. "We were playing some of Roy Brown's tunes, a

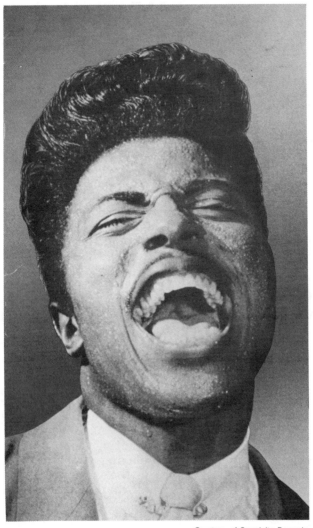

The fabulous Little Richard

lot of Fats Domino tunes, some B. B. King tunes and I believe a couple of Little Walter's and a few things by Billy Wright," remembered Little Richard.

After a few years of one-night stands in black southern nightclubs, Penniman began to change his style. He transformed himself from a traditional R & B singer into a wild-eyed, pompadoured madman who crashed the piano keys and screamed nonsensical lyrics at breakneck speed. Richard later recalled that "it was funny. I'd sing the songs I sing now in clubs, but the black audiences just didn't respond. They wanted blues stuff like B. B. King sings. That's what they were used to. I'd sing 'Tutti Frutti' and nothing. Then someone would get up and sing an old blues song and everyone would go wild."

On the advice of rhythm and blues singer Lloyd Price of "Lawdy Miss Clawdy" fame, Richard sent a demo tape of two rather subdued blues tunes to Art Rupe at Specialty Records in Los Angeles, which had recorded Price as well as R & B artists such as Roy Milton and Jimmy Liggins. The tape, according to Specialty's musical director Bumps Blackwell, was "wrapped in a piece of paper looking as though someone had eaten off it." Blackwell opened the wrapper, played the tape, and recommended that Rupe sign Little Richard.

Richard arrived in New Orleans during late 1955 for his first Specialty recording session. Reminisced Little Richard: "I cut some blues songs. During a break in the session, someone heard me playing 'Tutti Frutti' on the piano and asked about the song. We ended up recording it and it sold two hundred thousand copies in a week and a half." And a legend was born. During the next four years, Richard cut a wealth of rock standards, which defined the new music: "Long Tall Sally," "Slippin', and Slidin'," "Rip It Up," "Ready Teddy," "The Girl Can't Help It," "Good Golly Miss Molly," "Jenny, Jenny," "Keep a Knockin'," and "Lucille."

If anyone besides Little Richard could claim to be the father of rock-and-roll, it would be Chuck Berry. Berry, unlike almost all other R & B musicians, spent his youth in a sturdy, tree-lined, brick house in the middle-class outskirts of St. Louis. He first sang gospel at home with his family. As he wrote in his *Autobiography*, "Our family lived a block and a half from our church and singing became a major tradition in the Berry family. As far back as I can remember, Mother's household chanting of those gospel tunes rang through my childhood. The members of the family, regardless of what they were doing at the time, had a habit of joining with another member who would start singing, following along and harmonizing. Looking back I'm sure that my musical roots were planted, then and there."

The young Berry soon heard a different music on the radio. "The beautiful harmony of the country music that KMOK radio station played was almost irresistible," recalled Berry. By his teens, the now-fledgling guitarist had become a fan of Tampa Red, Arthur Crudup, and, especially, Muddy Waters.

After a stay in reform school and various odd jobs, which included work as a cosmetologist and an assembler at the General Motors Fisher Body plant, Berry turned to rhythm and blues. He obtained his first guitar from St. Louis R & B performer Joe Sherman, and in the early fifties he formed a rhythm and blues trio with Johnny Johnson on piano and Ebby Harding on drums that played "backyards, barbecues, house parties," and St. Louis bars such as the Cosmopolitan Club.

In the spring of 1955, Berry and a friend traveled to Chicago, then the mecca of urban blues: He watched the shows of Howlin' Wolf, Elmore James, and his idol, Muddy Waters. After a late-night set, Berry approached Waters for his autograph and got "the feeling I suppose one would get from having a word with the president or the pope." When asked about making a record, Muddy replied, "Yeah, see Leonard Chess, yeah, Chess Records over on Forty-seventh and Cottage." To Berry, Waters "was the godfather of the blues. He was perhaps the greatest inspiration in the launching of my career."

Chuck Berry took Muddy Waters's advice. The next day he rushed to the Chess offices and talked with Leonard Chess who asked for a demo tape of original songs within a week. Berry returned with a tape that included a country song, "Ida May." Chess, remembered Berry, "couldn't believe that a country tune (he called it a 'hillbilly song') could be written by a black guy. He wanted us to record that particular song." In the studio, Berry, on the advice of Willie Dixon, added "a little blues" to the tune, renamed it "Maybelline," and backed it with the slow blues, "Wee Wee Hours."

Berry convinced Chess to release "Maybelline," a country song adapted to a boogie-woogie beat, which hinted at the marriage between country and R & B that would reach full fruition with the rockabillies. Within weeks, Berry's upbeat song had received national airplay. The guitarist-songwriter followed with "Roll Over Beethoven (Dig These Rhythm and Blues)," "School Days," "Rock and Roll Music," "Sweet Little Sixteen," "Johnny Be Goode," "Rockin' and Rollin'," and an almost endless list of others. He embarked upon a whirlwind tour of the country, playing 101 engagements in 101 nights, where he perfected antics such as the duckwalk.

Berry's music, like that of Little Richard, took the jumpy R & B to an extreme and bridged the short gap between rhythm and blues and what became known as rock-and-roll.

THE GROWING LEGION OF ROCKERS

The market for the new sound expanded with the number of blacks who flooded into northern and western cities during and after World War II. The migrants, some of them having a little extra cash for the first time, looked for entertainment but faced a number of obstacles. "Harlem folks couldn't go downtown to the Broadway theaters and movie houses," recalled Ahmet Ertegun, cofounder of Atlantic Records. "Downtown clubs had their ropes up when they came to the door. They weren't even welcome on Fifty-Second Street where all the big performers were black. . . . Even radio was white oriented. You couldn't find a black performer on network radio. And when it came to disc jockeys on the big wattage stations, they wouldn't play a black record. We had a real tough time getting our records played—even Ruth Brown, who didn't sound particularly black."

For their leisure, some urban blacks frequented segregated clubs such as the Roosevelt in Pittsburgh, the Lincoln in Los Angeles, the Royal in Baltimore, Chicago's Regal, the Howard in Washington, and the now-famous Apollo Theater in New York City. The owners of Town Hall, the only dance hall for blacks in Philadelphia, claimed that "swollen Negro paychecks at local war plants and shipyards" helped to increase their profits. Other blacks frequented segregated taverns and demanded music by black artists on the jukeboxes. The majority of migrants, bound closer to home by their families, found entertainment through the record. As Ahmet Ertegun suggested, most "black people had to find entertainment in their homes—and the record was it." They bought 78-rpm discs by their favorite artists in furniture stores, pharmacies, shoeshine stands, and anywhere else they were sold.

Most favored the electrified R & B sound. "The black people, particularly the black people I knew," Art Rupe, the owner of Specialty Records, recalled of the late 1940s, "looked down on country music. Among themselves, the blacks called country blues 'field nigger' music. They wanted to be citified."

At first, only blacks bought R & B discs. Johnny Otis, a white bandleader who grew up in a black section of Berkeley and later helped many black artists rise to stardom, noticed the trend: "As far as black music was concerned we had what was known as race music. Race music was Big Bill Broonzy, Peetie Wheatstraw, and things like that. Now, these things were very much part of the black community but they didn't occur anywhere else and these cats could hardly make a living plying their trade." A successful rhythm and blues recording generally sold only four hundred thousand copies, and, according to Jerry Wexler of Atlantic Records, "sales were localized in ghetto markets. There was no white sale, and no white radio play."

But in the early 1950s, more and more white teenagers began to become aware of R & B. At first, young southern whites started to buy records by black artists. As Jerry Wexler of Atlantic observed in the early 1950s, "we became aware that southern whites were buying our records, white kids in high school and college." In California at the same time, Johnny Otis saw the changing composition of the R & B audiences, which were becoming dotted with white faces. In 1952, the Dolphin Record store in Los Angeles, which specialized in R & B records, reflected the trend, reporting 40 percent of its sales to whites. Eventually white teens in all parts of the country turned to rhythm and blues. In April 1955, Mitch Miller—then head of Columbia Records and later famous for the singalong craze he masterminded—complained that "rhythm and blues songs are riding high." This " 'rock and roll' began among

Negro people, was first recorded by Negro performers and had its following among Negroes in the South and also Negro urban areas in the North." But "suddenly," Miller noticed that "millions of white teenagers who buy most of the 'pop' records in America have latched onto rhythm and blues."

SOCIAL CHANGE AND ROCK AND ROLL

The sudden transformation that Miller observed, and later viciously criticized, can be explained by a number of social changes that occurred during the 1950s. Television made radio space available to more recording artists. Before the 1950s, network radio shows, many of them broadcast live, dominated the airwaves, and as Johnny Otis argued, "in the thirties and forties, black music was summarily cut off the radio." It "simply was not played, black music of any kind—even a Louis Armstrong was not played on the air." Television, curtailed during World War II, became more popular and affordable after the war. By 1953, more than 300 television stations in the United States broadcast to more than 27 million sets. By absorbing the network shows, television allowed black records to be played on the radio.

Many of the disc jockeys who spun R & B records became die-hard advocates of the music. B. Mitchell Reed, who still broadcasts on the leading Los Angeles rock station, KMET FM, became "enthralled with rock" in the 1950s and convinced the management to switch from a jazz format to rock when he "realized that the roots of the stuff that I was playing—the rock—had come from the jazz and blues I'd been playing before." Even earlier than Reed's conversion to rock, the Los Angeles "dean of the DJs," Al Jarvis, "wanted the black artists to be heard" and introduced them on his show.

Rock-and-roll's superpromoter was Alan Freed. Freed, a student of classical trombone and music theory, began his broadcasting career in New Castle, Pennsylvania, on the classical station WKST. After a four-year stint in Akron, Ohio, he landed a job in Cleveland in 1951 on the independent station WJW. Although hired to play classical albums, Freed witnessed the reaction of white teenagers to R & B as the music blared in a local record store and "went to the station manager and talked him into permitting me to follow my classical program with a rock 'n' roll party." He picked "Blues for Moondog," a King release by Todd Rhodes, for his theme song and named his show "The Moon Dog Rock 'n' Roll House Party."

Freed ceaselessly marketed the new music. In 1952 and 1953, the disc jockey organized racially integrated rock-and-roll concerts in the Cleveland area that met with enthusiastic responses. For the first, the "Moon Dog Coronation Ball," which included Charles Brown, the Moonglows, and the Dominoes, he sold eighteen thousand tickets for an auditorium that seated nine thousand and was forced to cancel the show. By 1954, the successful Freed landed the key nighttime spot on the influential New York station, WINS. While there, the DJ introduced thousands of young whites on the East Coast to black music, consistently befriending black artists recorded on the small, independent labels at the expense of the major, "all-white" companies. The movies in which he appeared—"Don't Knock the Rock," "Rock, Rock, Rock," and the now-famous "Rock Around the Clock," which caused riots in the United States and Europe—further familiarized white youths with R & B, now being called rock-and-roll by Freed.

Young teens listened to disc jockeys such as Freed on a new invention—the portable, transistorized radio. First developed in 1947 at the Bell Laboratory in New Jersey, it reached the general public by 1953. Within a decade, the hand-held radio was bought yearly by more than 12 million consumers, many of them teens. It offered teens on the move an inexpensive means of experiencing the exciting new music called rock-and-roll.

The car radio served the same purpose as the portable transistor model. Marketed initially in the 1950s, it became standard equipment within a few years. By 1963, music blasted forth from the dashboards of more than 50 million automobiles that sped down the highways and backroads of the country. The car radio introduced rock-and-roll to many teens who used the automobile in such rites of passage as the school prom and the first date. In 1959, a nervous, clammy-palmed youth, sitting next to his girlfriend and behind the wheel of his father's El Dorado, could hear Chuck Berry detail his exploits with Maybelline that occurred in a similar car. The car radio provided a bridge between rock-and-roll and a mobile, young, car-crazy generation.

The civil rights movement also made black-inspired rock more acceptable. In 1954, the year that the Canadian group, the Crew-cuts, made "Sh-Boom" into rock's first commercial success, the Supreme Court handed down *Brown v. the Board of Education of Topeka*. Convinced by the arguments of Thurgood Marshall, counsel for the NAACP and later a Supreme Court justice himself, the court unanimously banned segregation in public schools and ordered school districts to desegregate. "In the field of public education," Chief Justice Earl Warren contended, "the doctrine of 'separate but equal' has no place. Separate educational facilities are inherently unequal." By overturning the "separate but equal" doctrine of the 1896 *Plessy v. Ferguson* case, the court had strongly endorsed black rights and had helped to start a civil rights movement that would foster an awareness and acceptance of black culture, including the black-based rock and roll.

The number of youths who would feel the impact of the *Brown* decision was growing rapidly. In 1946, about 5.6 million teenagers attended American high schools. Ten years later, the number climbed to 6.8 million, and in 1960, to 11.8 million. Observers called it the "wartime baby boom." "No decrease is in sight this century," predicted a Census Bureau official in 1955. "We have come to consider it routine to report new all-time high records."

Many of these teens, living during prosperous times, had money in their pockets to spend on records. Between 1940 and 1954, the United States Gross National Product (GNP) rose from $200 billion to $360 billion, and the average yearly family income increased from about $5,000 to $6,200. Having more leisure time than during the war, most Americans spent much of this extra money on consumer items such as paperback novels, television sets, cameras, and electrical appliances. Teenage sons and daughters received sizeable allowances totaling more than $9 billion in 1957 and $10.5 billion in 1963. Rather than cameras or electrical gadgets, the youths bought records. In a 1960 survey of 4,500 teenage girls conducted by *Seventeen* magazine, the average teen had "a weekly income of $9.53, gets up at 7:43 A.M., and listens to the radio two hours a day." Craving the songs they heard, more than 70 percent of the girls bought records with their allowances. An affluent society, along with other factors, paved the way for the mass consumption of rock-and-roll.

By 1954, rock-and-roll was beginning to achieve a general popularity among white youths. Teens bought discs by Chuck Berry, Little Richard, and Fats Domino. Soon they started to dance to the music. When Ralph Bass, a producer for Chess Records, went on the road with black acts in the late 1940s and early 1950s, "they didn't let whites into the clubs. Then they got 'white spectator tickets' for the worst corner of the joint. They had to keep the white kids out, so they'd have white nights sometimes, or they'd put a rope across the middle of the floor. The blacks on one side, whites on the other digging how the blacks were dancing and copying them. Then, hell, the rope would come down, and they'd all be dancing together." Touring with Fats Domino in 1957 and 1958, Chuck Berry also saw audiences beginning to integrate: "Salt and pepper all mixed together, and we'd say, 'Well, look what's happening.' "

RACIST BACKLASH

The integration of white and black youths elicited a racist response from many white adults. In 1956, as white Southerners lashed out against desegregation and attacked civil rights workers, a spokesman for the White Citizens Council of Birmingham, Alabama, charged that rock-and-roll—"the basic, heavy-beat music of the Negroes"—appealed to "the base in man, brings out animalism and vulgarity" and, most important, formed a "plot to mongrelize America."

Other whites expressed their fear of race mixing by harping

about the sexual overtones of rock. Testifying before a Senate sub-committee in 1958, Vance Packard—author of *Hidden Persuaders*—cautioned that rock-and-roll stirred "the animal instinct in modern teenagers" by its "raw savage tone." "What are we talking about?" Packard concluded, quoting an article from a 1955 issue of *Variety*. "We are talking about rock 'n' roll, about 'hug' and 'squeeze' and kindred euphemisms which are attempting a total breakdown of all reticences about sex." *Cash Box* similarly editorialized that "really dirty records" had been "getting air time," and suggested that companies "stop making dirty R & B records." Russ Sanjek, later vice-president of Broadcast Music, Inc. (BMI), which initially licensed most rock songs, explained the white hysteria over possible white and black sexual relations: "It was a time when many a mother ripped pictures of Fats Domino off her daughter's bedroom wall. She remembered what she felt toward her Bing Crosby pin-up, and she didn't want her daughter creaming for Fats."

A few adults defended the music of their children. In 1958, one mother from Fort Edward, New York, found that rock eased the boredom of her housework: "After all how much pep can you put into mopping the floor to 'Some Enchanted Evening,' but try it to 'Sweet Little Sixteen' by Chuck Berry and see how fast the work gets done. (I know the above is silly, but I just had to write it because it really is true, you know.)" "Rock and roll has a good beat and a jolly approach that keeps you on your toes," she added.

To jazz innovator Count Basie, the uproar over rock reminded him of the racist slurs hurled at his music two decades earlier. After living through the "swing era of the late 1930s when there was a lot of screaming pretty much like the furor being stirred up today," he remembered "particularly one comment in the 1930s, which said 'jam sessions, jitterbugs, and cannibalistic rhythm orgies are wooing our youth along the primrose path to hell.' The funny thing is, a lot of the kids who used to crowd around the bandstand while we played in the 1930s are still coming around today to catch us. A lot of them are parents in the PTA, and leading citizens."

Many whites refused to accept the Count's logic. To waylay expected integration, they tried to outlaw rock-and-roll. The Houston Juvenile Delinquency and Crime Commission blacklisted thirty songs that it considered obscene, all of them by black artists, which included "Honey Love" by the Drifters, the Five Royales' "Too Much Lovin," "Work with Me Annie" by Hank Ballard and the Midnight-ers, and Ray Charles's "I Got a Woman." R & B singer Jimmy Witherspoon, living in Houston at the time, felt that "the blacks was starting a thing in America for equality. The radio stations and the people in the South was fighting us. And they were hiring program directors to program the tunes. . . . They banned Little Richard's tune ('Long Tall Sally') in Houston." In Memphis, station WDIA banned the recordings of thirty black rock-and-roll singers.

In some areas, violence erupted in response to the new music.

In April 1956 at a Nat King Cole concert, the White Citizens Council of Birmingham, equating jazz with R & B, jumped on the stage and beat the performer. Explaining the incident, Ray Charles said it happened because "the young white girls run up and say, 'Oh, Nat!' and they say, 'No, we can't have *that!'* Come on man, shit, that's where it is." At other rock-and-roll shows, Bo Diddley reminded interviewer Lou Cohen, that "we used to have funny things like bomb scares and stuff like that because we were in South Carolina where the K. K. K. didn't want us performing."

THE MUSIC INDUSTRY VS. ROCK AND ROLL

The music industry also organized against rock-and-roll. Crooners whose careers had taken nose dives because of the new music bitterly condemned it. Testifying before Congress in 1958, Frank Sinatra called rock "the most brutal, ugly, desperate, vicious form of expression it has been my misfortune to hear." He labeled rock and rollers "cretinous goons" who lured teenagers by "almost imbecilic reiterations and sly—lewd—in plain fact dirty—lyrics." By such devious means, he concluded, rock managed "to be the martial music of every sideburned delinquent on the face of the earth." A year earlier, Sammy Davis, Jr.—a black who had achieved success by singing in a style that differed little from Sinatra's—put it more succinctly: "If rock 'n' roll is here to stay I might commit suicide." At the same time, Dean Martin cryptically ascribed the rise of rock to "unnatural forces."

Disc jockeys who lost listeners from their pop and classical programs to rock-and-roll stations similarly spoke out against their competition. In 1955, Bob Tilton of WMFM in Madison, Wisconsin, called for "some records for adults that don't rock, roll, wham, bam, or fade to flat tones." To Chuck Blower of KTKT in Tucson, the year 1955, "with the tremendous upsurge of R & B into the pop crop— the almost complete absence of good taste, to say nothing of good grammar—this has been the worst and certainly the most frustrating pop year I have ever known." A *Billboard* survey in the same year indicated that "many jockeys believe the quality of the pop platter has seriously deteriorated in the past year. . . . Several jockeys are strongly opposed to the rhythm and blues influence in pop music."

Songwriters in the American Society of Composers, Authors, and Publishers (ASCAP) showed an equal disdain for rock. Because the new music usually was written by the performers themselves, professional songwriters began to scramble for work, and soon complained. Lyricist Billy Rose, then a board member of ASCAP, labeled rock-and-roll songs "junk," and "in many cases they are obscene junk much on the level with dirty comic magazines." Meredith Wilson, the songwriter of *Music Man* fame, charged that "rock and roll is dull, ugly, amateurish, immature, trite, banal and stale. It glorifies the mediocre, the nasty, the bawdy, the cheap, the tasteless." Mrs. Barbara Lehrman, a listener from Brooklyn, New York, supported Wilson's contention: "Let's give the music business back to the music men," she demanded in a letter to Senator John Pastore. "Let's clear the air of ear-splitting claptrap." To reassert their control, in 1953 ASCAP songwriters initiated a $150 million lawsuit against their competitor, the rock-oriented Broadcast Music, Inc., on the pretext of payola among the jockeys. It eventually ended in a Congressional subcommittee, but did little to squelch the popularity of rock music.

THE BLANCHING OF ROCK

Many record executives complained about and successfully undermined black rockers and their music. Some leaders of the music industry personally disliked rock-and-roll. RCA vice-president George Marek did not "happen to like [rock] particularly, but then I like Verdi and I like Brahms and I like Beethoven." As Ahmet Ertegun explained, "you couldn't expect a man who loved 'April in Paris' or who had recorded Hudson DeLange in the 30s when he was beginning in the business, to like lyrics like 'I Wanna Boogie Your Woogie,' and 'Louie, Louie.' He had always thought race music and hillbilly were corny, and so he thought rock 'n' roll was for morons."

More important than personal taste, established record executives feared the economic consequences of a new popular music that they did not control. Outdistanced by new, independent labels that had a virtual monopoly on rock acts by 1955, they worried about their share of the market, especially when white teens started to buy rock-and-roll records.

To reverse this trend, larger companies signed artists such as Pat Boone, who copied, or "covered" the songs of black artists with watered-down versions of the originals performed by whites. From 1954 to 1956, Boone, wearing a white sweater and white buck shoes, rose to prominence by covering R & B songs. He copied Fats Domino's "Ain't That a Shame," "At My Front Door" by the El Dorados, "Tutti Frutti" by Little Richard, the Flamingos' "I'll Be Home," "Long Tall Sally" again by Little Richard, and Ivory Joe Hunter's "I Almost Lost My Mind," among many others.

Boone many times toned down the originals. He changed Etta James's "Roll with Me, Henry" to the more bland "Dance with Me, Henry," and reworked T-Bone Walker's "Stormy Monday," substituting the phrase "drinkin' coca cola" for "drinkin' wine." When covering "Tutti Frutti," Boone explained, "I had to change some words, because they seemed too raw for me. I wrote, 'Pretty little Susie is the girl for me,' instead of 'Boys, you don't know what she do to me.' "

Other artists covered songs of R & B artists first released by independent labels. The McGuire Sisters copied "Sincerely" by the Moonglows; Dorothy Collins took Clyde McPhatter's "Seven Days"; Perry Como stole "Kokomo" from Gene and Eunice, as did the Crew Cuts, who covered the Penguin's "Earth Angel" and took their monster hit, "Sh-Boom," from the Chords. The Chicago-raised LaVern Baker, who in 1955 on Atlantic cracked the R & B market with "That's All I Need" and "Tweedle Dee," fell victim to many cover artists. "Imitation may be the sincerest form of flattery, but the kind of flattery I can do without," dryly noted the singer.

To sell these imitations, Columbia, Capitol, Decca, and RCA employed new marketing techniques. The companies placed their product on racks in suburban supermarkets which by 1956 sold $14 million worth of records and in another year sold $40 million of discs, almost 20 percent of all record sales. In addition, first Columbia and then RCA and Capitol started mail-order record clubs to further increase sales.

Many disc jockeys aided the majors in the purge of the independent labels. Although a few jockeys such as Alan Freed refused to spin covers, most gladly played "white" music. "It was a picnic for the majors," Ahmet Ertegun of Atlantic Records told an interviewer. "They'd copy our records, except that they'd use a white artist. And the white stations would play them while we couldn't get our records on. 'Sorry,' they'd say. 'It's too rough for us.' Or: 'Sorry, we don't program that kind of music.' " Similarly, Danny Kessler of Okeh Records, another independent, found that "the odds for a black record to crack through were slim. If the black record began to happen, the chances were that a white artist would cover—and the big stations would play the white record. . . . There was a color line, and it wasn't easy to cross."

Industry leaders even succeeded in banning some black artists from the airwaves. In one instance, CBS television executives discontinued the popular "Rock 'n' Roll Dance Party" of Alan Freed when the cameras strayed to a shot of black Frankie Lymon of the Teenagers dancing with a white girl.

The introduction of the 45-rpm record by the major companies helped undermine the power of the independents. Leon Rene of the small Exclusive Records outlined the effects of the move: "We had things going our way until Victor introduced the seven-inch vinyl, 45-rpm record, which revolutionized the record business and made the breakable ten-inch 78-rpm obsolete overnight. . . . Competition with the majors, however, forced the independent labels to use the seven-inch 45-rpm records, and they had to reduce the price of R & B records from a dollar five to seventy-five cents, retail. This forced many independent companies out of business."

Through all of these efforts, businessmen at the head of the major companies suppressed or at least curtailed the success of the independents and their black performers. The McGuire Sisters' copy of "Sincerely," for example, sold more than six times as many records as the Moonglows' original. In 1955 and 1956, the covers of such white artists as Pat Boone climbed to the top of the charts, while black artists received little fame or money for their pioneering efforts.

By the early 1960s, Wynonie Harris tended bar; Amos Milburn became a hotel clerk; and Muddy Waters, Howlin' Wolf, and Bo Diddley were forced to tour constantly to make a living. "With me there had to be a copy," complained Bo Diddley twenty years later. "They wouldn't buy me, but they would buy a white copy of me. Elvis got me. I don't even like to talk about it. I was Chess Records along with Muddy Waters, Koko Taylor, Etta James, Chuck Berry, Little Walter, Howlin' Wolf. Without us there wouldn't have been no Chess Records. I went through things like, 'Oh, you got a hit record but we need to break it into the white market. We need to get some guy to cover it.' And I would say, 'What do you mean?' They would never tell me it was a racial problem." Johnny Otis put the problem succinctly: Black artists developed the music and got "ripped off and the glory and the money goes to the white artists."

THE STORY OF ARTHUR "BIG BOY" CRUDUP

The saga of Arthur "Big Boy" Crudup bears testimony to Otis's charge. Crudup, born in Forrest, Mississippi, and working as a manual laborer in the fields, logging camps, sawmills, and construction projects until his thirties, headed to Chicago in 1941 and signed a contract with RCA, releasing over eighty sides between 1941 and 1956. The songs, including "Mean Ole Frisco Blues," "Rock Me Mama," "She's Gone," "That's All Right, Mama," and "My Baby Left Me," have been subsequently done by Elvis Presley, Creedence Clearwater Revival, Elton John, Rod Stewart, Canned Heat, Johnny Winter, and many others. But in the late 1950s Crudup quit playing: "I realized I was making everybody rich, and here I was poor."

In 1968, Dick Waterman, an agent and manager for many blues artists, fought for Crudup's royalties through the American Guild of Authors and Composers. He reached an agreement in 1970 with Hill and Range Songs, which claimed ownership of Big Boy's songs, for $60,000 in back royalties. Crudup and his four children traveled from their home in Virginia to New York City and signed the requisite papers in the Hill and Range office, a converted four-story mansion. John Clark, the Hill and Range attorney, took the papers to Julian Aberbach, head of Hill and Range, for his signature, while Waterman, Crudup, and his children "all patted each other on the back and congratulated Arthur that justice had finally

Arthur Crudup

been done." But, according to Waterman, "the next thing, John Clark comes back in the room, looking stunned and pale, and says that Aberbach refused to sign because he felt that the settlement gave away more than he would lose in legal action. We all waited for the punch line, for him to break out laughing and whip the check out of the folder. But it wasn't a joke. We sat around and looked at each other." Crudup, who once said "I was born poor, I live poor, and I'm going to die poor," passed away four years later, nearly destitute.

In only a few years, rock-and-roll, recorded and promoted by small independents, had become a major force in popular music. The major record and publishing companies, songwriters, and disc jockeys refused to allow independent labels and their black artists to enjoy the success that they deserved. As Mick Jagger of the Rolling Stones once observed: "Music is one of the things that changes society. The old idea of not letting white children listen to black music is true, 'cause if you want white children to remain what they are, they mustn't."

2

Elvis and Rockabilly

"I love the rhythm and beat of good rock and roll music and I think most people like it too. After all, it's a combination of folk or hillbilly music and gospel singing."

Elvis Presley

ROCKABILLY ROOTS

Elvis Presley, a kinetic image in white suede shoes, an oversized, white-checkered jacket over a jet-black shirt with an upturned collar, and *no tie*. He violently shook his black zoot-suit pants as he gyrated his hips and legs. A sneering, disdainful expression covered Presley's face, and his greased hair fell over his sweat-drenched forehead. The singer grabbed a microphone as if he were going to wrench it from its metal base and barked, snarled, whimpered, and shouted into it. Elvis warded off screaming fans who pulled at his loose pants, his suit, and his shirt, lusting to tear off a piece of the raw energy that burst forth. Swaggering across the stage, he sang a sexually charged music that fused a white, country past with the wild and suggestive beat of the black man. Elvis Presley, singing to hordes of adoring, frantic teens, delivered a music called rockabilly that would change the face of popular music.

White teenagers from poor southern backgrounds, growing up in the border states where black and white cultures stood face to face over a seemingly impassable chasm, delivered the pulsating mixture of black-inspired rhythm and blues and country and western known as rockabilly. They were teenagers such as Jerry Lee Lewis, who leapt on his piano, banged the keys with his feet, and heaved his jacket, and sometimes his shredded shirt, to the audience; the more subdued Carl Perkins, writer of "Blue Suede Shoes," "Boppin' the Blues," and many other classics; Johnny Cash, who launched his career with "The Ballad of a Teenage Queen," "Get Rhythm," and "Folsom Prison Blues"; Johnny Burnette, the cofounder of the crazed Rock and Roll Trio with brother Dorsey and Paul Burlison; the quiet, bespeckled Texan, Charles ("Buddy") Holly; and, of course, Elvis Presley, the pacesetter of the new music, whose raw edge drove the crowds to a frenzied insanity. Despite the warnings of many horrified adults, these poor southern whites spread the message of rock-and-roll to millions of clamoring teenage fans and vaulted to the top of the national charts.

Most rockabillies never dreamed of such success. Presley, the king of swagger, the musical embodiment of James Dean's celluloid image, grew up in a thirty-foot-long, two-room house in the poor section of Tupelo, Mississippi. His father, Vernon, sharecropped and worked odd jobs, while his mother, Gladys, did piecework as a sewing machine operator. When Elvis was born on January 8, 1935, one neighbor remembered that his parents "didn't have insurance and the doctor didn't believe in carrying his expectant mothers to the hospital, so Gladys stayed at home." During Elvis's childhood in Tupelo, noted a friend, the Presleys "lost their house and moved several times. They lived in several houses this side of the highway, on Kelly Street, then on Barry. Later the house on Barry was condemned. They was real poor. They just got by." In September 1948, the Presley family moved from Mississippi. As Elvis told it: "We were broke, man, broke, and we left Tupelo overnight. Dad packed all our belongings in boxes and put them on the top and in the trunk of a 1939 Plymouth. We just headed to Memphis. Things had to be better."

In Memphis, the standing of the Presleys did not improve initially. Vernon worked for a tool company, as a truck driver, and finally in 1949 landed a job as a laborer at the United Paint Company. Earning less than forty dollars a week, he paid the rent on an apartment in the Lauderdale Courts, a federally funded housing project. Elvis attended nearby Humes High School, "a lower poverty-type school, one of the lowest in Memphis," according to one of Presley's classmates. After graduating from Humes in 1953, he did factory work at the Precision Tool Company and then drove a truck for the Crown Electric Company until he turned to music. Jane Richardson, one of two home service advisors working for the Memphis Housing Authority, summed up the condition of the Presleys during their first years in Memphis: "They were just poor people."

Other rockabilly stars came from similar impoverished backgrounds. Jerry Lee Lewis, who scored hits in 1957 with "Great Balls of Fire" and "Whole Lotta Shakin' Goin' On," was born in September

1935 on a farm outside Ferriday, Louisiana. His father, the gaunt-faced Elmo, eked out a living doing carpentry work and by growing surplus produce on the farm. Johnny Cash was born on February 26, 1932, into a poor country family in Kingland, Arkansas. When Franklin D. Roosevelt's New Deal came to the South, the Cash family moved to Dyess, Arkansas, as part of a resettlement program for submarginal farmers. Johnny later enlisted in the Air Force and after his discharge sold refrigerators in Memphis. The boredom of the sales job prompted him to write the classic "I Walk the Line." Carl Perkins grew up only a few miles from Johnny Cash—according to Cash, "he on the Tennessee side of the Mississippi, I on the Arkansas side. We both lived on a poor cotton farm." When he wrote "Blue Suede Shoes," Perkins recounted, "me and my wife Valda were living in a government project in Jackson, Tennessee. Had the idea in my head, seeing kids in the bandstand so proud of their new city shoes—you gotta be real poor to care about new shoes like I did—and that morning I went downstairs and wrote out the words on a potato sack—we didn't have reason to have writing paper around."

THE ROCKABILLY SOUND

These poor youths combined the two indigenous musical forms of the rural American South: the blues and country music. Elvis Presley, as did the Delmore Brothers in the 1930s and Arthur ("Guitar Boogie") Smith in the 1940s, looked to both black and white music for inspiration. A member of the evangelical First Assembly of God Church in Tupelo, Elvis "used to go to these religious singings all the time. There were these singers, perfectly fine singers, but nobody responded to them. Then there was the preachers and they cut up all over the place, jumpin' on the piano, movin' ever' which way. The audience liked 'em. I guess I learned from them."

Elvis listened to such bluesmen of the Mississippi Delta as Big Bill Broonzy, B. B. King, John Lee Hooker, and Chester ("Howlin' Wolf") Burnett, hearing them on late-night radio and in the clubs along Beale Street in Memphis, one of the main thoroughfares of black musical culture in the South. According to blues great B. B. King, "I knew Elvis before he was popular. He used to come around and be around us a lot. There was a place we used to go and hang out on Beale Street. People had like pawn shops there and a lot of us used to hang around in certain of these places and this was where I met him."

The Presley sound also was steeped in the country and western tradition of the South—Roy Acuff, Ernest Tubb, Ted Daffan, Bob Wills, and Jimmie Rodgers. In late 1954, Elvis, then called the King of the Western Bop, played the Bel Air Club in Memphis with bassist Bill Black and guitarist Scotty Moore in Doug Poindexter's Starlite Wranglers. At that time, recalled Poindexter, "we were strictly a coun-

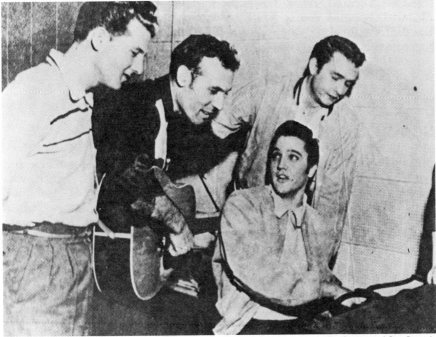

Million Dollar Quartet of Sun Records. From left to right: Jerry Lee Lewis, Carl Perkins, Elvis Presley, and Johnny Cash

try band. Elvis worked hard at fitting in, but he sure didn't cause too many riots in them days."

Presley's first recordings revealed his dual influences: a "race" number written by Arthur ("Big Boy") Crudup, "That's All Right, Mama," and a Bill Monroe country tune, "Blue Moon of Kentucky." As Paul Ackerman, *Billboard's* music editor, pointed out: "Often the difference between a country side and an R & B side is merely the use of strings as against the use of horns. The Presley sound might be called R & B without horns but with strings." Presley summed it up himself: "I love the rhythm and beat of good rock and roll music and I think most people like it too. After all, it's a combination of folk or hillbilly music and gospel singing."

The wild man Jerry Lee Lewis, who has never minced words, once defined the new music that fused R & B and country: "I play rock-and-*roll*," he insisted. "Don't ever call me a hillbilly. I'm a *rocker.*"

Ironically, at least to self-righteous Northerners, southern whites incorporated the black-inspired R & B into their music. "The breakthrough didn't come, as you might expect, in the North," observed Atlantic Record cofounder Ahmet Ertegun. "No, it was 'prejudiced' white Southerners who began programming R & B. They began playing Fats Domino, Ivory Joe Hunter, Roy Milton, Ruth Brown, Amos Milburn, because young white teenagers heard them on those top-of-the dial stations and began requesting them. What the hell was Elvis listening to when he was growing up?" Added Jerry Wexler, another one of the original forces behind Atlantic: "Despite the Ku Klux Klan and bloodshed, the Southern white is a helluva lot closer to the Negro psyche and black soul than your liberal white Northerner."

SUN RECORDS AND ELVIS

Many southern rockabillies recorded their brand of raucous black and white blues at the Sun Record Company in Memphis, which was owned by Sam Phillips. Phillips, growing up near Florence, Alabama, and working in the cotton fields as a boy, seldom noticed "white people singing a lot when they were chopping cotton, but the odd part about it is I never heard a black man who couldn't sing good. Even off key, it had a spontaneity about it that would grab my ear." He "got turned on to rock and roll immediately, when it was still rhythm and blues," he later related. "I always felt that rhythm and blues had a special viability." During the early 1940s, a young Phillips landed a job as a disc jockey at WLAY in Muscle Shoals, Alabama, moved to WLAC in Nashville, and ended at WREC in Memphis.

Phillips, earning certification as a radio engineer through a correspondence program, built his own recording studio in a converted radiator shop on Union Avenue in Memphis to record R & B artists, since, in his words, "there was no place in the South they could go to record, the nearest place where they made so-called race records—which was soon to be called rhythm and blues—was Chicago." He cut sides for such independent companies as Chess and Modern, with such performers as Howlin' Wolf, Big Walter Horton, Joe Louis Hill, Rosco Gordon (who began to combine R & B and country), B. B. King, and Jackie Brenston, who with the Ike Turner band cut "Rocket 88."

The R & B orientation of Sun Records began to change during the early 1950s. Many of the best black performers in Memphis, such as B. B. King and Howlin' Wolf, trekked to Chicago, the rhythm and blues capital of the world, and the remaining artists only sold a limited number of discs. Phillips, still in his twenties, also sought a younger audience. As he told *Rolling Stone* magazine, he wanted his records to appeal "most especially to young whites, young blacks and then thirdly to the older blacks. . . . There was just no music for young people then except for a few little kiddy records put out by the major labels." Faced with a declining business in R & B, Phillips confided to his secretary that "if I could find a white man who had the Negro sound and the Negro feel, I could make a billion dollars."

Elvis Presley made Sam Phillips's dream come true. In 1953, an eighteen-year-old Presley recorded the Ink Spots' "My Happiness" as a present for his mother at the Memphis Recording Service, a section of the Sun Studio where anyone could record a ten-inch acetate for four dollars. On a Friday in January 1954, he returned and cut his second disc—a ballad, "Casual Love," and a country tune, "I'll Never Stand in Your Way." Marion Keisker, the secretary at the studio, taped the takes and rushed them to her boss.

After a few weeks, Phillips telephoned Presley and made arrangements for some recording sessions. Presley, guitarist Scotty Moore, and bass player Bill Black struggled without results until finally a disgusted Phillips "went back to the booth. I left the mikes open, and I think that Elvis felt like, 'What the hell do I have to lose? I'm really gonna blow his head off, man.' And they cut down on 'That's All Right, Mama,' and, hell, man, they were just as instinctive as they could be."

Dewey Phillips, WHBQ disc jockey who had the R & B radio show "Red Hot and Blue," received the record from the Sun owner the next day. On July 10, 1954, recalled Phillips, Dewey "played that thing, and the phones started ringing. Honey, I'll tell you, all hell broke loose." The disc jockey then interviewed the new local sensation. In Dewey's words, "I asked him where he went to high school and he said Humes. I wanted to get that out, because a lot of people listening thought he was colored." Within ten days more than five thousand orders for the record streamed into the Sun offices, and the song hit the top position in the Memphis charts.

Elvis's live performances began to create hysteria. "In his first public show," Phillips remembered, "we played him at a little club up here at Summer and Medenhall. I went out there that night and introduced Elvis. Now this was kind of out in the country and way out on the highway, as they say. It was just a joint. Here is a bunch of hard-drinking people, and he ain't necessarily playing rhythm and blues, and he didn't look conventional like they did. He looked a little *greasy*, as they called it then. And the reaction was just *incredible*."

The mania continued unabated during Elvis' first tour of the South. On July 4, 1955, in DeLeon, Texas, fans shredded Presley's pink shirt—a trademark by now—and tore the shoes from his feet. One female admirer from Amarillo, Texas, suffered a gash in her leg at the concert. "But who cares if it left a scar," she told a *Newsweek* reporter. "I got it trying to see Elvis and I'm proud of it. This must be what memories are made of."

Country singer Bob Luman recalled similar hysteria at Kilgore, Texas. "The cat came out in red pants and a green coat and a pink shirt and socks," he told writer Paul Hemphill, "and he had this sneer on his face and he stood behind the mike for five minutes, I'll bet, before he made a move. Then he hit his guitar a lick, and he broke two strings. So there he was, these two strings dangling, and he hadn't done anything yet, and these high school girls were screaming and fainting and running up to the stage, and then he started to move

Photo by Alfred Wertheimer, used by courtesy of RCA Records

The young Elvis Presley, 1956

his hips real slow like he had a thing for his guitar. That was Elvis Presley when he was about nineteen, playing Kilgore, Texas. He made chills run up my back."

Presley, attracting die-hard fans, began to sell records. In early 1955, the singer had a local hit with "Good Rockin' Tonight." Later that year he regularly appeared on the radio program, "Louisiana Hayride" on KWKH in Shreveport, Louisiana and made his television debut on a local version of "Hayride," which propelled "Baby, Let's

Play House" to number 10 and "Mystery Train" to the top slot on the national country-and-western chart.

"THE KILLER"

Sam Phillips, buoyed by his success with Presley, began to record other young Southerners who had the same gritty, jumpy sound. A persistent Jerry Lee Lewis, nicknamed "The Killer" in high school, joined Sun in 1956. Influenced by both the gospel sound and country singer Jimmie Rodgers, Lewis first played piano publicly at the age of fourteen with a local country band in a Ford dealership parking lot. Five years later, a determined Jerry Lee headed for Memphis and met Jack Clement. The producer at the Sun studio, according to Lewis, "told me he didn't have time to make a tape with me, but I told him he was going to do it or I'd whip him. I had driven up to Memphis from Ferriday, Louisiana—286 miles. I sold 39 dozen eggs to pay for the gas. I said, 'You've got the time. I'm going to play the piano and you're going to put it on tape for Sam Phillips.' " He said, "Well, if you feel that strongly about it, you must be good."

When Phillips returned from a long-deserved vacation at Daytona Beach, Clement put Lewis's "Crazy Arms" on the sound system, and the Sun owner screamed, "Where the *hell* did that man come from? He played that piano with abandon," Phillips later remembered. "A lot of people do that, but I could hear between the stuff that he played and he didn't play, that spiritual thing. Jerry is very *spiritual*."

In December 1956, Lewis released the Sun-issued "Crazy Arms," which entered the lower reaches of the charts. For the next year, Jerry Lee backed a few lesser known Sun acts such as Warren Smith on "Miss Froggie" and the colorful Billy Lee Riley and his Little Green Men. Lewis helped Riley on "Flying Saucers Rock and Roll" and "Red Hot" and lured two of the Little Green Men to his own camp—drummer James Van Eaton and guitarist Roland James.

In 1957, Sam Phillips recorded Jerry Lee Lewis and his new band ripping through an earth-shattering version of "Whole Lotta Shakin' Goin' On" for his second Sun disc, which sold sixty thousand copies regionally soon after its release. Phillips, in dire financial straits, decided to put Sun's efforts behind the single. "I knew the only hope to make Sun a successful and big company was that we take Jerry Lee Lewis and put everything behind him and use his talent to create all the other Sun personalities," remarked Judd Phillips, Sam's brother and a Sun executive.

The promotion package included a spot on the popular "Steve Allen Show"—the close rival of the "Ed Sullivan Show"—which showcased Lewis frantically banging the keys, kicking the piano stool into the audience, and shaking his mop of curly blonde locks until he looked like Lucifer's incarnation. The teens in the audience erupted while the stage crew peered in disbelief. After the performance, the switchboard lit up: Scandalized voices screamed their dissatisfaction and shaky-voiced teenagers called to find out more about their new idol. In an uncharacteristic understatement, Lewis related: "Then I got on the Steve Allen Show and it busted wide open." Hits followed with "Great Balls of Fire," "Breathless," and "High School Confidential."

"BLUE SUEDE SHOES"

Lewis's success was matched by a steady stream of Sun rockabilly talents, among them guitarist-songwriter Carl Lee Perkins. Born in Tiptonville, Tennessee, on April 9, 1932, Perkins and his family moved near Jackson, Mississippi, where young Carl found work at a battery factory. Eight years later, in 1953, he bought his first guitar, a $150 Les Paul, and began to perfect a unique style. Since he seldom had the cash for new strings, he once told a reporter, "I'd slide along to where I'd had to tie a knot and push up on a string 'cause I couldn't jump over the knot. Maybe if I'd been wealthy and could have bought new strings, I'd have slid down it and not developed the pushing up on the strings and I'd have sounded like everyone else."

Carl produced a sound that resembled that of other rockabillies. He "liked Bill Monroe's fast stuff and also the colored guys, John Lee Hooker, Muddy Waters, their electric stuff. Even back then, I liked to do Hooker's things Monroe style, blues with a country beat and my own lyrics" and began to play music that sounded very much like Presley's. Bob Neal, then a disc jockey at Memphis radio station WMPS and later Presley's manager, recalled that he and Elvis saw Perkins perform "in the fall of 1954 and we were both struck by the sound Perkins was getting. It was very similar to Elvis's own." After hearing Presley's first Sun recording, Perkins himself felt that "it was identical to what our band was doing and I just knew that we could make it in the record business after that."

Perkins and his band, which included his brothers Clayton and Jay as well as W. S. Holland, signed with Sun in 1955 and began touring from the back of a truck, charging a dollar to watch the show. That year, the Perkins band released three singles for Sun: "Movie Magg," backed by "Turn Around"; "Let the Jukebox Keep Playing," with the hard-bopping "Gone, Gone, Gone"; and in December 1955, Perkins's smash "Blue Suede Shoes," which by April 1956 topped country-and-western, pop, and R & B charts.

Though it seemed as if he might wrest the rockabilly crown from the still-emerging Elvis, Perkins faced tragedy on March 21, 1956. On the way to New York City for appearances on the "Ed Sullivan Show" and the "Perry Como Hour," outside of Delaware, he was involved in a car crash that killed his brother, Jay and hospitalized Carl with a broken shoulder and skull. "I was a poor farm boy, and with 'Shoes' I felt I had a chance but suddenly there I was in the hospital," he recalled bitterly.

Perkins never attained the stardom of Presley who, according to Perkins, "had everything. He had the looks, the moves, the manager, and the talent. And he didn't look like Mr. Ed, like a lot of us did." "Elvis was hitting them with sideburns, flashy clothes and no ring on the finger. I had three kids," added Carl. When Presley hit the charts with his version of "Blue Suede Shoes," Perkins was known more for his songwriting than for his performing and his star began to fade.

JOHNNY CASH

Johnny Cash was the other important Sun rockabilly besides Elvis, Jerry Lee Lewis, and Carl Perkins. Son of a sharecropper, Cash joined the Air Force when, in his words, "I started writing songs. I wrote 'Folsom Prison Blues' in the Air Force in 1953. I played with a little group of musicians in my barracks. I was singing Hank Snow and Hank Williams songs with them before I ever tried to sing my own songs."

Cash was also attracted to the blues. "My favorite music," he recalled, "is people like Pink Anderson, Robert Johnson, the king of the Delta blues singers, Howlin' Wolf, Muddy Waters. . . . Those are my influences in music, those are the ones I really loved."

The songwriter signed with Sun Records in 1955 and developed his own sound. As Cash told *Musician* magazine, "I kind of found myself in those first months working in the studio at Sun. I discovered, *let it flow*." He first hit the charts with "Cry, Cry, Cry." Convincing Sam Phillips that he should record it rather than baritone singer Tennessee Ernie Ford, Cash followed with "Folsom Prison Blues." The next year, he remembered, "Elvis asked me to write him a song. . . . I just told a story about a shoeshine boy. I put it down and Elvis loved ['Get Rhythm']. But it came time for my next single release and Sam said, 'Elvis can't have that!' . . . So Sam released it with the 'Ballad of a Teenage Queen' which got the most play for a long time." Later in 1956, Cash recorded his signature song, "I Walk the Line," which eventually sold a million copies.

THE SUN ROCKABILLY STABLE

The Big Four of Sun—Presley, Jerry Lee Lewis, Perkins, and Johnny Cash—supported a battalion of lesser-known but nonetheless hell-bent rockabillies. Billy Lee Riley was probably the most promising. The wild Riley, a part-Indian who played guitar, harmonica, drums, and bass, formed the Little Green Men in 1955. He scored hits with "Flying Saucers Rock and Roll" and "Red Hot" and drove crowds to a frenzied pitch with his onstage antics. During one memorable performance, he hung from the waterpipes near the stage with one hand and clutched the microphone with the other, screaming the lyrics of a song until his face turned a bright pink color. Though the fans went berserk, Riley never achieved major recognition. He believed that his failure stemmed from the "distribution of Sun discs. They sent out a batch of discs all together and when there was a Perkins release, a Cash release and later Jerry Lee Lewis, the dee jays didn't want to be bothered with the rest of the bunch. The public could only afford so many at one time anyway."

Sonny Burgess, another slightly crazed rockabilly in the Sun fold, produced raw rock but failed to attract a national audience. A farm boy from Newport, Arkansas, Burgess heard of Sun's growing reputation and traveled to Memphis in 1955. His music, best exemplified in his minor hit "Red-Headed Woman," which sold ninety thousand copies, combined a country Arkansas heritage and black rhythm and blues: "Yes, I really liked R & B, Fats Domino, Jimmy Reed, Muddy Waters," Burgess told a reporter. Burgess's gritty, R & B–inspired voice possessed the demonic quality of the true rockabilly. Authors Colin Escott and Martin Hawkins called Sonny's music "loosely organized chaos."

Ray Harris, who cut "Come On Little Mama" for Sun in 1956, had the same style. Bill Cantrell, then a Sun employee, felt that "Ray wanted to be another Elvis. He couldn't sing and he wasn't good to look at but he didn't care. Man, he was crazy. You would go to visit him and hear him practicing there on Ogden from two blocks away. He would open the door wearing nothing but his overalls and dripping with sweat. He had an old portable tape recorder and he'd go back to singing and playing and sweating. In the studio he would throw himself around with his arms like windmills. That record 'Come On Little Mama' was a triumph for the guitar man Wayne Powers and drummer Joe Riesenthal. They had to keep up with the guy." *Billboard* just referred to the single as "excitable."

Not all possessed the passion of Ray Harris. Some Sun rockabillies such as Roy Orbison were forced by Sam Phillips into the Sun mold. Orbison, raised in Wink, Texas, formed the Wink Westerners, later renamed the Teen Kings while in high school. After a year of college, remembered the singer, "I met a couple of guys who had written 'Ooby Dooby' and what convinced me I was in the wrong place at the wrong time was I heard a record by a young fellow on the jukebox called 'That's All Right.' "

Orbison headed for Memphis and in March 1956 recorded the Sun-issued "Ooby Dooby." It sold nearly a half million copies, reached number 59 on the *Billboard* charts, and represented the best showing of a Sun disc, except singles by the Big Four of Sun. The singer, characterized by sunglasses, black clothes, and a near-operatic, high-pitched, ethereal voice, followed with "Rockhouse," but only reluctantly. Said Jack Clement: "The first artist Sam gave me to record was Roy Orbison. I recorded 'Rockhouse' with Roy and it was good but Roy was not into what the Sun studio was capable of back then." "I was writing more ballads then [1957]," confirmed Roy, "but I didn't bother to ask Sam to release them. He was the boss and there was no arguing. I made some demos of things like 'Claudette' but that was about it. I would never have made it big with Sun. They just didn't have the ways to get into the audience I wanted to go for." Orbison eventually signed with Monument Records and in the early 1960s achieved prominence with a series of songs with almost innocent lyrics that built to powerful, dramatic, emotional crescendos: "Only the Lonely," "Running Scared," "Crying," and "Oh, Pretty Woman."

Except for a few artists, such as Roy Orbison, who had been pushed in a direction inconsistent with their talents, by late 1956 Sam Phillips had achieved his goal. He had groomed a stable of white country boys who sang with the feeling of black men and the intensity of whirling dervishes, driving white teenage girls to hysteria.

THE DECCA CHALLENGE

The major record companies, especially after the success of Elvis Presley, noticed the rockabilly trend and tried to capitalize on it. Decca Records took the lead, signing Bill Haley and the Comets. Born in Michigan, Haley in 1949 became a disc jockey at WPWA in Chester, Pennsylvania, and for the show formed a band, the Four Aces of Western Swing. As the Ramblin' Yodeler, he recorded country music with the Four Aces and then the Down Homers and the Saddlemen. "My mother was a piano teacher," he told an interviewer. "My dad, who was from Kentucky, played mandolin. And I suppose that was where the country influence came from."

In 1950, Haley recorded a cover version of Jackie Brenston's "Rocket 88," which convinced him to combine country swing music with the R & B boogie-woogie, jump beat of Louis Jordan. "We'd begin with Jordan's shuffle rhythm," remembered Milt Gabler, the Comets' producer at Decca. "You know, dotted eighth notes and sixteenths and we'd build on it. I'd sing Jordan riffs to the group that would be picked up by the electric guitar and tenor sax, Rudy Pompilli. They had a song that had the drive of [Jordan's] Tympany Five and the color of country and western. Rockabilly was what it was called back then."

"We started out as a country western group, then we added a touch of rhythm and blues," Haley recalled. "It wasn't something we planned, it just evolved. We got to where we weren't accepted as country western or rhythm and blues. It was hard to get bookings for a while. We were something new. We didn't call it that at that time, but we were playing rock-and-roll."

After minor success with "Crazy Man Crazy" in 1952, Haley and the Comets signed with Decca in 1954. They first released "Rock Around the Clock," a song originally cut two years earlier by Sunny Dae, who scored only a minor hit with it. The group followed with a remake of Joe Turner's "Shake, Rattle and Roll" that hit the Top 10 in both the United States and Britain. In 1955, the Comets rereleased "Rock Around the Clock," which hit the top of the charts and caused riots worldwide when it was included on the soundtrack of *Blackboard Jungle,* a movie which captured the spirit of teenage rebellion embodied by rock during the mid-1950s. In the words of rock critic Lillian Roxon, the furor over "Rock Around the Clock" "was the first inkling teenagers had that they might be a force to be reckoned with, in numbers alone. If there could be one song, there could be others; there could be a whole world of songs and, then, a whole world."

Haley continued to churn out hits. During 1955 and 1956, he scored with twelve Top 40 records, including "See You Later Alligator," "Burn That Candle," "Dim, Dim the Lights," "Razzle-Dazzle," and "R-O-C-K." In 1957, he appeared in two movies, *Rock Around the Clock* and *Don't Knock the Rock* that featured his music.

Though predating Elvis and laying claim to the first rockabilly success, Haley never wrenched the rock crown from Presley. He delivered a smoother sound than the jagged-edged Presley music. The singer and his Comets also offered a tamer stage show. In 1956, Haley warned that "a lot depends on the entertainer and how he controls the crowd. The music is stimulating enough without creating additional excitement," an apparent jab at Elvis. Just as important, Haley's age and appearance—pudgy, balding, and thirty-two years old in 1957—compared unfavorably to that of the young, virile, swivel-hipped Elvis in the eyes of teenage rock fans driven by raging hormones.

Decca, hoping to gain a larger share of the teen market, signed the Rock 'n' Roll Trio to its Coral subsidiary. Growing up in Memphis, Johnny and Dorsey Burnette met Paul Burlison in 1953 at the Crown Electric factory, the same company for which Presley drove a truck. Initially they played in a Hank Williams style. But when Burlison backed Howlin' Wolf on a radio broadcast in West Memphis, the group started to blend country music with the blues.

Beale Street in Memphis "was really happening in those days, and my dad and his friends would go down there a lot and listen to the blues guys," remembered Billy Burnette, the son of Dorsey, who continued in the rockabilly tradition of his family. "They'd buy their clothes on Beale Street, at Lansky Brothers, where all the black people shopped. Right outside Memphis, there was a voodoo village, all black—real mystic kind of people. People who were into music would go over there and get charms and things like that. You know, a lot of real old line Southern people called my dad and my uncle white niggers. Nobody was doing rock-and-roll in those days except people they called white trash. When my dad and uncle started doin' it, they were just about the first."

The pathbreaking Trio caused disturbances throughout the South with "The Train Kept a Rollin'," "Rock Billy Boogie," "Tear It Up," and "Rock Therapy." In one incident, reported the Evansville, Indiana, *Courier* in late 1956, "all during Burnette's performance, the crowd of about two thousand persons kept up a continuous howl that all but drowned out the singer's voice." When Johnny Burnette tried to leave the stage, hundreds of wild-eyed girls attacked him and "tore his shirt to bits for souvenirs." According to the *Courier,* "the singer, who had all but exhausted himself in the performance, was in sad shape when he reached the car. 'I shoulda laid off that last 'Hound Dog,' ' he panted." In 1956, the Trio decided to quit their jobs and move to New York City with hopes of national success. When the young Southerners won first prize on Ted Mack's "Amateur Hour," Decca added the group to its roster. The Rock 'n' Roll Trio recorded one seminal album and disbanded.

The same year, Decca discovered Charles ("Buddy") Holly, a skinny teenager from Lubbock, Texas, who wore thick-rimmed glasses and a shy grin. Holly had been exposed to R & B through records and on radio programs such as "Stan's Record Rack" broadcast from Shreveport, Louisiana. As Holly's friend Bob Montgomery explained, "Blues to us was Muddy Waters, Little Walter, and Lightnin' Hopkins."

As with other rockabillies, Holly was also influenced by white country music, especially bluegrass and western swing. He listened to performers such as Hank Snow and Hank Williams, and in 1953, with friends Bob Montgomery and Larry Welborn formed a country music trio that performed at the Big D Jamboree in Dallas and regularly played on the radio as "The Buddy and Bob Show." By his sixteenth birthday, Buddy already had "thought about making a career out of western music if I am good enough but I will just have to wait and see how that turns out."

The new music of rock-and-roll changed Buddy's plans. In early 1955, when Elvis arrived in Lubbock for an engagement at the Cotton Club, Holly and Bob Montgomery drove the new sensation around town. Later that night at the concert, remembered a Lubbock local, Buddy and Bob "went over to talk to Elvis. Later Buddy said to me, 'You know, he's a real nice, friendly fellow.' I guess Buddy was surprised that Elvis was so normal and would talk to him so easily, because Buddy thought of Elvis as a big star and really admired him." The next day, Holly and his group backed Elvis at the grand opening of a local Pontiac dealership. "And when the next KDVA Sunday Party rolled around, Buddy was singing Elvis songs." Added Larry Holly, Buddy's brother, "He was on an Elvis Presley kick—he just idolized the guy. And, I mean, he sounded exactly like him. He did Elvis Presley things on the Jamboree." Holly, interested in leather work at the time, even crafted a wallet with "ELVIS" emblazoned in pink letters on it and in early 1956 left the wallet at Sun Studios as a present for Presley.

Holly incorporated Presley's style to create a unique sound. By 1957, when he formed the Crickets with Joe B. Mauldin on stand-up bass and drummer Jerry Allison, he had perfected a light, bouncy, bright rockabilly that bore traces of the unique Presley sound.

Holly took his distinctive sound to the small studio of producer

Norman Petty, who had already recorded hits for the Rhythm Orchids—"Party Doll" and "Stickin' with You," released under the names of singer Buddy Knox and bassist Jimmy Bowen. With Petty's help, the Crickets hit the charts in 1957 with "That'll Be the Day," the title taken from a John Wayne line in the movie, *The Searchers*. They followed with a series of fresh rockabilly tunes that became rock-and-roll classics: "Peggy Sue," "Maybe Baby," "Not Fade Away," "Rave On," and "Oh Boy."

ROCKABILLY SWEEPS THE NATION

Other record companies, hoping for a share of the rockabilly market, searched for their own acts. Capitol Records, a major label, signed Gene Vincent, the Korean War veteran, who was born Gene Vincent Craddock in the southern navy town of Norfolk, Virginia. With his band, the Bluecaps, Vincent in 1956 released the unforgettable "Be-Bop-a-Lula." According to the singer, he wrote the classic one day when he "and Don Graves were looking at this bloody comic book. It was called Little Lulu and I said, 'Hell, man, it's bebopalulu.' And he said, 'Yeah, man, swinging,' and we wrote the song. Just like that. And some man came to hear it and he bought the song for $25. Right. Twenty-five dollars! And I recorded it and told my friends that I was going to get a Cadillac, because all rock and roll singers had Cadillacs." From 1956 to 1958, in quest of his Cadillac, Vincent cut such rockers as "Dance to the Bop," "Bluejean Bop," "Race with the Devil," "She She Little Sheila," and "Crazy Legs."

Cadence Records, a small independent owned by Archie Bleyer, scored with the more country-influenced Everly Brothers. Sons of country stars Ike and Margaret Everly, the two brothers, Don and Phil toured with their parents and performed on the family radio show. In 1955, the duo headed for Nashville, where they wrote songs for a country music publisher and the next year joined the Grand Ole Opry.

In 1957, after being spotted by Cadence Record talent scout Wesley Rose, the duo signed with the label and climbed the charts almost immediately with "Bye Bye Love." The new sound—bright, warm harmonies largely a result of the Everlys' country backgrounds—contained traces of R & B. As Don pointed out, "I loved Bo Diddley; I told [country guitar master] Chet Atkins, 'That's what I want my guitar to sound like.' I said, 'Chet, have you heard Bo Diddley?' he said, 'Yeah.' 'What's he doing?' He said, 'Well, he's got an amplifier, but he's also got a tuned guitar.' The intro to 'Bye Bye Love' was inspired by Bo Diddley." The Everlys followed with the now-classic "Wake Up Little Susie," "All I Have to Do Is Dream," and "Bird Dog," racking up sales of $35 million by 1962.

Imperial, the label that featured Fats Domino as its star, snagged Ricky Nelson in the rockabilly sweepstakes. The son of jazz band-

The Everly Brothers in the studio

leader Ozzie Nelson, by 1952 Nelson played himself on his parents' television series, "The Adventures of Ozzie and Harriet." The young Nelson "used to listen to the radio and longed to be a recording artist. I wanted to be Carl Perkins. I used to go and buy every Sun record that I could get my hands on back in the Fifties 'cause they were such a really good sound."

In 1957, Nelson debuted as a singer on his parents' show, signed with Imperial, and sold a million copies of a Fats Domino cover, "I'm Walking." During the next few years, Ricky managed to end many of the segments on "Ozzie and Harriet" by belting out his latest song at the high school sock hop. Helped by the television show and guitarist James Burton, who later backed Elvis, Nelson racked up a series of

Elvis and Rockabilly **47**

hits such as "Travelin' Man," "Poor Little Fool," "Just a Little Too Much," "Believe What You Say," and "Hello Mary Lou."

Liberty Records jumped into the rockabilly field with Eddie Cochran. The son of two Oklahoma City country-western fans, in 1949 Eddie moved with his family to Bell Gardens, California. While thumbing through the racks of a local record store, Cochran met Jerry Capehart, who would be his songwriter-collaborator throughout his career. In 1955, the duo traveled to Nashville, signed with American Music, and recorded "Skinny Jim," which flopped. Trying to secure better distribution for their discs, Capehart flew to Los Angeles and convinced Si Waronker, president of Liberty Records, to invest in the rockabilly talent of Cochran. After releasing a few unsuccessful singles, in late 1958 Cochran alternated between an Elvis-like whimper and a gravel-voiced growl in an anthem of teenage frustration, "Summertime Blues." Cochran's bopping call to arms, nearing the top of the charts, struck a chord among teenagers, who were gaining increasing power by their numbers.

THE SELLING OF ELVIS PRESLEY

RCA Victor lured to its label the performer who became known as the king of rock-and-roll. In 1955, the company offered Sun Records thirty-five thousand dollars for the rights to Elvis Presley's recorded material. Sam Phillips accepted the money and surrendered all of the Presley tapes that Sun had produced. "I looked at everything for how I could take a little extra money and get myself out of a real bind," explained Phillips. "I mean I wasn't broke, but man, it was hand-to-mouth."

In January 1956, RCA began to merchandise Elvis, for the first time using the powerful new medium of television to sell rock-and-roll. Developed during the 1920s, televised images had been offered to the public by the end of the 1930s and after World War II had become much more available. By 1953, 328 stations broadcast to nearly 27 million sets in the United States. Only three years later, the number of stations nearly doubled, to 620, and the number of TV sets in American homes increased to 37 million, showing many programs that previously had been aired on radio. At the time television was dominated by three networks—the American Broadcast Company (ABC), the Columbia Broadcasting System (CBS), and the National Broadcast Company (NBC)—the last of which owned by RCA, the Radio Corporation of America.

RCA immediately slotted the photogenic Elvis for television, booking him for six Saturday night appearances on the Tommy and Jimmy Dorsey "Stage Show," a half-hour variety program hosted by the two big-band leaders preceding Jackie Gleason's "The Honeymooners" and competing with "The Perry Como Hour." After Presley

the most talked-about new personality in the last 10 years of recorded music

ELVIS PRESLEY

now on RCA Victor records with

I FORGOT TO REMEMBER TO FORGET
MYSTERY TRAIN...20/47-6357

Bob Neal, manager
under direction of Hank Snow Jamboree Attractions,
Col. Tom Parker, general manager
Box 417, Madison, Tennessee

RCA/Estate of Elvis Presley

The new sensation: ad for Elvis Presley, December 3, 1955

boosted the ratings of "The Stage Show," RCA scheduled the singer for "The Milton Berle Show" and "The Steve Allen Show."

By the end of the year, Ed Sullivan, who earlier had condemned Presley as "unfit for a family audience," agreed to pay the new rock star fifty thousand dollars for three appearances on his show, one of the two most popular television programs in America at the time.

Elvis and Rockabilly   **49**

Sullivan booked Presley for his first appearance on September 9, 1956. Fearing a backlash from his usual viewers, the television host ordered that Elvis be filmed from the waist up, allowing the teenage television audience to imagine the pelvic gyrations that took place off the screen. Creating one of the most legendary clips in television history, Sullivan attracted nearly 54 million viewers or almost 83 percent of the television audience to his show and helped lift Presley into national prominence. "Presley is riding high right now with network T.V. appearances," observed *Billboard*, and RCA's release of "Heartbreak Hotel" "should benefit from all the special plugging." A week later, the magazine reported that sales of the single had "snowballed," and in a few more weeks it reached the top of the national charts.

In the next few months, Presley hit the top of the charts with a number of songs, many of which he had sung on his television appearances: "I Want You, I Need You, I Love You," "Love Me Tender," "Hound Dog," "Don't Be Cruel," and "All Shook Up," the last two written by black songwriter Otis Blackwell, who had penned "Great Balls of Fire" for Jerry Lee Lewis.

Besides television, a new Top 40 format on radio helped promote Presley. It was pioneered in 1954 by radio chain owners Todd Storz and Gordon McLendon to rescue radio from a five-year decline that had been caused by the popularity of television. Top 40 radio involved an instant news concept, disc jockey gags and patter, and a limited play list of roughly 40 hits that disc jockeys spun in a constant rotation.

Top 40 radio, promoting the songs of only a few artists, fueled the meteoric rise of Elvis. "There was a huge change overnight," recalled Russ Solomon, the founder of the Tower Records chain. "Everybody was interested [in Presley]. At the same moment, Top Forty radio came into play. As a result there was a very dramatic change in the way you perceived selling records. Your hit titles became more and more important."

The marketing acumen of Colonel Thomas Parker contributed to Presley's hit-making success. Born in 1910, Parker got his start in carnivals. Since the circus life, according to the Colonel, "was a day-to-day living" he used his ingenuity to make money. For one of his ploys, he rented a cow pasture adjacent to the circus grounds and during the night herded the cows on the only road through the field, which served as the sole exit from the carnival. When unsuspecting circus-goers reached the exit the next day, they could either walk through ankle-deep manure or pay the Colonel a nickel for a pony ride through it.

By 1955, Parker had abandoned the circus and applied his ingenious techniques to the careers of such country singers as Roy Acuff, Minnie Pearl, Eddy Arnold, and Hank Snow. A year later, remembered one of Elvis's neighbors, the Colonel "in the most polished Machiavellian way" convinced Presley's parents to sign their son to his management company. "Colonel Tom was a salesman, I'll give him that. He sure knew how to sell." Almost immediately the Colonel began to market Elvis Presley to the media. "The Colonel doesn't sell Elvis to the public, dig?" Jon Hartmann, one of Parker's subordinates, later observed. "He sells Elvis to the people who sell to the public, and those are the media people—the television and motion picture personalities, the executives and businessmen who control the networks, the important radio people. It's like an endless trip for the Colonel. Elvis, as a product, always in the state of being sold."

In mid-1956, Hank Saperstein joined Tom Parker in the Presley media blitz. Saperstein had become successful in the advertising industry through his marketing efforts for television creations such as Lassie, Wyatt Earp, Ding Dong School, and the Lone Ranger. Not to be outdone by his competitors, he had even stuffed plastic blowguns in cereal boxes to increase the sales of Kellogg Cornflakes. Saperstein recognized the "universality" of the Presley appeal and began to plaster Elvis's name and picture on all types of products. By 1957, Saperstein and Parker had saturated the American market.

If a loyal fan so desired, she could put on some Elvis Presley bobby socks, Elvis Presley shoes, skirt, blouse, and sweater, hang an Elvis Presley charm bracelet on one wrist, and with the other hand smear on some Elvis Presley lipstick—either Hound Dog Orange, Heartbreak Hotel Pink, or Tutti Frutti Red. She might put an Elvis Presley handkerchief in her Elvis Presley purse and head for school. Once in the classroom, she could write with her green Elvis Presley pencil, inscribed "Sincerely Yours," and sip an Elvis Presley soft drink between class periods. After school she could change into Elvis Presley bermuda shorts, blue jeans, or toreador pants, write to an Elvis Presley pen pal, or play an Elvis Presley game, and fall asleep in her Elvis Presley pajamas on her Elvis Presley pillow. Her last waking memory of the day could be the Elvis Presley fluorescent portrait that hung on her wall. All told, the fan could buy seventy-eight different Elvis Presley products that grossed about $55 million by December 1957. In addition to 25 percent of Elvis's performance royalties, Colonel Parker received a percentage of the manufacturer's wholesale price on each item.

REACTIONS AGAINST THE PRESLEY MANIA

Many adults criticized the Presley mania. In one review, Jack Gould, the television critic for *The New York Times*, wrote: "Mr. Presley has no discernible singing ability. His specialty is rhythm, songs which he renders in an undistinguished whine; his phrasing, if it can be called that, consists of the stereotyped variations that go with a beginner's aria in a bathtub. . . . His one specialty is an accented movement of the body that heretofore has been primarily identified with the repertoire of the blonde bombshells of the burlesque runway. The gyration never had anything to do with the world of popular music and still doesn't." Jack O'Brien of the New York *Journal-American* agreed that "Elvis Presley wiggled and wiggled with such abdominal gyrations that burlesque bombshell Georgia Southern really deserves equal time to reply in gyrating kind. He can't sing a lick, makes up for vocal shortcomings with the weirdest and plainly planned, suggestive animation short of an aborigine's mating dance."

Others held similar opinions. Jack Mabley of *Downbeat* jazz magazine did not think "the fad of Elvis Presley is going to last much longer than the fad for swallowing goldfish." Addressing the House of Representatives, Congressman Robert MacDonald of Massachusetts viewed "with absolute horror" performers "such as Elvis Presley, Little Richard . . . and all the other hundreds of musical illiterates, whose noises presently clutter up our jukeboxes and our airways." *Time* magazine called Presley a "sexibitionist," who lived "off what most parents would agree is the fat of teenagers' heads," and *Look* accused him of dragging " 'big beat' music to new lows in taste." The magazine *America* pleaded with television and radio executives to "stop handling such nauseating stuff" so "all the Presleys of our land would soon be swallowed up in the oblivion they deserve." "Beware Elvis Presley," the magazine cautioned. Broadway composer Oscar Hammerstein, analyzing "All Shook Up," astutely noted that " 'bug' and 'shook up' don't rhyme. It's sloppy writing."

Fear of increasing juvenile delinquency underlay much of the backlash against Presley. The dark image of the alienated, shiftless, and violent street tough in a black leather jacket who dangled a cigarette from his lips had been popularized in books and films. The preoccupation with the teenage delinquent was reflected in such paperbacks as *Blackboard Jungle, Gang Rumble, The Hoods Ride In, Teen-Age Vice, Teen-Age Terror, D For Delinquent* and countless others. It also appeared in such movies as *The Wild One* (1954) which showcased Marlon Brando as the leader of a heartless motorcycle gang, and *Rebel Without a Cause*, released the next year, which starred James Dean who with Brando symbolized teenage rebellion.

Rebel Without A Cause, explained Stewart Stern, who wrote the screenplay, dealt with "the phenomenon of what was called in those days juvenile delinquency, happening not in families that were economically deprived but in middle-class families that were emotionally deprived. Partly, people felt it had to do with the war, the fact that so many women were working for the first time away from the home, that older brothers and fathers who would have been role models for the young weren't there, and the tremendous drive for material 'things.' " "When the kids saw that the material goods that were supposed to make their parents happy really didn't," continued Stern, "they began to doubt their parents' authority." "The lesson of *Rebel*," concluded the screenwriter, "was that if the kids could not be acknowledged or understood by their parents, at least they could be acknowledged by each other."

Threatened by the power of youth banding together, which they identified with juvenile delinquency, adults many times linked rock-and-roll to teen violence. On April 11, 1956, *Variety* connected rock to a "staggering wave of juvenile violence and mayhem. . . . On the police blotters, rock 'n' roll has been writing an unprecedented record. In one locale after another, rock 'n' roll shows, or disc hops where such tunes have been played, have touched off every type of juvenile delinquency." The Pennsylvania Chief of Police Association contended that rock music provided "an incentive to teenage unrest," and Pittsburgh Police Inspector Fred Good felt "wherever there's been teenage trouble lately, rock and roll has almost always been in the background." Entertainer Jackie Gleason put it succinctly, calling Elvis Presley "a guitar-playing Marlon Brando."

Teen riots served to increase fear of rock-and-roll delinquents and prompted officials to bar promoters from holding rock concerts in civic buildings. In San Jose, rock fanatics routed seventy-three policemen and caused $3,000 in damage, pressuring the mayor of nearby Santa Cruz to ban rock concerts. On May 3, 1958, violence erupted after an Alan Freed–hosted rock revue that had headlined Jerry Lee Lewis. When police turned on the house lights before the show ended, Freed huffed, "I guess the police here in Boston don't want you kids to have a good time," and teens streamed into the street. As *Time* reported, "all around the arena common citizens were set upon, robbed and sometimes beaten. A young sailor caught a knife in the belly, and two girls with him were thrashed. In all nine men and women were roughed up enough to require hospital treatment." Though, as *Time* admitted, "the arena site had been the site of frequent muggings in the past" and teens probably did not participate in the violence, Boston Mayor John Hynes barred rock-and-roll shows from the city. Officials in New Haven and Newark followed the Boston example, canceling scheduled Freed-sponsored shows. After a melee among 2,700 fans at a rock show, Mayor Roland Hines of Asbury Park, New Jersey, banned all rock concerts from city dance halls. Officials in nearby Jersey City did the same a few days later.

Others mobilized against Elvis Presley. In Nashville and St. Louis, angry parents burned effigies of Presley. In Ottawa, Canada, eight students of the Notre Dame convent were expelled for attending a local Elvis show. Yale University students handed out "I Like Ludwig [Beethoven]" buttons to counter the sale of "I Like Elvis" buttons. And a Cincinnati used-car dealer increased business with a sign that read: "We Guarantee to Break 50 Elvis Presley Records in Your Presence If You Buy One of These Cars Today."

Disc jockeys who broadcast classical and pop music also took action. In Halifax, Nova Scotia, station CJCH rigidly forbade the airplay of any Elvis discs. Nashville jockey "Great Scott" burned six hundred Presley records in a public park, and a Chicago station manager smashed Elvis 45s during a broadcast. In Wildwood, New Jersey, a local disc jockey started an organization to "eliminate certain wreck and ruin artists" such as Elvis.

Even religious leaders spoke out against Presley. Reverend William Shannon commented in the *Catholic Sun* that "Presley and his voodoo of frustration and defiance have become symbols in our country, and we are sorry to come upon Ed Sullivan in the role of promoter. Your Catholic viewers, Mr. Sullivan, are angry." Although he had never seen Elvis, evangelist Billy Graham was "not so sure I'd want my children to see" him. Reverend Charles Howard Graff of St. John's Episcopal Church in Greenwich Village called Elvis a "whirling dervish of sex," and Reverend Robert Gray of the Trinity Baptist Church in Jacksonville, Florida, believed Presley had "achieved a new low in spiritual degeneracy. If he were offered salvation tonight, he would probably say, 'No thanks, I'm on the top.'" In his sermon "Hot Rods, Reefers, and Rock and Roll," Gray warned the youth in his congregation not to attend an upcoming Presley show.

A few adults sided with Elvis. Alan Lomax, a collector of American folk songs who had trudged down South with his tape recorder and saved many traditional blues, contended that the trend toward rockabilly and Elvis was "the healthiest manifestation yet in native American music." Mae Boren Axton, the schoolteacher who wrote "Heartbreak Hotel" felt that Presley concerts allowed youths to release pent-up aggression in a socially acceptable manner.

ELVIS GOES TO HOLLYWOOD

RCA Victor and Colonel Parker responded to the reaction against Presley by modifying the singer's wild act. Presley's appearance on the "Steve Allen Show" provides an example. "We'd recognized the controversy that was building around Elvis and so we took advantage of it," remembered Allen. The host dressed Presley "in a tuxedo—white tie and tails—and [took] away his guitar. We thought putting Elvis in formal wardrobe to sing the song was humorous. We also asked him to stand perfectly still, and we positioned a real hound dog on a stool next to him—a dog that had been trained to do nothing but sit and look droopy." Elvis's respectable behavior on the show stood in marked contrast to his earlier hip-shaking performances and signaled the beginning of a change in image.

Throughout 1957 and 1958 and into the 1960s, Presley became more subdued. In September 1957, the rising star split with two members of his original band, Scotty Moore and Bill Black, who had helped pioneer the distinctive Presley sound. On subsequent records and in his thirty-one movies, starting with *Love Me Tender* and followed by such films as *G. I. Blues, Flaming Star, Wild Star, Blue Hawaii, Follow That Dream, Kid Galahad,* and *Girls! Girls! Girls!*

Elvis for the most part abandoned gut-bucket rockabilly for a soothing ballad style that reinforced his new image. "Elvis would go ahead with the program and get the picture done," remembered D. J. Fontana, the drummer who played with Elvis from 1954 to 1968. "You see, the Colonel's thought was *don't make any waves*; don't let me have to make a deal with these people."

The more mainstream Presley appealed to even more fans and sold even more albums, a total of over 250 million by the end of his career. In the history of recorded music, only Bing Crosby neared Elvis's mark with about 200 million records sold. Frank Sinatra, the bobby-socks sensation of the 1940s, sold only about 40 million discs.

With his newfound wealth, Elvis bought a fleet of Cadillacs, including one in his favorite color—pink, a $40,000, one-story ranch house in Memphis, and then a $100,000 mansion, Graceland, for himself and his parents. He purchased an airplane, a truckload of television sets, and hundreds of other gadgets.

Presley also began to receive awards of all types. In 1959, the Mississippi legislature passed a resolution that lauded Elvis as a "legend and inspiration to tens of millions of Americans" who "reaffirms a historic American idea that success in our nation can still be attained through individual initiative, hard work and abiding faith in one's self and his creator." A few months later, a joint session of the Tennessee legislature honored Presley.

The young, working-class Presley, ceaselessly marketed by RCA, was swept away by stardom. "My daddy and I were laughing about it the other day," he told a reporter in late 1956. "He looked at me and said, 'What happened, El? The last thing I remember is I was working in a can factory and you were still driving a truck.' We all feel the same way about it still. It just caught us up."

The rock star paid dearly for his fame. As his popularity increased, Elvis found it difficult to protect his privacy. "Even today [late Sixties] I'd be willing to bet a thousand dollars he could draw a hundred people in five minutes anywhere he went," mused Neal Matthews, one of the Jordanaires, Elvis's backup singing group. "And he knows this. It's bound to make him unhappy. He'd like to be able to walk down the street like a normal human being. He can't be a person like anybody else." The "only time he could get out, really, was at night, or if he had the night off. He'd rent a skating rink or a movie house and rent it for the whole night and he and whoever'd be around would go to the two, three movies after the movie theater had closed. That's the only kind of entertainment he had. He couldn't go out."

On his 1969 tour of Hawaii with Minnie Pearl, Minnie related, "There were five hundred women there and as we got out of the taxi, Elvis grabbed my arm and the women broke and mobbed us. I felt my feet going out from under me. . . . You know, everyone wants to be number one, but that one experience was enough to convince me I don't want it." As Minnie Pearl and her husband enjoyed the Hawaiian sun, "Elvis never got out of his room except to work. They say he came down in the middle of the night to swim. He couldn't come down during the day. He had the penthouse suite on the top of that thing there and we'd get out and act crazy, having the best time in the world, and we'd look up there and Elvis would be standing at the window, looking down at us."

Eventually the isolation began to affect Presley. "You know, you all are lucky," Presley told D. J. Fontana and his wife in 1968. "I'm so tired of being Elvis—I don't know what to do. I just wish I could do something else."

A depressed Elvis sometimes became violent. He destroyed several television sets, pool cues, jukeboxes, and cars. "The temper was the hardest thing to take," one friend recalled. "One day he'd be the sweetest person in the world, the next day he'd burn holes in you with his eyes." As singer Johnny Rivers concluded, Elvis "had created his own world. He had to. There was nothing else for him to do." His retreat into himself ended in drug excess and a premature death in 1977.

Elvis Presley had been trapped by success. The gyrating, sneering Elvis, who taunted his audiences and worked them to a fever pitch, had given way to a more haggard performer bloated by drugs and alcohol and adorned by extravagant, sequined costumes, who sang ballads to the well-dressed clientele of Las Vegas nightclubs and in arenas across the country. Sometimes, the old magic sneaked through the weary flesh, but most of the original vibrancy and vitality had disappeared. Elvis was transformed from an innocent country boy who belted out a new kind of music with animalistic intensity to a well-groomed, multi-million-dollar product. The change, starting when Presley signed with RCA and becoming more pronounced during the sixties, spelled the end of rockabilly. Soon, teenage crooners schooled by Dick Clark would vie for the mantle of the King.

3

Dick Clark, Don Kirshner,

and the Teen Market

**"I hope someday that somebody will say that in the
beginning stages of the birth of the music of the Fifties,
though I didn't contribute in terms of creativity, I helped
keep it alive."**

Dick Clark

"Elvis in the army, Buddy dead, Little Richard in the ministry, and
Berry nabbed by the Feds," became the chant of a bewildered rock-
and-roll generation. Bursting upon the music scene just three years
earlier, by 1959 rock-and-roll had lost many of its heroes. Elvis
Presley had been inducted into the army, Buddy Holly had been
tragically killed, Little Richard had suddenly joined a fundamental-
ist religious sect, and Chuck Berry had been jailed at a time when
rock and roll was becoming an important part of American culture
as well as a burgeoning part of the record industry.

Two young entrepreneurs—Dick Clark and Don Kirshner—
produced a new crop of idols and a fresh batch of songs for rock-
starved teens. Beginning in 1957, Clark found photo-ready,
well-groomed "Italian stallions," promoted them on his television
show, and almost single-handedly created the Philadelphia sound.
Only the payola scandal slowed Clark's success. A music publisher
in the Tin Pan Alley tradition, Kirshner assembled teams of young,
talented songwriters in the Brill Building in New York City and
from 1960 to 1963 churned out hundreds of tunes that he placed
with scores of budding girl groups. For nearly three years, he helped

set the direction of rock. From 1958 to 1963, in the absence of the king and his court, two businessmen reshaped rock-and-roll and made it respectable.

LOST IDOLS

During the late 1950s, rock-and-roll fans either lost or rejected their heroes. In October 1957, the flamboyant Little Richard renounced his jeweled bracelets and wild parties for the ministry of the Seventh Day Adventist Church. Richard had frequently threatened to quit rock. Chuck Conners, the drummer in Little Richard's band, remembered that Richard "had been talking about giving up rock 'n' roll and devoting his life to God for a long time." Then, on his way to Australia, Little Richard looked out the window of his plane, and the engines seemed to burst into flames, doused only by the saving efforts of yellow angels. A few days later, in Sydney, on the fifth day of a two-week tour, Richard walked away from rock and roll during the middle of a show and in front of forty thousand fans. As he told it, "that night Russia sent off the very first *Sputnik* [the Soviet Union's first artificial earth satellite in outer space]. It looked as though the big ball of fire came directly over the stadium about two or three hundred feet above our heads. It shook my mind. It really shook my mind. I got up from the piano and said, 'This is it. I am through. I am leaving show business to go back to God.' " True to his word, Richard deserted his fans for Jehovah. Said the singer: "If you want to live for the Lord, you can't rock and roll too. God doesn't like it." Not until 1964 during a tour of England did Little Richard again raise the standard of rock.

A month later, twenty-two-year-old Jerry Lee Lewis married his thirteen-year-old third cousin, Myra Gale Brown, who was the daughter of Lewis's bass player. It was Lewis's third marriage. Though a relatively common practice in the rural South—"I know lots of people married to thirteen-year-olds," Lewis said at the time—the marriage caused promoters to cancel the twenty-seven shows scheduled for Lewis's 1957 tour of England. During his first appearance after the marriage, the crowd greeted the rockabilly star with silence and then sporadic heckling. "I sho' hope yawl ain't half as dead as you sound," Lewis shouted to the crowd. "Go home, crumb, baby snatcher," the audience yelled back. For more than a decade, the public censured the "Killer," who gravitated more and more toward country music.

On March 24, 1958, the king of rock-and-roll, Elvis Presley, entered the armed forces for a two-year stint. On orders from his manager, Colonel Parker, he refused to sing for the army, and spent his time in Bremerhaven, Germany, where he met his future wife, Priscilla Beaulieu. When discharged in January 1960, Presley concentrated on motion pictures, and only in 1968 returned to the stage.

The next year, two of rock's pioneers left the stage. Chuck Berry was forced from the rock scene by a ruling from a federal court. In 1959, a fourteen-year-old girl accused the rocker of transporting her from Texas to St. Louis for immoral purposes after Berry fired her as a hat check girl in his St. Louis club. Testimony at the trial, which dragged on for nearly two years, revealed that the girl had been a prostitute when Berry first met her and that she had come willingly to St. Louis. A judge initially found Berry guilty, but a retrial was scheduled because the magistrate referred to the performer as "this Negro." The jury in a second trial convicted Berry of a violation of the Mann Act and sentenced him to two years in the federal penitentiary at Terre Haute, Indiana.

A different sort of tragedy occurred on February 3, 1959. Rockabilly singer and songwriter Buddy Holly, the shy, bespectacled youth from Texas, died in a plane crash near Mason City, Iowa, after a show during a Midwestern tour. J. P. Richardson, the disc jockey known as the Big Bopper, who in 1958 hit the charts with "Chantilly Lace," and the seventeen-year-old sensation Richie Valens (a.k.a. Richard Valenzuela), who had just scored hits with "La Bamba" and "Donna," were killed in the same crash.

An automobile accident robbed rock-and-roll of two other talents. On April 17, 1960, after a successful tour of England, Eddie Cochran, Gene Vincent, and Sharon Sheely, Cochran's girlfriend, who subsequently wrote many of Ricky Nelson's hits, rode to the airport in a chauffeured limousine. En route near Chippenham, Wiltshire, a tire blew out, the driver lost control, and the car smashed into a lamppost. Within hours, Cochran died of multiple head injuries at Bath Hospital. Sheely and Vincent survived, but the accident destroyed Vincent's career.

THE BOOMING TEEN MARKET

Rock-and-roll tragedy occurred amid booming economic conditions. During the 1950s, the gross national product (GNP), the indicator of U.S. economic growth, rose from $213 billion to $503 billion. The personal per capita income in the country increased from $1,526 in 1950 to $2,788 ten years later, an increase of 82 percent. Throughout the decade, unemployment fluctuated between 4 and 5.5 percent.

The recording industry, reinvigorated by rock-and-roll, shared in the general prosperity. Record sales in the United States skyrocketed from $189 million in 1950 to nearly $600 million by the end of the decade. The industry sold almost half of all discs through mail-order clubs and in supermarkets, which by the 1950s had replaced the corner store. In 1959, the industry chalked up almost $200 million in sales of 45-rpm records, which usually were oriented to the rock audience. Though over 5,000 record labels competed for a share of the market, four major companies—RCA Victor, Columbia, Decca, and Capitol—racked up nearly 75 percent of the sales.

Reflecting a postwar trend in U.S. business, the record industry even expanded into the international market with rock-and-roll. RCA vice-president George Marek observed in 1959 that "rock-and-roll is popular not only in this country but it has swept the world, the world where there are no broadcasting stations even: It is relatively popular in conservative England, in Australia, India, Germany, wherever you go." A Decca press release of the early 1960s described the state of the music business: "The recording industry, a fledgling during the heyday of vaudeville, has shown a steady, remarkable growth until today it stands as a major factor in the world's economy."

DICK CLARK AND AMERICAN BANDSTAND

Dick Clark, a marketing genius from upstate New York, delivered new stars to the swelling numbers of rock-and-rollers. Born in 1929, Richard Augustus Clark II attended Syracuse University and studied advertising and radio, getting, in his words, a "sound education in business administration." In 1951, he landed a part-time job as an announcer for station WOLF, and then worked for his father, who was station manager at WRUN in Utica. A short while later, Clark decided to take a job at WFIL in Philadelphia, first announcing a radio show of popular and classical music. He later wrote: "I was a great pitchman. I sold pots and pans, vacuum cleaners, diamond rings, Mrs. Smith pies, the works. Eventually I landed the Schaefer Beer account. I did one hell of a beer spot."

In July 1956, Clark moved to WFIL's television station and hosted Philadelphia "Bandstand" which showcased local high school students dancing to popular hit records. He replaced disc jockey Bob Horn, who, in October 1952 had launched the program and four years later had resigned after adverse publicity surrounding two drunken driving citations.

Dick Clark initially knew little about the rock-and-roll music that the program highlighted. During his first "Bandstand" appearance as a regular, Clark remembered, he arrived on the "set at two that afternoon with only a foggy notion of what the kids, music, and show were really about." "I don't understand this music," he confessed to record promoter Red Schwartz.

The new moderator of "Bandstand" quickly became familiar with the new music and its commercial potential. "The more I heard the music the more I enjoyed it; the more I enjoyed it, the more I understood the kids," he later related. "I knew that if I could tune into them and keep myself on the show, I could make a great deal of money." Clark—voted by his high school classmates as the "Man Most Likely to Sell the Brooklyn Bridge"—felt that behind his "bland twenty-nine-year-old face lay the heart of a cunning capitalist" who wanted to "defend my right and your right to go to a church of our choice, or to buy the record of our choice."

Clark's business savvy transformed a local telecast into a national phenomenon. To get sponsors for the show, he "traveled the advertising agency circuit on Madison Avenue" and eventually snagged the lucrative Beechnut Spearmint Gum account. After that success, *Advertising Age* predicted that Dick Clark "may replace Arthur Godfrey as the number-one personal salesman."

"Bandstand," built upon a solid advertising base by Clark, was nationally televised as "American Bandstand," premiering on August 5, 1957, on sixty-seven stations coast to coast to more than eight million viewers. The show aired from Philadelphia for ninety minutes every weekday afternoon and on Monday nights from 7:30 to 8:00 P.M.. It featured 150 teenagers in the audience, many of whom danced to the popular hits and listened to the smooth patter of Dick Clark. "It's been a long, long time since a major network has aimed at the most entertainment-starved group in the country," Clark told *Time* magazine. "And why not? After all, teenagers have $9 billion a year to spend."

Droves of teenage girls responded to Clark's brand of rock-and-roll. After school hours, hordes of pubescent girls rushed home and feverishly tuned into "American Bandstand." Usually with their best girlfriend or sister, they danced to the music on their living room floors, identified with the regular dancers, and fantasized about stardom on the dance floor of "American Bandstand." The girls flooded the show with up to 45,000 letters a week and helped the program gross $500,000 a year and net ratings that equaled the combined ratings of the two rival networks. "We love it," gushed one girl from Charleston, West Virginia. "When I hear a Beethoven symphony I don't feel anything. When I hear our kind of music, I feel something way down deep, like oatmeal." In the absence of major rock stars and working on the new medium of television, the farsighted Clark had created a rock-and-roll that emphasized the audience as much as the music.

Clark and "American Bandstand" brought a respectability to rock that had not existed with the lowdown, greasy rockabillies. Clark himself portrayed a prim, clean-cut image. *Newsweek* referred to him as "genial and softspoken," and *Time* characterized the announcer as "personable and polite, he manages to sound as if he really means such glib disc jockey patter as, 'Let me pull up a hunk of wood and sit down with you.'"

The dancers and performers featured on "American Bandstand" reflected the clean-cut demeanor of the host. Clark insisted upon a dress code, forcing boys to "wear a jacket and tie, or a sweater and tie. Nobody dressed that way in real life, but it made the show acceptable to adults who were frightened by the teenage world and their music. Girls couldn't wear slacks, tight sweaters, shorts, or low-necked gowns—they had to wear the kind of dresses or sweaters and skirts they wore in school. No tight toreadors or upturned collars." *Newsweek* approvingly reported that "Clark enforces strict rules: No smoking, no tight sweaters or dresses, no slacks, no hats or overcoats, no gum chewing. He also carries a supply of safety pins for 'sent' kids who come undone." "We've never had an incident," Clark boasted to *Time* in 1958.

To further purge sexuality from the airwaves, the announcer refused to say 'going steady' and banned the Alligator and Dog dances "as too sexy." "We just didn't deal with sex," Clark later wrote. As music writer Arnold Shaw concluded, "Clark was, in fact, the great tranquilizer of the era, reassuring parents by his suave manners that rock-and-roll was not bad and transforming the youngsters on his show into sunshine biscuits."

One of Clark's books on teenage etiquette, *To Goof or Not to Goof,* exemplified his moderation of teenage rebellion. The dust jacket read: "How to have morals and manners and still have fun." The contents dealt with such burning questions "to successful teenaging" as "Where do your elbows go when you're not eating?" "How long should it take to say good night to a girl? To her father?" "Do nice girls call up boys?" and "How far is friendly?"

CLARK'S CREATIONS

Dick Clark created a stable of Italian, Philadelphia-bred performers whom he groomed, promoted, and cast as the stars of his show. One such idol was Fabian. One day in 1957 a South Philadelphia policeman, Dominick Forte, suffered a heart attack on the street. Bob Marcucci, co-owner of Chancellor Records offered help and noticed Forte's fourteen-year-old son, Fabian. Impressed with Fabian's resemblance to Elvis Presley, the manager gave the youth voice and etiquette lessons for two years and then without much success tried to sell his new commodity by buying full-page ads in the trade papers of the music industry.

In 1959, Dick Clark agreed to promote Fabian, who lip-synched "Turn Me Loose," "Tiger," and the Elvis Presley imitation, "Hound Dog Man" on "American Bandstand." Though feeling that the singer "got screams though he couldn't sing a note," Clark transformed Fabian from a $6-a-week drugstore clerk into an overnight sensation. Within a year, Clark had enabled the Philadelphia teen to sell almost a million copies of his signature song, "Tiger," appear on "The Ed Sullivan Show," and be covered in *Time* magazine.

Dick Clark also launched the career of Frankie Avalon, another regular on "American Bandstand." Born Francis Avallone, Avalon played trumpet for the Philadelphia group, Rocco and the Saints, and in 1958 debuted his solo single, "DeDe Dinah," which reached the number 7 slot on the charts. Through repeated appearances on "American Bandstand," the teen scored hits with such songs as "Venus" and "Why." Remarked Frankie about "Venus": "Dick got behind it and it sold a million and a half copies. He's the greatest."

Bobby Rydell, born Robert Ridarelli in Philadelphia, followed his friend Frankie Avalon on the path to stardom. Also a member of Rocco and the Saints, Rydell started a solo career in 1958 that was unsuccessful until he joined "American Bandstand" a year later. In 1959 he scored hits with "Kissin' Time," "Volare," and "Swingin' School" and within four years chalked up nineteen Top 30 chartbusters. Along with Fabian and Frankie Avalon, Bobby Rydell became an "American Bandstand" produced teen idol who defined the Philadelphia sound, a teenage version of the smooth ballads delivered by such Italian crooners of the 1940s and early 1950s as Frank Sinatra, Perry Como, and Dean Martin.

Clark also brought to fame Ernest Evans, another Philadelphia product who became known as Chubby Checker and popularized an international dance craze. In the summer of 1960, Clark noticed a black couple on "American Bandstand" "doing a dance that consisted of revolving their hips in quick, half-circle jerks, so their pelvic regions were heaving in time to the music." "For God's sake, keep the cameras off that couple. . . . It looked like something a bellydancer did to climax her performance," Clark screamed to his producer, Tony Mammarella.

The announcer soon realized the commercial potential of the dance and suggested that Cameo Records, a company owned partially by Clark, cover Hank Ballard's 1959 "The Twist." For a singer the company chose Chubby Checker, a chicken plucker at a poultry shop who had attended high school with Fabian and Frankie Avalon. In 1960 "American Bandstand" played Checker's "The Twist" until it hit the top of the charts and earned the butcher's helper $822,459 from 1960 to 1962. A new dance craze, started on the program, accompanied the song. To do the dance, instructed rock critic Lillian Roxon, "you put one foot out and pretend you're stubbing out a cigarette butt on the floor with the big toe. At the same time, you move your hands and body as though you're drying every inch of your back with an invisible towel. That's the twist." The twist craze reached international proportions and spawned a series of records: "The Twist" by Ray Anthony and the Bookends, the Isley Brothers' "Twist and Shout," Ray Henry's "Twist Polka," "Twist with Bobby Darin," Sam Cooke's "Twistin' the Night Away," "Twist with the Ventures," "Twistin' with Duane Eddy," and many others.

Dick Clark marketed other dances and their theme songs on

his television show. "Many of these dances," admitted the announcer, "came out of Philadelphia and were associated with songs done by artists on Cameo Records." Chubby Checker sang to the Hucklebuck, the Pony, the Limbo, and the Fly. Bobby Rydell popularized the Fish. The white, Philadelphia doo-wop group, the Dovells, introduced the Bristol Stomp and the Continental, and singer Dee Dee Sharp exhorted television viewers to do the Mashed Potato.

Though creating teen idols and dance steps for his television viewers, Clark remained at center stage. He received the attention of the trade publications and the popular press. *Time* labeled him "the Pied Piper of the teenagers."

Even the teens themselves swooned over Clark. During the first year of "American Bandstand" more than 300,000 fans requested Clark's photo, and in 1958 *Life* printed a revealing shot of an awestruck 16-year-old, June Carter, "reassuring her great moment, touching the cheek Dick Clark has just kissed." *Life,* carrying an article about the announcer and the army-bound Elvis Presley, described the power of Clark in the headline: "The Dictator at Home and the King at War."

For Clark, popularity led to wealth. The announcer collected a sizeable salary each year for his work on such television programs as "American Bandstand," the "Dick Clark Show," a concert format started in 1958, and "Dick Clark's Caravan of Stars" begun in 1959. Beside his regular salary, he earned $50,000 a year spinning discs at record hops which led to the formation of his first corporation, Click. Clark slowly gained interest in such record companies as Chancellor which featured Fabian and Frankie Avalon, Cameo-Parkway which recorded Bobby Rydell, Chubby Checker, and the Dovells, Swan Records, Jamie Records, Chips Record Distributing Corporation, Globe Records, and Hunt Records. He also owned the copyrights to over 160 songs including "At the Hop," "Party Time," "January Music," and "Sixteen Candles" and controlled the Mallard Pressing Corporation. All told, Dick Clark held at least some share in thirty-three corporations. By April 8, 1958, *Time* reported that "television's newest rage consists of a jukebox full of rock 'n' roll records, a studio full of dancing teenagers and Dick Clark, a suave young (28) disc jockey full of money."

THE PAYOLA SCANDAL

Clark's interlocking interests became painfully public during the payola investigations of 1959 and 1960. Payola, or play for pay, had been an accepted practice in the music industry dating to the vaudeville era. "It was an era of outright payola," wrote Abel Green, editor of *Variety.* "From the opening acrobatic act, which plugged *Japanese Sandman, Dardanella* or some other instrumental while making with the hand-to-hand gymnastics, through the rest of the bill, there was little that the then powerful Vaudeville Managers Protective Association and the Music Publishers Protective Association could do to kayo it." "Historically, payola is an outgrowth of a music business tradition—song plugging," agreed Paul Ackerman, the music editor of *Billboard.*

The payola investigations of 1959 and 1960 began with fraud on television. In November 1959, Charles Lincoln Van Doren admitted before the House Special Committee on Legislative Oversight that he had been given answers in advance as a contestant on NBC's "Twenty-One" quiz show. "I would give almost anything I have to reverse the course of my life in the last three years," he told the committee. Reeling from the revelation, the networks discontinued many game programs: NBC canceled "Tic Tac Dough" and "The Price Is Right"; CBS eliminated all quiz shows from its schedule and fired the president of the network, who had been closely associated with "Quiz Kids," "Stop the Music," and "The $64,000 Question," the most popular show in America.

The scandal spread to the music industry with the prodding of the American Society of Composers, Authors and Publishers (AS-CAP), a song-licensing concern that, through the 1950s, had attacked the interlocking interests of radio, network television, and the record companies represented by the rival licensing agent, Broadcast Music, Inc. (BMI). Concerned about rock performers such as Little Richard and Chuck Berry, who wrote their own material, the professional songwriters of ASCAP used the payola investigation as a forum to lash out bitterly against BMI and the rock-and-roll it licensed. The songwriters hired Vance Packard, author of *Hidden Persuaders,* who tried to demonstrate "that the rock and roll, hillbilly, and Latin American movements were largely engineered, manipulated for the interests of BMI, and that would be the point, that the public was manipulated into liking rock and roll." Rock music, Packard continued, "might be best summed up as monotony tinged with hysteria," which could not be sold to the discerning public without payola. "What do you think is going to happen to rock and roll songs?" asked ASCAP member and well-known songwriter Oscar Hammerstein. "There seems to be something funny to me that these songs have been so popular, so much more popular than any other new songs that have been produced, and yet don't live. They die as soon as the plug stops."

Congressmen in charge of the investigation, hoping to impress their conservative constituencies during an election year, joined in the attack on rock-and-roll. "Suppose John Smith owns a record company and then buys a broadcast station," postulated the counsel for the committee. "Suppose he dumps its personnel and its good music format to put on his own label, generally only rock and roll. . . . Now, that's not in the public interest." Without payola, "a lot of this so-called junk music, rock 'n' roll stuff, which appeals to the teenagers would not be played," stressed Congressman John Bennett of Michigan. "The good music did not require the support, the good music did not require the payment of payola," added Representative John Moss of California. Such "trash" as rock music had been "pushed" on unsuspecting teens.

The committee focused on disc jockeys who played rock-and-roll. Boston jockey Norm Prescott told the House committee that "bribery, payola, has become the prime function of this business to get the record on the air at any cost," and that he had taken almost $10,000 from various record distributors. Another Boston announcer, WBZ's Dave Maynard, admitted that a record distributor had helped finance his 1957 Mercury station wagon and his 1959 Buick, and had given him $6,817 in cash. Alan Dary, also of WBZ, received cash, a hi-fi, liquor, and carpeting for his master bedroom. By 1960, investigators announced that 207 rock disc jockeys in forty-two states had accepted more than $263,000 in payola. President Dwight Eisenhower instructed the committee, headed by Oren Harris of Arkansas, "to clean up this whole mess."

Some rock dee jays immediately felt repercussions from the payola investigation. In Detroit, Tom Clay of station WJBK was fired after he admitted to taking $6,000 in a year and a half. After defending payola "as part of American business," WJBK jockey Jack LeGoff lost his job. Don McLeod of the same station was fired two days later. In Boston, three top disc jockeys on the rock station WILD—Stan Richards, Bill Marlowe, and Mike Eliot—found themselves unemployed. And in New York, premier rock announcer Alan Freed was dismissed by WABC when he admitted that he had taken $30,650 from six record companies. Complained a bitter Freed, "what they call payola in the disc jockey business they call lobbying in Washington."

Dick Clark, perhaps the most prominent rock announcer at the time, came under especially close scrutiny. As Representative John Burnett of Michigan put it: "I think it is pretty convincing that Clark was involved with payola as all other disc jockeys, but on a much larger scale." Congressman Peter Mack of Illinois called him "the top dog in the payola field," and Representative John Moss of California began to refer to the investigations as "Clarkola."

Clark escaped the payola investigation with his job and reputation intact. Wearing a blue suit, a button-down shirt, and black loafers, the announcer uncategorically informed the House committee in April 1960 that "I have never agreed to play a record in return for payment in cash or any other consideration." When grilled about spinning records of artists who recorded for companies in which he owned an interest, a cool Clark replied softly that "I did not consciously favor such records. Maybe I did so without realizing it." The host of "American Bandstand," seldom promoting performers who wrote their own material and projecting an air of respectability to the Congressional investigators, slipped through the committee unscathed. At the end of his testimony, he was told by Chairman Oren Harris: "You're not the inventor of the system or even its architect. You're a product of it." "Obviously," Harris concluded, "you're a fine young man."

Alan Freed, a tireless champion of black performers who wrote their own songs and had created rock-and-roll, did not fare so well. As the payola investigation ended in 1960, an unemployed Freed was charged with commercial bribery in connection with payola by an eight-member grand jury in New York. Blackballed by the music industry after the payola scare, the former disc jockey, penniless, stood trial in December 1962 and pleaded guilty to two counts of commercial bribery. He was fined $300 and given a six-month suspended sentence. Less than two years later, on March 16, 1964, Freed was charged with income tax evasion during 1957 to 1959 by another grand jury which ordered him to pay the Internal Revenue Service almost $38,000 in back taxes. Later in the year, a broken, unemployed, despondent Alan Freed entered a California hospital, suffering from the effects of alcoholism. On January 20, 1965, he died at the age of 43.

DON KIRSHNER TAKES CHARGE

The payola investigation had an immediate impact upon rock-and-roll. As the established tunesmiths in ASCAP had hoped, songwriters became a dominant force in the new music. Ironically, from 1960 to 1963, a new breed of songsmiths nurtured by New York music publisher Don Kirshner outdistanced recognized Tin Pan Alley songwriters to corner the teen market. They produced romantic lyrics and upbeat melodies for and about teenage girls and placed the songs with gospel-influenced, black girl groups, which gradually became more popular than the white, male, Italian teen idols of the Dick Clark era.

Don Kirshner masterminded the takeover of rock by the songwriters. The son of a Bronx tailor, Kirshner began to write songs professionally in 1958 and hoped to reshape Tin Pan Alley for the expanding teen market. As he remembered, "my idols at the time were Max and Louis Dryfuss, who had built [the music publishing firm of] Chappell Music. I had watched some of the old movies they were in, like *Night and Day* and *Rhapsody in Blue* and had observed them molding the greats like Gershwin, Rodgers and Hammerstein, and Lerner and Lowe." "My philosophy—my dream," he related, "was that we were approaching a new era in the music business with room for new people to accomplish what the Dryfusses had. And I believed that if I got the chance to sit behind a desk in the music business, I'd be the guy to accomplish that."

Chasing his dream, in 1958 a twenty-one-year-old Don

Kirshner along with Al Nevins, guitarist for the pop group, the Three Suns, established Aldon Music. "Our concept," pointed out Kirshner, "was to build new writers." The business partners rented office space across the street from the famed Brill Building at 1619 Broadway, which housed the well-known publishing firms so important to the pop music of Tin Pan Alley. "The Brill Building," reminisced songwriter Mike Stoller who collaborated with Jerry Leiber on a number of songs recorded by Elvis Presley and the Coasters, "had music publishers on every floor. Frequently in the Brill Building writers would go to peddle their songs and they'd go from door to door trying to sell them."

Kirshner quickly discovered teams of young songwriters who challenged the established firms across the street. One afternoon, just two days after he had opened his door for business, the new music publisher "was sweeping the floor with a short-sleeve shirt on." Two aspiring writers and high school chums, Neil Sedaka and Howie Greenfield, walked into the office. As Kirshner recalled, "they had just been turned down by Hill and Range [publishers] upstairs. They asked to see me. I said, 'I'm the guy!' They said, 'Come on you're kidding us.' But they figured they had nothing to lose, so they proceeded to play six incredible songs: 'Stupid Cupid,' 'The Diary,' and 'Calendar Girl' and a few others." Kirshner took the team to the home of a friend, pop singer Connie Francis, who recorded and hit the charts with "Stupid Cupid" and later in 1958 scaled the charts with another Sedaka-Greenfield tune, "Fallin'."

Neil Sedaka, unlike almost all the other songwriters at Aldon, began to record his own material. After the Connie Francis hits, Sedaka, who was a classically trained pianist, began to sense that the singers who recorded his songs "couldn't feel it the way I could. I used to play songs for people and then play the record, and they would say, 'We like the way you do it better.' "

In 1959 Al Nevins took Sedaka to RCA executive Steve Schoals who told the nineteen-year-old songwriter: "Yes, we are looking for more teenage attractions because of our immense success with Elvis. Being that you write songs, you are very interesting." A few weeks later, RCA signed Sedaka and recorded "The Diary," which after a $100,000 promotional campaign became Sedaka's first hit as a singer. During the next three years, Sedaka followed with the chartbusters "Breaking Up Is Hard to Do," "Calendar Girl," "Stairway to Heaven," "Happy Birthday Sweet Sixteen," and "Oh, Carol," the last written in 1959 for his girlfriend, Carole Klein.

Carole Klein, who later became known as Carole King, helped write Aldon Music's first smash hit, which set the direction of the company for the next three years. King had learned piano at the age of four and in high school formed her first band, the Co-sines. While attending Queens College in New York, she met Gerry Goffin who started to write songs with her.

The King-Goffin team soon joined Aldon Music and began to

compose Tin Pan Alley songs designed especially for teens. Goffin told *Time,* "Lyrics will hurt a song if they're too adult, too artistic, too correct. You should shy away from anything too deep or too happy."

In 1960, the King-Goffin duo, by then fixtures at Aldon Music, composed the teen ballad "Will You Love Me Tomorrow." Kirshner brought the song to Mitch Miller, then the head of Artists and Repertoire (A&R) at the powerful Columbia Records and suggested that pop balladeer Johnny Mathis sing the song. Miller, a stalwart in the music establishment, rejected the offer of the fledgling new publisher. Since, as Kirshner explained, the "A&R man was very big, and two men controlled the industry: Mitch Miller and Milt Gabler of the Decca Group," the co-owner of Aldon took the song to a New Jersey–based, independent company, Scepter Records. He approached label owners Florence Greenberg and Marv Schlacter "for a group they had called the Shirelles," a black, all-girl act that recorded the song. Within a few months, "Will You Love Me Tomorrow" became a number 1 hit.

The success of "Will You Love Me Tomorrow" brought a renewed confidence to Don Kirshner. As he told it, the song "created Scepter Records. I mean it was a real major hit. And effectively I had the feeling that we had the power to create record companies as well because the key to me as a publisher was always the song."

THE GIRL-GROUP SOUND

Kirshner not only created record companies but helped define the girl-group sound through two of his most successful songwriting teams, Barry Mann-Cynthia Weil and Ellie Greenwich-Jeff Barry. The four songwriters had joined about thirty other young tunesmiths at Aldon Music during the early 1960s. "It was insane," recalled Barry Mann. "Cynthia and I would be in this tiny cubicle, about the size of a closet, with just a piano and chair; no window or anything. We'd go in every morning and write songs all day. In the next room Carole [King] and Gerry [Goffin] would be doing the same thing, and in the next room after that Neil [Sedaka] or somebody else. Sometimes when we all got to banging on our pianos you couldn't tell who was playing what."

The two teams, sequestered in their cubicles, in 1962 and 1963 crafted a number of songs for two of the premier black girl groups, the Ronettes and the Crystals. Mann and Weil wrote the hits "Uptown" and "He's Sure the Boy I Love" for the Crystals and "Walking in the Rain" for the Ronettes. The more prolific Greenwich-Barry team authored "Baby, I Love You" and "Be My Baby" for the Ronettes, "Da Doo Ron Ron" and "Then He Kissed Me" for the Crystals and "The Boy I'm Gonna Marry" and "Wait Till My Baby

Gets Home" for Darlene Love, who sang lead vocal on most of the Crystals' hits.

The songwriters provided the gospel-influenced Crystals and Ronettes with tunes that appealed to the teen market. Darlene Love (a.k.a Darlene Wright), described by Ellie Greenwich as "a typical 60s soulful street gospel singer," complained that "many of the singers [in the girl groups] that sung those songs didn't really want to sing them. We called them bubblegum songs. The lyrics were really not even teenage. I say kid, you know 10 to 12, the market was geared for them."

Phil Spector, owner of Philles Records which recorded the Crystals and Ronettes, surrounded the teen-oriented, gospel-flavored tear-jerkers of Aldon Music with a wall of sound to create distinctive, girl-group music. Spector, born in the Bronx, moved to Los Angeles with his mother when his father died. After a short-lived success with a rock combo, the Teddy Bears, he found employment with independent producers Lester Sill and Lee Hazelwood, who in 1960 sent Spector to New York. In 1961 the twenty-one-year-old Spector and Lester Sill formed the New York–based Philles Records, which Spector owned solely by 1962.

While recording the Crystals and the Ronettes for Philles, the producer perfected his now-famous wall of sound, which involved multiple instrumentation. Ronnie Spector, the lead singer of the Ronettes who later married and then divorced the producer, remembered that "everything was done double. I mean where most people have one guitar or one drummer we had two of everything, so that's what made that wall of sound." "Well, I know that Phil's favorite composer was Wagner, no question, power, bigness," commented Ellie Greenwich. "And a few times when I'd gone over, Phil had an office on the main floor of a building and he had an apartment upstairs, and very often he would be upstairs in his one room listening with the speakers blasting, conducting. Wagner was his idol and Wagner was power and bigness and heavy and all that and I think he was going after that in his records." Spector himself called the new sound "a Wagnerian approach to rock and roll; little symphonies for the kids." The power of Spector's production that surrounded gospel-flavored songs of teenage romance resulted in the bright, upbeat, almost ethereal girl-group sound.

THE DREAM

The rags-to-riches success stories of the girl groups added to the romantic appeal of the music for thousands of school-age girls. The Crystals, a group of Brooklyn teens, had been discovered by Phil Spector while auditioning in New York City. The Shirelles had begun singing at school shows and at parties and in 1958 had been signed to Scepter Records by Florence Greenberg, the mother of one of their high school classmates, Mary Jo Greenberg. The Chantels, five New York teens who sang in the cherub choir of a local Catholic grade school, were signed to a contract, when a talent scout inadvertently heard them harmonizing at a Frankie Lymon concert. In 1958, they hit the charts with "Maybe." The Shangri-las, one of the few white girl groups of the era, grew up in a tough section of Queens and began singing together by their early teens. One day, producer Shadow Morton, a friend of Ellie Greenwich, happened to hear the three girls—Mary Weiss and the Ganser twins, Marge and Mary Ann—and signed them to the new Red Bird label. In 1964, when Mary was only fifteen, the group hit the top of the singles charts with "Leader of the Pack."

The discovery of the Ronettes—sisters Veronica and Estelle Bennett and cousin Nedra Talley—probably offered teenage girls the most heartfelt story. After a show at the Peppermint Lounge in New York, Ronnie Bennett casually walked into a bar and saw Phil Spector sitting at the piano. Their eyes fastened upon one another, and Spector softly asked Ronnie to sing. After a few bars, the producer exclaimed, "That's the voice, that's the voice I've been looking for."

Such tales of instant stardom coupled with the dramatic, romanticized music of the girl groups created the fantasy among many young girls that they too could become famous. "You see them coming from the cities, mostly groups, off the streets, hanging around Tin Pan Alley on Broadway near the Brill Building," noticed Phil Spector at the time. "They're usually between 16 and 19, anxious to record, anxious to be a singer." Although few traveled to New York in search of their dreams, millions of girls lay in their beds, listened to their transistor radios, and fantasized about impending stardom. Jerry Leiber, who with Mike Stoller started Red Bird Records in 1964 to capture girl groups on vinyl, characterized the era as "very naive, very innocent, full of hope, full of fantasy, full of promise." *Life* magazine referred to the new rock as "a fairy tale called the pop-record business" and identified Don Kirshner as "the grand wizard of the fairy tale."

The fantasies of teenage girls helped Don Kirshner establish a music-publishing empire. "The fastest rising phenomenon in the business is a Tin Pan Alley octopus called Aldon Music Inc., which has 35 boys and girls busy night and day composing songs," reported *Time* in March 1963. A few months later, *The Saturday Evening Post* renamed Tin Pan Alley as "Teen Pan Alley" and told its readers that "Broadway's Brill Building, once the home of jelly-jowled, gray-headed music publishers, is now being refurbished with youthful executives who have grown up to no other kind of music than the beat of today. . . . One of the typical—and prime—figures in youth's take-over of the pop record business is a onetime unsuccessful songwriter named Don Kirshner whose knack for picking up songs has earned him a $225,000 palace in New Jersey." By the end of the year, Kirshner had sold hundreds of songs that dominated the rock charts and grossed millions of dollars.

In 1963, Don Kirshner and partner Al Nevins sold Aldon Music. "The money just kept rolling in, and the hits kept rolling in," shrugged Kirshner "and you walk away at 28 years of age with a $2 million dollar check with your partner, it's difficult to turn down." Kirshner left for a lucrative job in the Columbia Screen Gems Television Music Division, where he supervised the record- and music-publishing interests of the company. He had left Aldon just when the surf had begun to rise.

4

Surfboards and Hot Rods:
California, Here We Come

"We sang about California and being young."

Dean Torrance

Eureka, a Greek word meaning "I have found it," was selected in 1850 as a motto by state legislators when California became the thirty-first state at the end of the great gold rush. Especially during the late 1950s and early 1960s, it aptly characterized the sentiments of the droves of migrants from the Midwest and the East Coast who traveled to California with hopes of sun, fun, and jobs. A new indigenous music, a bright, bouncy sound that glorified beaches, bikinis, and hot rods, embodied and promoted the California myth.

THE NEW AMERICAN EMPIRE

Postwar California had advantages over most other states. It enjoyed an abundance of natural resources including lumber, oil, boron minerals, mercury, thorium concentrates, and tungsten. In 1961, the state produced more fruit, vegetables, sugar beets, seed crops, walnuts, and almonds than any other state and topped the number two farm state, Iowa, by more than $700 million in total produce. California, which offered scores of white-collar jobs to its inhabitants, by the early 1960s secured about 25 percent of all prime government defense contracts and space program money. In the computer-chip age, the state procured almost half the $6 billion in Defense Department research-and-development contracts in 1961, and during the 1950s attracted 200 electronic firms such as Western Electric, Raytheon, Remington Rand, Zenith, and Motorola to the aptly named Silicon Valley. Probably most important, the state, third only to Alaska and Texas in size, boasted a wide range of terrains and climates from the desert of Death Valley to the damp, forested mountains in the north, from the central farm valley to the beaches of Malibu.

The resources of California, especially a healthy economy and the sunny, balmy climate of the southern part of the state, drew throngs of migrants after the war. In 1940, the population of the state stood at almost 7 million. Within ten years, it had increased to 10.6 million, bolstered by many Texans and Oklahomans who had come to California during the war for employment in government factories. People continued to stream into California during the next decade, until by 1960 the population mushroomed to more than 15.8 million. By late 1962, with its population expanding by 1,700 daily, California had reached more than 17 million inhabitants and had become the most populous state in the Union. About 60 percent of the people lived in the ten southernmost counties of the state. According to then-Governor Edmund "Pat" Brown, the rapid population growth "is the greatest mass migration in the history of the world."

Many of the migrants looked for the mythical California of fun and prosperity that had been promulgated by the press. In a late-1962 article, "What to Know About and Look For," *Life* focused upon the "bigness, bustle and boom" of California. It promised its readers a per capita income 25 percent above the national average, a "wide open" job market, "plenty" of houses equipped with swimming pools, 160 state parks (a third of which were beaches), and supermarkets and roadside stands that would "stagger most easterners." At the same time, *Newsweek* emphasized the "happy hedonism" of the California transplants. "Californians take their relaxation seriously," it asserted. "Unassuming and carefree, they break with the staid ways of their former communities, dip freely into credit for financing luxury items, and start experimenting in weird and wonderful ways." Concluded a writer in a September 1962 issue of *Look*, California "presents the promise and the challenge contained at the very heart of the original American dream."

SURFING U.S.A.

A buoyant surf music, born amid the California boom, reflected and promoted the myth of the California wonderland. It glorified one of the most attractive elements of the California myth—the sun-drenched, Southern California beaches dotted with tanned, blonde, bikini-clad beauties.

Surfing, the sport of Hawaiian kings, was introduced to California at the turn of the century. In 1959, the sport received a boost from the movie *Gidget*, a tale about a young girl who spends a summer on the beach and falls in love with two surfers. Cliff Robertson, one of the male leads in the film, even started a surfboard business. "One day," he remembered, "production on the picture got held up while we waited for a shipment of boards to come in from Honolulu, and I got to thinking why couldn't the West Coast support a surfboard industry." With a partner, Robertson established a surfboard-manufacturing company in Venice, California. "We drew some blueprints, bought some raw materials and started to turn out ten or twelve boards a month."

The innovations of two other surfboard companies, Hobie Surfboards in Dana Point and Sweet's Surfboards in Santa Monica, further popularized the sport. Hobie Alter and Dave and Roger Sweet replaced the heavy wooden board with a lightweight polyurethane foam strip coated with Fiberglass and glossed with a polyester resin that could be handled more easily and was accessible to teens.

Almost immediately, young people in Southern California armed themselves with the foam plastic boards and took to the waves. In late September 1961, *Life* commented that "now the surf that sweeps in on the beaches bears flotillas of enthusiasts standing on long buoyant boards. . . . Surfing has become an established craze in California. There are some 30,000 [teenagers who] revel in the delights of mounting their boards on waves hundreds of feet out and riding them in." "If you're not a surfer," explained one high school boy, "you're not 'in.' If you're a good surfer, you're always in. All you've got to do is walk up and down the beach with a board and you've got girls."

By August 1963, reported *Time*, "every weekend an estimated 100,000 surfers paddle into the briny on 7 ft. to 12 ft. balsa or polyurethane boards, struggle upright into a precarious balance with nature, and try to catch the high breakers coming in." "Ninety percent are beginners," calculated Bill Cooper, executive secretary of the U.S. Surfing Association. "Half of them give it up in a year or two, but then there are more."

The new legion of predominantly male, teenage surfers began to develop their own culture, dressing and speaking in a distinctive way. At high school, the bleach-blonde surfers wore Pendleton shirts, sandals, white, tight and somewhat short Levis, and baggies—very large, loose boxer-style shorts. Once school was over, they jumped into an oversized station wagon with wooden sides ("woodie"), which transported their "polys" (surfboards), drove to the beach, and dashed toward the ocean. They ran with their "sticks" (surfboards) into the "soup" (the foaming water near the beach) and tried to catch a wave. Some would only "fun surf" on three to six feet waves. Other, more daring, surfers would carry their "big guns" (surfboards designed for riding tall waves) into the water, pick up a "hairy" wave (fast wave that is difficult to surf) and "shoot" (ride) it, sometimes "hot dogging" (performing tricks) to impress the "bunnies" (girls) on shore. All surfers showed disdain for the poorly skilled or fraudulent, to whom they referred as "gremlins" or "kooks." After packing up and going home, they could read magazines such as *Surfer* and *Surfer Illustrated* or watch such surf-fanatic films by director Bruce Brown as *Slippery When Wet* (1960) and *Barefoot Adventure* (1962) or the more commercial *Beach Party* (1963), *Muscle Beach Party* (1964), and *Bikini Beach* (1964), all starring two Dick Clark regulars, Frankie Avalon and Annette Funicello.

THE SOUND OF SURF

The surfing culture listened to its own music, which originated with Dick Dale and his Deltones. Born in Beruit, Dale (a.k.a. Richard Monsour) grew up on the Southern California coast and joined the hordes of young surfers. Also a guitar enthusiast who had released a few traditional-sounding singles in 1959, Dale worked closely with Leo Fender, the manufacturer of the first mass-produced, solid-body electric guitar and the president of Fender Instruments, to improve the Showman amplifier and to develop the reverberation unit that would give surf music its distinctively fuzzy sound. Dick Dale fused his two passions, surfing and the guitar, to create a new music for the surf fanatics. "There was a tremendous amount of power I felt while surfing and that feeling of power was simply transferred into my guitar when I was playing surf music," he recalled. "I couldn't get the feeling by singing, so the music took an instrumental form."

During the summer of 1961, Dale and his band unveiled the new surf sound during weekend dances at the Rendezvous Ballroom in Balboa, California. The guitarist told an interviewer that "they said nobody would come to my dances because the Ballroom was too far away and nobody will drive that distance."

Loyal surfers traveled the distance to hear their own music. The Rendezvous Ballroom in Balboa, remembered Pete Johnson, later a member of the surf group The Belairs, "held well over 1,000 and Dale's sound was, in a word awesome! The music was huge and throbbing, especially when combined with all those sandals stomping on the wooden floor." By late 1961, when he first arrived on the West Coast, disc jockey and producer Jim Pewter found that "the word was 'Let's go to a Dick Dale dance,' so my girl and I motivated to the Rendezvous and checked it out, only to return again and again."

Courtesy of Capitol Records

The Beach Boys: kings of the wild surf

Dick Dale and the Deltones released records for the surf crowd. In September 1961, "Let's Go Trippin' " topped the California charts and edged into the national Top 100. Dale followed with "Surfbeat," "Surfing Drums," and "Shake 'n' Stomp," and in 1962 produced the classic surf instrumental "Miserlou." In February 1963, Capitol Records recorded Dale and pegged him the King of the Surf Guitar. The same year, the guitarist landed a spot in the William Asher movie *Beach Party* and by 1963 had become a California celebrity.

THE BEACH BOYS

The Beach Boys brought surf music to national prominence. Raised in the suburb of Hawthorne, California, the boys—leader Brian Wilson, his brothers Carl and Dennis, cousin Mike Love, and Al Jardine, a friend of Brian's—formed in 1961 and played as Kenny and the Cadets, Carl and the Passions and usually the Pendletons, the last a name that referred to the brand of shirt worn by most surfers.

The band smoothed the rough edges of the fuzzy, twanging surf instrumental. As with Dick Dale, the boys favored a swinging, fifties, electric guitar sound. " 'Rock Around The Clock' shocked me," Brian Wilson once told a reporter. "I mean, I was so electrified by the experience—that song was really it." The group polished the raw distortion of fifties rock with glossy harmonies gleaned from such white vocal groups as the Four Freshmen. The blend resulted in a bright, airy, snappy sound that embodied the California myth and, as with the girl-group sound, reflected the general optimism of the Kennedy presidency.

The Wilson brothers recorded their new sound in 1961 with the help of their father, Murry Wilson, who managed a heavy-machinery import business and in his spare time composed songs. When asked by music publisher Hite Morgan about new song-writers, Murry suggested Al Jardine, who spoke with the publisher and agreed to record a demo for him.

In late 1961, Jardine appeared at the session with the complete band. "We've written a song about the surfing sport and we'd like to sing it for you," pestered the Wilson brothers. Morgan quietly listened to the tune and exclaimed, "Drop everything; we're going to record your song. I think it's good." Within two hours, in Morgan's single-track studio the group recorded "Surfin'." Morgan took the demo to the local Candix label, owned by Herb Newman, who released the record in December 1961 and changed the name of the group from the Pendletons to the Beach Boys. Commented Mike Love about the name change: "We didn't even know we were the Beach Boys until the song came out. It was that kind of thing. We could have said, 'No, we're not going to be the Beach Boys.' " Within weeks, "Surfin'" topped the California charts and reached number 75 on the national Top 100.

Good luck temporarily deserted the Beach Boys. Two months after the success of "Surfin', " the Beach Boys entered Hite Morgan's studio and recorded four more songs: "Surfin' Safari," "The Beach Boys Stomp," "Judy," and "Surfer Girl," the last two written by Brian for his girlfriend, Judy Bowles. Before it could release the songs, Candix Records, plagued by financial difficulties, ceased operations. Murry Wilson, by this time the manager of the group, played the demos to Decca, Liberty, and Dot Records, all of which rejected the songs because, in the estimation of an executive at Dot, "surfing music was a flash in the pan." Al Jardine, disgusted with the failures, quit the band and entered dental school.

Murry Wilson finally brought the demos to Nick Venet of Capitol Records. After listening to the songs, the producer rushed into the office of his supervisor, Voyle Gilmore, and boasted, "Boss, I've got a double-sided smash for Capitol." The label signed the Beach Boys and released "Surfin' Safari," which reached number 14 on the national charts. Later in the year, Capitol followed with an album of the same name.

In May 1963, Capitol released the breakthrough Beach Boys album, *Surfin' U.S.A.*, which featured on the cover an action photo of a surfer cutting a path across a thirty-foot wave and included a headline that hailed the Beach Boys as "the No. 1 surfing group in the country." "Surf's Up! Here come the Beach Boys," Nick Venet proclaimed in the liner notes on the album. "Here's the group that started the surf-dancing craze all over the country—even in places where the nearest thing to surf is maybe the froth on a chocolate shake." Venet promoted the "brawny, sun-tanned" Beach Boys as "nationwide symbols for the exhilarating sport that has taken America by storm."

The Beach Boys applied their trademark harmonies to the title song on the album, "Surfin' U.S.A." a note-for-note reworking of Chuck Berry's "Sweet Little Sixteen," which hit the number 3 slot on the national charts. The other selections on the album included covers of Dick Dale's "Miserlou" and "Let's Go Tripping" and other odes to surfdom such as "Lonely Sea," "Surf Jam," and "Noble Surfer." The album established the Beach Boys as the kings of surf, and *Surfin' U.S.A.* helped to spread the surfing craze throughout the nation.

During the next few months, the Beach Boys fortified their reputation. In late 1963, they scored with "Surfer Girl" and in 1964 topped the charts with "I Get Around." The group reflected and enforced the California myth with their next two chartbusters, "Fun, Fun, Fun" and "California Girls." By early 1964, the Beach Boys had brought a bright, bouncy surf music that extolled the sun and fun to teens throughout the nation.

JAN AND DEAN

Jan and Dean delivered the same message of the California surf to American teenagers. Becoming friends at University High School in Los Angeles where they had football lockers next to one another, Jan Berry and Dean Torrance began their partnership by recording standard teen ballads. In 1959, they reached the Top 10 with "Baby Talk" and appeared on the nationally televised "American Bandstand." They followed with such paeans to teenage love as "Heart

Jan and Dean, courtesy of EMI Records

and Soul," "Julie," "A Sunday Kind of Love," "There's A Girl," and "We Go Together."

The duo joined the ranks of surfdom in 1963 with the help of the Beach Boys. "When 'Surfin'' came out," recalled Dean, "we heard it and liked it. I think we sensed that it was going to be good for business." Because both "Jan and I were physically involved with surfing, it was just natural that we became involved with the music."

In early 1963, Jan and Dean became converted to surf music when they performed with the Beach Boys. The Beach Boys first played a few songs, including "Surfin'" and "Surfin' Safari," and Jan and Dean followed with three or four songs. When met by an enthusiastic reaction from the predominately male crowd, Jan and Dean asked the Beach Boys, "Hey do you want to do your set again, and we'll sing with you guys?" "Gee, you'll sing our songs," responded an awestruck Brian Wilson. "Sure," replied Dean, "I think your songs are really fun to sing." Jan and Dean backed the Beach Boys for two numbers, and the crowd went wild.

The collaboration convinced Jan and Dean to include a surf song on their upcoming album, which featured the song "Linda." As Dean told it, record producer Lou Adler suggested " 'Why don't you take Linda surfing, and do an album called *Jan and Dean Take Linda Surfing*. That gets it all in there.' " Dean agreed but "didn't know any surfing songs except the two that the Beach Boys had done." He called Brian Wilson and asked if the group would play the instrumental parts to "Surfin' " and "Surfin' Safari" on the album. Brian, Dean recalled, "was just totally knocked out that we were going to record his songs! He said, 'Sure, I'll get the guys' " who dashed to the studio. While at a session, Brian sang the opening line of a new song and offered it to Jan and Dean. The duo added lyrics and recorded it as "Surf City," a song that in 1963 went to the top of the charts and, as part of the California myth of abundance, promised "two girls for every boy." The next year, they followed with "Ride the Wild Surf" and "Sidewalk Surfin'."

By the end of 1963, surf music had become a national craze. The Surfaris recorded "Wipe Out," which reached number 2 on the national charts. Modeling their sound after Dick Dale, the Chantays hit the Top 5 with "Pipeline." Duane Eddy, the king of twang, recorded "Your Baby's Gone Surfin'," the Midwestern Trashmen cut "Surfin' Bird," and the Astronauts from Colorado released "Surfin' with the Astronauts." A spate of other surf-inspired albums emerged: *Surfin' with the Challengers, Surfin' Bongos, Surfin' with the Shadows*, the Markett's *Surfers Stomp, Surfbeat* by the Surfriders, and *Surf Mania* by the Surf Teens. Chess Records even released the album *Surfin' with Bo Diddley*, without informing the R&B guitarist. By the mid-1960s, the California surf had definitely risen.

DRAG CITY

Many of the surfer groups glorified another aspect of the sprawling Southern California landscape—the automobile. By the early 1960s, a maze of highways connected the inhabitants of Southern California. "California," *Life* informed its readers in October 1962, "has 1,000 miles of freeways and blueprints for many more. It has 850 miles of expressways and 2,400 miles of multilane highways."

The tangle of roads forced most Californians to own at least one automobile. "In California, a car is like an extra, highly essential part of the human anatomy," explained *Life,* which estimated that the 8.5 million cars in the state, positioned bumper-to-bumper, would extend over 27,000 miles. The magazine equated life in California without an automobile to "a fate roughly equal to decapitation."

The importance of cars in California led to an automobile subculture that, as with the surfer subculture, involved distinctive dress and language. Teenagers, mostly males, lusted for their first automobile. Rather than a staid station wagon, they cast their eyes upon "asphalt eaters" (dragsters) such as Cudas (Plymouth Barracudas) or GTOs (Grand Turismos) propelled by such huge engines as the rat motor (a 427-cubic-inch Chevy engine) or the Chrysler Hemi (a 426-cubic-inch engine equipped with hemispherical combustion chambers). Like cowboys on their horses in a California of another era, teens with greased hair and tight black pants would drive their machines to seldom-used roads and wait for a competitor to drag (race). They would anticipate the flash of a light, "drop the hammer" (release the clutch quickly) and speed away, "shutting down" (defeating) an opponent. By the end of the 1950s, the dragsters could race legally on such strips as the one at the Orange County Airport near Santa Ana. "Kids love dragging a car," gushed noted auto customizer Ed Roth at the time, "I mean they really love it."

The hot rod subculture was promoted through the press and film. Bob Petersen and Bob Lindsay, two young hot rodders living near Los Angeles, in 1947 published the first issue of *Hot Rod* magazine, which would become standard reading for car-crazed California youth. Casting hot rodders as juvenile delinquents on wheels, such movies as *Hot Rod Girl* (1956), *Dragstrip Girl* (1957), *Hot Rod Gang* (1958), *Dragstrip Riot* (1958), and *Teenage Thunder* (1959) further popularized drag racing among an element less clean-cut than the surfer crowd.

Roger Christian, a Los Angeles disc jockey who was tagged "Poet of the Strip," helped surfer bands such as the Beach Boys write songs about dragsters, even though die-hard surfers considered hot rodders, or "ho-dads" as they called them, to be rivals. "Roger was a guiding light for me," revealed Brian Wilson of the Beach Boys. After Christian's late-night radio show, Brian and the disc jockey would "go over to Otto's, order a hot fudge sundae and just . . . whew! talk and talk." "Roger is a real car nut," he told *Life* in 1964. "His normal speech is only 40 percent comprehensible. And he has a tremendous knack for rhyming things with *carburetor*." Christian and Brian Wilson first collaborated on "Shut Down," which became a Top 20 hit. They continued their partnership with "Little Deuce Coupe," "Car Crazy Cutie," "Don't Worry Baby," and "Spirit of America," the last of which celebrated Craig Breedlove's three-wheeled, 7,800-pound jet car.

Roger Christian began to compose songs for Jan and Dean. In 1963, at the request of Jan, Christian and Brian Wilson wrote "Drag City" for the duo, which reached the Top 10. The disc jockey penned most of the other songs on the album of the same name, including "Hot Stocker," "I Gotta Drive," "Schlock Rod," and "Dead

Man's Curve," which became prophetic in 1966 when Jan Berry smashed his Stingray into a parked truck at 65 mph on Whittier Boulevard in Los Angeles and sustained serious brain damage. "For the finest reproduction," wrote Roger Christian in the liner notes for *Drag City*, "this recording should be played on a chrome reversed turntable driven by a full-blown turntable motor equipped with tuned headers. Transmission of power should be through a four-speed box with a floor stick." The "Poet of the Strip" had, in his own words, effected "the merger of Jan and Dean and the car craze."

By 1964, several other bands had jumped on the car craze bandwagon. The Rip Chords, a studio band formed by Bruce Johnston, a neighbor of Jan Berry, and which included guitarist Glen Campbell, scored with "Hey, Little Cobra." The Nashville-based Ronny and the Daytonas hit with "G.T.O." Jerry Kole and the Stokers released the album, *Hot Rod Alley*; a group called the Hot Rodders cut "Big Hot Rod"; and Riverside Records recorded actual drag races and committed the sounds to vinyl. Even car customizer Ed Roth, backed by a studio band, recorded an LP, *Rods and Ratfinks*, under the name Mr. Gasser and the Weirdos. By November 1964, *Life* noted the prolifieration of "love songs to the carburetor."

By 1964, jangling harmonies celebrated the California myth. "I think we had a lot to do with the population rush to California," asserted Beach Boy Al Jardine. "People hearing the Beach Boys' songs envisioned California as sort of a golden paradise where all you did was surf and sun yourself while gorgeous blondes rubbed coconut oil on your back." "We sang about California and being young," agreed Dean Torrance. "They seemed to go together. In the Sixties everyone wanted to go to California, or so it seemed, and it was the time of the youth movement, too. Our records, of course, were directed to the young; they were obviously teenage songs. Who else would be hanging out at the beach or driving hot rods around?" "Lyrics," continued Torrance, "don't mean shit. I'm talking about the kind of music we do, not the kind Bob Dylan or someone else does." As Jan and Dean promoted "Surf City," folk singers in New York City such as Bob Dylan were singing about another America where blacks protested and died for their civil rights.

5

Bob Dylan and the New Frontier

"There's other things in this world besides love and sex that're important."

Bob Dylan

Early on a Saturday night in 1961, a twenty-year-old singer carrying an oversized guitar case walked into a dimly lit coffeehouse, Gerde's Folk City in Greenwich Village, New York City. He was dressed casually: worn brown shoes, blue jeans, and a black wool jacket, covering a plain yellow turtleneck sweater. A jumble of rumpled hair crowned his head, which was topped by a black corduroy Huck Finn cap. He pressed his lips together tightly and glanced at the tables of patrons, who sipped espresso and seemed to be arguing feverishly about current events. The singer looked serious and exhibited a nervousness that a friend had earlier tried to calm with four jiggers of Jim Beam bourbon. He slowly mounted the stage, opened his case, and carefully took out an old, nicked, six-string acoustic guitar, which he treated like an old friend. He fixed a wire harmonica holder around his neck and pushed a harmonica into place. As the singer stood alone on stage, motionless, a hush descended upon the coffeehouse.

The audience, mostly white middle-class college students, many of them attending nearby New York University, politely applauded the singer. For a moment, the scene appeared to epitomize Eisenhower gentility and McCarthy repression: boys with closely cropped hair, button-down shirts, corduroy slacks, Hush Puppy shoes, and cardigans; and rosy-cheeked girls dressed in long skirts, bulky knit sweaters and low-heeled shoes who favored long, straight, well-groomed hair.

The singer shattered the genteel atmosphere when he began to strum a chord and sing. He was young Bob Dylan, who had just recently arrived in New York City to sing songs of social protest.

Many college-age youths raptly listened to Bob Dylan deliver his hymns of social protest. As civil rights marchers protested in Birmingham and as President John F. Kennedy announced plans for a New Frontier, they heard the stirring message of Bob Dylan, who leveled his guitar at racism and the hypocrisy of corporate America. By 1963, the first baby boomers had entered college and were starting to become aware of the world around them.

SONGS OF PROTEST

The foundation for the protest song of the 1960s was laid at the turn of the century by the International Workers of the World (IWW). Members of the group, known as Wobblies, first penned protest songs in the United States as part of their drive to achieve equality for American workers. While marching in demonstrations, the radical unionists sang from the *Little Red Songbook*, first published in 1909 at Spokane, Washington, and compiled by organizers Ralph Chaplin and the legendary Joe Hill, a Swedish immigrant who was later executed in Utah for his political beliefs. The Wobblies adopted as their anthem Chaplin's "Solidarity Forever," a protest song set to the music of the "Battle Hymn of the Republic": "They have taken untold millions that they never toiled to earn/ But without our brain and muscle not a single wheel can turn/ We can break their haughty power, gain our freedom when we learn/ That the Union makes us strong/ Solidarity forever!"

Woody Guthrie continued the legacy of the protest song after federal and state authorities raided and closed IWW offices during the Red Scare that followed World War I. Born in July 1912 to a poor family in Okemah, Oklahoma, Woodrow Wilson Guthrie left home at sixteen and drifted through the Southwest during his teens, working as a newsboy, a sign painter, spittoon washer, and farm laborer. While visiting his uncle Jeff Guthrie in Tampa, Texas, during 1929, the young Woody learned to play guitar. The youth played on street corners and continued to work odd jobs until 1937, when he became the host for a program on the Los Angeles radio station KFVD, on which he read radical newspapers over the air. Within two more years he moved to New York City and began writing a daily column for the Communist *People's Daily World* and the *Daily Worker.* In 1940, Guthrie recorded for folklorist Alan Lomax, who taped the singer for the Library of Congress and who three years later would do the same with Muddy Waters.

After a two-year stint in the merchant marines during World War II, Guthrie packed his bags and returned to New York City, where he penned many of his 1,000 songs which included "This Land Is Your Land." "I don't sing any songs about the nine divorces

Pete Seeger, folk singer whose influence helped revive folk tradition

of some millionaire playgal or the ten wives of some screwball," he later explained. "I've just not got the time to sing those kinds of songs and I wouldn't sing them if they paid me ten thousand dollars a week. I sing the songs of the people that do all of the little jobs and the mean and dirty hard work in the world and of their wants and their hopes and their plans for a decent life." The motto emblazoned on his guitar summed up his message: "This Machine Kills Fascists."

Pete Seeger joined Woody Guthrie, roaming the countryside to sing songs to the American worker. Born on May 3, 1919, in New York City to a musical family, Seeger quit Harvard University during the 1930s and worked with Alan Lomax. In 1940 he founded the Almanac Singers. After serving in World War II Seeger formed a musician's union, People's Songs, Inc., which attracted 3,000 members, including Woody Guthrie. In 1948 Seeger formed the Weavers, a group which popularized folk songs such as "On Top of Old Smokey," and "Good Night Irene."

The Guthrie-style protest song fell into disrepute during the McCarthyite witch hunt. During the early and mid-1950s, Senator Joseph McCarthy of Wisconsin doggedly pursued Communist sympathizers. He progressively accused more and more public figures of Communist tendencies, eventually creating a hysterical, crisis atmosphere. The Wisconsin Senator criticized left-wing entertainers such as Woody Guthrie and Pete Seeger, who were blackballed by the networks and recording industry.

THE FOLK REVIVAL

Folk music reappeared around 1960, when the number of college students increased. In 1956, 3.2 million students attended college in schools across the country. Four years later, almost 4 million studied within the ivy halls.

These college-age youths searched for an alternative to the popular, romanticized hit singles of Don Kirshner's songwriters who composed for the young teen market. "Today," observed *Look* in early 1961, "the 15 to 20-year-olds, especially those in college, are showing their musical curiosity in ways that don't appear on single-record popularity charts." "Weary of the more and more juvenile level of 'pop' music, frustrated by the dearth of good Broadway show tunes, and slightly befuddled by the growing complexity of jazz," reported the magazine a few issues later, college students were "ready to turn solidly folknik."

The Kingston Trio started the folk revival. Formed in 1957 by three college students, Bob Shane, Nick Reynolds, and Dave Guard, the Trio scored a number-1 hit in 1958 with "Tom Dooley," a song written by North Carolina banjo player Frank Proffitt. The threesome, following with a series of successful albums for Capitol Records, which in four years grossed $40 million, surpassed Frank Sinatra as Capitol's number-1 moneymaker. By June 1960, *Time* called the "rockless, roll less and rich" trio the "hottest group in U.S. popular music."

The Kingston Trio projected a safe, corporate image. "They are 'sincere' without being 'serious,' " reported singer Will Holt about the Trio in 1961. "They are the kids who sing Saturday nights at fraternity house parties, and the audience gets the comfortable feeling that anyone can do it." Pictures in the national magazines featuring the well-groomed, well-dressed Trio at poolside with their wives further promoted the image of stability.

The wholesome Trio profited from their success. In 1962, the threesome averaged $10,000 per concert in a large hall, earned nearly $300,000 in record sales, and grossed $1.7 million in total earnings. Marketed by manager Frank Werber who, according to *Business Week* proved "there's a small fortune to be coined from the folksong craze," the group established Kingston Trio Inc., a ten-company investment firm that owned an office building in San Francisco, a land-development concern, a restaurant, a concert-promotion agency, and a group of music-publishing companies. "When we fight nowadays," one of the Kingston Trio told *Time* in 1960, "it's mostly about business—what to invest in."

The commercial success of the Kingston Trio encouraged other apolitical, clean-cut folkies to form singing groups. In 1959, thirty-six-year-old Lou Gottlieb, who earned a Ph.D. in musicology from UCLA, actor and University of Chicago graduate Alex Hassilev, and twenty-nine-year-old Glenn Yarbrough began to sing as the Limeliters. Within a year, the group commanded $4,000 a week for their performances and recorded a top-selling album of traditional French, Portuguese, and English folk songs. "If the button-down, scrubbed-looking, youthful Kingston Trio are the undergraduates of big-time U.S. folksinging," *Time* reported in June 1961, "the Limeliters are the faculty."

The next year, ten folksters banded together into the blatantly commercial New Christy Minstrels. "When I chose our people," explained founder Randy Sparks, "I made it a point to shy away from questionable people. I looked for the All-American boy or girl who had no political complaints and no sexual problems anyone would be interested in." The "sporty, clean New Christy Minstrels," reported *Time*, offered "a bland mix of broad harmonies, familiar tunes, corny humor and just enough of the folk music spirit to cash in on the most avid adult record buyer." The group sold over 100,000 copies of its first album and in 1963 hit the Top Twenty with "Green Green." In 1964 Sparks sold his interest in the group for $2.5 million.

The commercial folk boom ironically led to the rediscovery of traditional folk. "Commercialization has actually helped folk music," claimed Pete Seeger in 1963. "It revived interest in it in the cities where it had almost died. Country interest never really stopped. Now, there are kids all over the nation plinking their banjos, and folk music is a living, vibrant thing again." College-age youths began to listen to Seeger, the reformed Weavers, the spiritual singing of Odetta, and Jean Ritchie, who sang Appalachian folk tales to her own accompaniment on the dulcimer. They became interested in the spirited bluegrass style of such guitar pickers as Bill Monroe, Doc Watson, and Earl Taylor, and discovered the electric blues of Muddy Waters, John Lee Hooker, and Howlin' Wolf.

By the early 1960s, folk music in all its varied forms had become a craze. "Like, I mean, it's not esoteric anymore," gushed Israel Young, head of Greenwich Village's Folk Center, in late 1961. Coffeehouses began to open in Boston, Chicago, Minneapolis, Denver, and San Francisco. Folk fans could sip mocha java and listen to minstrels at The Know Where in Joliet, Illinois, The Fourth Shadow in Fort Wayne, Indiana, the Jolly Coachman in Council Bluffs, Iowa, and The Third Man and The Crooked Ear in Omaha, Nebraska. College-age folk fans, having more money than young teens, discarded the 45-rpm hit singles for long-playing albums of their favorite groups, which helped double sales of the LP from 1956 to 1961. Beginning in April 1963, eleven million folk fans watched "Hootenanny," a nationally broadcast, Saturday-night television show which each week took viewers to a folk concert on a different campus. "Yesterday, it was the esoteric kick of history buffs and music scholars. Today, it's show business," *Look* told its readers in 1963. "With a hoot and a holler, folk music has taken over from coffeehouse to campus to prime-time television."

CIVIL RIGHTS ON A NEW FRONTIER

The growing clamor of black Americans for civil rights coincided with and shaped the burgeoning folk music scene. On February 1, 1960, four black students from the Agricultural and Technical College in Greensboro, North Carolina, entered a variety store, made several purchases, and sat down at the lunch counter reserved for whites, ordering coffee. Although refused service and told to leave, the students remained at the counter until the store closed. This tactic of passive resistance, the sit-in, attracted national attention to the civil rights movement and for the first time attacked segregation in privately owned facilities.

Sit-ins spread to other cities. On October 19, 1960, a group of blacks marched into the all-white Magnolia Room of Rich's Department Store in Atlanta and refused to leave. Leader Martin Luther King, Jr., was sentenced to four months of hard labor in the Reidsville State Prison for his part in the incident. As some blacks argued in the *Atlanta Constitution,* "We do not intend to wait placidly for those rights which are already legally and morally ours to be meted out to us one at a time."

The next year, sit-ins, picketing, and boycotts ended segregation of restaurants and beaches. In Oklahoma City, Savannah, Atlanta, Louisville, and Norfolk, blacks used sit-ins to desegregate lunch counters and restaurants. In Chicago, passive resistance opened a beach that had previously been available to whites only. A weekend sit-in around the courthouse square in Monroe, North Carolina successfully ended segregation in city facilities.

In 1961 civil rights demonstrators employed a new tactic, the freedom ride. In May, the Congress of Racial Equality (C.O.R.E.), an interracial direct-action group founded in 1942, boarded members on buses in the North and sent them on "freedom rides" into the South to challenge the segregation of interstate travel facilities. Despite the warnings of federal officials to Alabama Governor John Patterson, the riders were brutally attacked by white racists in Anniston, Birmingham, and Montgomery, Alabama. When arriving in the segregated bus terminal in Jackson, Mississippi, more than 300 of the "freedom riders," mostly college students, ministers, and professors, were arrested and jailed.

Trouble exploded next in Albany, Georgia. On December 10, 1961, youths in the Student Non-Violent Coordinating Committee (SNCC) walked into the all-white lobby of the Albany railway station, sat down, and waited until local authorities arrested them on charges of disorderly conduct. The next week, Martin Luther King, Jr., head of the Southern Christian Leadership, traveled to Albany and led 700 civil rights adherents in a march to protest the arrest of the students. After authorities arrested King, blacks in Albany began to boycott the local bus system, which relied heavily upon black riders. Within forty days, they successfully forced the bus company to cease operations.

The demand for civil rights among black Americans escalated, turning violent in 1963. On April 3, protesters in Birmingham, Alabama marched for fair employment and desegregation, led by Martin Luther King, Jr., and Fred Shuttlesworth, president of the Alabama Christian Movement for Human Rights. The demonstrators slowly increased in numbers, reaching more than 3,000 in a month. On May 3, the marchers were assaulted by police, who unleashed dogs, wielded electric cattle prods, and used fire hoses to disperse them and achieve an uneasy peace. A week later, when racists bombed the house of a demonstrator and a black-owned motel, blacks spilled out into the streets and confronted police, pelting them with bricks and bottles. By May 12, when the violence ended, they had wrecked dozens of automobiles, burned six small stores, and gutted a two-story apartment building. The riot in Birmingham quickly spread to other cities such as Tallahassee, Nashville, and Cambridge, Maryland.

Racist-inspired violence erupted in June. That month, racists

Sixties idealism reflected in Kennedy for President campaign button

in Jackson, Mississippi, ambushed and killed near his home Medgar Evers, the Mississippi field secretary of the National Association for the Advancement of Colored People (NAACP). Police in Danville, Virginia, arrested 347 protesters and injured 40 others when they turned fire hoses on the crowd. Racists shot and killed white civil rights crusader William Moore, who was walking near Attalla, Alabama, with a sign demanding equal rights. They pelted with rocks and herded into jail ten freedom riders who attempted to continue Moore's march. By early July 1963, authorities had arrested almost 14,000 civil rights advocates, who participated in 758 demonstrations in eleven states.

On August 28, 1963, 200,000 white and black civil rights partisans converged on Washington, D.C. They marched to the steps of the Lincoln Memorial to listen to ten civil rights leaders, including Martin Luther King, Jr. "I have a dream," intoned King, "that one day this nation will rise up and live out the true meaning of its creed, 'we hold these truths to be self-evident that all men are created equal.' " "I have a dream," King continued in a mounting fervor, "that one day on the red hills of Georgia the sons of former slaves and the sons of former slave owners will be able to sit down together at the table of brotherhood. I have a dream that one day even the state of Mississippi, a state sweltering with the heat of injustice, sweltering with the heat of oppression, will be transformed into an oasis of freedom and justice."

President John F. Kennedy, elected in 1960, offered civil rights crusaders hope that King's dream could become reality. The young, energetic Kennedy assured the nation that the United States was approaching a "new frontier . . . a frontier of unknown opportunities and perils—a frontier of unfilled hopes and threats" that was "not a set of promises—it is a set of challenges. It sums up, not what I intend to offer the American people, but what I intend to ask of them." In his inaugural speech, the president specifically focused on "human rights to which this nation has always been committed and to which we are committed today at home."

Kennedy supported the demands for equal rights. On September 20, 1962, as part of an ongoing effort to desegregate public schools, Kennedy sent federal troops to the University of Mississippi in Oxford, at which James Meredith, a black air force veteran, attempted to enroll. When resisted by state troops mobilized by Governor Ross Barnett, Kennedy federalized the Mississippi national guard and on national television appealed to the students at the University to accept desegregation. After a racist-inspired riot left two dead, the president ordered a guard of U.S. marshals to protect James Meredith, who began to attend classes.

In June 1963, the president sent federal troops to the University of Alabama to safeguard two new black enrollees, Vivian Malone and James Hood. He ordered federal marshalls to dislodge Alabama Governor George Wallace, who physically positioned himself in the front doorway of a university building and denounced "this illegal and unwarranted action of the Central Government." In a televised broadcast after the Wallace incident, Kennedy told the nation that the civil rights question was "a moral issue . . . as old as the Scriptures and . . . as clear as the American Constitution." He committed his administration to the proposition "that race has no place in American life or law."

Kennedy took further action after protests in Birmingham and their aftermath. "The events in Birmingham and elsewhere," he declared, "have so increased the cries for equality that no city or state or legislative body can prudently choose to ignore them." The President proposed wide-reaching civil rights legislation to guarantee equal access to all public facilities, to attack employment discrimination based on race, and to empower the Attorney General to file suit on behalf of individuals whose civil rights had been violated.

Many college students pledged their energies to the new frontier of racial equality. They perceived Kennedy, the youngest elected president in U.S. history, as an energetic visionary who stood in sharp contrast to the grandfatherly Dwight Eisenhower. College-age youth felt an affinity to the Harvard-educated president, who surrounded himself with academics such as Harvard professor Arthur Schlessinger, Jr., and in his inaugural address told a national audience that "the torch has been passed to a new generation of Americans."

College students devoted themselves to Kennedy's program for civil rights. "This generation of college students has begun to react against being treated like adolescents," reasoned a writer in a 1961 issue of *The New Republic*. "They have been willing to associate themselves with nonconformist movements, despite warnings by parents and teachers that such activities will endanger their personal as well as their job security." Driven by a Kennedy-inspired idealism, college students became freedom riders, marched for desegregation, and gathered in Washington, D.C., to demand equality.

BOB DYLAN: THE MUSIC OF PROTEST

The convergence of the civil rights movement and folk music on the college campuses led to the mercurial rise of Bob Dylan and his brand of protest folk music. Born on May 24, 1941, to the owner of a hardware store in Hibbing, Minnesota, Robert Allen Zimmerman grew up near the Mesabi copper range. Being Jewish in an area that, in his words, "had a certain prejudice against Jews," Dylan felt isolated. As a high school girlfriend of Dylan's, Echo Star Helstrom, later confided: "The other kids, they wanted to throw stones at anybody different. And Bob was different. He felt he didn't fit in, not in Hibbing." "I see things that other people don't see," Dylan told a reporter from *The Saturday Evening Post*. "I feel things that other people don't feel. It's terrible. They laugh. I felt like that my whole life. . . . I don't even know if I'm normal."

To cope with the isolation, Dylan turned to music. He first listened to "Hank Williams one or two years before he died. And that sort of introduced me to the guitar." As with thousands of other youths at the time, Dylan "late at night used to listen to Muddy Waters, John Lee Hooker, Jimmy Reed, and Howlin' Wolf blastin' in from Shreveport. It was a radio show that lasted all night. I used to stay up until two, three o'clock in the morning."

Bob Dylan, a fan of both country and R & B, almost naturally embraced the new music of rock-and-roll. When *Rock Around the Clock* showed in Hibbing, Dylan shouted to a friend outside the

Bob Dylan.

theater, "Hey, that's our music! That's written for us." He began to idolize Little Richard and then Elvis Presley and "saw Buddy Holly two or three nights before he died. I'll never forget the image of seeing Buddy Holly on the bandstand. And he died—it must have been a week after that. It was unbelievable." By his freshmen year in high school, Dylan formed "a couple of bands" including the Golden Chords, which played rock-and-roll at local functions.

Dylan turned to folk music when it reached the Midwest. "I heard a record—the Kingston Trio or Odetta or someone like that," he remembered, "and I sort of got into folk music. Rock and roll was pretty much finished. And I traded my stuff for a Martin [acoustic guitar] that they don't sell anymore." In 1959, he began to perform traditional folk music and bluegrass in coffeehouses around the University of Minnesota under the name of Dillon and then Dylan.

Bob Dylan encountered his most pervasive influence while in

Minneapolis. As he told it, "I heard Woody Guthrie. And when I heard Woody Guthrie, that was it, it was all over . . . He really struck me as an independent character. But no one ever talked about him. So I went through all his records I could find and picked all that up by any means I could." "Woody was my god," declared the young singer. In December 1960, he eventually traveled from Minnesota to New York City and frequently visited the dying Guthrie. Dylan's first album, recorded in November 1961 for four hundred dollars, included a song dedicated to Woody.

In Greenwich Village at such clubs as Gerde's Folk City, the Gaslight Coffeehouse, and the Village Gate, Dylan began to sing his own songs of social protest. Remembered Terri Thal, who was then married to folk guitarist Dave Van Ronk, "He was beginning to think about and talk about people who were being trod upon [by 1961]. Not in any class way, but he hated people who were taking people. He had a full conception of people who were being taken, and he did read the newspapers, and that's what came through in 'Talkin' Bear Mountain' and 'Talkin' New York," both in the Guthrie style of talking blues."

Some observers suggested that Suze Rotolo, Dylan's girlfriend, influenced him. "Dylan's girlfriend at the time, Suze Rotolo, worked as a secretary for the civil rights group CORE and probably caused Dylan to write 'The Ballad of Emmet Till,' " remarked Thal. Recalled someone then in the Village, "Suze came along and she wanted him to go Pete Seeger's way. She wanted Bobby to be involved in civil rights and all the radical causes Seeger was involved in. . . . She influenced Bobby considerably, that way."

Composing songs about current, pressing issues such as civil rights rather than singing traditional or commercialized folk, Dylan politicized sixties folk music with his second album, *Freewheelin.'* The album, released in May 1963, showed a picture of Suze Rotolo on Bob's arm as they ambled down a windswept New York City street on a gray winter day and featured "Blowin' in the Wind," which became an anthem for the civil rights movement. "The idea came to me that you were betrayed by your silence," Dylan told some friends about the song. "That all of us in America who didn't speak out were betrayed by our silence. Betrayed by the silence of the people in power. They refuse to look at what's happening. And the others, they ride the subway and read the *Times,* but they don't understand. They don't know. They don't even care, that's the worst of it." Dylan told of the ordeal of James Meredith at the University of Mississippi in "Oxford Town," composed "Hard Rain's A-Gonna Fall" about the Cuban missile crisis in October 1962, penned "Talkin' World War Three Blues," a humorous but somber picture of life after a nuclear holocaust, and blasted government leaders in the vitriolic "Masters of War." At the time, the singer felt that "there's other things in this world besides love and sex that're important," too. People shouldn't turn their backs on them just because they ain't pretty to look at. How is the world ever going to get better if we're afraid to look at these things?"

Dylan continued to pen protest songs for his next album, *The Times They Are A-Changin'*, released in February 1964. Besides the title song, which became a battle cry of the emerging social revolution, he chronicled the struggle for civil rights in "The Lonesome Death of Hattie Carroll" and wrote about the murder of civil rights leader Medgar Evers in "A Pawn in Their Game." John Hammond, the record executive who signed Dylan to Columbia Records in 1961, believed that the singer "was thinking and talking about injustice and social problems. Bobby really wanted to change things. He was uptight about the whole setup in America, the alienation of kids from their parents, the false values. From my leftist point of view, he was just superb, and it was real."

Dylan reinforced his politicized music by a number of public demonstrations. On May 12, 1963, he refused to perform on the "Ed Sullivan Show," when CBS banned him from singing "Talkin' John Birch Society Blues." On July 6 he gave a concert outside Greenwood, Mississippi with Pete Seeger to promote black voter registration initiated by the Student Non-Violent Coordinating Committee. Later in the month he appeared on a local New York television program dealing with "freedom singers." In August, Dylan marched on Washington for equal rights with Martin Luther King, Jr.

Bob Dylan began to serve as the focal point for a community of protest singers. Eric Anderson, known for his "Violets of Dawn," felt "the whole scene was generating a lot of vibes, and Dylan had the heaviest vibes of them all. Dylan was sowing the seeds of the decade." To Joan Baez, herself active in the protest movement, "Bobby Dylan says what a lot of people my age feel but cannot say."

JOAN BAEZ

Joan Baez was Bob Dylan's female counterpart in folk protest. The daughter of a Mexican-born physicist and a Scotch-Irish mother, the dark-skinned Baez faced racial discrimination at an early age. When living as a girl in Clarence Center, New York, a town of 800 people, she felt that "as far as the [townspeople] knew we were niggers."

Baez moved with her family to Boston where, during the late 1950s, she began to perform traditional folk songs in coffeehouses around Harvard, such as Tulla's Coffee Grinder. In 1959 Baez debuted to 13,000 people at the first Newport Folk Festival. "A star was born," wrote Robert Shelton in *The New York Times* after the performance, "a young soprano with a thrilling lush vibrato and fervid and well-controlled projection." Baez continued to attract a following, selling out a Carnegie Hall performance two months in advance. By 1962, *Time* referred to Joan "as the most gifted of the newcomers to the folk scene" and featured her on the cover of its November 23rd issue.

The singer, though composing few of her own songs, took a decidedly political stance. She sang such topical songs as the anti-war "Strangest Dream" and a parody of the House UnAmerican Activities Committee, which ceaselessly tracked supposed Communist sympathizers. The singer refused to appear on ABC's "Hootenanny" when the show blacklisted Pete Seeger and rejected more than $100,000 in concert dates during a single year because, as she told *Time,* "folk music depends on intent. If someone desires to make money, I don't call it folk music." In 1963, Baez demonstrated in Birmingham for desegregation and in August marched on Washington, D.C. "I feel very strongly about things," Joan told *Look* in 1963. "Like murdering babies with fallout and murdering spirits with segregation. I love to sing and, by some quirk, people like to hear me. I cannot divide things. They are all part of me."

THE SINGER-ACTIVISTS

A few other folk singers followed the path of protest. Texas-born Phil Ochs, the son of a Jewish army physician, attended Ohio State University, where he won his first guitar by betting on John Kennedy in the hotly contested 1960 presidential election. A year later, he composed his first song, "The Ballad of the Cuban Invasion" about the American invasion of Cuba at the Bay of Pigs, and joined a radical singing group called the Sundowners or, sometimes, the Singing Socialists, with roommate Jim Glover, who later became half of the pop duo, Jim and Jean. In 1962, Ochs dropped out of Ohio State over censorship of the school paper and journeyed to New York City to start his folk-protest career in earnest. According to Phil, he attended the 1963 Newport Folk Festival "with the Freedom Singers, Dylan, Baez, the songwriters' workshop, where the topical song suddenly became the thing. It moved from the background to the foreground in just one weekend."

Ochs, looking for a forum to propagate his radical ideals, churned out protest songs dealing with the issues of the day. His first album, *All the News That's Fit to Sing,* released by Elektra in April 1964, included "Thresher," "Too Many Martyrs," "The Ballad of William Worthy," "Talking Cuban Crisis," and "Talking Vietnam." Said Ochs: "I was writing about Vietnam in 1962, way before the first anti-war marches. I was writing about it at a point where the media were really full of shit, where they were just turning the other way as Vietnam was being built." Subsequent albums delivered other protest hymns, such as "The Ballad of the AMA," "Freedom Riders," "Ballad of Oxford, Mississippi," "Draft Dodger Rag," and "I Ain't Marching Anymore."

Phil Ochs backed his words with action. In 1964, when he heard that the bodies of three murdered civil rights workers had been found buried under an earthen dam, he headed for Mississippi. Ochs later traveled to Hazard, Kentucky, to help striking miners engaged in a bloody struggle with mine owners who were trying to bypass provisions of the Mine Safety Act. Phil's song "No Christmas in Kentucky" became a battlecry among the workers. When Phil and folksinger Tom Paxton played a benefit for the miners, members of the John Birch Society and the Fighting American Nationalists picketed the concert with placards that read "Agrarian Reformers Go Home."

Tom Paxton raised his voice in protest in other instances. Born in Chicago, young Paxton traveled to Oklahoma with his family and then served a stint in the army. In the early 1960s he moved to New York City, where he became radicalized and joined the folk protest circle of Bob Dylan. In 1964 he landed a recording contract with Elektra and followed the lead of Dylan, offering a series of protest songs in *Ramblin' Boy*. The next year, he recorded one of his most political albums, *Ain't That News,* which included "Lyndon Johnson Told the Nation," "Buy a Gun for Your Son," "We Didn't Know," and "Ain't That News." Explained Paxton about the title song: "When the poor (again, with the help of the students) are making the first hesitant steps toward organization; when Negroes, disenfranchised for years, are lining up by the thousands to register to vote; when mass demonstrations and teach-ins protest this government's foreign policy; when after the long sleep of the Eisenhower years you find heated dialogues and demonstrations throughout the country—that's news."

DYLAN'S DISENCHANTMENT

The folk protest movement began to fragment in late 1963 after the assassination of President John Kennedy. On November 22, in Dallas, a rifleman shot and killed the president, who was riding in a motorcade with his wife, Jackie, and Texas Governor John Connelly and his wife. The assassination sent shock and then horror throughout the nation, which mourned a president who had symbolized energy, action, and optimism.

Folk musicians felt especially disillusioned with overt political activism. Phil Ochs sensed "a definite flowering-out of positive feelings when John Kennedy became president. The civil rights movement was giving off positive vibrations. There was a great feeling of reform, that things could be changed, that the government cared, that an innovator could come in. . . . Things looked incredibly promising. Then came the Bay of Pigs, the beginnings of Vietnam and the assassination. It ruined the dream. November 22, 1963, was a mortal wound the country has not yet been able to recover from."

Dylan experienced the same pain and confusion after the assassination. As folksinger Eric Andersen told it, "You can't separate Dylan from history in the sense of what was going down, the way he reacted to a chain of events. The first being Kennedy's death; I think that got him out of politics. . . . Kennedy, he was sort of like the shadow of the flight . . . and then that bird got shot out of the sky and everyone was exposed, naked to all the frightening elements, the truth of the country. It had flown, that force had lost out. And people were depressed."

Dylan also began to move away from protest as he became more successful. The national press began to notice Dylan during the early 1960s. In 1962, *Newsweek* tagged him "the newest rage" in folk music, and *Time* sarcastically mentioned Bob Dylan who delivered "his songs in a studied nasal that has just the right clothespin-on-the-nose honesty to appeal to those who most deeply care." The next year the influential folk magazine *Little Sandy Review* called him "our finest contemporary folk songwriter."

Bob Dylan attracted national prominence when he signed with manager Albert Grossman, who was a major impetus in the folk revival. In 1957, Grossman opened one of the first folk clubs, The Gate of Horn, in Chicago and two years later helped George Wein launch the first Newport Folk Festival. In 1960 he met folksinger Peter Yarrow, whom he signed to a management contract and brought together with one-time Broadway singer Mary Travers and stand-up comic Paul Stookey, to form Peter, Paul and Mary.

Grossman's new creation hit the charts in May 1962, with "Lemon Tree" and five months later cracked the Top 10 with Pete Seeger's "If I Had a Hammer," which brought folk protest to a national audience. In 1963, the trio received from their manager a Bob Dylan song, "Blowin' In the Wind," which reached number 1 on the charts and lifted its composer into the national spotlight.

After gaining national exposure, and in the wake of the Kennedy assassination, Dylan started to become somewhat disillusioned with political activism. "I agree with everything that's happening," he told writer Nat Hentoff over dinner in October 1964, "but I'm not part of no Movement. If I was, I wouldn't be able to do anything else but be in 'the Movement.' I just can't sit around and have people make rules for me. . . . Those [protest] records I already made," said Dylan, referring to his first three albums,' "I'll stand behind them but some of that was jumping on the scene to be heard and a lot of it was because I didn't see anybody else doing that kind of thing. Now a lot of people are doing finger-pointing songs. You know—pointing at the things that are wrong. Me, I don't want to write for people anymore. You know—be a spokesman." Dylan began to criticize Joan Baez for her involvement with the Institute for the Study of Nonviolence at Carmel, California, established to "root out violence in ourselves and in the world." By 1965, Dylan abruptly informed a *Newsweek* reporter that "I've never written a political song. Songs can't save the world. I've gone through all that. When you don't like something, you gotta learn to just not need that something."

In place of social protest, Dylan crafted complex, personal and sometimes cryptic songs. "I have to make a new song out of what *I* know and out of what *I'm* feeling," he told Nat Hentoff. "I once wrote about Emmett Till in the first person, pretending that I was him. From now on, I want to write what's inside me." *Another Side of Bob Dylan,* recorded in the summer of 1964, featured such free association as "Chimes of Freedom" and repudiated the composer's folk protest in "My Back Pages." "I think it is very, very destructive music," complained Joan Baez at the time about Dylan's new orientation. "I think he doesn't want to be responsible for anybody, including himself."

Dylan's next album, *Bringing It All Back Home,* released in early 1965, abandoned folk protest for an electric rock. It included a rock-and-roll rhythm section and highlighted such bitter, dark songs as "Subterranean Homesick Blues," "She Belongs to Me," "Maggie's Farm," "Gates of Eden," and "It's All Right Ma (I'm Only Bleeding)." His next LP, *Highway 61 Revisited,* also released in 1965, included the impressionistic, beat-inspired poetry of "Desolation Row," "Queen Jane Approximately," "Ballad of a Thin Man," and "Like a Rolling Stone" which hit the number 2 spot on the charts. On July 25, 1965, at the Newport Folk Festival, Dylan unveiled his electric sound and his new brand of songwriting to the folk community who heartily booed their former leader. "I wouldn't mind so much if he sang just one song about the war," lamented Irwin Silber, the editor of the radical folk magazine *Sing Out!*

FOLK ROCK

Many groups mimicked the electric sound and sometimes borrowed the songs of Dylan to create what critics termed folk rock. The Byrds, probably the premier folk rockers, were formed in 1964 by Roger McGuinn, who at one time had been a member of the Limeliters and the Chad Mitchell Trio. Besides McGuinn, the group consisted of bassist Chris Hillman, drummer Michael Clarke, and guitarist Gene Clark, who had been a member of the New Christy Minstrels and had met the other member of the group, David Crosby, at the Troubador Club in Los Angeles on a hootenanny night. They hit the top of the charts with a version of Dylan's "Mr. Tamborine Man" which featured bouncy vocal harmonies and a 12-string guitar. The group followed with electrified versions of Dylan's "Spanish Harlem Incident," "All I Really Want to Do," and "Chimes of Freedom" as well as "Turn, Turn, Turn," a song adapted by Pete Seeger from the Book of Ecclesiastes.

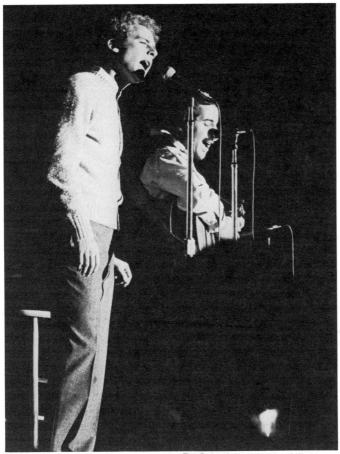

The Daily *of the University of Washington*

Simon and Garfunkel

Other groups became successful with the folk-rock formula of electrified folk and Dylan songs. In 1965, the ebullient Turtles, a band that had switched from surf music to folk in 1964, hit the Top 10 with "It Ain't Me Babe." Paul Simon and Art Garfunkel were two high school friends who in 1957 had attracted notice as Tom and Jerry with "Hey Schoolgirl" and appeared on "American Bandstand." In 1964 after experiencing the folk boom they reemerged with a collegiate image and an album of soft harmonies, *Wednesday Morning, 3 A.M.*, that showcased Dylan's "Don't Think Twice" and Simon's composition, "Sounds of Silence," which the next year became a number 1 hit when Columbia Records remixed the track, adding drums, percussion and electric guitar.

As Simon and Garfunkel scaled the charts, in 1965 a husband-wife team, Sonny and Cher, released the million-selling, Dylan-sounding "I Got You Babe." Cher, a former backup singer for the Ronettes, scored a solo hit with Dylan's "All I Really Want To Do." Mimicking Dylan by wearing a denim cap and using a racked harmonica, Donovan Leitch of Scotland became the British answer to Dylan. Though scoring an acoustic hit in Britain with "Catch the Wind" in 1965, Donovan first achieved success in the United States the next year with an electric "Sunshine Superman" and "Mellow Yellow." The Lovin' Spoonful which in the mid-1960s hit the Top 10 with "Do You Believe in Magic?" "You Didn't Have to Be So Nice," "Daydream," and "Summer in the City," attributed their sound to Bob Dylan. Dylan, insisted John Sebastian who had backed several folk groups in Greenwich Village before forming the Spoonful, acted as "a force on our music, just like the 'Star Spangled Banner.' We all heard it." By the end of 1965, various folk rockers had recorded forty-eight different Dylan songs, most of them concerned with topics other than protest. According to *Newsweek,* "healthy, cheap, moral or venal, folk rock is what's happening at this moment in the dissonant echo chamber of pop culture."

The folk-rock explosion, epitomized by the Byrds, also exhibited an influence from across the Atlantic. "I did feel that the real folk scene was in the Village," remembered Roger McGuinn. "But the Beatles came out and changed the whole game for me. I saw a definite niche, a place where the two of them blended together. If you took Lennon and Dylan and mixed them together, that was something that hadn't been done." Though believing that "Dylan was real and the Beatles were plastic," McGuinn grafted the bouncy, jangling harmonies of the moptops from Liverpool onto Dylanesque folk. As with a few other folk rockers, the Byrds reflected the pervasive influence of the Beatles who were conquering America and changing the sound of rock-and-roll.

6

The British Invasion of America

"We were just the spokesmen for a generation."

Paul McCartney

Friday, February 7, 1964, at the Kennedy International Airport, New York, New York. Outside, a mass of screaming teenagers covered the rooftop of one portion of the airport. The crowd, mostly pubescent girls, had been waiting for more than eight hours in the frosty winter air. They considered themselves lucky; only those with special passes had been permitted on the roof, along with dozens of uniformed security police.

Inside the terminal, huddled around the gate, which admitted incoming passengers from London, more than nine thousand teenage girls, adorned with bouffant hairdos, oversized jewelry, and their mothers' makeup, shoved, clawed, and pushed each other in a mad attempt to get to the arrival entrance. They were separated from their goal only by a thin, white nylon rope and a few airport guards. As the minutes passed slowly and the intensity mounted, the crowd was comforted by a voice from a transistor radio: "It is now 6:30 A.M. Beatle time. They left London 30 minutes ago. They're out over the Atlantic Ocean heading for New York. The temperature is 32 Beatle degrees."

Four of the passengers on Pan American flight 101 felt uneasy. "We did all feel a bit sick," remembered one. "Going to the States was a big step. People said just because we were popular in Britain, why should we be there?" Asked another: "America's got everything, George, so why should they want us?" A third: "I was worrying about my hair as well. I'd washed it, but when it had dried, it had gone up a bit." The fourth, the oldest and the leader of the group, sat silent and motionless in his seat.

As the plane neared its destination, a few wild screams broke the tense silence. Then an entire chorus of cries from girls on the rooftop alerted the crowd inside the arrivals building. In a few moments, the frenzied wails of pent-up teenage passion sent tremors throughout Kennedy International, increasing at a deafening rate. The girls started to half-chant, half-sing, "We Love You Beatles, Oh Yes We Do."

The plane landed safely and reached the hangar. Scurrying attendants pushed a platform toward the jet, the door swung open, and passengers started to descend the steps. Employees of Capitol Records shoved Beatle kits complete with wigs, autographed photos, and a button with the message: "I Like the Beatles" at them. At last, four young Englishmen, who sported button-down, Edwardian suits from Pierre Cardin and mushroom-shaped haircuts, walked out. After almost 200 years, the British had again invaded the United States. This time they would emerge as the victors. The Beatles had arrived in America.

The four lads from Liverpool—John, Paul, George, and Ringo—dashed toward a chauffeured airport limousine. They leapt in the car, locked the doors, and rode toward the terminal, assaulted by hundreds of girls, who hurled themselves at the slow-moving automobile, clinging to the hood, the roof, and the sides. As they inched away, the foursome saw, pressed against the windows, the contorted faces of teenage fans who tried to catch a glimpse of their heroes before they were pulled away by yet another admirer.

The foursome broke loose from the crowd and headed toward the airport complex. After a short press conference, the Beatles jumped back into the limousine and sped down the Van Wyck Expressway, reaching Manhattan about an hour and a half later. Though swarmed by hundreds of fans when the car stopped at New York's plush Plaza Hotel, the Beatles managed to pry the doors open and somehow make it into the hotel lobby, where they were escorted to a twelfth-floor room. There they discovered three screaming girls in the bathtub and called room service for help. Throughout the night and the next few days, the Beatles were protected by armed guards from ingenious girls who climbed the fire escapes and from conspiring groups of teens who checked in at the hotel, using the names of their well-to-do parents to penetrate the twelfth floor. Outside, the boys heard fans keep a twenty-four-hour vigil by chanting "We Want the Beatles, We Want the Beatles."

On Sunday night, the new idols from across the Atlantic came into full view. Late in 1963, Ed Sullivan, the square-faced, stocky, show-business impresario, had witnessed a near-riot at the London airport, where more than 15,000 screaming fans descended upon the terminal, delaying the Queen and Prime Minister Sir Alec Douglas-Home in order to welcome the Beatles back from a trip abroad. Impressed, Sullivan told *The New York Times,* "I made up my mind that this was the same sort of mass hit hysteria that had characterized the Elvis Presley days." He hurriedly located Brian Epstein, the dapper, brilliant manager of the group, and for less than twenty thousand dollars booked the Beatles for three appearances on his show.

On February 9, 1964, Sullivan showcased the Beatles. Seven hundred twenty-eight wild teenagers packed into the studio from which the Sullivan show was broadcast. They had battled 50,000 others for tickets to the show that featured the Beatles. When Sullivan introduced the foursome—"and now, the Beeeatles!"—the room erupted. Girls with checkered skirts and Macy blouses let out primal screams and pulled their hair, thrusting themselves toward the front of the stage or leaning perilously over the balcony. Some simply fainted. Few noticed that one of the microphones had gone dead. All eyes fastened on Paul bobbing back and forth as he played a left-handed bass guitar; Ringo, smiling as he brushed the drum-skins; John, yelling the words over the din; and a rather dour George, the youngest, skinniest member of the group, just looking down at the neck of his lead guitar. The screaming intensified. Explained one girl in the crowd: "You really do believe they can see you and just you alone, when they're up on stage. That's why you scream, so they'll notice you. I always felt John could see me. It was like a dream. Just me and John together and no one else." The show, ending amidst the wails, had been extremely successful. More than 60 percent of all viewers had tuned into the program, and more than 73 million people across the nation had witnessed the event.

From New York City, after playing two sets at Carnegie Hall to 12,000 screaming fans, the Beatles rode the King George train to Washington, D.C. On Wednesday, February 11, at 3:09 P.M., amid a storm that dropped ten inches of snow, they arrived in the nation's capital. The band emerged from the train, hurriedly made their way down a platform "behind a wedge of Washington's finest," and reached the main concourse of Union Station. "For hours," *The Washington Post* reported, "teenagers had been drifting into Union Station—many of them from National Airport, where the Beatles before the show had been scheduled to arrive . . . In the concourse, the teenagers, perhaps 2,000 strong, lined the barriers, breathed on the glass, hung through the bars, even climbed the gates." The Beatles, heads down in combat fashion, snaked through the crowd with the help of the police, who pushed and shoved the oncoming torrent of fans. Screamed one girl to the police as they dragged away her friend, "You can't throw her out, she's president of the

Beatles Fan Club." Finally, John, Paul, Ringo, and George broke through the crowd and leapt into a waiting, limousine. They sped toward the Washington Coliseum, which was jammed with 8,092 wild-eyed teens. "From the moment the Beatles were led to the stage by a phalanx of policemen," the *Post* informed its readers, "the din was almost unbearable." Reporter Leroy Aarons compared the noise to "being downwind from a jet during takeoff." During the performance, frantic, distraught girls began mercilessly to pelt their heroes with jelly beans. Explained George: "It was terrible. They hurt. They don't have soft jelly babies in America but hard jelly-beans like bullets. Some newspaper had dug out the old joke, which we'd all forgotten about, when John had once said I'd eaten all his jelly babies."

From Washington, the Beatles flew to Miami, where they were greeted by four bathing beauties, a four-mile-long traffic jam, and 7,000 screaming teens who shattered twenty-three windows and a plate glass door in a tumultuous attempt to touch their idols. The group played for a raucous audience in Miami, then headed toward New York City, where they upstaged the president. In an article entitled "LBJ Ignored as New York Crowds Chase Beatles," *Billboard* reported that "President Lyndon B. Johnson visited here late last week, but the arrival was overshadowed by the Beatles invasion. Few were aware of the president's presence in their midst, but no one could miss the fact that Britain's Beatles had descended upon the town. Radio, TV, and all other communication media were filled with Beatles clamors. At Kennedy Airport here, Beatles' greeters began lining up at 4 A.M. Friday to await the group's arrival this afternoon."

By the time the Beatles left New York for London on February 16, the entire nation had been afflicted with Beatlemania. Head-

Hysterical Beatles' fans, 1964

lines in the staid *Billboard* told the story: "The U.S. Rocks and Reels from Beatles Invasion"; "Chicago Flips Wig, Beatles and Otherwise"; "New York City Crawling with Beatlemania"; and "Beatle Binge in Los Angeles." In nine days, during the Beatles' brief visit, Americans had bought more than 2 million Beatles records and more than $2.5 million worth of Beatles-related goods. They purchased blue and white Beatles hats; Beatles T-shirts and beach shirts; Beatles tight-fitting pants; Beatles pajamas and three-button tennis shirts; Beatles cookies; Beatles egg cups; Beatles rings, pendants, and bracelets; a pink, plastic Beatles guitar with the pictures of the four lads stamped on it; a plethora of Beatles dolls including inflatable figurines, six-inch hard rubber likenesses, painted wood dolls that bobbed their heads when moved, and a cake decoration in the form of the Beatles. Others snapped up Beatles nightshirts; countless Beatles publications; Beatles ice-cream sandwiches covered with a foil Beatles wrapper; Beatles soft drinks; and Beatles wigs, which Lowell Toy Company churned out at fifteen thousand a day. Seltaeb (Beatles spelled backwards), the American arm of the Beatles manufacturing company, NEMS, even planned for a Beatles' motor scooter and a Beatles' car.

THE MODS AND THE ROCKERS

Beatlemania had its genesis in the postwar baby boom and an economic depression that spawned gangs of British working-class youths. As with the United States, England experienced a baby boom immediately after World War II. "That was the Bulge, that was England's Bulge," Pete Townshend, the lead guitarist for The Who, told a reporter. "All the war babies, all the old soldiers coming back from the war and screwing until they were blue in the face— this was the result. Thousands and thousands of kids, too many kids, not enough teachers, not enough parents." As in the United States, by 1963 the mass of baby boomers had become teenagers ready for rock music.

At the same time, England faced economic hardships. Crippled by the war, it continued to enforce wartime rationing until 1954 and tried to rebuild with little help from wartime allies. "World War II went on there for another nine years after it finished everywhere else," recalled Keith Richards of the Rolling Stones. "I remember London, huge areas of rubble and grass growing."

During the mid- and late-1950s, many British baby boomers, unlike their American counterparts, faced hard times upon finishing school at 15 or 16. In March 1964 Harold Wilson, a Labour Party leader from Liverpool and later Prime Minister, regarded "as deserving of the utmost censure and condemnation a system of society which, year in, year out . . . cannot provide employment for its school-leavers." The youths felt especially directionless because of the change in English conscription laws. The draft "ended," remembered Ringo Starr, "and so at 18 you weren't regimented. Everyone was wondering what to do."

The idle working-class teens began to form rival gangs: the Rockers and the Mods. The Rockers, modeling themselves after the tough Teddy Boys of the 1950s, wore black leather jackets, tight-fitting pants, and pointed boots or suede shoes. They greased their hair in a pompadour style and sometimes put on sunglasses in beatnik fashion, roaring down the streets on motorcycles.

The Modernists, shortened to Mods, favored "teenage Italian-style clothes," according to Townshend, himself a Mod. They had "short hair, money enough to buy a real smart suit, good shoes, good shirts; you had to be able to dance like a madman. You had to be in possession of plenty of pills all the time and always be pilled up [especially with Drynamil, an amphetamine commonly known as a 'purple heart']. You had to have a scooter covered in lamps. You had to have like an army anarack to wear." The Mods sometimes adopted different fashions weekly. "One outfit might be 12 quid, a week's wages, and the next fucking week you'd have to change the whole lot," recalled Townshend. As with the Rockers, the Mods "were nothing. They were the lowest, they were England's lowest common denominators. Not only were they young, they were also lower-class young," added the guitarist. "Most Mods were lower class garbagemen, you know, with enough money to buy himself Sunday best."

The gang experience fostered a sense of belonging among British youths. Pete Townshend knew "the feeling of what it's like to be a Mod among two million Mods and it's incredible. It's like being— suddenly you're the only white man in the Apollo [Theater in Harlem]. Someone comes up and touches you and you become black. It's like that moment, that incredible feeling of being part of something which is really much bigger than race and much bigger than—it was impetus. It covered everybody, everybody looked the same, and everybody acted the same and everybody wanted to be the same. It was the first move I have ever seen in the history of youth towards unity, towards unity of thought, unity of drive and unity of motive." "Any kid," said Townshend, "however ugly or however fucked up, if he had the right haircut and the right clothes and the right motorbike, he was a Mod. He was a Mod!"

The Mods and the Rockers, each bound together by common appearance, fought one another for dominance. During the Easter weekend of 1964 at Clacton-on-Sea, Essex, a few hundred "young scooter riders" from the eastern and northeastern parts of London attacked motorcycle gangs of Rockers. According to D. H. Moody, chairman of the Urban District Council, "they insulted passers-by, lay in the middle of the road to stop traffic, jumped onto cars and destroyed and damaged property. The girls were almost as bad and [one witness] had seen five of them try to knock a child off his bicycle." "At one stage," reported the *London Times,* "there was almost a battle on the seafront with missiles of all descriptions being thrown." The police intervened and arrested more than a hundred rioters, who the *Times* called a "collection of uncivilized youths with no respect for persons, property, or the comfort of other people." In explaining the incident, Labour's chief front bench spokesman, Fred Willey, observed that the "general complaint of those who took part was that there was nothing for them to do. They came from housing estates with far too few social amenities and were expected to spend their time in amusement arcades. . . . The present government regarded working-class adolescents as fair game for blatant exploitation by commercial interests."

On May 17, 1964, trouble broke out in the Kent resort of Margate and at Brighton. More than 800 Mods, arriving "on scooters bristling with headlights and badges," fought 200 leather-jacketed Rockers. The *Daily Express* painted a terrifying picture: "There was dad asleep in a deckchair and mum making sandcastles with the children when the 1964 boys took over the beaches at Margate and Brighton yesterday and smeared the traditional scene with more bloodshed and violence." Fumed Dr. George Simpson, Margate Court Chairman, "these long-haired, mentally unstable petty little sawdust Caesars seem to find courage, like rats, by hunting only in packs." By Tuesday, May 18, when the clashes subsided, "at least 40 youths had been arrested," the *Daily Mirror* informed its readers. "And there was blood on the sand."

THE WHO

Many of these warring youths, having time and lacking direction, turned to music. "My opinion why music suddenly shot out of England in the Sixties is that we were the first generation that didn't get regimented and didn't go into the army," explained Beatle drummer Ringo Starr. "Music was a way out. We all wanted to leave. Everyone wanted to fly. Music was my way. Back then every street had a band. You could hear it all over. Everyone was playing, and mostly it sounded real bad, but we were playing. We all picked up guitars and drums and filled our time with music." "Had not the government stopped the draft," echoed Dave Clark, "there would have been no Dave Clark 5, no Beatles, no Stones."

The rival Mods and Rockers had definite musical preferences. "The groups that you liked when you were a Mod were The Who," bragged Pete Townshend. "That's the story of why I dig the Mods, man, because we were Mods and that's how we happened." Peter Meadon, the early manager of The Who and the founder of the Mod band the Ace Faces, in 1963 convinced The Who, then called the High Numbers, to adopt a Mod image. Said Meadon: "I had this dream of getting a group together that would be the focus, the entertainers for the Mods; a group that would actually be the same people onstage as the guys in the audience. . . . an actual representation of the people." Roger Daltrey fit the image with his "French crewcut" and "Townshend identified with the Mod scene immediately."

In 1964, the High Numbers recorded two Mod anthems for their first single, "Zoot Suit," a compendium of Mod fashion, and "I'm the Face," a reworking of bluesman Slim Harpo's "Got Love If You Want It." The band had released "the *first authentic* Mod record" asserted a press release, "a hip, tailored-for-teens R & B oriented shuffle rocker . . . with a kick in every catchphrase for the kids of the fast-moving crowd . . . to cause an immediate rapport between the High Numbers and the thousands of young people like themselves. In a nutshell—they are the people."

Late in 1964, the band began to reflect the Mod image to an even greater extent. After firing Meadon, they enticed Kit Lambert, the son of classical composer Constant Lambert, and Chris Stamp, the brother of actor Terence Stamp, to become co-managers. On the advice of their new managers, band members went, recalled drummer Keith Moon, "to Carnaby Street with more money than we'd ever seen in our lives, like a hundred quid each. . . . We weren't into clothes, we were into music. Kit thought we should identify more with our audience. Coats slashed five inches at the side. Four wasn't enough. Six was too much. Five was just right." The band returned with garb that would become their trademark: Bull's-eye T-shirts; and pants, shirts, and jackets cut from the British flag. The group renamed themselves The Who and played for sixteen consecutive Tuesdays at the London Marquee Club, a Mod hangout owned by Ziggy Jackson, where, according to Moon, the band "blew open the doors of the Marquee to rock." To complete The Who image, Townshend contributed the first of his many compositions, "My Generation," which became the battle cry of the Mods. "That's my generation, that's how the song 'My Generation' happened, because of the Mods," Townshend explained.

The members of The Who grew up in the same working-class neighborhoods as other London Mods. Roger Daltrey, lead singer and organizer of the group at the age of fifteen, Townshend, and bassist John Entwhistle were raised in Shepard's Bush, a dilapidated suburb of West London. Before The Who gained notoriety, its members worked as manual laborers—Daltrey for five years as a sheet metal worker, and Townshend and Entwhistle at various odd jobs. Keith Moon, the ebullient madman of The Who, who met an untimely death in 1978, grew up in Wembley and joined the band when he wandered into the Oldfield Hotel one day to listen to their act. Noticeable with his "dyed ginger hair and a ginger cord suit," Moon asked the band if he could play with them during one number. In the words of the drummer, "they said go ahead and I got behind this other guy's drums and did one song—'Road Runner.' I'd several

Pete Townshend of The Who

drinks to get me courage up and when I got onstage I went arrggg-Ghhhh on the drums, broke the bass drum pedal and two skins, and got off. I figured that was it. I was scared to death. Afterwards I was sitting at the bar and Pete came over. He said: 'You . . . come 'ere.' I said, mild as you please: 'Yes?' And Roger, who was the spokesman then, said: 'What are you doing next Monday?' I said: 'Nothing.' I was working during the day, selling plaster. He said: 'You'll have to give up work . . . there's this gig on Monday. If you want to come, we'll pick you up in the van.' I said: 'Right.' And that was it."

The Who's sound captured the anger and rebelliousness of the English Mods. Roger Daltrey screamed the lyrics of a song, backed by Townshend's crashing chords, the thumping bass of Entwhistle, and Moon's propulsive drumming. Townshend, the writer of most of the band's material, felt that The Who's brand of rock-and-roll "is a single impetus and it's a single force which threatens a lot of crap which is around at the moment in the middle class and in the middle-aged politics or philosophy." Townshend's guitar-smashing antics and Moon's destruction of his drum kit accentuated the rebellious spirit of the band. Though not attracting attention in America until the late 1960s with the rock opera *Tommy,* The Who became the most popular band among British Mods.

The Mods also listened to the Small Faces. Steve Marriott of the Faces remembered that "we started out doing little clubs and weddings, but because we were Mods we were asked to play London clubs like the Flamingo. We were a bit dubious about it, 'cause we weren't very good. . . . But all the London management started watching the Mod following we were getting. The only other band really doing that was The Who, and they were pretty successful."

THE EARLY BEATLES

One Rocker group, made up of rowdy youths from Liverpool, changed rock-and-roll history. Formed in 1959, the Quarrymen, as they were first called, then Johnny and the Moondogs, the Silver Beatles, and finally just the Beatles, started their musical careers in the Cavern Club of Liverpool. The next year they traveled to Hamburg, Germany, to back up singer Tony Sheridan. Within two more years the Beatles had become the rage of England and by 1964 they had become worldwide celebrities.

The Beatles, as with The Who, came from working-class families. Abandoned by his father and mother, John Winston Lennon grew up with his aunt Mimi and as a boy joined a Rocker gang that "went in for things like shoplifting and pulling girls' knickers down." Paul McCartney, the son of a cotton salesman, lived in a half house—"They were such small, diddy houses, with bare bricks inside," he later reminisced. The youngest of the Beatles, George Harrison, was the son of a bus driver and began an apprenticeship as an electrician at the age of sixteen. Drummer Ringo Starr, born Richard Starkey, told a reporter that his family had "always been just ordinary, poor working class." When her husband deserted the family, Ringo's mother worked as a barmaid to support her child. At fifteen, Ringo landed a job as a messenger boy for the British Railways.

The four Liverpool youths adopted a Rocker image. To his aunt, Lennon seemed to be "a real Teddy boy." "I wasn't really a Ted, just a Rocker," Lennon insisted. "I was imitating Teds, pretending to be one. I was never a real one, with chains and real gangs. If I'd met a proper Ted, I'd have been shit-scared." Paul spent hours styling his pompadoured hair and choosing the clothes that fit Rocker fashion. Worried that his son would "turn out a Teddy boy," Jim McCartney "said over and over again that [Paul] wasn't going to have tight trousers. But he just wore me down." George Harrison "used to go to school with his school cap sitting high on top his hair. And very tight trousers," remembered his mother. "Unknown to me, he'd run them up on my machine to make them even tighter. I bought him a brand new pair once and the first thing he did was to tighten them. When his dad found out, he told him to unpick them at once. 'I can't Dad,' he said. 'I've cut the pieces off.' George always had an answer." As a band, the Beatles affected a Rocker image, wearing black-and-white cowboy shirts with white tassels dangling from the pockets, leather jackets, and pointed cowboy boots.

The quasi-Western attire indicated a major musical influence on the Beatles: American rockabilly. Although covering such Chuck Berry tunes as "Rock and Roll Music" and "Roll Over Beethoven," the band initially modeled its sound after Elvis Presley. "Nothing really affected me until Elvis," John Lennon remembered. "I had no idea about doing music as a way of life until rock 'n' roll hit me. It was *Rock Around the Clock,* I think. I enjoyed Bill Haley, but I wasn't overwhelmed by him. It wasn't until 'Heartbreak Hotel' that I really got into it." McCartney felt that Presley "was the biggest kick. Everytime I felt low I just put on Elvis and I'd feel great, beautiful. I'd no idea how records were made and it was just magic. 'All Shook Up'! Oh, it was beautiful." "Elvis changed my life," added Ringo Starr, epitomizing the attitude of Britain's baby boomers. "He was the first teenager in my life. Johnnie Ray, Frankie Laine and Bill Haley were my early heroes, around '54. But they were always a bit like me dad. Elvis was the first real lad who came out. The kid. He totally blew me away, I loved him so." When Malcolm Evans, later a road manager for the Beatles, first heard the group at the Cavern Club, he felt that they "sounded a bit like Elvis."

The Beatles idolized other rockabilly stars as well. In 1959, as a Silver Beatle, George Harrison changed his name to Carl Harrison after one of his heroes, Carl Perkins. On tour with Perkins in 1964, John Lennon told the rockabilly star that "we got all your records! We slowed 'em down from 45 to 33 [to learn them]." When told by Perkins that the Beatles sounded "a lot like the old Sun Records," remembered Carl, John jumped off the couch, put "both arms around me and kissed me on the jaw." At another point in their early years, the foursome called themselves the Foreverly Brothers in honor of the Everly Brothers. *Variety* spotted the influence years later. "Mullarkey," read one story. "The Beatles are dishing up a rock-and-roll style that was current in this country ten years ago and that is still typical of such groups as the Everly Brothers." The name the group eventually adopted reflected the rockabilly connection. As John told a reporter, "I was looking for a name like the Crickets [Buddy Holly's band] that meant two things.

From Cricket I went to Beatles. . . . When you said it, people thought of crawly things; when you read it, it was beat music."

MANAGER BRIAN EPSTEIN

The Beatles, playing an English brand of rockabilly music and influenced by R & B, the English music hall tradition, and washboard-and-fiddle skiffle music, became famous through the efforts of Brian Epstein. Epstein, born in September 1934 into a wealthy family, was raised in a five-bedroom house in Childwall, one of Liverpool's most exclusive residential areas. He began a successful career as a salesman in two of his father's stores: a furniture shop and the North End Music Enterprises. "I enjoyed selling as well, watching people relax and show trust in me," he said. "It was pleasant to see the wary look dissolve and people begin to think there were good things ahead for them and I would be the provider." After expanding his father's record retailing business, Epstein turned his attention to the Beatles, a group he had heard about in one of his music stores. As he told it, "I suppose it was all part of

Courtesy of Capitol Records

The Beatles

getting bored with simply selling records. I was looking for a new hobby. The Beatles at the same time, though I didn't know it and perhaps they didn't either, were also getting a bit bored with Liverpool." In 1961 Brian Epstein became the manager of the Beatles, getting a 25 percent share of their net revenues.

To make the band more palatable to the general public, Epstein changed their Rocker image. When he first saw them at the Cavern Club, he thought that "they were a scruffy crowd in leather." The Beatles "were not very tidy and not very clean. They smoked as they played and they ate and talked and pretended to hit each other." Brian tried to "clean our image up," John Lennon remarked years later. "He said our look wasn't right. We'd never get past the door at a good place. We just used to dress how we liked, on and off stage. He talked us into the suit scene." Said Epstein himself: "First I got them into trousers and sweaters and eventually into suits." Besides changing their appearance, said Pete Best, the Beatles' drummer before Ringo joined the group, the manager forced the band to "work out a proper program, playing our best numbers each time, not just the ones we felt like playing." After Epstein had finished molding the four Liverpudlians, noticed Malcolm Evans, "the image of the Beatles was so good and nice."

To sell the band, Epstein brought in other professionals from the music business. He approached George Martin, an executive with the Parlophone branch of the Electrical Music Industry (EMI) who on September 11, 1962, recorded the Beatles' first British release, "Love Me Do" and "P.S. I Love You." Epstein, who "didn't know how you promoted a record," enlisted the services of Tony Barrow, a publicity man for Decca Records. By May 1963, the manager had set up the machinery to make the Beatles a national sensation.

THE TOPPERMOST OF THE POPPERMOST

As with most working-class youths, the Beatles initially wanted money and fame. Scarred by the insecurity of his childhood, John "wanted to be popular. I wanted to be the leader. It seemed more attractive than just being one of the toffees." "All I wanted was women, money, and clothes," Paul later confessed. In discussing his financial future with Paul, George said that he "felt he was going to make a lot of it [money]. He was going to buy a house and a swimming pool, then he'd buy a bus for his father." As a group, the Fab Four dreamed of stardom. In 1961, remembered George, "we still used to send up the idea of getting to the top. When things were a real drag and nothing was happening, we used to go through this routine: John would shout, 'Where are we going, fellas?' We'd shout back, 'To the Top, Johnny.' Then he would shout, 'What Top?' 'To the Toppermost of the Poppermost, Johnny!' "

The Beatles soon achieved their goal. They first became well known in Liverpool. By late 1962, remembered Maureen Cox, Ringo's first wife, admirers "used to hang around the Cavern all day long, just on the off chance of seeing them. They'd come out of the lunch time session and just stand outside all afternoon, queuing up for the evening show. . . . It was terrible, the mad screams when they came on. They went potty." News spread quickly. More than 5,000 squealing teens mobbed a Beatles' performance and caused a riot in Manchester. At Newcastle-upon-Tyne, more than 4,000 die-hards lined up in front of a concert hall at three o'clock in the morning to secure tickets for an evening Beatles show. Dr. F. R. C. Casson, a psychologist who tried to explain the phenomenon for the readers of *The London Times,* likened "Beatlemania to the frenzied dancing and shouting of voodoo worshippers and the howls and bodily writhing of converts among primitive evangelical sects in the southern states of America." "Beat music," Dr. Casson said, "has a rhythmic stimulation on the brain. A similar result of rhythmic stimulation is seen in some types of epileptic fit which may be caused by rapidly flickering light."

On October 13, 1963, the band gained national exposure when they performed at the London Palladium. More than 15 million television viewers watched thousands of young Londoners claw at each other to get into the Beatles' concert. "From that day on," insisted press agent Tony Barrow, "everything has changed. My job has never been the same again. From spending six months ringing up newspapers and getting 'no,' I now had every national reporter and feature writer chasing *me.*" Within two more weeks, on November 4, the Beatles performed for the Queen at the Royal Variety Performance and solidified their reputation. Following the heavy-set singer Sophie Tucker, whom Paul called the Beatles' favorite American "group," they elicited screams and moans with "Till There Was You," "Twist and Shout," and "She Loves You." During one number, John asked the audience to clap. "Those upstairs, just rattle your jewelry," he added, looking up toward the royal box. The following Sunday, 26 million Britons witnessed the escapade while sitting in front of their television sets.

By December 1963, manufacturers started to offer Beatles products—one firm in Peckham selling Beatles sweaters, "designed specially for Beatles people by a leading British manufacturer with a top-quality, two-tone Beatles badge." The Beatles fan club swelled to more than 800,000 members, and the foursome sold a million copies of two singles, which featured "I Want to Hold Your Hand" and "She Loves You." The band's first British album, *Please Please Me,* topped the British charts for more than six months. By the end of 1963, the Fab Four had sold eleven million records and $18 million worth of Beatles goods.

Public opinion responded favorably to the clean-cut Beatles. The *Daily Mirror* argued that "you have to be a real sour square not to love the nutty, noisy, happy, handsome Beatles." From a different political wing, *The Daily Worker* of the British Communist Party commented that the "Mersey sound is the voice of 80,000 crumbling houses and 30,000 people on the dole." Although Conservative politician Edward Heath first criticized the Beatles' language as "unrecognizable as the Queen's English," he later told an interviewer: "Who could have forecast only a year ago that the Beatles would prove the salvation of the corduroy industry" as thousands emulated the band in its trouser style. Prime Minister Sir Alec Douglas-Home called the group "our best export" and "a useful contribution to the balance of payments." Even the Queen complimented the Beatles. "So young, fresh, and vital," she cooed.

Amid such praise, Brian Epstein began to question his marketing tactics. He feared overexposure: "At first sight the endless discussion in the newspapers of the Beatles' habits, clothes, and views was exciting. They liked it at first and so did I. It was good for business. But finally it became an anxiety. How long could they maintain public interest without rationing either personal appearances or newspaper coverage? By a stringent watch on their bookings and press contacts we just averted saturation point. But it was very close. Other artists have been destroyed by this very thing."

The band members started to doubt the value of stardom as they began to pay the price of success. Ringo Starr complained about the loss of friendships and the diminishing control he exercised over his own life. "There were so many groups in Liverpool at one time that we often used to play just for each other, sitting in on each other's sessions, or just listening. It was a community on its own, just made up of groups." But when the Beatles became popular nationally, "it broke all the community up. People start hating each other." Moreover, Ringo felt slighted when George Martin replaced him with a session drummer on "P.S. I Love You." "Nobody said anything. What could the others say, or me? We were just lads, being pushed around. You know what I mean. They were so big, the London record company and all that. We just did what we were told." At about the same time, John believed that the band had relinquished too much control. In Liverpool, he later told an interviewer, the Beatles "felt embarrassed in our suits and being very clean. We were worried that our friends might think we'd sold out—which we had, in a way."

THE BEATLES INVADE AMERICA

Despite their doubts, the Beatles prepared for even greater success in America. Epstein paved the way for the British invasion, convincing Capitol Records to spend $50,000 dollars on a "crash publicity program." The company plastered five million "The Beatles Are Coming" stickers on buildings, fences, and telephone poles in every state, and printed a million copies of a four-page tabloid about the Fab Four. Capitol executives pressed one million units of a promotional, seven-inch Beatles interview record, which gave radio listeners the impression that the Beatles had personally contacted every disc jockey in the country. They also convinced many of the major weekly publications to run stories on the British foursome before their arrival: *Time* covered the group in its November 15, 1963, issue; *Newsweek* did so three days later; and on January 31, 1964, *Life* published a color spread entitled "Here Come The Beatles." By February 7, 1964, Brown Meggs, director of eastern operations for Capitol Records, told *The New York Times* "I have been on full-time Beatles duty since—the date is indelibly imprinted on my mind—January 6 when I returned from vacation. All this came at once, everything happened in a tremendously concentrated period. I'm awfully tired, but Beatles only come once in a decade, if that." Voyle Gilmore, a vice-president of Capitol, summed up the efforts of his company: "There was a lot of hype."

When the Beatles arrived in New York City on February 7, 1964, Beatlemania had swept the United States. Entering the charts at number 83, by February 1 "I Want to Hold Your Hand" had replaced Bobby Vinton's "There! I've Said It Again" in the number-1 slot. The song remained in the top position for seven weeks. The third week of February 1964, contended *Billboard*, "was the week that was the Beatles'. First in the platter polls, first in the press, first in police protection, and the first in the hearts of New York teenagers, who upset the mechanics of John F. Kennedy Airport, the Plaza, a CBS-TV studio, Penn Station, and Carnegie Hall ever since the foursome arrived from London."

Some adults disapproved of the new rage. After the Sullivan show, the *Herald Tribune* called the Beatles "75% publicity, 20% haircut and 5% lilting lament." To the *Daily News,* "the Presleyan gyrations and caterwauling were but lukewarm dandelion tea compared to the 100-proof elixir served up by the Beatles." Disregarding his personal ban on Sunday television viewing, evangelist Billy Graham watched the Beatles on the "Ed Sullivan Show" and believed that the performance revealed "all the symptoms of the uncertainty of the times and the confusion about us." Ray Block, orchestra leader on the Sullivan program, prophesied that the band "wouldn't last longer than a year," and actor Noel Coward said: "I've met them. Delightful lads. Absolutely no talent." Concert critic Louis Biancolli summed up the adverse reaction to the Beatles: "Their effect is like mass hypnosis followed by mass nightmare. I never heard anything like what went around me. I've read about the bacchantes and corybantes in wild Greek rites screaming insensately. They were antique squares compared to these teenage maenads."

Most media commentators, however, welcomed the clean-cut, well-tailored Beatles and their aristocratic manager. *Time* wrote that "the boys are the very spirit of good clean fun. They look like shaggy Peter Pans, with their mushroom haircuts and high white shirt collars, and onstage they clown around endlessly." The *1964 Yearbook* of *World Book Encyclopedia* singled out the Beatles' "rambunctious and irreverent sense of fun" and the stuffy *Yearbook* of *Collier's Encyclopedia* likened the foursome to "Little Lord Fauntleroys."

Newsweek probably best captured the majority opinion when it labeled the Beatles "a band of evangelists. And the gospel is fun. They shout, they stomp, they jump for joy and their audiences respond in a way that makes an old-time revival meeting seem like a wake. . . . The Beatles appeal to the positive, not negative. They give kids a chance to let off steam and adults a chance to let off disapproval. They have even evolved a peculiar sort of sexless appeal: cute and safe. The most they ask is: 'I Want to Hold Your Hand.' " The fun-loving Beatles seemed a perfect antidote to the pessimism that had engulfed America after John F. Kennedy's death a few months earlier.

The "cute and safe" Beatles, appealing to a vast audience, scored fantastic successes in America. Shortly after their tour of the United States, Beatle John Lennon released his book *In His Own Write*, which nudged Ian Fleming's latest James Bond thriller from the top of the best-seller list and won Lennon an invitation to the prestigious Foyles Literary Lunch on Shakespeare's four-hundredth birthday. Some compared the book to James Joyce's classic *Finnegans Wake*. Almost simultaneously, the Beatles released a full-length motion picture, *A Hard Day's Night*. "The idea was to make it as quickly as possible and get it out before their popularity faded," admitted director Richard Lester. The timing was superb. Even historian and JFK speechwriter Arthur Schlesinger, Jr., lauded the movie as "the astonishment of the month" by a group who embodied the "timeless essence of the adolescent effort to deal with the absurdities of an adult world." In its first six weeks, the film earned $5.6 million in rental fees.

A few months later, in 1965, the Beatles returned to the States for another tour: It included a stint at New York's Shea Stadium, where the Fab Four lured 55,000 rabid fans who paid $304,000— "the greatest gross ever in the history of show business" up to that time, according to promoter Sid Bernstein.

In Seattle, a typical explosion of mayhem erupted over the second coming of the Beatles. When the foursome arrived in town, they faced screaming, clawing teenagers. Escorted by a police motorcade, they immediately sped to Room 272 of the Edgewater Inn, which had been secured with barbed wire and sawhorse barricades. While in their room, Ringo, George, Paul, and John sorted through the hundreds of letters from their fans that had been mailed to the

Courtesy of Seattle Times

Seattle welcomes The Beatles, 1965

Edgewater, ate a few of the cookies and cakes that Beatles die-hards had baked, and fished from a window that overlooked Elliot Bay.

They finally emerged from the hotel into the damp Seattle air that night, when they ran from the hotel lobby and jumped into a limousine bound for the Coliseum. Marty Murphy, a twenty-five-year-old switchboard operator at the Edgewater Inn, rode with the Beatles, dragged into the car by Brian Epstein, who desperately needed help with two terrified Beatles secretaries. According to her account, "the limousine started moving. Now I could understand

120 The British Invasion of America

why the Beatles had looked so scared when they arrived. When we got to the barricade, I have never been so frightened in my life. These children had their faces pressed up against the car, all bent out of shape. They were crying, screaming, 'Touch me! Touch me!' They were saying that to me, and they didn't even know who I was. Finally, the limousine got to the Coliseum." When the Beatles leapt onstage and started to play, remembered police officer Noreen Skagen, "I only sort of heard the music; the screaming was just too loud. The Beatles themselves looked very tense, pale, scared. . . . We had to have a regular flying wedge with our then-TAC squad to bring them into the Coliseum and on stage. The entire audience charged the stage when the Beatles were ready to leave. We were constantly dragging hysterical youngsters who had gone berserk. Back then, it wasn't a matter of drugs or alcohol. It was hysteria. The girls were in love. They would say, 'I have to talk to them! You don't understand!' "

After the performance, the police bundled up the Fab Four in blankets, put them on stretchers and carried them through the crowd to a Red Cross van, which escaped the wild hordes who demanded their heroes. About the entire episode the *Seattle Times* wrote: "Seattle seethed with uncontrollable hysteria, terrifying noise and danger in a real-life nightmare last night. This was the Beatles' show. For 30 incredible minutes, those in the jam-packed Seattle Center Coliseum had the feeling of being sealed in a crazed capsule pitching through the chasms of space." A similar hysteria gripped other cities on the Beatles' tour which by the end of 1965 had reaped more than $56 million in the United States alone.

Besides publicity and talent, radio contributed to the Beatles' triumphant sweep of America. In 1964, during Beatlemania, one record executive in a company that had no Beatles releases complained that "stations are playing our records like spot commercials between Beatles tunes." "What sells records is radio," explained Brown Meggs of Capitol. "The Beatles got unbelievable radio play. There wasn't a single market in the country in which airplay wasn't simply stupendous."

The intensity and magnitude of Beatlemania in America resulted from the postwar baby boom. In 1964, millions of pubescent and pre-pubescent Beatlemaniacs were part of the over 43 million youths who had been born between 1947 and 1957. They lusted for an identity and, en masse, latched onto the Beatles as a symbol of unity. As one Beatles' fan told a reporter as she stood vigil in 1964 outside a hotel where her heroes resided, "I'm here because everyone else is here." Though youths had idolized Elvis Presley, the mass hysteria surrounding Beatlemania could only have occurred during the mid-Sixties when the decade of baby boomers had become young teens. "We were just the spokemen for a generation," explained Paul McCartney.

THE MERSEY BEAT SOUND

In the mid-1960s the often-played, well-publicized, talented Beatles conquered the American music market by appealing to the baby-boom generation and paved the way for other British groups, some of them linked to Brian Epstein. "The biggest thing the Beatles did was to open the American market to all British artists," contended British promoter Arthur Howes, who planned the early Beatles' tours of England. "Nobody had ever been able to get in before the Beatles. They alone did it. I had brought over lots of American stars, but nobody had gone over there." By February 1964, *Variety* told its readers, "Britannia ruled the airwaves." "The advent of the [Beatles] now has shattered the steady, day-to-day domination of made-in-America music here and abroad." During 1964, British rock bands had sold more than $76 million worth of records in the United States. Bill Harry, editor of the English music magazine *Mersey Beat,* explained that "the beat career is the equivalent of becoming a boxer in the beginning of the century—the only way into the luxury world."

Some of the British groups had grown up with the Beatles in Liverpool. Gerry Marsden, a truck driver who was a neighbor of the Beatles, in 1959 formed a band called the Pacemakers. Under the watchful eye of manager Brian Epstein who signed the group in June 1962, Gerry and the Pacemakers established a following at the Cavern Club in Liverpool, frequently playing on the same bill as the Beatles. In 1963 they climbed to the top of the British charts with a song written for the Beatles, "How Do You Do It?" and followed with the chart-toppers, "I Like It" and "You'll Never Walk Alone," ending the successful year with an appearance on the British television show, "Saturday Night at the London Palladium." In May 1964 Gerry and the Pacemakers debuted in America on the "Ed Sullivan Show" which helped promote the group's best-selling U.S. single, "Don't Let the Sun Catch You Crying." They capped their career in 1965 by starring in the movie, *Ferry across the Mersey.*

Members of another Epstein act, Billy J. Kramer and the Dakotas, rose from their working-class backgrounds to stardom. Billy J. Kramer (a.k.a. William Ashton), a worker for the British Railways, originally sang with a group called The Coasters, but teamed with a Manchester combo, the Dakotas, on the advice of Epstein who signed the Liverpudlian in late 1962. Observed *The Big Beat,* an English fan magazine in 1964: "The marriage of the zing singing of Billy J. to the true-beat accompaniment of the Daks has proven a brilliant stroke on the part of Epstein. These boys just have to step onto the stage and the fans go wild!" Though not having "the greatest voice in the world" according to producer George Martin, Billy J. Kramer hit the charts in June 1963 with "Do You Want To Know a Secret?," a track from the Beatles' first album, and the same month toured the United Kingdom with the Beatles. Two months later, he followed with the chart-topper, "Bad To Me," a song written by John Lennon specifically for Kramer. The group hit the British Top Ten with two Lennon/McCartney originals, "I'll Keep You Satisfied" and "From a Window" and in mid-1964 broke into the American market with "Little Children."

The Searchers, another Liverpool group, rode the crest of the Beatles' success. Formed in 1961 and named after a John Wayne movie, the group began performing regularly at such Liverpool clubs as the Cavern, the Casbah and the Hot Spot, eventually becoming the house band at the Iron Door. In August 1963 they topped the British singles chart with a remake of the Drifters' "Sweets for My Sweet." After an April 1964 appearance on the "Ed Sullivan Show" and amid Beatlemania, the Searchers scaled the American charts with their best-selling record, a remake of "Needles and Pins."

Together, the Beatles, the Searchers, Gerry and the Pacemakers and Billy J. Kramer delivered the Liverpool "Mersey Sound." Alex Korner, who with Cyril Davies started the sixties British blues scene, found that "there was a certain brashness about the Liverpool music, which stamped it almost immediately—they played it the way they speak English, you know! You could definitely tell a Liverpool group. The Mersey sound was basically a guitar sound: lead guitar, rhythm guitar, bass guitar, and drums was the basic Liverpool set-up."

Groups from other parts of Great Britain invaded America with a sound similar to the Mersey beat. From Manchester, a dingy, smokestacked industrial center much like Liverpool, came Freddie Garrity and the Dreamers. Quitting his job as a milkman, Freddie and his Dreamers hit the British charts in 1963 with "If You Gotta Make a Fool of Somebody," "I'm Telling You Now" and "You Were Made for Me," becoming popular on English television for their comic act. In February 1964 the band appeared on the American television programs, "Hullaballoo," and "Shindig," which promoted, "Do the Freddie."

In early 1965, Wayne Fontana and the Mindbenders, another amalgam of Manchester youths, scored a hit with "The Game of Love." Fontana (a.k.a. Glyn Geoffrey Ellis), who took his stage name from his record company, quit his job as a telephone engineering apprentice and formed a band during an audition at the Oasis Club in Manchester. He named the group The Mindbenders after a horror film that was then playing in a local theater. Besides their 1964 hit, The Mindbenders charted with a sequel, "A Groovy Kind of Love."

The Hollies proved to be more long-lasting than most other Manchester beat bands. The group was started by Graham Nash and singer-guitarist Allan Clarke who first met in grammar school and later became the Two Teens. After a few name changes, including the Guytones and the Deltas, the duo added three other members in 1963 and labeled themselves the Hollies after their musical hero, Buddy Holly. Signed by an EMI producer who saw them perform at the Cavern Club in Liverpool, the band first hit the British charts in early 1964 with "Stay" and followed with the Top Ten "Just One Look," "Here I Go Again," "Yes I Will," "I'm Alive" and the Beatles' "If I Need Someone." In 1965 during a tour of America, they worked fans to a frenzy at New York City's Paramount Theater and on such television shows as "Shindig," "Hullabaloo," and "The Smothers Brothers Show," charting with "Bus Stop."

Herman's Hermits, another Manchester band, capitalized on the beat music craze. Formed in 1963 by frontman Peter Noone, the band was signed to EMI Columbia by producer Mickie Most who noticed a facial resemblance of Noone to John F. Kennedy. The next year the group charted on both sides of the Atlantic with "I'm Into Something Good" which featured Noone backed by such session musicians as Jimmy Page and John Paul Jones, later of Led Zeppelin. In 1965 they followed with a string of upbeat hits which included "Silhouettes," "Mrs. Brown You've Got a Lovely Daughter," "Just a Little Bit Better" and a revival of the British music hall tune, "I'm Henry the Eighth, I Am."

The Dave Clark Five, from the Tottenham section of London, initially posed the most serious threat to the commercial dominance of the Beatles. Teaming together to raise money for Dave Clark's rugby team, in 1964 the Five toured America, appearing on the "Ed Sullivan Show." "The power of the man and his show were unbelievable," later explained Clark who like the Beatles had been inspired by "Little Richard, Elvis Presley, Fats Domino, all those great rockers." "Within the course of seven days we were household names and ended up having five records on the charts at once." The DC5 hit the charts on both sides of the Atlantic with "Glad All Over," "Bits and Pieces," "Can't You See That She's Mine" and "Because." The liner notes on their American debut album predicted that "the Tottenham sound of the Dave Clark Five is on its way towards overthrowing the reign of the Beatles in this country." The next year they copied the Fab Four and branched out into films, acting in *Catch Us If You Can* and charted with "Over and Over" and "I Like It Like That."

THE MONKEES

Two American producers took advantage of the Mersey beat craze by creating the Monkees, a prefabricated version of the Beatles. Observing the success of Richard Lester's Beatle film, *A Hard Day's Night,* Bob Rafelson and Bert Schneider, the son of the then president of Columbia Pictures, formed Raybert Productions. They placed an ad in the major Hollywood trade papers which called for "four insane boys, age 17-21, want spirited Ben Frank's types" for "acting roles in new TV series." In a month, the duo auditioned 437 hopefuls including folk rocker Stephen Stills and mass murderer Charles Manson.

The producers picked four photogenic, energetic, largely inexperienced applicants: Robert Michael Nesmith, an unknown folk singer; Mickey Dolenz who as a child had played "Corky" in the TV series, *Circus Boy*, and more recently had played in a California garage band; Greenwich Village folk singer Peter Thorkelson, shortened to Tork; and David Jones, the most experienced of the four, who had appeared on Broadway as the Artful Dodger in *Oliver*, had played a drug-crazed youth on the TV program, *"Ben Casey"* and had released an album of pop songs, some of which he performed on the same "Ed Sullivan Show" at which the Beatles had debuted.

In late 1965 Rafelson and Schneider secured $225,000 from Jackie Cooper, the former child actor who headed the television subsidary of Columbia Pictures, for a pilot TV series. "It all went great," Rafelson told *Time* the next year. "NBC bought the series 24 hours after it saw the pilot and sold it to two sponsors 72 hours later."

The producers quickly began to groom their new product. They hired underground film director William Frawley to provide intensive acting lessons for the group. "At first they were embarrassed, they were stiff and they were a little raw," Frawley told *Saturday Evening Post*. "We would roll over on the floor, sometimes, and do animals. 'You're a crab. Talk the way a giraffe would talk. Deal with an elephant. Now, talk the way a teapot would talk.' It was like a training period to free them physically, to start to use their bodies in a new way." After three months of lessons, in June 1966 the Monkees ventured in front of a television camera.

Rafelson and Schneider also shaped the Monkees musically. After unsuccessful attempts to have the Monkees write songs and play them, the team approached former music publisher Don Kirshner, the president of Screen Gems-Columbia music and its new record label, Colgems. "The boys didn't relate," explained Kirshner at the time. "I was looking for a driving, exciting, frantic young sound. There was no sound to the Monkees." Having little time to develop and record 22 songs for an album and five TV shows, he "brought in Goffin and King, Mann and Weil, Sedaka and Greenfield, the Tokens and Neil Diamond and created songs for the group. On most of the records I did with the Monkees, Carole King and Neil Diamond would sing background" and studio musicians such as Glen Campbell, Leon Russell and James Burton would play the instruments. "The music had nothing to do with us," complained Michael Nesmith.

Though prefabricated, the look and sound of the Monkees started to sell. They hit the top of the charts with their debut, "The Last Train to Clarksville" and followed with four number-1 albums.

By late 1966 the group attracted 10 million viewers every Monday night for their television program, received 5,000 fan letters a day and sold over $20 million in Monkees merchandise including shirts, slacks, raincoats, sweaters, comic books, trading and playing cards, dolls, lunch boxes, stuffed animals, games, hats, bubblegum, shoes, charms, guitars and puppets. "We're advertisers," enthused Mickey Dolenz. "We're selling a product. We're selling Monkees."

The success of the Monkees had been patterned after the Beatles. Before releasing the Monkees debut LP, the band's label spent $100,000 on an ad campaign involving 76 advance men who distributed thousands of posters proclaiming "The Monkees Are Coming" and provided preview records to disc jockeys. The name of the group had been calculatedly misspelled as had the Beatles and the first Monkees single included several "no-no-no" choruses to substitute for the Beatles' "yeah-yeah-yeah." The group's management even published a *Monkees Monthly* magazine similar to the many fanzines dealing with the Beatles such as *Beat Monthly* and *Beatles Monthly*. "The teens have bought the Monkees," a Raybert official proclaimed in early 1967. "They're the American Beatles." *Newsweek* called the band members "direct videological descendants of the Beatles" and *Time* in early 1967 commented that "less than a year ago, a team of wily promoters ran the Beatles through a xerox machine and came up with the Monkees."

THE BRITISH BLUES INVASION

The success of the Beatles paved the way for the acceptance of more blues-oriented English groups. The Yardbirds, formed in 1963 as the Metropolitan Blues Quartet, debuted on record with a cover of bluesman Billy Boy Arnold's "I Wish You Would," backed Sonny Boy Williamson on a 1963 tour of England and first charted with Don & Bob's R & B standard, "Good Morning Little School Girl." When in 1965 the band lost guitarist Eric Clapton who felt the Yardbirds were deserting the pure blues, they added guitarists Jeff Beck and then Jimmy Page to score blues-based Top 10 hits in Britain and America with "For Your Love" and "Heart Full of Soul." They hit the next year with "Shapes of Things" and "Over Under Sideways Down."

From the Muswell Hill region of London, a northern working-class suburb, came the Kinks. Formed in 1963 by blues and R & B enthusiasts Ray and Dave Davies, Peter Quaife, and Mike Avory, the band unsuccessfully debuted with Little Richard's "Long Tall Sally." In late 1964 they topped the charts with "You Really Got Me" which almost defined power-chord rock. Dave Davies explained to *Melody Maker* that the distinctive sound originated because at that time "I was never a very good guitarist . . . so I used to experiment with sounds. I had a very small amplifier which distorted badly." The Kinks followed with the crunching "All Day and All of the Night" before turning toward a softer, more Beatlesque sound based upon a skiffle, music-hall influence.

In 1962, Manfred Mann (a.k.a. Michael Lubowitz) teamed with Mike Hugg to become the Mann-Hugg Blues Brothers. After being greeted by wild receptions at the London Marquee Club, the duo added three more members and emerged as Manfred Mann and the Manfreds or, in the United States, as just Manfred Mann. In 1964, the band wrote "5-4-3-2-1," the popular theme of the British rock television show, "Ready, Steady, Go!," and topped the charts with a remake of the Exciters' "Do Wah Diddy Diddy." The band subsequently covered such R & B standards as Muddy Waters's "Got My Mojo Working," "Smokestack Lightning" by Howlin' Wolf, and Willie Dixon's "I'm Your Hoochie Coochie Man."

The Animals, a group of poor youths from a mining town in northern England and named for their wild stage behavior, played a convincing brand of British R & B. In 1962, jazz organist Alan Price joined with lead guitarist Hilton Valentine, bassist Bryan "Chas" Chandler, drummer John Steel and Eric Burdon, whose voice captured the raw, deep pain of black American bluesmen. Price was pushed in the direction of rhythm and blues by the new musicians, especially Burdon, who, according to the *New Musical Express,* had "written out hundreds of lyrics by artists like Mose Allison and Chuck Berry. On the first page he had written the word *Blues* in his own blood. He had cut his finger especially for it." In their first two years the Animals attracted a following at the Club-a-Go-Go in their hometown of Newcastle-on-Tyne. Price remembered that "we used to play everything from the blues to Chico Hamilton, and it used to swing like the clappers." After moving to London in 1964, the band reworked the folk blues "The House of the Rising Sun" into a million-selling hit. They then revived John Lee Hooker's "Boom Boom" and "I'm Mad Again," "Don't Let Me Be Misunderstood," first released by jazz/blues singer Nina Simone and Sam Cooke's "Bring It on Home to Me" and triumphantly toured the United States in the fall of 1964.

George Ivan Morrison and his group, Them, were equally dedicated to American R & B. Raised in Ulster by parents who were blues and jazz enthusiasts, Van Morrison grew up listening to the likes of John Lee Hooker, Muddy Waters, Leadbelly, and Sonny Boy Williamson. At fifteen, he dropped out of school and joined a band called the Monarchs, which headlined at the R & B Club in Belfast. In 1965 the stocky Morrison formed the group Them which charted with "Baby, Please Don't Go" and "Here Comes the Night," and recorded "Gloria." Though hardly cracking the charts with "Gloria," the band defined a sound which would be emulated by thousands of garage bands in the United States during the next few years.

THE ROLLING STONES

The Rolling Stones, first managed by a publicist for the Beatles, Andrew Loog Oldham, became the most successful and talented of the R & B revival bands. As with the Beatles, the Stones became interested in rock music through American rockabilly. Mick Jagger "had been singing with some rock-and-roll bands, doing Buddy Holly," guitarist Keith Richards remembered. "Buddy Holly was in England as solid as Elvis. Everything that came out was a record smash number one. By about '58 it was either Elvis or Buddy Holly." Richard himself was "really listening to what was coming over the Atlantic. The ones that were hitting hard were Little Richard, and Presley, and Jerry Lee Lewis." He "was rockin' away, avoidin' the bicycle chains and razors in those dance halls." And when *Blackboard Jungle* with the music of Bill Haley and the Comets showed in London, Richards found that "people were saying 'Did ya hear that music, man?' Because in England we had never heard anything: the BBC controls it and won't play that sort of music. But everybody our age stood up for that music and the hell with the BBC."

Members of the Rolling Stones soon began to uncover the blues roots of rockabilly. Keith Richards heard "Broonzy first. . . . Then I started to discover Robert Johnson and those cats." The multi-instrumentalist Brian Jones, initially the impetus behind the group, one day heard "Elmore James, and the earth seemed to shudder on its axis. . . . The blues was real. We only had to persuade people to listen to the music, and they couldn't help but be turned on to all those great old blues cats." Mick Jagger, who started out by singing in a band called Little Boy Blue and the Blue Boys, similarly "was crazy over Chuck Berry, Bo Diddley, Muddy Waters, and Fats Domino, not knowing what it meant, just that it was beautiful."

One day in London, recalled Richards, "I get on this train one morning and there's Jagger—and under his arm he has four or five albums. . . . He's got Chuck Berry, Little Walter, Muddy Waters." The two talked about their mutual passion for R & B and in a few weeks, with a friend, Dick Taylor, formed a band called the Glimmer Twins, which laid "down some of this Chuck Berry and Little Walter stuff. No drummer or anything, just two guitars and a little amplifier. And suddenly in '62, just when we were getting together, we read this thing about a Rhythm and Blues Club starting in Ealing."

Alexis Korner's Blues Incorporated had made the Ealing Blues Club prominent. "Alexis and Cyril Davies were the only ones really playing blues in London at that time," remembered Stones drummer Charlie Watts who originally played with the Korner band. "Cyril was a great harmonica player; he made a couple of very good records 'Country Line Special' was one. He and Alexis got together while Alexis was playing with Chris Barber who had one of the biggest trad bands." By 1962 the two formed Blues Incorporated and landed a regular Saturday night job at the Ealing Club which attracted such blues enthusiasts as Richards, Jagger and Brian Jones who occasionally performed with Korner and Davies.

In mid-1963, Keith Richards, Mick Jagger and Brian Jones, together with Dick Taylor and drummer Tony Chapman, formed the Rolling Stones, moving into a run-down apartment in the downtrodden district of King's Road. They debuted on July 12 at the Marquee Club in London as a replacement for Blues Incorporated. By the end of the year, Charlie Watts replaced Chapman as drummer and bassist Bill Wyman joined when Taylor quit, solidifying a lineup which would remain intact for nearly thirty years. "We wanted to sell records for Jimmy Reed, Muddy, John Lee Hooker," explained Keith Richards. "We were disciples—if we could turn people on to that, then that was enough. That was the total original aim."

The material chosen by the early Stones indicated their blues orientation. For their first single, recorded in March 1963, they covered Chuck Berry's "Come On" and Muddy Waters' "I Wanna Be Loved." Their first American album, *England's Newest Hitmakers*, included Slim Harpo's "I'm a Kingbee," "Carol" by Chuck Berry, Willie Dixon's "I Just Wanna Make Love to You," and Jimmy Reed's "Honest I Do." Subsequent albums exposed teenage record buyers to such R & B classics as "You Can't Catch Me" and "Talkin' about You" (Chuck Berry), "Little Red Rooster" (Willie Dixon), "Mona" (Bo Diddley), and "Look What You've Done" (Muddy Waters). The Stones recorded many of these cuts at the legendary Chess studio in Chicago. "Chuck Berry wandered in while we were recording 'Down the Road Apiece,' " a wide-eyed Bill Wyman told a reporter for the *New Musical Express*, "and he said to us: 'Wow, you guys are really getting it on.' Muddy Waters was also there." Even the name of the band—the Rolling Stones—came from a tune penned by Muddy Waters, and in April 1963 the *Record Mirror* characterized the Stones as "genuine R and B. As the traditional jazz scene gradually subsides, promoters of all kinds of teen-beat entertainments heave a long sigh of relief that they have found something to take its place. It's rhythm and blues . . . and to the Station Hotel, Kew Road, the hip kids throw themselves around to the new jungle music like they never did in the more restrained days of traditional. And the combo they writhe and twist to is called the Rolling Stones."

THE STONES TURN RAUNCHY

As a strategy to capture a larger following, the Stones and their manager consciously created a contrast to the Beatles: the raunchy, crude, offensive Rolling Stones. At first the band appeared to be like most other British invasion bands. When in June 1963 they performed on "Thank Your Lucky Stars," a British television program, the Stones wore checkered suits. "You have to make some compromises," Andrew Loog Oldham instructed the group, sounding like his one-time boss, Brian Epstein. "Just to get started in this business you have to compromise a bit." As Keith Richards later told it, the manager "tried to tidy us up. . . . There are photographs of us in the suits he put us in, those dog-toothed checked suits with the black velvet collars."

Oldham's tactics backfired. Looking like any other British band during their first tour of the United States, which started in June 1964, the Stones received scant notice. They first appeared on a segment of "Hollywood Palace" that happened to be hosted by Dean Martin. After the Stones chugged through their versions of "I Just Want to Make Love to You" and "Not Fade Away," a twisted-faced Martin, eyes rolling upward, asked the audience, "Aren't they great?" He continued: "They're off to England to have a hair pulling contest with the Beatles. . . . Their hair is not that long—it's just smaller foreheads and higher eyebrows." When a trampolinist finished his act, Martin added: "That's the father of the Rolling Stones. He's been trying to kill himself ever since." To a distraught Brian Jones, Dean Martin "was just a symbol of the whole tour for us."

Mostly, the band played to empty seats. In San Antonio, Texas, the crowd clamored for an encore by a trained monkey over one by the Rolling Stones. "We all wanted to pack up and come home," confessed Bill Wyman. The colorful Keith Richards remembered "Nebraska, we really felt like a sore pimple in Omaha. On top of that, the first time we arrived there, the only people to meet us off the plane were twelve motorcycle cops who insisted on doing this motorcade thing right through town. And nobody in Omaha had ever heard of us. We thought, 'Wow, we've made it. We must be heavy.' And we get to the Auditorium and there's 600 people there in a 15,000-seat hall."

To avoid a complete disaster, Oldham quickly changed his course of action and manufactured an opposite to the neat, smiling Beatles. "It was perfect, just perfect," Oldham told Jagger after a press conference, at which the Stones had given flippant and insulting replies to American journalists. "They're going to plaster your pictures and your terrible, terrible statements all over the papers. Those dirty Rolling Stones, that's what you are. The opposite of those nice little chaps, the Beatles. It's working, it's sure as hell working. We're gonna make you famous." "The long-haired, dirty-rebel image was pushed on us here in the States," Richards contended. In 1965 Jagger added: "That's what we wanted you Americans to think, that we were dirty and raunchy. That was our image over there. If those dumb American birds dig that kind of shit, why shouldn't we do it?"

To refine the image, Oldham engineered a few changes. He downgraded piano player Ian Stewart to roadie. "Well, he just doesn't look the part, and six is too many for [fans] to remember the faces in the picture," Oldham told Richards at the time. The manager shaved a few years off the ages of each Stone in their official biography, making them teens again. He then convinced his label, London Records, to blitz the media. Read one ad in *Billboard,* "They're great! They're outrageous! They're rebels! They sell! They're England's *hottest.*"

The rest of the media soon picked up on the cue. In 1964 the *News of the World* carried an article headlined "Would You Let Your Daughter Go Out with a Rolling Stone?" and pictured the band as "symbols of rebellion . . . against the boss, the clock, and the clean-shirt-a-day routine." The Stones, it continued, looked like "five indolent morons, who give one the feeling that they really enjoy wallowing in a swill-tub of their own repulsiveness." Even *Melody Maker* and the *New Musical Express* described the group as "the ugliest pop group in Britain" and "the caveman-like quintet." In 1964, *Time* interviewed Keith Richards who told the magazine that he hoped "to be sitting in a country house with four Rolls-Royces and spitting at everyone."

The new, rebellious image of the Stones dovetailed with their second tour of America in the autumn of 1964, making it a smashing success. Their October performance on the Ed Sullivan program ended in such chaos that the host babbled: "I promise you they'll never be back on our show. . . . Frankly, I didn't see the Rolling Stones until the day before the broadcast. They were recommended by my scouts in England. I was shocked when I saw them. It took me seventeen years to build this show; I'm not going to have it destroyed in a matter of weeks. Now the Dave Clark Five were nice fellows—they are gentlemen and performed well." *Newsweek* pegged the Stones as a "leering quintet" obsessed with pornographic lyrics. One concerned woman wrote to *Time* magazine: "We like the Beatles because they have rhythm, enthusiasm, and a good sound. After listening to the groans, pants, and frankly dirty words of the Rolling Stones and a few other sick groups, one begins to wonder where they dig up a DJ to play such garbage."

Such adult criticism of the band predictably pushed rebellious American teenagers into the Stones' camp. Keith Richard at the time felt an "energy building up as you go around the country. You find it winding tighter and tighter, until one day you get out halfway through the first number and the whole place is full of chicks screaming. We'd walk into some of these places and it was like they had the Battle of the Crimea going on—people gasping, tits hanging out, chicks choking, nurses running around." "There was a period of six months in England we couldn't play ballrooms anymore because we never got through more than three or four songs every night," added Richards. "Chaos. Police and too many people in the places fainting. They used to tell us, 'There's not a dry seat in the cinema.' And the bigger it got, America and Australia and everywhere it's exactly the same number." Beatle George Harrison noticed by 1966: "It's become the in thing for adults to say the Beatles are good or the Beatles are funny, it's in for adults to like us. So the real hip kids—or the kids who think they are—have gone off us. The in thing for those kids now is to be a Stones fan, because their parents can't stand the Rolling Stones." The income of the band reflected their growing popularity: It skyrocketed from about $150 a week in early 1963 to almost $800 a week a year later.

The Stones also changed their sound to correspond to their image. Pressured in part by Andrew Oldham, who, according to Richards, "had never listened to an R & B record in his life," Richards and Jagger pushed aside the versatile Brian Jones and began to concentrate on their own material, which combined pop conventions with Chicago-style blues. In their first three albums, Jagger told interviewer Ed Rudy, the Stones found "that American songs are better for ourselves. The songs that Keith and I write . . . we give to other people. They're mostly ballads." By their fourth LP, *Out of Our Heads,* which was recorded in mid-1965, the band had started to move toward the R & B–influenced hard rock sound of the rebellious, chart-topping "Satisfaction" which, according to Mick Jagger, dealt with "my frustration with everything. Simple teenage aggression." With the 1966 *Aftermath,* Jagger-Richards' compositions such as the murky incantations of "Paint It Black" and the misogynist venom of "Under My Thumb" and "Stupid Girl" had almost totally replaced R & B covers. By the end of the year, the Rolling Stones vied with the Beatles for the rock-and-roll crown.

THE PRICE OF SUCCESS

The Rolling Stones, as well as the Beatles, found the intensity of success overwhelming. The frantic pace of touring and churning out two or three albums a year eventually led Keith Richards, who needed some escape from the pressure, to heroin addiction. Success had the same effect on Richard's common-law wife, Anita Pallenberg, and Marianne Faithfull, Jagger's rich girlfriend, who in 1964 gained musical notice with her version of "As Tears Go By" and fifteen years later delivered the bitter, cutting testament, *Broken English.* In 1966, Mick Jagger suffered from a nervous exhaustion. And for Brian Jones, who turned to drugs and alcohol after he lost his influence in the Stones, stardom ended in 1969 at the bottom of a swimming pool.

George Harrison felt that in Liverpool the Beatles "were doing shorter hours, but it was still as enjoyable. We were part of the audience. We lived our lives with them. We never rehearsed an act. . . . Then came touring, which was great at first, doing an even shorter, more polished act and working out new songs. But it got played out. We got in a rut, going round the world. It was a different audience each day, but we were doing the same things. . . . No one eventually enjoyed touring. You can't really. Once you've got to manufacture it, it doesn't work." He vowed never to do it again: "Never in this life or any other life. I mean, a lot of the time it was fantastic, but when it really got into the mania it was a question of either stop or end up dead." The usually sanguine Paul McCartney told a reporter that "to go from being a kid living on the street on some council-estate [public-housing] project to become very famous is a big change. Living with all the trappings of that isn't an easy adjustment; your privacy has to go a bit. It is a bit humiliating sometimes."

John Lennon gave the most bitter assessment: "I came out of the fuckin' sticks to take over the world it seemed to me. I was enjoying it, and I was trapped in it, too. I couldn't do anything about it, I was just going along for the ride. I was hooked, just like a junkie." One "has to completely humiliate oneself to be what the Beatles were." Added Lennon, who with McCartney formally disbanded the band in 1970: "Since I was 22, I was always 'supposed to.' I was supposed to write a hundred songs by Friday, supposed to have a single out by Saturday, supposed to do this or that. I became an artist because I cherished freedom—I couldn't fit into a classroom or an office. Freedom was the plus for all the minuses for being an oddball! But suddenly I was obliged to a record company, obliged to the media, obliged to the public. I wasn't free at all!" The guitarist contended that "I was always waiting for a reason to get out of the Beatles from the day I filmed *How I Won the War* [in 1966]. I just didn't have the guts to do it. The seed was planted when the Beatles stopped touring and I couldn't deal with not being onstage. But I was too frightened to step out of the palace. That's what killed Presley. The king is always killed by his courtiers. He is overfed, overindulged, overdrunk to keep him tied to his throne."

The Beatles had paid the price of success, but had risen to dizzying heights that no other rock performer had scaled. From 1964 to 1966 their music, along with the sounds of other British bands that invaded America, blasted from the radios of almost every American teenager. Yet, in the mid-1960s, even though they still commanded a huge following and easily sold a million copies of each record they produced, the Beatles had to contend with a new force that exploded from Detroit.

7

Motown: The Sound of Integration

"This organization is built on love."

Berry Gordy

"This organization is built on love," thirty-five-year-old Berry Gordy, the founder of Motown Productions, told *Newsweek* in early 1965. "We're dealing with feeling and truth."

Gordy, sounding much like Martin Luther King, Jr., created a music empire that exemplified the peaceful integration advocated by King and reflected the progress of the civil rights movement. The black-owned-and-operated Motown was established a year before the first sit-in demonstration and achieved moderate success during the civil rights strife of the early 1960s. The Detroit-based company, using the assembly-line techniques of the nearby auto factories, became a major force in popular music from late 1964 to 1967 when civil rights partisans won a series of significant legislative victories. It was the first label that successfully groomed, packaged, marketed, and sold the music of black artists to the white American masses.

MOTOWN: THE EARLY YEARS

Berry Gordy started in the music industry as a producer and song-writer. Born in Detroit in 1929, Gordy became interested in songwriting as a youth. "I did other things," he remembered. "I was a plasterer for a while in my father's business, took a job on an automobile assembly line. But I always wrote songs." In 1957, Gordy had his first success with the song "Reet Petite," which was recorded by Detroit-born Jackie Wilson who had at one time replaced Clyde McPhatter as the lead singer of the Dominoes. The next year he penned the million-selling "Lonely Teardrops" for Wilson and established the Jobette Music Publishing Company. At the same time, Gordy began to produce such records as the Miracles' "Get a Job" and "You," Eddie Holland's first single, and Brian Holland's "Shock."

In 1959, the same year that Don Kirshner started Aldon Music, Berry Gordy borrowed $700 from his sister, rented an eight-room house at 2648 West Grand Boulevard, and founded the Motown Record Corporation, which would issue records under a variety of labels. "If I ever get this house and get it paid for," Gordy told his sister Esther at the time, "I'll have it made. I'll live upstairs, I'll have my offices down in the front part, and I'll have a studio out back where I can make demonstration records or masters to sell to record companies."

Gordy first began to record artists on the rhythm and blues-oriented Tamla Records. "When Berry first started the company," recalled Mable John, the first female recording artist signed to Tamla, "it had an air of being a rhythm and blues and pop company, but I was basically a blues singer." Gordy scored a minor hit with the first Tamla release, Marv Johnson's "Come to Me," and later in his first year of operation co-wrote and released "Money," which was recorded by Barrett Strong and climbed to the number-2 position on the R & B chart. In September 1959, the Motown founder recorded "Bad Girl" by young William "Smokey" Robinson and the Detroit-born Miracles, which reached number 93 on the pop charts with the help of national distribution by Chess Records.

Gordy became convinced by Smokey Robinson that Motown should distribute its own records. "When I started," Gordy told *Black Enterprise*, "we licensed our singles to other companies such as United Artists. Smokey Robinson gave me the idea to go national with my own product; my attorneys and other people said it was madness, that I shouldn't do it because a hit would throw me into bankruptcy since [we were] undercapitalized." In 1960, Gordy co-wrote and distributed "Shop Around" by Smokey Robinson and the Miracles, which hit the top of the charts and established Motown as an important independent company.

Throughout the next four years, Berry Gordy continued to produce hits by capitalizing on the girl-group craze. In 1959, sixteen-year-old Mary Wells, who had written a song for Jackie Wilson, approached the Motown founder. Unable to write music, she sang the song to Gordy, who immediately signed the teenager and released her version of "Bye Bye Baby," which hit the Top 10 on the R & B chart in 1960. Two years later, Wells teamed with Smokey Robinson who by now wrote and produced for Tamla and hit with "The One Who Really Loves You," "You Beat Me to the Punch," and "Two Lovers." The next year, she recorded "Laughing Boy" and "Your Old Stand By." In 1964, Wells topped the pop charts with "My Guy."

Gordy also won a spot on the charts with the Marvelettes. "We were discovered at a talent show in Inkster [Michigan]," recalled Wanda Young who with Gladys Horton founded the group. "One of our teachers arranged an audition for us with Motown, even though we didn't even win the contest. This was around 1961 and there were five of us then." The group signed with the label and released "Please Mr. Postman," written by Marvelette Georgeanna Dobbins, which became Motown's first number 1 hit. The next year the Marvelettes charted with "Playboy," "Beachwood 4-5789," "Someday, Someway," and "Strange I Know." In November 1962, the group toured the South in a bus and five cars as part of the first Motortown Revue and, according to Katherine Anderson of the Marvelettes, "did what we could to play for integrated audiences."

Berry Gordy, encouraged by his success with the Marvelettes, recorded another group of girls from Detroit, Martha and the Vandellas. Martha Reeves, Annette Sterling, Rosalind Ashford and Gloria Williamson sang as the Del-Phis while in high school and recorded the forgettable "Won't You Let Me Know" for Chess. In 1960, Reeves accepted a job at Motown as a secretary and, when Mary Wells failed to appear for a recording session, convinced the company to record her group, now called the Vels. Though selling so few copies of their first Motown release that a disgusted Gloria Williamson quit the group, the persistent quartet sang backup vocals on a number of Motown hits, including "Hitch Hike" and "Stubborn Kind of Fellow" by Marvin Gaye, a romantic balladeer who had sung in the doo-wop group, the Moonglows, and in 1961 had joined Motown. In 1963, amid the girl-group explosion, Martha and the Vandellas first hit the charts with "Come and Get These Memories" and followed with the number 1 "Heat Wave" and the sound alike, "Quicksand." The next year, they recorded the memorable "Dancing in the Streets," which almost reached the top of the pop charts, and along with hits by Mary Wells and the Marvelettes, identified Motown as a major source of the girl-group sound.

CIVIL RIGHTS IN THE GREAT SOCIETY

The civil rights movement, which began in the 1950s and escalated during the early 1960s, in 1964 and 1965 resulted in significant achievements that were reflected in the distinctive Motown sound.

On July 2, 1964, Congress passed the most sweeping civil rights legislation since the Civil War. The Civil Rights Act established a sixth-grade education as a minimum voting requirement and empowered the attorney general to protect the voting rights of all citizens. It forbade discrimination in such public places as restaurants, hotels, bathrooms and libraries, created an Equal Employment Opportunity Commission and a Community Relations Service that would help communities solve racially based problems, banned discrimination in federally funded programs, and authorized technical and financial aid for school desegregation. The same year, Congress ratified the Twenty-fourth Amendment to the U.S. Constitution, which outlawed the poll tax in federal elections.

Congress enacted the Voting Rights Act the next year when violence erupted in Selma, Alabama. Early in 1965, Sheriff James G. Clark forcibly resisted a voter-registration drive in Dallas County, Alabama, where no blacks had voted in years. He collected a posse wielding whips, clubs, and canisters of tear gas to disperse peaceful demonstrators, two of whom were murdered. Martin Luther King, Jr., and 3,200 equal-rights partisans, protected by the Alabama National Guard, marched fifty miles from Selma to Montgomery to protest the blatant discrimination and violence. "No tide of racism can stop us," King exhorted 25,000 listeners in Montgomery after the completion of his five-day march.

Disturbed by the events in Selma, President Lyndon Johnson proposed greater voting safeguards for blacks and, in the words of the civil rights anthem, promised Congress that "we shall overcome." Congress complied with a law that banned the unfair literacy tests used in the South to disenfranchise blacks and authorized the attorney general to dispatch federal examiners to register voters in areas where local examiners discriminated on the basis of color. By the end of the year, nearly 250,000 blacks registered to vote for the first time.

President Lyndon Johnson also promised a Great Society "where the city of man served not only the needs of the body and the demands of commerce but the desire for beauty and the hunger for community." He encouraged America to ask "not only how much, but how good; not only how to create wealth, but how to use it; not only how fast we are going, but where we are headed."

To achieve his dream, Johnson pushed through Congress a series of bills designed to eradicate economic inequality. In 1964, Congress passed the Economic Opportunity Act, which declared a "war on poverty." It created the Office of Economic Opportunity, which included a Job Corps for high school dropouts, a Neighborhood Youth Corps for unemployed teens, the Volunteers in Service to America (VISTA) that was a domestic version of the Kennedy-established Peace Corps, a Head Start Program for disadvantaged children, and the Upward Bound Program that prepared the poor to attend college.

The same year, Congress enacted the Criminal Justice Act, which provided the indigent with adequate legal representation. It passed the Food Stamp Act to provide groceries to needy families and ratified the Housing Act, which authorized $1 billion for urban renewal of the inner cities. Congress also agreed to cut taxes by $11.5 billion in two years, which Lyndon Johnson called "the single most important step that we have taken."

In 1965, Congress continued to legislate reforms. It passed the Elementary and Secondary Education Act, which earmarked more than $1.3 billion for the improvement of school districts that had desegregated. It also created Medicare, which provided medical and hospital insurance to the aged. Coupled with civil rights legislation, the new laws of the Great Society provided poor blacks with hope of a better future and seemed to be a giant step toward the dream of Martin Luther King, Jr.

THE SOUND OF INTEGRATION

In 1964, Berry Gordy assembled the parts of a music machine to create a distinctive Motown sound, which reflected and furthered the integration of blacks into white America. Gordy had always supported the peaceful integrationist program of Martin Luther King, Jr., who once had paid a brief visit to the Motown offices. In 1963, he had released a recorded version of King's "I Have a Dream" speech, delivered on the steps of the Lincoln Memorial at the end of the march on Washington. "Motown was a very strong backer of Martin Luther King's total program," asserted Motown producer Mickey Stevenson. "Berry felt that our job in Detroit was to make blacks aware of their culture, of the problems and some of the ways out of the problems. We'd showcase our artists to young kids at the Greystone Ballroom and it gave us a chance to get the youngsters off the street and see what our image was about. . . inspiring them a little to maybe live up to that imagery. Motown was a tremendous avenue of escape and hope."

Gordy, the son of a black entrepreneur who hoped for the upward mobility of blacks, specially groomed and cultivated streetwise teens from Detroit to make them acceptable to mainstream America. In 1964, he hired Maxine Powell, who formerly had operated a finishing and modeling school, to prep his performers. "The singers were raw," remembered Powell. "They were from the streets, and like most of us who came out of the [housing] projects, they were a little crude: Some were backward, some were arrogant. They had potential, but they were not unlike their friends in the ghetto. I always thought of our artists as diamonds in the rough who needed polishing. We were training them for Buckingham Palace and the White House, so I had my work cut out for me."

Powell tried to turn the Motown artists into polished professionals. "Many of them had abusive tones of voice, so I had to teach them how to speak in a nonthreatening manner," she explained. "Many of them slouched, so I had to show them what posture meant. Some were temperamental and moody; I would lecture them about their attitude . . . I chose which clothes were best for them as well. We used to call them 'uniforms,' and before we had them specially made, I would have to choose outfits that would compliment all of the people in a group, which wasn't easy. As far as makeup, I worked with all of the girls on wigs, nails, and that sort of thing. And on stage technique, I taught them little things like never turning their backs to an audience, never protruding their buttocks onstage, never opening their mouths too wide to sing, how to be well-rounded professionals." She also taught them the art of the inoffensive interview. "I had to force these lessons," Powell concluded. "The youngsters often had to be pushed and shoved."

A few months after adding Maxine Powell to the staff, Berry Gordy hired choreographer Cholly Atkins. Atkins, a well-known dancer in the 1930s and 1940s who had performed in the Cotton Club and the Savoy Ballroom, tried to teach the Motown groups to move gracefully. "What I was really trying to do with them was to teach them physical drama, which most of them had no respect for," he said. "My methods for the Motown artists was that I always wanted them coming from someplace and going to someplace." Within a year, boasted Atkins, "we had the best-looking artists in the record business."

Atkins worked with Maurice King, who served as the executive musical director. King, who had arranged shows at Detroit's Flame Show Bar for years and had worked with such jazz artists as Billie Holiday and Dinah Washington, taught the Motown acts about stage patter. "My rehearsals were conducted like a class, a noninterupted class," he recalled.

By the mid-1960s, Berry Gordy had assembled a Motown team that could take poor black youths from Detroit and teach them to talk, walk, dress, and dance like successful debutantes and debonair gentlemen. "I'm sure that blacks were wearing tuxedos, top hats, wigs and eyelashes before Berry Gordy came along but not with the popular music we were recording, and not for the same reasons," observed one Motown staffer. "We really wanted young blacks to understand that you do not have to look like you came out of the ghetto in order to be somebody other blacks and even whites would respect when you made it big. They'll believe you had a rough childhood; you don't have to prove it to them by looking like hell."

Berry Gordy combined the polished image of the Motown acts with a gospel-based music that could appeal to the American mainstream. "Blues and R & B always had a funky look to it back in those days, and we at Motown felt that we should have a look that the mothers and fathers would want their children to follow. We wanted to kill the imagery of liquor and drugs and how some people thought it pertained to R & B" explained Motown producer Mickey Stevenson. "I did not like blues songs when choosing material for our artists, and Berry agreed with that," continued Stevenson. "We enjoyed John Lee Hooker and B.B. King just as much as the next guy, but we would reject anything that had a strong blues sound to it."

In place of blues and R & B, Gordy favored a distinctive music grounded by an insistent, pounding rhythm section, punctuated by horns and tamborines and featuring shrill, echo-laden vocals that bounced back and forth in the call-and-response of gospel. Building upon his experience with girl-group sound, he produced a full sound both reminiscent and expanding upon Phil Spector's wall of sound. Aiming for the mass pop market, Gordy called the music "The Sound of Young America" and affixed a huge sign over the Motown studio that read, "Hitsville U.S.A."

THE SUPREMES ON THE ASSEMBLY LINE

The Supremes fulfilled Berry Gordy's dream of a polished black act that sang gospel-based pop to both blacks and whites. Born in Detroit and meeting in the low-income Brewster housing project, Diana Ross, Mary Wilson, Florence Ballard, and Betty Travis began singing together in high school. They sang as the Primettes at sock hops and in 1960 won first prize at the Detroit/Windsor Freedom Festival talent contest. Early the next year, after pestering Motown staffers for a few months, the group, which included Barbara Martin who replaced Betty Travis, signed to Motown and on the advice of Berry Gordy changed their name. "One day I was working at my desk," recalled Motown songwriter Janie Bradford, "and Berry came up to me and said, 'I'm changing the name of this group called the Primettes, four giggly little girls. Come up with a name.' So I thought it over and came up with three names, put them in a hat on little slips of paper. Florence picked the Supremes."

The newly signed act had little success initially. Late in 1961, the Supremes recorded "I Want a Guy," which attracted so little attention that Barbara Martin quit the group. During the next two years, the group recorded over forty songs, of which only twelve were released and met with limited success.

Around 1964, when Mary Wells left the company, Motown began to polish the Supremes. It sent the girls to Maxine Powell who taught them proper etiquette and attire. "We spent only about six months working with Mrs. Powell, but anything we learned would be incorporated the same day," recalled Mary Wilson. "We would be out eating something, and if one of us accidentally picked up her chicken with her fingers, the other two would say, 'remember what Mrs. Powell said.' " The company also provided the group with lessons from music director Maurice King and choreographer Cholly Atkins.

The Supremes, groomed by the Motown organization, scaled the charts in 1964. After the minor hit, "When the Love Light Starts Shining through His Eyes," the year before, the group recorded "Where Did Our Love Go," which was released just fifteen days after the passage of the momentous Civil Rights Act and by the end of the year topped both the pop and R & B charts. On December 24, 1964, the Supremes made their first of twenty appearances on the "Ed Sullivan Show," which had introduced both Elvis Presley and the Beatles to the American public. The Supremes, appearing in sleek, light-blue chandelier gowns, embodied the Motown image of the slick, cultivated black entertainer and became overnight pop stars.

Berry Gordy, using methods practiced in the Detroit auto factories, ensured the continued success of the Supremes by assembling the parts of a hit-making machine that included standardized songwriting, an in-house rhythm section, a quality-control process, selective promotion, and a family atmosphere reminiscent of the camaraderie fostered by Henry Ford in his auto plant during the early twentieth century. "I worked in the Ford factory before I came in the [record] business, and I saw how each person did a different thing," Gordy reasoned. "And I said, 'Why can't we do that with the creative process?' It was just an idea of coming in one door one day and going out the other door and having all these things done."

The song-writing team of Brian Holland, Lamont Dozier, and Eddie Holland, joining forces in 1962, perfected the formula of success that they discovered with their composition "Where Did Our Love Go?" From late 1964 to 1967, they wrote a series of number-1 hits for the Supremes which rivaled the chart success of the Beatles and included "Baby Love," "Come See About Me," "Stop! In the Name of Love," "Back in My Arms Again," "I Hear A Symphony," "You Can't Hurry Love," "You Keep Me Hangin' On," and "Love Is Here and Now You're Gone." "When 'Where Did Our Love Go' hit for the Supremes," remembered Lamont Dozier, "we knew we had stumbled onto a sound. You'll notice that we patterned 'Baby Love' and 'Come See About Me' right after the first hit. In fact, all the Supremes' big hits were really children of 'Where Did Our Love Go?' "

The different singles also sounded remarkably similar because of the in-house rhythm section known as the Funk Brothers who played on almost all major Supremes recording sessions. In 1964, Earl Van Dyke, a former be-bop jazz pianist who had toured with R & B singer Lloyd Price, became the leader of the studio band. He played with drummer Benny Benjamin and bassist James Jamerson, who had backed Jackie Wilson and the Miracles. Together with a few other musicians who joined them occasionally in the studio, the Funk Brothers provided the trademark percussive beat of the Motown sound.

Berry Gordy attempted to maintain the consistent quality of Motown material by conducting weekly meetings that scrutinized possible releases. "The quality control meetings on Fridays were real intense," remarked Motown songwriter Ron Miller. "All of the writers, producers, and many of the executives gathered in Berry's office, and he would play everyone's songs. And then he went around to everyone there and asked them for their opinion. It was brutal."

Berry Gordy carefully promoted the songs that were released through means which kept the slick Motown image intact. Besides spots on the "Ed Sullivan Show," he snagged appearances for the Supremes on such mainstream television programs as "The Dean Martin Show," "The Tonight Show," "Hollywood Palace," a special presented by black crooner Sammy Davis, Jr., and the Orange Bowl Parade. For concerts, Gordy favored such posh settings as the Copacabana in New York, which hosted the Supremes in July 1965, the Yale University prom of 1965, which featured jazz great Duke Ellington and the Supremes, and exclusive Las Vegas hotels such as the Flamingo where the Supremes performed in 1967. He even asked established entertainers such as Sammy Davis, Jr. and Broadway star Carol Channing to write the liner notes for Supremes' albums.

Gordy retained control of the successful group by creating a family atmosphere at the company. In 1965, like a watchful father, he limited each Supreme to a $100 weekly allowance and funnelled the rest of their $300,000 profit for the year into a joint bank account. The Motown owner refused to allow the girls to date and, to fend off possible suitors, gave each girl a diamond ring. "They're Christmas presents from Gordy," Florence Ballard told *Newsweek* about her ring in 1965. "Someone saw mine the other week," chimed Mary Wilson. "He said, 'Oh, you're engaged.' I said, 'Yeah. To Motown.' "You have to be very strict with young artists," asserted Berry Gordy, sounding like a stern father. "That instills discipline."

THE MOTOWN STABLE

Berry Gordy's paternal, production-line approach produced other successful performers such as the Temptations. In 1957, the fifteen-year-old, Detroit-raised Otis Williams started a street-corner doo-wop group with a few friends including Elbridge Bryant. Two years later, he invited teenager Melvin Franklin to join and named the group the Elegants, then the Questions, and finally the Distants, who released "Come On" on Warwick Records. Later in 1959, on the advice of local Detroit promoter Milton Jenkins, the group added Eddie Kendricks and Paul Williams and renamed themselves the Primes.

In 1960, between sets at a local club, Williams walked into the bathroom, where he met Berry Gordy, who complimented the group and eventually signed them to Motown by the end of the year. Renamed the Temptations when signed by Gordy, the group from 1960 to 1964 released several singles, which met only moderate success.

Berry Gordy shaped the Temptations into the Motown image and placed them on the charts by 1964. He replaced their processed hair styles with carefully cropped Afros, discarded their casual clothes for top hats and tails, inserted such standards as "Old Man River" into their repertoire, and added the precise choreography of Motown dance master Cholly Atkins to their stage show.

When David Ruffin replaced Elbridge Bryant, the refurbished Temptations recorded the Smokey Robinson composition, "My Girl," an answer to the Mary Wells hit, "My Guy," that topped both the pop and R & B charts in early 1965. The group remained on the charts with a series of songs including "Since I Lost My Baby" and "Get Ready" by Smokey Robinson and "Ain't Too Proud To Beg," "Beauty Is Only Skin Deep," and "(I Know) I'm Losing You," all by Eddie Holland and Norman Whitfield who, with Robinson and the Holland-Dozier-Holland team formed the legendary Motown songwriting-production crew.

The Motown songwriting-production team revived the careers of other former doo-woppers, the Four Tops. The group, Levi Stubbs, Renaldo Benson, Lawrence Payton, and Abdul Fakir, grew up together in Detroit during the late 1940s and in 1953 banded together as the Four Aims, which released "Could It Be You" in 1956 on Chess Records. The vocal group began to back jazz vocalist Billy Eckstine and in 1960 signed with Columbia and recorded the unsuccessful "Ain't That Love." They signed with Riverside Records and recorded "When Are You," which also failed to chart. "We were working," recalled Abdul Fakir, "perfecting our craft and just out there hustling. Guess you could say were we getting ready for the Chairman."

Chairman Berry Gordy signed the group in 1964, dressed them in tuxedos and paired them with the songwriting team of Holland-Dozier-Holland, who wrote "Baby I Need Your Loving," a smooth, gospel-flavored composition that hit the number 11 slot on the pop charts. Gordy continued to provide the Four Tops with Holland-Dozier-Holland material, including the number-1 pop hits "I Can't Help Myself" and "Reach Out I'll Be There" and other chartbusters such as "Shake Me, Wake Me (When It's Over)," "Standing in the Shadows of Love," and "Seven Rooms of Gloom." As with the Supremes and the Temptations, the Four Tops benefited from the Motown finishing school, the dance classes, the music direction and the promotion and became a slick, popular act that appealed to both white and black audiences.

During the mid-1960s, Berry Gordy had established a music empire that included eight record labels, a management service, and a publishing company and grossed millions of dollars a year. From 1964 through 1967, Motown placed fourteen number-1 pop singles, twenty number-1 singles on the R & B charts, forty-six more Top Fifteen pop singles, and seventy-five other Top Fifteen R & B records. In 1966 alone, 75 percent of all Motown releases hit the charts. "It is no coincidence," observed a British newspaper columnist in 1965 amid a Motown tour of England, "that while 10,000 Negroes are marching for their civil rights in Alabama, the Tamla-Motown star is on the ascendent." Berry Gordy, putting into action the program of peaceful integration, had created one of the most commercially successful black-owned enterprises and certainly the most successful black-owned record company.

In 1967, the Motown empire began to decline. A few days before a scheduled performance by the Supremes at the Hollywood Bowl in April, Berry Gordy fired Florence Ballard, who had become jealous of the increasingly prominent position of Diana Ross and replaced her with Cindy Birdsong. The next year in July, he discharged David Ruffin of the Temptations and substituted Dennis Edwards. The same year, Gordy quarreled about royalty rates with the songwriting-production team of Holland-Dozier-Holland, who quit the company and filed suit against Motown. By 1968, when the inner cities exploded in rage and thousands of young college students took to the street to protest the war in Vietnam, the Motown machine had begun to slow down.

8

Acid Rock

"We have a private revolution going on."

A handbill distributed from the Blue Unicorn,
a coffeehouse in the Haight

"Everybody's relaxing and not afraid to speak out and not afraid not to wear a tie to work," asserted Marty Balin, one of the founders of the Jefferson Airplane, which took off in San Francisco during the mid-1960s. "The one word I can think of is love, even though that sounds like a cliche, but that's where it's at, it's uninhibited, coming out emotion. It's like the twenties. The twenties were really a start and at the end of it, they had all these great creative different things come out of it. I really feel it's the same. It's the most moving generation since the twenties. In creativity. And out of this are going to come many wonderful artists and people and thinkers. Even the philosophy of the day is being changed by what's happening now."

Speak out, love, creativity, moving generation, uninhibited, happening now became the bywords of a new era. In the wake of the British invasion, thousands of middle-class, college-educated youths clustered around San Francisco Bay to demonstrate to the country, and eventually to the world, that love could replace war, sharing could replace greed, and community could supercede the individual.

These San Francisco visionaries strove for nothing less than a total transformation of America which they demanded immediately. As Jim Morrison, lead singer of the Doors, screamed: "We want the world, and we want it *now.*"

A new hybrid of rock-and-roll reflected and helped propagate the new culture. Named after a strange new drug, LSD, acid rock broadcast the word of hippiedom from the epicenter, San Francisco, to the hinterlands. Unlike the working-class British invaders who used music to entertain, the West Coast bands such as the Jefferson Airplane, the Doors, the Grateful Dead, Quicksilver Messenger Service, and countless others (1,500 by one count) led the youth movement that consciously withdrew from America's 9-to-5, workaholic society and tried to create an alternative community built upon love. From 1965 to 1967, the vanguard of rock-and-roll had a mission.

THE BEATS

The social upheaval of hippiedom had its origins with the Beats, who had wandered from their homes in New York City to San Francisco's North Beach more than a decade earlier. In 1951, Jack

The Daily *of the University of Washington*

Poet Allen Ginsberg: a bridge between the Beats and the Hippies

Kerouac, the Columbia football star-turned-writer, planted the seeds of the Beat Generation when he bummed around the country with the ever-energetic, ever-adventuresome Neal Cassady and told of their travels in his book *On the Road*. The same year, poet Lawrence Ferlinghetti left New York for San Francisco because "it was the only place in the country where you could get decent wine cheap." Two years later he opened the prime beatnik haunt in North Beach, City Lights Bookstore. In 1953 Allen Ginsberg migrated to San Francisco on the advice of his friend Neal Cassady, and two years later organized the first public appearance of the Beat Generation—a poetry reading advertised as "Six Poets at the Six Gallery," at which Ginsberg premiered his controversial poem "Howl." In 1957, Kerouac finally published *On the Road,* to the critical acclaim of *The New York Times*.

The Beats formulated a countercultural philosophy based upon tenets of Eastern religion. Their metaphorical name—Beat—suggested the quest for beatitude that could be discovered in Zen Buddhism. It also referred to the patron saints of the movement, the drifters, who shed the trappings of institutional society and gathered in places such as New York City's Bowery. Although appearing "beat down" and downtrodden to "straights," the bums symbolized the freedom that the avant-garde so dearly cherished. As one writer put it, the beatniks "chased the unwashed American dream." Finally, the term reverberated to the cool jazz of Miles Davis, Lennie Tristano, and Gerry Mulligan that wafted from the coffeehouse hangouts of the Beat writers.

Congregating in San Francisco and New York City's Greenwich Village, these countercultural literati lambasted traditional American values. Beat comic Lenny Bruce satirized the marketing of the Lone Ranger and the wiles of the Avon lady. In his once-banned *Naked Lunch* (1959), William S. Burroughs, the literary genius who had inherited the Burroughs adding machine fortune, wove together powerful, graphic images of a decaying society: "Smell of chili houses and dank overcoats and atrophied testicles. . . . A heaving sea of air hammers in the purple brown dusk tainted with rotten metal smell of sewer gas." Ginsberg penned such drug-inspired poems as "Howl," which the San Francisco Police Department first declared obscene, then banned and confiscated.

In place of traditional bourgeois values, the Beats preached a cultural relativism. "We love everything," explained Kerouac. "Billy Graham, the Big Ten, Rock and Roll, Zen, apple pie, Eisenhower—we dig it all." Believing no value to be absolute, the Beats felt that morality depended upon the individual. As one Beat argued, "I stay cool, far out, alone. When I flip it's over something *I* feel, only me."

Such an ethos led to experimentation with sex and drugs, especially marijuana and amphetamines, which Kerouac mentioned in *Dharma Bums*. "They had no interest in building a greater America, in fighting Communism, in working at a career to buy hundred-dollar suits and dresses, color television sets, a house in the suburbs, or a flight to Paris," observed writer Burton Wolfe. "In fact, they laughed at those goals. Some brew, a few joints, a sympathetic partner in the sack, a walk in the park, an afternoon of lying in the sun on the beach, a hitchhike trip to Mexico—this was all there was."

The anti-institutional values of the Beats led to a reaction from more traditional quarters. Right-wing F.B.I. director J. Edgar Hoover, turning literary critic in 1959, reviewed Lawrence Ferlinghetti's poem "Tentative Description of a Dinner Given to Promote the Impeachment of President Eisenhower," concluding "it appears that Ferlinghetti may possibly be a mental case." A month later, the Alcoholic Beverages Commission declared "Beatnikland" a "problem area" and refused to issue any more liquor licenses. Other, more violent critics bombed the women's restroom at the Co-Existence Bagel Shop, a favorite gathering spot for the San Francisco Beats which, along with The Place, closed down shortly thereafter. By the end of 1959 Eric Nord, one of the most visible West Coast Beat writers, told a courtroom, "the Beat Generation is dead. I don't go to North Beach anymore."

THE REEMERGENCE OF THE BEATS: THE NEW YORK CONNECTION

Some of the Beats reappeared on the cultural scene to parent the psychedelic movement during the mid-1960s. On the East Coast, at St. Mark's Place in Greenwich Village in 1965, Beat poets Tuli Kupferberg, Ken Weaver, and Ed Sanders, the editor of *Fuck You: A Magazine of the Arts*, started the Fugs. "We used to read at the Metro, on Second Avenue," recalled Kupferberg. "After the readings, we'd go to the Dom, on St. Mark's Place . . . where lots of young people would go. The jukebox had Beatles and Stones albums on it, and some of the kids would dance. Once they started, the other paper-assed intellectuals tried to get up and dance, too. And Ed Sanders got the idea it might be good to try to combine some of our poetry with rock music."

The band caricatured American society, in the process using the verse of William Blake in "How Sweet I Roamed from Field to Field" and the prose of William S. Burroughs in "Virgin Forest." Allen Ginsberg described the countercultural message of the group in the liner notes on the Fugs' second album, released in 1966. "The United States is split down the middle," he contended. "On one side are everybody who make love with their eyes open, maybe smoke pot and maybe take LSD and look inside their heads to find the Self-God Walt Whitman prophesied for America. . . . Who's on the other side? People who think we are *bad.* . . . Yogis and Beatles say there is no other side. 'We can get along.' Can we? NOW sings

Sanders and the Fugs come camping and screaming along, out in the open where every ear can hear the soul politics ecstasy message—They've put it in Front. . . . The Fugs came to tell the truth that was only dreamy till they opened their mouths for Whitmanic orgy yawp. Group Grope, Dirty Old Man, Skin Flowers and Frenzy! Teenagers rise up and understand. When they scream 'Kill for Peace' they're announcing publicly the madness of our white-haired crazy governments." The poet concluded: "The Bible says that when Christ comes back, 'every eye shall see.' Now every ear can hear, and when the Fugs break thru the monopoly blockade and their image is broadcast on National Television, every kid in America and most white-haired old suffering men will turn them on with Relief at last and every eye shall see."

Velvet Underground drew inspiration from the same Beat source. In 1964, at a party in New York City, songwriter Lou Reed met John Cale, who had been performing with an avant-garde classical ensemble. The two decided to form a band and with guitarist Sterling Morrison and drummer Angus MacLise began playing as the Primitives at local clubs.

Courtesy of RCA Records

Lou Reed

Avant-garde artist Andy Warhol helped the band achieve notoriety. After meeting Reed and Cale through mutual friends in 1965, Warhol agreed to manage the band, adding singer Nico and drummer Maureen Tucker, who replaced MacLise. He showcased the band, named the Velvet Underground after a pornographic novel, at his Factory and added them to his multimedia extravaganza, the Exploding Plastic Inevitable. "He was the catalyst," remarked Reed of Warhol years later.

The band, dominated by Reed, played a Beat-inspired music. Reed, who had studied at Syracuse University with Beat poet Delmore Schwartz, crafted songs that dealt with the down-and-out themes of Beat fiction—heroin addiction in "I'm Waiting for the Man" and the rushing "Heroin," and cocaine in "Run, Run, Run." In one Velvet album, Reed led the listener through the adventures of a girl named Candy, who roamed the cultural underground assisted by her junkie boyfriend. The sexual and drug-related themes of the Velvet Underground, Reed later mentioned, were "only taboo on records. Let's keep that in mind. Movies, plays, books, it's all there. You read Ginsberg, you read Burroughs."

THE HAIGHT-ASHBURY SCENE

The Beats resurfaced in San Francisco to inspire the hippies as *San Francisco Examiner* writer Michael Fallon first called them in September 1965. At the first hippie gathering, held at Longshoremen's Hall near Fishermen's Wharf on October 16, 1965, wrote journalist Ralph Gleason, "long lines of dancers snaked through the crowd for hours holding hands. Free-form improvisation ('self-expression') was everywhere. The clothes were a blast. Like a giant costume party." Amid the revelry whirled a long-haired, bearded Allen Ginsberg.

Three weeks later, on November 6, Allen Ginsberg appeared at the Appeal, a benefit rock concert for the San Francisco Mime Troupe, an avant-garde theater group managed by Bill Graham. He brought his Beat friends, the Fugs, who flew in from New York for the event, mingling with hundreds of free-minded participants who lived in the surrounding Haight Ashbury district near San Francisco State College. At the end of the evening, Ginsberg chanted as the Hashbury hippies cleaned the Mime Troupe loft.

For three days in late January 1966, Beat writer Ken Kesey, author of *One Flew Over the Cuckoo's Nest* (1962), and his band of free spirits known as the Merry Pranksters, hosted the Trips Festival, which attracted 6,000 people. For the event, they enlisted the services of the Grateful Dead and Big Brother and the Holding Company, set up five movie screens, on which they projected a mind-boggling combination of colors and shapes, and spiked the punch with a little LSD, a concoction that became known as the kool-aid acid test. At the festivities, Kesey stalked the floor dressed in a space helmet and a jumpsuit and periodically composed free-form poetry on an overhead projector. Eyewitness Ralph Gleason saw one man "bandaged all over, with only his eyes peeking out through dark glasses, carrying a crutch and wearing a sign: 'You're in the Pepsi generation and I'm a pimply freak.' Another long-haired exotic dressed in a modified Hell's Angels' leather jerkin that had 'Under Ass Wizard Mojo Indian Fighter' stenciled on his back. Several varieties of Lawrence of Arabia costumes wandered through." At one point Neal Cassady, the Beat High Priest, who had appeared in Kerouac's *On the Road* as Dean Moriarty and had inspired the Indian in Kesey's *Cuckoo's Nest,* "stood for a while upstairs and then swung out and over the back of the balcony railing, scaring everyone who saw him, as they expected him to slip and fall to the floor." Cassady would reappear at countless Grateful Dead concerts to deliver amazing free-associational monologues as preludes to the performances. He also sat at the helm of the psyche-delic bus that took Kesey and the Merry Pranksters on a symbolic trip across the country that later inspired the Beatles' Magical Mystery Tour.

Neal Cassady especially influenced the Grateful Dead, the premier psychedelic band. "There's no experience in my life yet that equals riding with Cassady in like a '56 Plymouth or a Cadillac through San Francisco or from San Jose to Santa Rosa," remembered Jerry Garcia, lead guitarist for the Dead. "He was the ultimate *something*—the ultimate person as art." "When I fell in with Ken Kesey and Neal Cassady, it seemed like home sweet home to me," added Bob Weir, another Dead guitarist. "We picked up a lot from those guys. Particularly from Cassady."

Other Beats helped organize the "First Human Be-In," which took place in Golden Gate Park Stadium on January 14, 1967. Allen Ginsberg, painter Michael Bowen, playwright Michael McClure, po-etess Lenore Kandal, and poet Gary Snyder helped stage the multi-colored community gathering, which attracted 20,000 people on an unseasonably warm day. Early in the morning Ginsberg and Synder opened the proceedings by conducting an ancient Hindu blessing ritual, the dakshina, around the Polo Field to ensure its suitability for the coming pilgrimage. Throughout the day, hippies danced on the grass to the sounds of the Grateful Dead, the Jefferson Air-plane, and Quicksilver Messenger Service. "The costumes were a designer's dream, a wild polyglot mixture of Mod, Paladin, Ringling Brothers, Cochise and Hell's Angels' Formal," wrote Ralph Gleason in the *San Francisco Chronicle.* "The poets read. Allen Ginsberg (who may yet be elected president) chanted and Gary Snyder sat on the stage and joined in. Bells rang and balloons floated in the air. A man went around handing out oranges and there were sandwiches and candy and cookies. No one was selling anything." The celebration ended when Gary Snyder blew on a conch shell, the ritual instrument of the Yamabushi sect of Japanese Buddhism, and Allen

Ginsberg led a chant of "Om Shri Maitreya" to the Coming Buddha of Love.

When news of these remarkable events spread to the burgeoning ranks of college-aged baby boomers, the psychedelic ranks in San Francisco began to swell. "Like, Wow! There was an explosion," remarked Jay Thelin, co-owner with his brother Ron of The Psychedelic Shop, which served as the briefing center for hippie initiates to the city. "People began coming in from all over and our little information shop became sort of a clubhouse for dropouts and, well, we just let it happen, that's all." By 1967, 50,000 hippies resided in or near the Haight-Ashbury district of San Francisco.

THE HIPPIE CULTURE

Many who flocked to the Haight were baby boomers who had grown up in educated, middle-class homes. Most of the hippies, wrote journalist Hunter Thompson, who lived in San Francisco at the time, "were white and voluntarily poor. Their backgrounds were largely middle class; many had gone to college." According to a report by a San Francisco State sociologist, H. Taylor Buckner, 96 percent of the Haight hippies were between the ages of sixteen and thirty, 68 percent had attended college for a time, and 44 percent had a father who had earned a college degree.

The hippies, as with the Beats, criticized the bourgeois values with which they had been raised. "The standard thing is to feel in the gut that middle-class values are all wrong," remarked one hippie. "It's the system itself that is corrupt," added another. "Capitalism, communism, whatever it is. These are phoney labels. There is no capitalism or communism. Only dictators telling people what to do." The hippies, remarked Peter Cohan of the Haight, "are the fruit of the middle class and they are telling the middle class they don't like what has been given them."

The hippies, raised in an age of relative affluence, attacked the materialistic American culture that had been accepted by their Depression-bred parents. "I have no possessions," remarked Joyce Ann Francisco of the *San Francisco Oracle,* the preeminent psychedelic newspaper published by Ron Thelin in the Haight. "Money is beautiful only when it is flowing. When it piles up it's a hangup." "I could have a job selling real estate in Tahoe for $400 a week anytime, but that isn't what I want," agreed Jay Thelin of the Psychedelic Shop. The residents of the Haight, noticed historian Arnold Toynbee when he toured the District during spring 1967, "repudiate the affluent way of life in which making money is the object of life and work. They reject their parents' way of life as uncompromisingly as Saint Francis rejected the rich cloth merchants' way of life of his father in Assisi."

Many hippies challenged the dominant values concerning obscenity. Morning Glory, a long-haired, twenty-two-year-old hippie, felt that the "human body is a beautiful thing. It should be displayed. I want people to see what I look like, and I want to see what they look like without a bunch of clothes covering them up. Nude, everybody is in the same bag, the same economic class."

Such a freewheeling attitude toward nudity, coupled with the use of the birth control pill by over 6 million women by 1966 a decade after its introduction to the general public, led to a rejection of sexual taboos. As early as 1965, Haight residents started the Sexual Freedom League to confront traditional standards concerning sex. Within two years, hundreds of youths engaged in premarital sex with many partners, continuing a trend that had intensified with the Beats. "The 60s will be called the decade of the orgasmic preoccupation," predicted Dr. William Masters, the director of the Institute for Sex Research at Indiana University. "Young people are far more tolerant and permissive regarding sex."

In opposition to the middle class, the hippies dressed differently. Most wore long hair, which caused consternation among their elders. "As for bad vibrations emanating from my follicles, I say great," wrote James Simon Kunen in the *Strawberry Statement*. "I want the cops to sneer and the old ladies to swear and the businessmen to worry." To further distance themselves from a materialistic culture, the hippies favored tattered clothing, went shoeless, and bought bluejeans, contributing to the doubling of the sales of Levi Strauss jeans from 1963 to 1966.

By challenging authority, the hippies hoped to create an atmosphere that engendered freedom of individual expression. "We have a private revolution going on," read a handbill distributed by the Blue Unicorn, a coffeehouse in the Haight. "A revolution of individuality and diversity that can only be private."

The hippies turned to mind-expanding drugs to enhance their individual potentials. Most rolled marijuana or the more expensive hashish into joints or smoked the weed Indian-style in pipes. In 1965, Haight residents organized the Legalize Marijuana movement (LEMER), which held meetings at the Blue Unicorn. By the end of the decade, more than 96 percent of the hippies in the Haight had smoked marijuana and more than 10 million youths had tried the drug.

Another drug, the hallucinogen LSD, defined the hippie experience. Legal until October 6, 1966, "acid" fragmented everyday perception into a multitude of melting shapes and vibrant colors. "The first thing you notice is an incredible enhancement of sensory awareness," related Timothy Leary, the ex-Harvard professor who edited the *Psychedelic Review*, organized the LSD-based League for Spiritual Discovery, and became the most visible popularizer and high priest of acid. "Take the sense of sight. LSD vision is to normal vision as normal vision is to the picture of a badly tuned television set. Under LSD, it's as though you have microscopes up to your eyes, in which you see jewel-like, radiant details of anything your eye falls upon. . . . The organ of the Corti in your inner ear becomes a trembling membrane seething with tattoos of sound waves. The vibrations seem to penetrate deep inside you, swell and burst there. . . . You not only hear but *see* the music emerging from the speaker system like dancing particles, like squirming curls of toothpaste."

Timothy Leary contended that the drug experience resulted in altered, introspective states that expanded individual consciousness. In September 1966, comfortably lying on a mattress in his headquarters, a sixty-four-room mansion in Millbrook, New York, about thirty-five miles from Woodstock, he outlined the various states of consciousness to *Playboy:* "The lowest level of consciousness is sleep—or stupor, which is produced by narcotics, barbiturates and

Timothy Leary: the guru of LSD

our national stuporfactant, alcohol. The second level of consciousness is the conventional wakeful state, in which awareness is hooked to conventional symbols: flags, dollar signs, job titles, brand names, party affiliations and the like. . . . In order to reach [the third level], you have to have something that will turn *off* the symbols and open up your billions of sensory cameras to the billions of impulses that are hitting them. The chemical that opens the door to this level has been well known for centuries. . . . It is marijuana. . . . But we must bid a sad farewell to the sensory level of consciousness and go on to the fourth level, which I call the cellular level. It is well known that the stronger psychedelics such as mescaline and LSD take you *beyond* the senses into a world of cellular awareness. During an LSD session, enormous clusters of cells are turned on, and consciousness whirls into eerie panoramas for which we have no words or concepts." Leary advised readers to "turn on, tune in and drop out."

Many heeded Leary's advice. "Grass and LSD are the most important factors in the community," remarked Jay Thelin. "You should acquaint yourself with all of the consciousness-expanding drugs. I turn on every Sunday with acid, and I smoke grass everyday, working continuously with an expanding consciousness." "The only way to understand," agreed Gabe Katz of the *Oracle*, "is to turn on. The chemicals are essential. Without them you can ask a million questions and write a million words and never get it." On October 6, 1966, when legislation outlawing LSD took effect, hundreds of residents in the Haight staged a Love Pageant to assert the "inalienable rights" of "freedom of the body, the pursuit of joy, and the expansion of consciousness." In 1966, an official from the Food and Drug Administration estimated that more than 10 percent of all college students had ingested LSD and more than 90 percent of youths in the Haight had taken the drug. Many of the hippies had obtained LSD from chemist Augustus Owsley Stanley III, the grandson of Senator A. Owsley Stanley of Kentucky, who had produced and distributed an estimated 15 million acid tabs and sometimes dispensed them free at events such as the Trips Festival.

With their newfound consciousness, the hippies embraced the beliefs of past, less technological civilizations, real or imagined, to create a counter-culture. Some followed the example of the Beats by looking for salvation in the mysteries of the Orient. One San Francisco free spirit expounded that "society feeds us machines, technology, computers and we answer with primitivism: the I Ching, the Tibetan Book of the Dead, Buddhism, Taoism. The greatest truths lie in the ancient cultures. Modern civilization is out of balance with nature." Many hippies adopted the teachings of Zen popularizer Alan Watts, and some joined Hare Krishna when in January 1967 the International Society for Krishna Consciousness moved to the Haight and Allen Ginsberg declared that a Hare Krishna mantra "brings a state of ecstasy."

Attempting to recapture a lost innocence, some tried to recreate the popular image of the noble American Indian. They slipped into moccasins and sported fringed deerskin jackets, headbands, feathers, and colorful beads. As with Native Americans during a ceremony, many hippies painted their faces and bodies for festive occasions. In September 1965, the Committee Theater in the Haight staged a multimedia extravaganza, "America Needs Indians," and a few months later took their show to the acid tests. In January 1967, organizers of the Human Be-In in Golden Gate Park called the event a "Pow Wow" and a "Gathering of Tribes," advertising it with a poster that pictured a Plains Indian on horseback clutching a blanket in one hand and an electric guitar in the other. The *San Francisco Oracle* philosophized that "the white-eye who once annihilated the buffalo must now, in an action-reacted, be saved from slaughtering himself by the Indian incarnate."

Even though most Native Americans such as Robert Costo, president of the American Indian Historical Society, believed that the hippies practiced a "certain insidious exploitation of the Indian which is the worst of all," residents of the Haight created a cult of tribalism. "For one of the yearly Tribal Stomp dances at the Avalon, we gave everyone a little leather thong with a little Indian bell and a long white turkey feather tied to it," recalled Chet Helms, manager of the dance hall. "I can't tell you how effective that thematic favor was. It made everyone a member of the tribe."

Some, adhering to the notion of tribalism, banded together in communal living arrangements. At Drop City near Trinidad, Colorado, twenty-two Midwestern hippies built and lived in geodesic domes constructed from automobile hoods. Roughly forty miles from San Francisco near Sebastopol, more than fifty hippies communally farmed the thirty-one-acre Morningstar Ranch. Morningstar founder Lou Gottlieb, who held a Ph.D. in musicology and had played in the folk group the Limeliters, envisioned the Ranch as "an alternative for those who can't make it in the straight society and don't want to. . . . This sort of thing could be a beautiful alternative for people who are technologically unemployable and for other people it would be a retreat where they could come and re-create, I mean really re-create themselves. I can see ten Morningstars in every state, where people from straight society would come to live for a while in the 'alternative society,' a whole different culture based on non-competition." In the Haight itself, contended a study by a San Francisco State sociologist, more than 25 percent of the hippies lived with ten or more people.

Some hippies, believing in a noncompetitive, tribalistic society, shared their resources with others. The Diggers, most of them former members of the San Francisco Mime Troupe who named themselves after a seventeenth-century society of English agricultural altruists, provided free food, shelter, and transportation to needy hippies in the Haight-Ashbury District. A Digger leaflet distributed at the October 1966 Love Pageant advertised "free food, everyday, free food, it's free because it's yours." The Prunes in Cleveland, the Brothers in Seattle, and the Berkeley Provos followed the Digger example.

Even the shopkeepers in the Haight exhibited a community spirit. On November 23, 1966, the *San Francisco Examiner* told its readers that "the hip purveyors of painting, poetry, handcrafted leather and jewelry along Haight Street, having been blackballed by the Haight Merchants' Association, have formed their own Haight Street Merchants' Association, HIP for short." Once organized, HIP established a job cooperative to cope with the incoming hippies and provided free legal advice. Psychedelic Shop owners Jay and Ron Thelin additionally devoted over a third of their shop's floor space to a "calm center," where hippies could meditate, rap, or sleep. By the middle of 1967, the hippies had created an identifiable, vaguely defined counter-culture based upon a loose-knit community of individuals who focused upon self-expression.

By the mid-1960s, hundreds of newspapers were established to promulgate the counter-cultural ethos. In 1964, Art Kunkin started the *Los Angeles Free Press,* an underground newspaper, which was modeled after the *Village Voice* in New York. In late 1966, the *San Francisco Oracle* published the first of thirteen issues, unveiling a non-news, art-oriented format and a psychedelic look of vibrant, random colors and swirling typefaces perfected by hip artist Rick Griffin. "Our philosophy at the time was that newspapers are a lie," remembered *Oracle* editor Allen Cohen. "We were going to make the newspaper format a joke that would show everyone that newspapers were destroying sensibilities, causing paranoia and fear. We were going to fill our newspaper with art, philosophy, poetry and attend to this change of consciousness that was happening in the Haight-Ashbury and, we hoped, the world." The *Oracle* staff wanted to "serve as vehicles for the forces that were emerging." By 1967, when the Underground Press Syndicate (UPS) was founded, four other major underground tabloids printed stories about sex, drugs, and revolution: *The East Village Other, The Paper* in East Lansing, Michigan, the *Berkeley Barb,* and the *Fifth Estate* in Detroit. Two years later, more than 200 underground newspapers printed stories about the counter-culture that reached nearly a million readers.

ACID ROCK: THE TRIP BEGINS

A legion of rock bands, playing what became known as acid rock, stood in the vanguard of the movement for cultural change. The *Oracle* defined rock music as a "regenerative and revolutionary art, offering us our first real hope for the future (indeed, for the present) since August 6, 1945." "Rock and roll," announced *Rolling Stone*, which had been established in 1967 by Berkeley dropout Jann Wenner and journalist Ralph Gleason "is more than just music. It is the energy center of the new culture and the youth revolution." Even handbills distributed to promote the Trips Festival in January 1966 hinted that "maybe this is the ROCK REVOLUTION."

Not surprisingly, psychedelic music had its basis in Dylanesque folk. "I began as a folk musician. I went to New York and I heard Dylan when he was at Gerde's. And I was very impressed by, I don't know what it was, his youth I guess, his exuberance," mentioned Marty Balin who had played in the Los Angeles folk group, the Town Criers. "So I decided to come up here and started up here [San Francisco]. I went through a million different guys and then I saw Paul [Kantner]. He was walking into a folk club [The Drinking Gourd]. I just saw him, and I said, 'That's the guy.' I just knew it. He had a twelve-string and a banjo and he had his hair down to here and an old cap." The duo asked a few other musicians to join their band and then, according to lead guitarist Jorma Kaukonen, the group was "thinking of names, trying to think of some sort of name that would imply a whole different way of looking at things." They settled on the Jefferson Airplane.

The Grateful Dead, another major exponent of acid rock, grew from folk roots. "When the whole folk music thing started, I got caught up into that," remembered Jerry Garcia. "When Joan Baez's first record came out I heard it and I heard her finger picking the guitar, I'd never heard anything like it before so I got into that and I started getting into country music, into old-time white music. Mostly white spiritual stuff, white instrumental music and I got into finger style, the folk-music-festival scene, the whole thing. And I was very heavy into that for a long time and I sort of employed a scholarly approach and even went through the South with tape recorders and stuff recording bluegrass bands. I spent about three years playing bluegrass banjo, that was my big thing and I almost forgot how to play the guitar during that period of time. And then I got into a jug band, we got a jug band going and I took up the guitar again and from the jug band it was right into rock and roll. . . . I was sort of a beatnik guitar player." "Bob Weir, who plays rhythm," continued Garcia, "did the whole folk-blues coffeehouse thing. That was his thing. And he also played jug and kazoo in the jug band [Mother McCree's Uptown Jug Champions] when we were playing. And he's a student, you might say. His musical leader was Jorma [Kaukonen]." Concluded Garcia: "Like here on the West Coast, the guys that are into rock 'n' roll music have mostly come up like I have . . . like me and Jorma for example . . . up through folk music." In early 1965, folkies Garcia and Weir joined with blues enthusiast Ron "Pig Pen" McKernan, drummer Bill Kreutzmann and bassist Phil Lesch to form the band, The Warlocks, which was renamed the Grateful Dead later that year.

Poster for a Jefferson Airplane show at the Fillmore

Acid Rock **159**

Other acid rockers rose through the ranks of folk. Peter Albin, the impetus behind Big Brother and the Holding Company, had organized folk concerts during the early 1960s with his brother, Rodney. David Freiberg, the unofficial leader of Quicksilver Messenger Service, learned guitar in 1963 amidst the folk craze, and onetime fellow band member, drummer Dino Valenti, had worked for several years as a folk singer in Greenwich Village, writing the classic, "Hey Joe." In 1964, Country Joe McDonald "came to become a folksinger with the beatniks in San Francisco" and formed a jug band with Barry Melton, a friend of Peter Albin, shortly before he teamed up with the Fish to deliver his politically minded brand of psychedelic rock. Likewise, lead guitarist Robby Kreiger, lead guitarist of the Doors, which formed in late 1965 with Kreiger, fellow Psychedelic Ranger John Densmore on drums, singer Jim Morrison and organist Ray Manzarek, had started a jug band during his stay at the University of California at Santa Barbara.

Unlike the acoustic strummings of early Bob Dylan, the acid rockers amplified their message to glass-shattering levels. Jerry Garcia thought of it as "a sensory overload. . . . It's very loud." The San Francisco bands also favored extended guitar solos and distorted guitar feedback and added some blues riffs, a dash of country-western, and traces of Indian ragas to create the heralded San Francisco sound.

ROCK-AND-ROLL REVOLUTION

The new sound came from middle-class youths. Grace Slick, the daughter of a Chicago investment banker, attended the exclusive Finch College where, in her words, she became a "regular suburban preppy." Fellow Airplane member Jorma Kaukonen was the son of a foreign service official. Jim Morrison, the son of a rear admiral, had enrolled in the Theater Arts Department at UCLA, where he met pianist Ray Manzarek. John Cipollina, the guitarist for Quicksilver Messenger Service, had become interested in music through his mother, a concert pianist, and his godfather, Jose Iturbi, a well-known classical pianist. Peter Albin of Big Brother and the Holding Company grew up in suburban San Francisco, the son of a magazine editor-illustrator.

These middle-class youths wanted to overturn the social order in which they had been raised. Jim Morrison, lead singer of the Doors, professed an interest "in anything about revolt, disorder, chaos. It seemed to me to be the road toward freedom—external revolt is a way to bring about internal freedom." "When I sing my songs in public," he told *The New York Times,* "that's a dramatic act, but not just acting as in theater, but a *social* act, real action." As he sang in one song, he hoped to "break on through to the other side." Grace Slick of the Jefferson Airplane hoped for "a whole

The Doors

turnaround of values." Chet Helms, the transplanted Texan who opened the Avalon Ballroom in the Haight because he "liked to dance" and who became the manager of Big Brother and the Holding Company, "was very interested in the scene's potential for revolution. For turning things upside down, for changing values."

As with the hippies in general, the psychedelic rockers challenged restrictive middle-class values, especially those dealing with sex. The Fugs, never hiding their intentions, belted out "Boobs Alot," "Group Grope," and "Dirty Old Man." Their name itself raised the eyebrows of the sexually inhibited. Reveling in the same theme, the Doors hit the charts with "Love Me Two Times," "Hello I Love You," "Love Her Madly," and their biggest hit, "Light My Fire." Morrison, who characterized himself as an "erotic politician," faced legal charges when he supposedly exposed himself on stage in Florida. The outspoken Grace Slick, who delivered such songs as "Somebody to Love," confessed, "it doesn't matter what the lyrics say, or who sings them. They're all the same. They say, 'Be free—free in love, free in sex.' " "The stage is our bed and the audience is our broad," added Marty Balin of the Airplane. "We're not entertaining, we're making love."

Many psychedelic bands renounced the competitive, corporate structure of American society in general and of the recording industry in particular. Jerry Garcia of the Grateful Dead resented "being just another face in a corporate personality. There isn't even a Warner 'brother' to talk to. The music business and the Grateful Dead are in two different orbits, two different universes." The Dead, added Stephen Stills of Buffalo Springfield and later of Crosby, Stills and Nash, "were the first people, I don't know whether it was acid or what, to come to that realization where they really didn't give a shit whether they made it or not." "The record companies sell rock and roll records like they sell refrigerators," complained Paul Kantner of the Jefferson Airplane. "They don't care about the people who make rock or what they're all about as human beings any more than they care about the people who make refrigerators." Max Weiss, owner of Fantasy Records in the Bay area, characterized the San Francisco bands as "good but a little crazy. They are absolutely non-commercial."

Opposed to a faceless commercialism, bands such as the Grateful Dead and the Airplane began to stage free concerts. "We don't do what the system says—make single hits, take big gigs, do the success number," Dead manager Rock Scully told an interviewer. "The summer of '67, when all the other groups were making it, we were playing free in the park, man, trying to cool the Haight-Ashbury." "The first thing that really hit me hard was the Grateful Dead were playing a lot of gigs for nothing," Eric Clapton, a former Yardbirds guitarist, remembered of his first visit to San Francisco. "That very much moved me. I've never heard of anyone doing that before. That really is one of the finest steps that anyone has taken in music yet, aside from musical strides. I guess that sums it up, what I think about San Francisco, what the Grateful Dead are doing. There is this incredible thing that the musical people seem to have toward their audience: they want to give."

The emphasis upon sharing determined the role of band members. David Getz, drummer for Big Brother and the Holding Company, remembered that "the whole philosophy of the psychedelic scene was to consciously avoid making anyone the star, focusing more on the interaction between the audience and the band, and trying to create something together. That's how the energy happened."

Most San Francisco bands felt a cameraderie with one another. "All of the bands were very close," remembered Mickey Hart of the Grateful Dead. "The Quicksilver and the Grateful Dead and Big Brother and the Airplane. We were like sister bands. We'd be over at each other's houses, see each other all day long, party at night. There were no hassles about who was going to open the show or close the show. It seemed like when we played with one of our sister bands, our compadres, we always played a little better for each other."

The cooperative feeling within bands sometimes extended to their own living arrangements. The members of the Grateful Dead lived communally in the Haight District at 710 Ashbury Street. Quicksilver Messenger Service roomed together in a house near the Dead headquarters. For a time, the Jefferson Airplane lived together in the Haight at 2400 Fulton Street.

Many acid rockers discovered the cooperative alternative to a competitive society through LSD. "Along came LSD and that was the end of that whole world. The whole world just went kablooey," related Jerry Garcia. "It changed everything, you know, it was just—ah, first of all, for me personally, it freed me, you know, the effect was that it freed me because I suddenly realized that my little attempt at having a straight life and doing that was really a fiction and just wasn't going to work out."

Rather than an isolated individual in a competitive context, Garcia realized his relationship with the universe through acid. "To get really high is to forget yourself," he asserted. "And to forget yourself is to see everything else. And to see everything else is to become an understanding molecule in evolution, a conscious tool in the universe."

As the avenue to understanding a new social order, mind-expanding drugs became the centerpiece of acid rock. They inspired the names of many West Coast bands, including the Loading Zone; Morning Glory; the Weeds; the Seeds; and the Doors, the last name taken from a phrase of poet William Blake quoted by Aldous Huxley in a book about a mescaline experience, *The Doors of Perception*.

Many San Francisco bands extolled psychedelic drugs in their songs. The Jefferson Airplane delivered the Haight-Ashbury anthem, "White Rabbitt": "One pill makes you larger and one pill makes you small, and the ones that mother gives you don't do anything at all. Go ask Alice when she's ten feet tall," sang Grace Slick while the Airplane churned out a sinister, electric drone in the background. She continued: "When the men on the chessboard get up and tell you where to go. You just had some kind of mushroom and your mind is moving low. Go ask Alice, I think she'll know." Then Slick launched into her piercing vibrato: "When logic and proportion have fallen softly dead, and the white knight's talking backwards and the red queen's lost her head, remember what the door mouse said, FEED YOUR HEAD, FEED YOUR HEAD." By 1969, a distraught Art Linkletter, whose daughter had overdosed on LSD, charged that at least half of all rock songs were "concerned with secret messages to teenagers to drop out, turn on, and groove with chemicals." A year later, Vice-President Spiro Agnew complained that much of "rock music glorified drug use."

Drugs defined the function of some psychedelic bands. According to Jerry Garcia, "The Grateful Dead is not for cranking out rock and roll, it's not for going out and doing concerts or any of that stuff, I think it's to get high."

Light shows at dances in the Haight simulated the LSD experience. The projection of light through liquid pigments in motion to create ever-changing expressionistic light shows had been discovered in 1952 by San Francisco State professor Seymour Locks as he prepared for a national conference of art educators. Through the efforts of Beatnik art student Elias Romero, who witnessed some of Locks's first shows, hipsters such as Bill Ham, Anthony Martin, and Ben Van Meter learned the craft and adapted it to the hippie subculture. By 1966, dances in the Haight normally held in Chet Helm's Avalon Ballroom or the Fillmore Theater rented by ex-Mime Troupe manager Bill Graham featured light shows of melting colors, which mimicked an LSD experience.

The poster art advertising the gatherings consisted of the same swirling designs. Based upon the style of early twentieth-century artist Alfred Roller, the posters featured thick, distorted letters that melted together against a bright, solid-color background. They were crafted by self-taught Haight artists such as Wes Wilson, Stan Mouse (a.k.a. Miller), Rick Griffin, Alton Kelley, Victor Moscoso, and Greg Irons.

The dance halls which the psychedelic posters advertised began to appear in other parts of the country. Philadelphia had the Electric Factory, Boston its Tea Party, the Kinetic Playground, where Chicago hippies flocked, and the Grand Ballroom in Detroit. In New York, baby boomers who had their minds expanded went to the Electric Circus and the Fillmore East, which Bill Graham had designed as an East Coast alternative to the San Francisco original.

The acid-inspired dance music reached youths throughout the country through airplay on FM radio. Not produced for the Top 40 play list of AM radio, the meandering psychedelic sounds first aired on the freewheeling San Francisco station KMPX on the programs of such disc jockeys as Larry Miller and Tom Donahue. "Somewhere in the dim misty days of yore, some radio station statistician decided that regardless of chronological age, the average mental age of the audience was 12 1/2, and Top 40 AM radio aimed its message directly at the lowest common denominator," sniped Donahue. "The disc jockeys have become robots performing their inanities at the direction of programmers who had succeeded in totally squeezing blips and bleeps and happy, oh yes, always happy sounding cretins who are poured from a bottle every three hours." To eradicate the "rotting corpse stinking up the airwaves," the San Francisco jockey used FM radio to air songs that lasted more than three minutes; began to spin entire albums; discontinued the breakneak delivery of the Top 40 disc jockeys; and played songs by the new groups of the Bay area. When confronted by an unhappy owner and a strike at KMPX, Donahue and his staff took their hip format to KSAN which poster artist Alton Kelley described as a "community drum."

By 1967, acid rock had scaled the charts. The Jefferson Airplane, the first Haight band signed by a major label, in June 1967 hit number 3 with *Surrealistic Pillow*, an album that involved Jerry Garcia as musical advisor and showcased vocalist Grace Slick, who had replaced original singer Signe Anderson. The same year, the Grateful Dead cracked the charts with its self-named debut LP. By the next year, Quicksilver Messenger Service too made the chart with its first album. The Doors, probably the best-selling West Coast band, in early 1967 neared the top of the charts with its debut and followed with a string of hits that included "People Are Strange," "Love Me Two Times," "Hello I Love You," and "Touch Me."

Other bands jumped on the psychedelic bandwagon. In 1967, the lovable, mop-topped Beatles released two albums, *Magical Mystery Tour*, a concept album and movie modeled after Ken Kesey's travels in his psychedelic bus, and *Sgt. Pepper's Lonely Hearts Club Band*, which included the cryptic "Lucy in the Sky with Diamonds," LSD for short. Later that year, the bubbly Paul McCartney admitted that he had taken LSD. The Beatles began to study transcendental meditation with Maharishi Mahesh Yogi, and George and Pattie Harrison, wearing heart-shaped granny glasses and paisley frocks, took a ceremonial tour of the Haight district. In 1967, the Rolling Stones released *Their Satanic Majesties' Request,* a psychedelic album featuring a three-dimensional cover, and Mick Jagger joined the Beatles in transcendental meditation. Eric Burdon of the Animals, after abandoning the blues for psychedelia, told *Melody Maker*, "It wasn't me singing. It was someone trying to be an American Negro. I look back and see how stupid I was." Adorned in vibrantly colored shirts and love beads, Burdon sang such odes to hippiedom as "San Franciscan Nights" and "Monterey." Even Dick Clark changed with the times and masterminded a movie, *The Love Children,* which starred a young Jack Nicholson and featured music by such psychedelic bands as the Seeds and the Strawberry Alarm Clock.

THE DECLINE AND FALL OF HIPPIEDOM

Counter-culture rock and hippiedom itself had a short-lived heyday, falling victim to its own drug-based logic. Many hippies, initially using drugs to increase awareness and open alternative realities, became wasted addicts. As some youths repeatedly tried to delve deeper and deeper into their own consciousness with LSD, they became isolated and detached from their own bodies. In the street vernacular, these hippies "burned out." Others became hooked on drugs that seemed to promise freedom. By 1967, many Haight residents had become methedrine or "speed" addicts who, according to Dr. Ellis D. ("LSD") Sox, the San Francisco public health director, cost the city $35,000 a month for treatment. "You had a lot of people talking to posts," remembered Travis Rivers, then owner of the Print Mint, which sold psychedelic posters in the Haight. "They were ripping one another off, because it costs a lot of money once you get strung out on speed."

Some of the major figures in the Haight drug culture fell prey to the guns of gangland. On August 3, 1967, John Kent Carter, a dealer known as "Shob," was found murdered, his arms hacked off at the elbows. Three days later, William "Superspade" Thomas ended in a sleeping bag with a bullet through his head at the bottom of a cliff in Marin County.

The saga of Skip Spence provides a moving testimony to the perils of drug experimentation. Alexander ("Skip") Spence was the original drummer for the Jefferson Airplane, composing "Blues from an Airplane." When he quit the Airplane to form the pathbreaking psychedelic band Moby Grape, he began to overindulge in psychedelics. Confided Skip: "Acid was like heaven, a moment of God, inspiring, tragic. I must have taken it a hundred times, a thousand times." One day Spence reached too high. He woke up in a hospital: "An overdose where I died and was brought back to life." Today the scraggly, unwashed ex–rock star lives in San Jose, where he spends his seven-dollar-a-day allowance from the state. At night, when he does not confine himself to the psychiatric ward of the San Jose hospital, Spence stays alone in a dingy, rundown room in Maas Hotel. Sometimes he speaks to Joan of Arc. Once in a while, he is visited by Clark Kent, "civilized, decent and a genius." And on a few thick, intense, San Jose summer nights, Spence meets his "master," who materializes with startling revelations. Says Spence, delivering his own autobiography, "I'm a derelict. I'm a world savior. I am drugs. I am rock and roll."

A deterministic psychedelic world view, unlocked by mind-expanding drugs, made hippiedom susceptible to cooptation. Most hippies such as Jerry Garcia considered themselves "conscious tools of the universe" who were directed by "cosmic forces" that bound disparate individuals and events into a logical pattern. They believed in an almost preordained "flow" that would sweep everyone into a psychedelic community.

Businessmen, more interested in individual gain than in universal cooperation, began to exploit the counter-culture. During the first months of 1967, more than twenty shops opened their doors in the Haight Ashbury District to accommodate the tourist traffic. The Pall Mall Lounge began to market "Love Burgers," and one store began to sell hippie costumes to weekenders—scraggly wigs for $85 and beards for $125. Even the Greyhound Bus Company started a "Hippie Hop" in San Francisco, advertised as "the only foreign tour within the continental limits of the United States." "Haight Street is no longer fun," complained Tsvi Strauch, an original hippie proprietor in the Haight. "Many of us are getting away from it because of all the plastic hippies and tourists that are fouling up the whole scene. They've made a mess of it."

On October 4, 1967, Jay Thelin closed the Psychedelic Shop, a hub of the Bay area counter-culture, and posted a sign on the front door: "Be Free—Nebraska Needs You More." Two days later, a procession of original hippies in the Haight district loaded a coffin full of beads, peace signs, flowers, and other symbols of their lifestyle and publicly burned it, announcing the "death of hippie, loyal son of media." The same day, the Fugs coordinated a similar procession in the East Village, memorializing the hippie culture.

Even acid rock, the music of the counter-culture, became part of the recording industry. Though complaining about the corporate structure of the music industry, the psychedelic rockers readily signed contracts with the major record labels who tried to sell the psychedelic sound. "We found we couldn't sell the Grateful Dead's records in a traditional manner," said Joe Smith, at the time president of Warner-Reprise. "You couldn't take your ad in *Billboard* and sell a record that way. . . . The packaging was important. The cult was important. Free concerts where you handed out fruits and nuts were important" as well as exposure on the underground club circuit, the campuses, and FM radio. Gil Frieson, then vice-president of A & M Records, assembled a Standard American Promotional Package—"billboards on Sunset Strip and Broadway, full-page advertising in the underground press, the trades, and various other outlets; radio spots and a promotional tour with all expenses paid by the label." "It's funny, the group out there on the stage preaching a revolutionary message, but to get the message to the people, you gotta do it in the establishment way," complained Bill Siddons, manager of the Doors.

Smaller businessmen also cashed in on acid rock. In 1965 Wolfgang Wolodia Grajanka, a businesslike, politically minded, thirty-five-year-old emigre who had changed his name to Bill Graham, decided to organize the psychedelic groundswell in San Francisco into a business. After organizing two benefit concerts as the manager of the San Francisco Mime Troupe, Graham decided to concentrate his efforts on the concert scene, coordinating the Trips Festival for Ken Kesey and his Merry Pranksters. By March 1966, Graham had secured a three-year lease on the Fillmore which, as with the Avalon Ballroom, became a popular dance hall in the Haight. He also began to manage the Fillmore house band, the Jefferson Airplane. Although never "a great fan of high volume rock and roll, and a lot of it was nonsensical to me," Graham took pride in his organizational abilities. "I was always, 'Well, I took your ticket and you came here expecting something, and I want to have that,' he recalled. "I want the food to be hot and the drinks to be cold." "Bill Graham was the star of the 60s," asserted Marty Balin of the Airplane. "In the beginning there was great talent, but there were no sound systems. No microphones. Graham came along and changed it. He made the performers a stage. He was what Alan Freed was to the 50s." By the end of the decade, Graham's organizational abilities had built a lucrative business including concert operations, a national talent-booking agency that represented the Grateful Dead and the Jefferson Airplane, among others, and two record labels—San Francisco and Fillmore.

By late 1967, acid rock and the counter-culture it exemplified had been drawn into the competitive society it attacked. The psychedelic baby boomers, armed with flowers and well-meaning platitudes, would soon confront the M-1 rifles of National Guardsmen, who would turn the brightly colored hopes of hippiedom into a dark nightmare of war-torn campuses.

9

Fire From the Streets

"Soul is sass, man."

Claude Brown

Four o'clock on a muggy, steamy Sunday morning in Detroit, July 22, 1967. A crowd of young blacks clustered around a pack of police squad cars on Twelfth Street, the heart of the city's West Side ghetto. As each of the blacks pressed against sweaty backs and arms to get a better view of the action, blue-shirted, white-faced policemen herded seventy-four captives into paddy wagons. The arrested blacks had been accused of drinking after-hours booze at the United Community League for Civic Action, which also offered sermons on the spreading gospel of Black Power. After finishing their job, the policemen jumped into the squad cars, revved the engines, and started to move out of the area. Someone in the crowd flung a full wine bottle through the air, which shattered the windshield of Tenth Precinct Sergeant Arthur Howison's Ford. Howison slammed on the brakes and leapt into the street. He was pelted first by a few stones, then by a barrage of rocks and bottles. The police officer ducked back into the car and sped off, followed by the angry mob.

The crowd multiplied as it made its way down Twelfth Street until it had grown to 3,000 agitated men, women, and youths. Someone grabbed a brick from the pavement and hurled it through the window of a grocery store. People swarmed toward the jagged open-

169

ing. They poked out the rest of the glass in the window frame with sticks, jumped into the store, and began gathering armloads of meat, bread, and canned goods. One man struggled with an entire side of beef. "I've always wanted to be a butcher," he told an onlooker.

Around daybreak, some teens overturned a line of garbage cans and set the trash on fire. Another man threw a homemade firebomb into a shoe store that already had been sacked. Summer breezes fanned the flames, which spread to adjoining buildings. Within a few hours, columns of fire engulfed East Detroit and spread across Woodward Avenue into the west part of the city. Williams's Drug Store and Lou's Men's Wear, along with hundreds of other buildings, disappeared in flames. "It looks like 1945 in Berlin," reported a dejected Mayor Jerome Cavanaugh.

Rioting and looting continued for the next four days. Enraged blacks ravaged thousands of stores, searching for food, clothing, furniture, and liquor. They only spared storefronts that had been marked "Soul Brother" or "Afro All the Way." Fires set by the rioters gutted fourteen square miles of Detroit, causing an estimated $500 million in damages. "Man, this is crazy," one older black told *Newsweek*. "We're burnin' our own houses up. Where these poor people going to live now?" "This is madness," echoed another homeowner. "Why do they have to burn our houses? That's not right. Goddamn. And there's not a house burning in Grosse Point [a white, middle-class suburb of Detroit]. This has got to stop." But other blacks in the Motor City, unemployed and confined to dilapidated slums, were impatient for the reforms promised by the Civil Rights Act of 1964 and predicted more trouble. Said one twenty-two-year-old youth: "We're tired of being second-class. We've been asking too long. Now it's time to take. This thing ain't over. It's just beginning."

The authorities responded to the rioting with armed force. During the first day of troubles, Mayor Cavanaugh unleashed his 4,000-man police force on the ghetto. When police proved inadequate, Michigan Governor George Romney mobilized 7,300 state troopers and National Guardsmen armed with tear gas, grenade launchers, M-1 rifles, submachine guns, M-48 tanks, and Huey helicopters. "I'm gonna shoot anything that moves and is black," vowed one young Guardsman. The next day, President Lyndon Johnson airlifted Task Force Detroit, a 4,700-man paratrooper unit commanded by Lt. General John L. Throckmorton, who had served as a deputy to General William Westmoreland in Vietnam. All told, an army of 16,000 government men marched into Detroit to quell the tumult. The city had become an armed camp divided into war zones, cordoned off by barbed wire, and patrolled by helmeted troops in their khakis.

After the fires had been stamped out and the smoke had cleared, the authorities counted 42 dead, 2,250 injured, and 5,557 arrests. Most of the casualties were black men. On national television, President Johnson pleaded that the "violence must be stopped—quickly, finally and permanently. There are no victors in the aftermath of violence. . . . We have endured a week such as no nation should live through: a time of violence and tragedy."

The flames of Detroit spread to other areas. Rioting occurred in other Michigan cities such as Pontiac, Saginaw, Flint, Grand Rapids, Albion, and Kalamazoo. Incited by Black Power activists such as H. Rap Brown, who threatened, "If America don't come around, we're going to burn America down," trouble broke out in urban areas across the nation. During the last days of July, looters sacked stores in the black neighborhoods of Phoenix, Hartford, Passaic, Poughkeepsie, and South Bend. The next month, four nights of violence ripped Milwaukee, leaving four dead and over a hundred injured. Blacks in nearby Chicago took to the streets, and riots scarred Providence and Wichita. By the end of August, race riots had torn apart more than seventy cities and had left a trail of eighty-six dead, thousands injured, and blocks of charred rubble. One government report estimated that 41 percent of the cities with populations of more than 100,000 had experienced racial violence. The press called it the "Long Hot Summer."

On April 4, 1968, the murder of black leader Dr. Martin Luther King, Jr., triggered another wave of violence. "When White America killed Dr. King," sneered black militant Stokely Carmichael, "she declared war on us. . . . We have to retaliate for the deaths of our leaders. The executions of those deaths are going to be in the streets." Carmichael proved to be prophetic. A few hours after the King assassination, Washington, D.C., burst into flames. As described by *Newsweek,* the more than 700 fires in the national capital, the worst conflagration in the city since the British burned it during the War of 1812, "made Washington look like the besieged capital of a banana republic, with helmeted combat troops, bayoneted rifles at the ready guarding the White House, and a light machine-gun post defending the steps of the Capitol." President Lyndon Johnson activated more than 15,000 troops—more than twice the size of the U.S. garrison that defended Khe Sanh in Vietnam—to quiet the disorders. In three days of rioting, the death toll reached ten and property damage exceeded $13.3 million.

Other black urban areas exploded upon receiving news of the King assassination. In Kansas City, six rioters died and sixty-five were injured. Chicago's riot, quelled by 5,000 federal troops and 6,700 National Guardsmen, left eleven dead, ninety-one injured, and miles of burned-out buildings. By the end of the week, 168 cities had erupted into violence; 5,117 fires had been started; about 2,000 shops had been ransacked; $40 million worth of property had been destroyed; and forty-six people, mostly black, had died. It took almost 73,000 Army and National Guard troops to quell the disturbances. In 1967 and 1968, many American blacks had dramatically reasserted their collective identity, an identity born in slavery and shaped by a century of discrimination. They called the reclaimed identity *soul*.

SOUL MUSIC

Soul music reflected the militant search for a black identity. The term *soul* had been used by American blacks during the fifties to suggest a black identity. In a vague sense, it defined the essence of being black in America. Be-bop musicians had soul: In 1957, horn-man Lou Donaldson recorded *Swing and Soul;* the next year saxophone great John Coltrane released *Soultrane;* trombonist Bennie Green cut *Soul Stirring* (1958) and *Hornful of Soul* (1959); trumpeter Blue Mitchell played *Blue Soul* (1959); and saxophonist Johnny Griffin led a *Big Soul-Band* (1960). When bop gave way to hard bop during the early sixties, Eldridge Cleaver noted in *Soul on Ice* that many referred to the sound as "soul music."

Around 1965, as the black ghettos of Watts and Harlem erupted in violence, many blacks started to equate soul with the struggle to reassert black dignity in the face of continued discrimination. "Soul is sass, man," wrote Claude Brown, author of *Manchild in the Promised Land.* "Soul is arrogance. Soul is walkin' down the street in a way that says, 'This is me, muhfuh'. . . . Soul is that uninhibited, no, *extremely* uninhibited self-expression that goes into practically every Negro endeavor. That's soul. And there's a swagger in it, man." Rock critic Arnold Shaw came to the same conclusion in *The World of Soul:* "Soul is black, not blue, sass, anger and rage. It is not just feeling but conviction. Not just intensity but involvement. A force as well as a style, an accolade as well as identification. It is an expressive explosiveness, ignited by a people's discovery of self-pride, power and potential for growth." Emphasizing the value of the black heritage, blacks began to regard collard greens, black-eyed peas, and sweet potato pie as soul food. Fellow blacks became soul brothers and soul sisters, and rhythm and blues became soul music.

Some of the "soul" performers had been involved in R & B long before it underwent a name change. James Brown, "Soul Brother Number One," released his first record, "Please, Please, Please," with his Famous Flames in 1956. Two years later, he scaled the R & B charts with "Try Me," and in 1960 he reworked the Five Royales' "Think" for a hit.

By 1963, when he recorded the now legendary album *Live at the Apollo,* Brown had perfected a stunning stage act complete with a backup band and vocal group known as the James Brown Revue. In a typical performance, the singer leapt on stage wearing skintight black pants, a half-unbuttoned, dark-blue satin shirt, and a purple cape. Without missing a beat, his head jerking to the music,

James Brown

he suddenly jumped into the air, landed in a perfect split, and bounced back up to his feet. Before the audience recovered, Brown was snaking across the floor or twirling in midair.

Ray Charles, considered to be the "Genius of Soul" in the mid-sixties, initially gained fame in R & B. Born Ray Charles Robinson in 1930, Charles traveled from his hometown of Albany, Georgia, to Seattle in 1947 to play cocktail-swing piano in the Nat King Cole style at such venues as the Elks Club, the Rocking Chair, and the Black and Tan. In 1949, on Swingtime Records, he cut his first disc, "Confessing the Blues," and two years later followed with the R & B hit "Baby, Let Me Hold Your Hand." In the next few years he toured with blues growler Lowell Fulson, R & B singer Ruth Brown, black comic Moms Mabley, and Eddie "Guitar Slim" Jones. In 1952 Atlantic Records, a leading company in the R & B field, bought Ray's contract from Swingtime for $2,000. During late 1953 in New Orleans, remembered Jerry Wexler, then vice-president of Atlantic Records, and Atlantic president Ahmet Ertegun "ran into Ray at Cosimo's famous small studio, and Ray asked us to please do a session with him. . . . This was the landmark session because it had Ray Charles originals, Ray Charles arrangements, a Ray Charles band." The session produced the single "Don't You Know." The singer-pianist quickly followed with "I've Got a Woman," one of his most notable hits. During the rest of the fifties, he scored repeatedly with "Blackjack," "Come Back," "Fool for You," "Greenbacks," and "This Girl of Mine" in 1955; "Drown in My Own Tears," "Hallelujah, I Love Her So," "Lonely Avenue," and "Mary Ann" the next year; and "Right Time" and "What'd I Say" in 1959. By the turn of the decade, Ray Charles had firmly established himself as a major figure in R & B.

Wilson Pickett, although not as prominent in the fifties as Ray Charles, had roots in early R & B. One day in 1959, as Pickett lounged on his porch strumming a guitar and singing, Willie Scorefield, a member of the R & B group the Falcons, happened to pass by. According to Pickett, Scorefield walked up to him and said, " 'Man, you got a good voice,' and invited me to come to the next rehearsal. That's when I found I could sing rhythm and blues." In the next few months, Pickett wrote and recorded with the Falcons the hits "I Found a Love" and "You're So Fine."

Otis Redding, recognized as "The King of Soul" by some, initially drew his inspiration from Little Richard. In an unlikely success story, which took place in 1962, Redding drove some friends, Johnny Jenkins and the Pinetoppers, to the Stax studio in Memphis for a recording session. As Redding told it, "They had 30 minutes left in the studio and I asked if I could do a song." "He did one of those heh, heh baby things," recalled Stax president Jim Stewart. "It was just like Little Richard. I told them the world didn't need another Little Richard. Then someone suggested he do a slow one. He did 'These Arms of Mine.' " Impressed by the song, Stewart signed Redding and released it. In 1964, Redding cut *Pain in My Heart,* a mixture of Little Richard screamers and Sam Cooke–type ballads.

Most soul artists, like R & B performers in the fifties, started their careers in the church. Wilson Pickett had sung in small-town gospel groups before he joined the Falcons and described his own style as "a gospel melody, not nothing pretty, a funky groove with lines that mean something." Otis Redding, the son of a minister, had sung in a church choir as a young boy. "Otis and I were very close," remembered Katie Webster who played piano for Redding. "It was a spiritual thing. Both our fathers were ministers, and we would read the Bible together." As youngsters, both Sam Moore and Dave Prater (later teaming up as Sam and Dave), had joined Baptist choirs and had toured with gospel groups in their teens.

James Brown had played organ and drums during the forties for various gospel outfits. "I sang gospel in prison," recalled the singer. "Once I got out I joined Sarah Byrd's group, the Gospel Starlighters, and it was here I got acquainted with her brother Bobby" who became a Famous Flame when Brown switched to secular music in 1954.

Ray Charles's music reflected his religious upbringing. He changed the Pilgrim Travelers' "I've Got a New Home" to "Lonely Avenue," shortened "Nobody But You, Lord" to "Nobody But You," and exulted in gospel screams in "Hallelujah, I Love Her So." Remarked Eric Burdon of the Animals, Ray "knows which church songs to take to his music and he changes the words slightly and makes hits out of them. By changing the words, I mean taking out the words 'God,' 'Christ' and 'Lord' and putting in their place 'woman' 'honey' and 'child.' " Added bluesman Big Bill Broonzy about Ray Charles, "He's cryin', sanctified. He's mixing the blues with the spirituals. He should be singing in a church."

Aretha Franklin, the chunky, five-foot-five-inch dynamo dubbed "Lady Soul," had a direct connection to the church. Her father, the Reverend Clarence L. Franklin, served as the pastor of Detroit's 4,500-member New Bethel Baptist Church and recorded more than seventy albums of fiery, blues-drenched sermons. Two white-uniformed nurses commonly stood guard at the aisles of New Bethel Baptist to aid parishioners who were overcome by the emotionally draining message of the minister. As a youth, Aretha came into contact with such gospel greats as James Cleveland and Mahalia Jackson, and at a funeral of an aunt she witnessed Clara Ward belt out a powerful rendition of "Peace in the Valley." At that moment, the minister's daughter later recollected, "I wanted to become a singer." Aretha began to learn gospel from James Cleveland: "He

Photo from Atlantic Records album

Aretha Franklin

showed me some real nice chords and I liked his deep, deep sound. There's a whole lot of earthiness in the way he sings, and what he was feelin', I was feelin', but I just didn't know how to put it across. The more I watched him, the more I got out of it." Soon Aretha joined a traveling gospel troupe organized by her father, and she premiered in it until signing with Columbia Records. The soul of Aretha Franklin had matured in the church.

Rhythm and blues, nurtured in church choirs, became known as soul music in the mid-sixties as many black Americans discovered a sense of self-esteem. In July 1965, station WOL in Washington, D.C., attracting primarily black listeners, began to call itself "soul radio," and local disc jockey Fred Correy labeled himself "Soulfinger." *Soul* magazine commenced publication. In 1965 and 1966, Otis Redding perfected his style with *Soul Album, Dictionary of Soul,* and *Otis Blue (Otis Redding Sings Soul),* the last including the hit "Respect."

After a series of hits during the early and mid-1960s, related Brown, "I got the name 'Soul Brother Number One.' The word 'soul' by this time meant a lot of things—in music and out. It was about the roots of black music, and it was a kind of pride thing, too, being proud of yourself and your people. Soul music and the civil rights movement went hand in hand, sort of grew up together."

Atlantic Records recorded most of the soul artists who became popular in the inner cities of America. In 1965, Wilson Pickett left the Double LL label and moved to Atlantic. That year he cut "In the Midnight Hour" in Memphis. Wicked Pickett, as he became known, followed it with "634-5789," "Funky Broadway," "Land of a Thousand Dances," and "Mustang Sally." Percy Sledge, the Alabama farm boy who had chopped cotton as a youth, joined the Atlantic stable and in 1966 topped the R & B charts with "When a Man Loves a Woman." Sam and Dave, the "Double Dynamite" soul duo from Miami, were signed by Atlantic's Jerry Wexler. In 1965, they hit with "You Don't Know Like I Know." The next year they scored with "Said I Wasn't Going to Tell Nobody," "You Got Me Hummin'," "When Something Is Wrong," and their trademark, "Hold On, I'm Coming." Atlantic also distributed Stax-Volt artists, who included Otis Redding.

During 1965 and 1966, Atlantic soul acts primarily won acceptance from African-Americans. Otis Redding, for example, broke attendance records at shows in Harlem and Watts and in 1966 grossed $250,000 on a month-long rhythm and blues tour. Percy Sledge's "When A Man Loves a Woman" stood on top of the R & B charts. James Brown bought a bright red Sting Ray, a fleet of Cadillacs, and a wardrobe of 150 suits and 80 pairs of shoes from the money he had amassed from an almost exclusively black audience. In the mid-sixties, while white rock-and-rollers listened to the Beatles, acid rock, or white covers of R & B songs, blacks took pride in a gritty soul sound performed by blacks. "It's SOUL, man,

SOUL," exclaimed black disc jockey Magnificent Montague in *Billboard*. "Now what is soul? It's the last to be hired, the first to be fired, brown all year-round, sit-in-the-back-of-the-bus feeling. You've got to live with us or you don't have it. The Black Brothers are the mainstay of our pop music today. Artists like John Lee Hooker, Otis Redding and others are heavy soul—one thing our English friends can't imitate."

BLACK SOUL IN WHITE AMERICA

The inner-city explosions during the late 1960s made many Americans, especially those raised during the civil rights era, more aware and more interested in black culture. Though causing a white backlash in some quarters, for many the 1967 riots in Detroit led to a better understanding of black Americans. Discrimination "hurts them real bad. I'd probably be rioting right with them," a Texas salesman told *Time* magazine. "It degrades [the black man] which no one likes. Therefore it is natural [for them] to fight back," echoed a California truck driver. Mrs. Margaret Lamb, a widow from Owensboro, Kentucky, told *Time:* "It makes you wonder that they do as good as they do the way people treat them sometimes. You see things that make you wonder why they put up with it."

Besides realizing the plight of black America, many whites even adopted elements of black culture. Some began to look for soul food restaurants. Students, protesting for their own causes, showed support for militant Black Power groups such as the Black Panthers. Black studies classes in history, psychology, English, and anthropology sprouted up on many campuses. And young rockers started to buy soul records. The year "1967 saw the greatest emergence of the blues in recent pop history. It was the year in which rhythm and blues became the music of the charts and the year in which 'soul' became the popular music of America," exclaimed Jon Landau, rock writer and later manager of Bruce Springsteen.

Black soul crossed over to white America with Aretha Franklin. Aretha had signed with John Hammond of Columbia in 1960. Mitch Miller, the Columbia executive who had assailed rock in the fifties, gave her voice lessons, hooked her up with Barbara Streisand's arranger, Bob Mersey, and assigned her such sappy material as the show tune "If Ever I Would Leave You" and Al Jolson's "Rock-A-Bye My Baby with a Dixie Melody." By 1966 a dissatisfied Aretha had found only moderate success and was in debt to Columbia.

Late in 1966, when her contract with Columbia expired, Jerry Wexler of Atlantic signed the singer. As Wexler told it, "One day, I happened to be in Muscle Shoals doing a Wilson Pickett session, and I got a call from [a friend] in Philadelphia. All she said was

'Call this number, *now!*' It was Aretha. I had never spoken to her, but I called her and that was it."

Within a few months, Aretha recorded for Atlantic *I Never Loved a Man the Way That I Love You,* which included the single "Respect." "Respect," an R & B hit for Otis Redding two years earlier, took on an added importance in 1967. The song, belted out by the Detroit native Aretha Franklin, hit the streets as the ghetto of the Motor City exploded into flames. To whites it seemed to epitomize the renewed self-pride that blacks had discovered. The song sold more than 1 million copies in ten months and brought black soul to white America.

In 1967, Aretha again hit the charts with "Dr. Feelgood," "A Natural Woman," "Baby, I Love You," and "Chain of Fools." She won the Best Female Vocalist of the Year Award. Early the next year, Detroit Mayor Jerome Cavanaugh declared Aretha Franklin Day, and Aretha solidified her reputation among whites as the soul spokeswoman, with her rendition of "Think," which ended with the singer crying, "Oh, Freedom, Freedom, Freedom, ya, Freeeeeedom."

Other soul singers began to sell amid the rioting. In 1967, Wilson Pickett's *Greatest Hits,* which included "In the Midnight Hour," started to sell among rockers. Sam and Dave scored a crossover success with *Soul Men,* and *Billboard* published the first of an annual supplement, *The World of Soul.* Otis Redding, who had died in December 1967, when his twin-engine Beechcraft plane plunged into an icy lake outside Madison, Wisconsin, won posthumous accolades for the chart-topping "Dock of the Bay." The King of Soul, who had received little attention from the white media during his lifetime, won a Grammy award for Best Male Vocalist of 1968. Percy Sledge's "When a Man Loves a Woman" began to be played on rock radio and Atlantic Records began to accumulate a fortune. In July 1967, *Time* calculated that "Manhattan-based Atlantic, with such singers as Aretha, Wilson Pickett and Sam and Dave, can now sell more records in a week (1,300,000) than it did in six months in 1950." Remarked Jerry Wexler in 1968: "The young white audience now digs soul the way the black does." Soul had become the music of white America.

10

Militant Blues On Campus

"The pop scene has become a roaring, pulsating paradox of sound — the white man singing the black blues."

Time magazine

In early May 1968, at 2:30 A.M., 1,000 New York City policemen approached the Morningside Heights campus of Columbia University. They moved onto the campus in police vans and squad cars, sealed off the entrances to the university, and, on orders from Commissioner Howard Leary, marched toward five buildings that had been occupied by student rebels to protest the university's affiliation with the Institute for Defense Analysis. As they began to dislodge student militants, the police encountered resistance. At Fayerweather Hall, they clubbed and kicked angry students and bystanding newsmen such as columnist Walter Winchell. By mid-morning, the police had dispersed the students from the buildings, arresting 698 and injuring 120. To noted anthropologist Margaret Mead, who had taught at Columbia for forty-eight years, the police action signaled "the end of an epoch."

The protests at Columbia sparked trouble at other colleges and universities. More than 500 students at Princeton demonstrated in support of students at Columbia. At Stony Brook, fifty student mili-

The Daily of the University of Washington

Student protest on campus

tants staged a seventeen-hour sit-in to express their sympathy. More than 200 Temple University students picketed university buildings in the wake of the Columbia protests. By the middle of June, as the inner cities burst into violence, estimated a National Students Association report, almost 40,000 students engaged in 221 major demonstrations at 101 colleges and universities.

The student protest intensified in August at the National Democratic Convention in Chicago. To protest the war in Vietnam, 10,000 young reformers traveled to the Windy City for the opening

Vietnam protest demonstration

of the convention on August 26. They were organized by David Dellinger of the National Mobilization Committee to End the War in Vietnam, Tom Hayden and Rennie Davis, founders of the Students for a Democratic Society (SDS), and Jerry Rubin of the Youth International Party (Yippie) which, according to its leader, "merged New Left politics with a psychedelic lifestyle. Our lifestyle — acid, long hair, freaky clothes, pot, rock music, sex — is the Revolution. Our very existence mocks America. The old order is dying. The Democratic Party is dying. While it dies, we will celebrate the Festival of Life. Come to Chicago! We are the politics of the future."

As the student militants flooded into Chicago armed with backpacks and flowers, Chicago Mayor Richard Daley readied the city for battle. The mayor, who had recommended that looters be maimed and arsonists be killed the previous year during a race riot, heavily barricaded the Amphitheatre, the site of the convention. He activated 6,000 National Guardmen, requested and received 6,000 federal troops armed with bazookas, barbed wire, and tanks, and placed 12,000 Chicago policemen on twelve-hour shifts. After encountering stiff resistance from the organized students, Daley planned a strategy of confrontation which, according to a subsequent report, created a "police riot." When the Democrats left on August 29, Daley's police force had injured 198 and arrested 641 protesters. The trial of eight protest leaders, labeled by *Rolling Stone* as the "trial of the new culture," created greater visibility and support for the student protest movement.

Protests continued the next year. In May 1969, 3,000 students at the University of California, Berkeley, tried to remove a chain that university officials had roped around a grassy lot known as People's Park. Ronald Reagan, then governor of California, calling the action "a deliberate and planned attempt at confrontation," activated 2,000 National Guardsmen who gassed the unsuspecting students from a helicopter and with birdshot killed one onlooker, wounded 30 protesters, and arrested 800 others. Even *Time* magazine called the reaction a "crushing repression."

More of the seven million university students across the country marched in protest. In 1969, disturbances occurred at state universities in Maryland, Delaware, and Minnesota. Students faced the police in major confrontations at San Francisco State, Duke University, Queens College in New York, Dartmouth College, and even at Harvard University, the bastion of academic respectability. At the University of Wisconsin at Madison, students protested the war in Vietnam by building 435 crosses which they planted in rows on the lawn of the main administration building. The organizer of the demonstration wanted to show that "students really are faced with death." By the end of 1969, millions of students had taken to the streets, and more than 700,000 of the militants had banded together in 350 chapters of the radical Students for a Democratic Society (SDS).

Radicalized to a large extent by the war in Vietnam and the establishment of the first lottery drawing to draft men into the armed forces since 1942, the militant American youths became interested in a hard-edged rock. Rather than the folk-based, airy, acid rock, they began to listen to the angry, slashing, piercing sounds of British and American guitar heroes and the gut-wrenching Chicago blues of such legends as B. B. King, Muddy Waters, and Howlin' Wolf, who provided a context for the white guitar masters. Faced with police clubs and tear gas, they turned to the music of an oppressed race. "The blues are bigger now than ever — ten times bigger," John Lee Hooker noticed in late 1968. "You know why it's bigger? Because all the college kids are digging it now. Ten years back the blues was just in a certain area, it was the blues lovers only. But nowadays all the kids are digging the blues — the college kids."

THE PSYCHEDELIC BLUES

Jimi Hendrix, a poor, half-black, half-Indian from a broken home in Seattle, bridged the gap between psychedelia and the urban blues. On the cover of his 1967 debut album, *Are You Experienced?* Hendrix and his band appeared to be the quintessential flower children. Hendrix wore bright yellow hip-huggers and a red, pink, and yellow paisley shirt under a white vest, which had two openings around the chest that let two red eyeballs peek out. Around his neck, Hendrix sported a vibrant orange, tufted scarf. Bass player Noel Redding favored a double-breasted, yellow felt sportcoat with flowers emblazoned on it, and drummer Mitch Mitchell had white-and-blue-

Courtesy of Alan Douglas and Warner Brothers Records

Jimi Hendrix and The Moving Sidewalks, whose members included ZZ-Top guitarist Billy Gibbons

striped trousers, a yellow scarf, and a white, red, and yellow tie-dyed shirt. The group stood against a backdrop of blood-red trees.

Hendrix and the Experience also freely experimented with drugs. "I fully admit that drugs controlled our music," Noel Redding later admitted. "Whether it was true or not, we felt we had to be stoned to play properly. Good dope equalled good music." Hendrix, identifying with the drug culture of the sixties, used such titles as "Are You Experienced?" and "Stone Free" for two of his songs on the British issue of his first album.

Despite his use of psychedelic drugs, Jimi Hendrix unleashed an updated version of the gut-wrenching electric blues that belied his hippie image. The young Hendrix had listened to Chicago electric blues players such as Muddy Waters, Howlin' Wolf, and Elmore James. After being discharged as a paratrooper from the 101st Airborne Division in 1961, he and fellow paratrooper Billy Cox began to play around Nashville, backing such blues acts as Nappy Brown, Slim Harpo, and Ironing Board Sam. For the next three years, he backed such R & B greats as Little Richard, James Brown, Jackie Wilson, and B. B. King. In 1964, Hendrix relocated to New York City, where he performed with the Isley Brothers and soul singer Curtis Knight.

In late 1966, Hendrix formed the Experience and amazed European audiences with an act modeled on such former employers as Little Richard and James Brown. At the Paris Olympia, he twisted, rolled, shook, and writhed in perfect time to every half-note of the thunderous electric blues. During the next few months, the guitarist staged similar shows for spectators at Stockholm's Tivoli, the Sports Arena in Copenhagen, and the Saville Theater in London.

Hendrix delivered a loud, angry electric blues that characterized the violence of the era. Using various electronic devices such as the wah-wah peddle, the fuzz box, and feedback at almost deafening levels, the guitarist pioneered a harsh, thrashing style of electric blues. Explained Hendrix of the sound: "Lots of young people now feel they're not getting a fair deal. So they revert to something loud, harsh, almost verging on violence; if they didn't go to a concert, they might be going to a riot." "He revolutionized the blues," contended Billy Cox who played with the guitarist in the Band of Gypsys in 1970. "He took it to another level."

Hendrix also exemplified the militant era through his stage show. At the 1967 Monterey Pop Festival, where he first attracted American acclaim, he finished his set with a thrashing, tortured version of the Troggs' "Wild Thing." As the last notes of the song blasted the audience from a column of nine amplifiers and eighteen speakers, Hendrix ceremonially doused his guitar with lighter fluid and set it on fire. In an article about Hendrix that referred to the Experience as a "triptych of smirking simian faces" led by the "hirsute Hendrix, called 'Mau Mau' in one British paper," *Newsweek* commented that "the Experience's destruction is inevitable rather than accidental, the surfacing of a violent streak that has always run through rock and roll, the spontaneous and impulsive violence of the young."

Other paisleyed guitar heroes hit the American scene. Cream appeared on stage in eye-boggling outfits, but played sorrowful riffs that came from the London and Scottish working class where members Eric Clapton, Jack Bruce, and Ginger Baker had been raised. The trio had individually started out in various blues units: Drummer Ginger Baker had driven the Graham Bond Organization; Jack Bruce had played his six-string bass for Graham Bond, Manfred Mann, and John Mayall; and Clapton, idolizing Muddy Waters and Little Walter, had perfected a piercing guitar sound in the Yardbirds and John Mayall's Bluesbreakers before joining Cream. In June

Courtesy of Warner Brothers Records

Eric Clapton

1966, Ginger Baker approached Clapton about forming a group which, upon the guitarist's suggestion, included Jack Bruce on bass and vocals.

As with Hendrix, Cream delivered a high-volume, jazz-tinged version of the electric blues. They first released the album, *Fresh Cream,* which included Muddy Waters's "Rollin' and Tumblin'," "I'm So Glad" by Skip James, and "Four Until Late" by legendary bluesman Robert Johnson. The group followed with *Disraeli Gears,* their U.S. breakthrough that contained a number of originals in the blues tradition. After hearing the album, Rose Clapp, Clapton's grandmother who had raised him, felt that Eric had "always been a lonely boy and his music still gives me that feeling about him." Said the guitarist about his music: "Rock is like a battery that must always go back to the blues to get recharged." After attending a May 1968 concert on the band's final tour, Ian Whitcomb wrote in the *Los Angeles Times* that "there were no antics — no planned trouser-splitting — from Eric Clapton, Ginger Baker, or Jack Bruce; just great cataleptic hunks cut from the aged blues and pummeled out, slit up, reshaped, thoroughly examined by the violent guitars and drums."

Jeff Beck, another guitar hero who had formerly played with the Yardbirds, produced a hard-edged blues. After splitting from the Yardbirds in 1967, Beck formed his own group, which included blues

Courtesy of Cam Garrett/S.C.V.D. Studio

Jeff Beck of the Yardbirds

shouter Rod Stewart. The guitarist, though dressed in paisley shirts and bell-bottomed, multicolored pants, reworked such blues standards as Willie Dixon's "You Shook Me" and "I Ain't Superstitious" in a tumultuous, shattering style. He characterized his second LP, *Beck-Ola*, a collection of blues-drenched originals and rock standards such as "All Shook Up," as "heavy music."

Alvin Lee, the blues fanatic who fronted Ten Years After, produced a loud, aggressive electric blues. He first drew attention to his guitar mastery when he backed John Lee Hooker at the Marquee Club in London. In 1965, he formed the blues-oriented Jaybirds with bass player Leo Lyons and drummer Ric Lee. A year later, the band added Chick Churchill on keyboards and changed their name to Ten Years After. In 1967, the band released their first LP which, though on the cover featured psychedelic art and a blurred picture of the paisley-clothed band, delivered biting renditions of such blues as Sonny Boy Williamson's "Help Me" and Willie Dixon's "Spoonful." The group developed their blues style on such albums as the 1969 *Ssssh* and *Cricklewood Green* released the next year, both of which reached the Top 20.

THE REBIRTH OF THE BLUES

During the late sixties, some young, white blues performers raised in the American South delivered a straight-ahead electric blues without psychedelic trappings. Many of the blues fanatics came from Texas.

Texan Janis Joplin drifted from her middle-class home in Port Arthur to San Francisco, where she sang in blues bars and coffeehouses. At the time, the singer remembered that "they were playing that 50s crap on the radio. It seemed so shallow, all oop-boop. It had *nothing*. Then I heard Leadbelly and it was like a flash. It *mattered* to me. . . . When I started singing, blues is all I sang."

In 1966, Joplin joined Big Brother and the Holding Company, which she transformed from one of the original psychedelic bands into a blues unit that showcased her saddening, razor-sharp cries of anguish. As with so many young American blues artists of the late sixties, Joplin first surprised the rock-and-roll world at the 1967 Monterey Pop Festival. The next year, her first Columbia release, *Cheap Thrills*, reached the million-dollar mark in sales within a few months and her reputation started to grow.

In 1970, Joplin delved deeper into the blues. She dumped her one-time psychedelic band and assembled the Kosmic Blues Band, which charted with one LP. On a visit to Philadelphia in August, she bought a headstone for the unmarked grave of blues great, Bessie Smith, probably Joplin's greatest influence. Despite the raves of journalists and her financial success, Joplin continued to feel the blues. "Someday," she confided to an interviewer, "I'm going to write

The Daily *of the University of Washington*

Janis Joplin belting out the blues

a song about making love to 25,000 people in a concert and then going to my room alone."

Johnny Winter, raised in Beaumont, Texas, played the blues for years before attracting national attention. After starting a number of blues-rock outfits with his brother, Edgar, Winter traveled to Louisiana and then to Chicago, where he backed local blues greats. He returned to Texas and played the Georgia-Florida blues circuit and produced a demo tape that included such blues standards as Howlin' Wolf's "Forty-Four," "Help Me" by Sonny Boy Williamson, and Muddy Waters's "Rolling and Tumblin'."

In 1968, Winter began to reap the rewards of his efforts. In a

Rolling Stone review of the Texas blues scene, the guitarist was referred to as "a hundred-and-thirty-pound cross-eyed albino with long, fleecy hair, playing some of the gutsiest fluid blues guitar you have ever heard." A few weeks later, Winter was signed by East Coast club owner Steve Paul, who rushed to Houston after reading the article. In 1969 Johnny Winter, by then signed to Columbia, debuted with a best-selling album that showcased piercing, cutting blues originals. "I'd been put down for years for singing the blues and suddenly everyone liked me and wanted to hear me," shrugged Winter in 1969.

ZZ Top followed the path of their fellow Texan. In the early 1960s, guitarist Billy Gibbons listened to "all the Little Richard stuff, Larry Williams's 'Short Fat Fanny,' Jimmy Reed, T-Bone Walker, B.B. King, the usual line-up of R & B stars." In 1967, he formed a psychedelic band, The Moving Sidewalks, which had a minor hit with "99th Floor" and in June 1968 opened for Jimi Hendrix. After The Moving Sidewalks disbanded in 1969, Gibbons joined with bassist Dusty Hill and drummer Frank Beard, die-hard blues rockers who had played together in American Blues, to form ZZ Top.

Johnny Winter provided inspiration to early ZZ Top. "Johnny Winter certainly deserves mention in this conversation because he led the way for so many with his blues guitar interpretations," Billy Gibbons told an interviewer. "We were immediately able to grasp the music through Johnny's performances in Beaumont and elsewhere. The way he did it was something; he ripped it up." Added Dusty Hill: "Johnny and also Edgar jammed with Frank and me in Houston clubs way back when we had blue hair for our old band, American Blues."

ZZ Top, signed to London Records in 1970, released their first LP, a collection of blues rockers and reworked gospel songs. They toured the South constantly, developing a cult following that supported their second LP. By 1973, when they released the Top-10 album *Tres Hombres,* the band had become one of the most successful touring blues bands. "We have not only been fans of the blues for a long time," remarked Billy Gibbons, "but we've really tried to study and deliver it with some kind of forceful feeling."

Steve Miller offered another brand of Texas blues. As a youth, he met T-Bone Walker, who provided him with "my basic lead phrasing." In 1961, after backing Jimmy Reed in a Dallas bar, Miller traveled from his Texas home with friend Boz Scaggs to the University of Wisconsin in Madison, where they formed a white blues group, the Ardells. In 1964, he migrated to Chicago, where he backed blues greats Howlin' Wolf, Muddy Waters, and James Cotton and organized a blues band with Barry Goldberg. "Texas and then Chicago," Miller told a reporter, "where I spent some time learning Chicago blues and by the time I got to San Francisco [in 1966] I realized I had picked up a whole lot of Chicago blues."

The Steve Miller Band

In San Francisco the guitarist formed the Steve Miller Blues Band that sounded, in the words of a reviewer, like "huge sheets of steel violently shaken." In 1968, after appearing at the Monterey Pop Festival and backing Chuck Berry on his *Live at the Fillmore* album, the band signed with Capitol Records and released *Children of the Future*. The next year, Miller won critical approval and commercial success with *Sailor*.

Canned Heat, from nearby Los Angeles, also began to attract fans. Brought together in 1965 by singer Bob ("The Bear") Hite and guitarist Alan Wilson, Canned Heat initially had trouble finding work. "Nobody would hire us because we were blues," complained Hite, who in the sixties rabidly collected more than 70,000 blues records. In 1968, after the group surfaced at the Monterey Pop Festival, the band began to gain recognition. They signed to Liberty Records and hit the charts with the single "On the Road Again." The next year, the group neared the Top 10 with the single "Going Up the Country." In 1971, after a series of successful, blues-drenched LPs, Canned Heat recorded with one of their idols, John Lee Hooker.

The Allman Brothers delivered electric blues from the Deep South. In 1965, brothers Duane and Gregg Allman, raised in Florida, played as the Allman Joys, recording a commercially unsuccessful version of Willie Dixon's "Spoonful." Two years later they moved to Los Angeles and signed with Liberty Records as Hourglass. After two LPs, Hourglass disbanded and Duane moved to Muscle Shoals, Alabama, providing background guitar for Wilson Pickett, Aretha Franklin, and Percy Sledge.

In 1969, Duane Allman formed a new band with brother Gregg, Dickey Betts on second guitar, Berry Oakley on bass, and drummers Butch Trucks and Jaimoe Johanson. The next year, the Allman Brothers released their debut album, which sold well in the South. They backed Jimi Hendrix and B. B. King at the Atlanta Pop Festival and released a second album that reached the Top 40. By 1971, when the band released the top-selling *Live at the Fillmore East*, it had become the spearhead of what critics termed southern rock, paving the way for bands such as Lynyrd Skynyrd and the Marshall Tucker Band.

Some bands, such as Creedence Clearwater Revival began to infuse their music with a political message. In his San Francisco home during the beat era, amid the stirrings of hippiedom, bandleader John Fogerty listened to the records of Muddy Waters, Howlin' Wolf, Elvis Presley, and Carl Perkins. By 1959 he joined with his brother Tom and high school classmates Stu Cook and Doug "Cosmo" Clifford in bands called The Blue Velvets, the Golliwogs, and finally Creedence Clearwater Revival. The band, mixing Chicago electric blues with early rockabilly into a driving concoction that Fogerty labeled "swamp music," covered such rhythm and blues classics as "I Put a Spell on You" by Screaming Jay Hawkins and Little Richard's "Good Golly Miss Molly." It repeatedly scored hits with a string of originals such as "Proud Mary," "Born on the Bayou," "Green River," "Bad Moon Rising," and "Down on the Corner."

During the late sixties, Fogerty increasingly turned to social commentary. He penned such antiwar songs as "Effigy," "Fortunate Son," and "Who'll Stop the Rain," which mirrored the sentiments of young rockers, who feared being drafted and sent to the unpopular and escalating war in Vietnam. "Some folks are born, made to wave the flag, ooh, they're red, white and blue," sang the gravelly voiced Fogerty in "Fortunate Son." "When the band plays 'Hail to the Chief,' they point the cannon at you. Some folks inherit star-spangled eyes, ooh, send you off to war, and when you ask them how much should we give, the only answer's more, more more. It ain't me, it ain't me, I ain't no military son. It ain't me, it ain't me, I ain't no fortunate one."

The Motor City 5 (MC5) used their loud, fast blues to effect political change. Formed by five high school friends in Detroit in 1967, the band played to the rioters at the 1968 National Democratic convention. According to manager John Sinclair, the organizer of the White Panther Party, the group was "totally committed to the revolution, as the revolution is totally committed to driving people out of their separate shells and into each other's arms."

Sounding like a hoarse-voiced black preacher, Sinclair delivered one of the most rousing exhortations in rock history to kick off an MC5 concert: "Brothers and sisters, I want to see a sea of hands out there, let me see a sea of hands. I want everybody to kick up some noise. I want to hear some revolution out there, brothers, I want to hear a little revolution!" The crowd, clapping when Sinclair had begun, became more agitated. "Brothers and sisters, the time has come for each and every one of you to decide whether you are going to be the problem or whether you are going to be the solution," the manager continued. "You must choose, brothers, you must choose. It takes five seconds, five seconds of decision, five seconds to realize your purpose here on the planet. It takes just five seconds to realize that it's time to *move,* it's time to *get down with it.* Brothers, it's time to testify, and I want to know, are you ready to testify? *Are you ready?"* screamed Sinclair to a wild crowd that was jumping on the auditorium chairs. "I give you a testimonial — the MC5." The band launched into a near-deafening version of a hard-edged blues called "Rambling Rose."

By the end of the Sixties, bands such as the MC5, Canned Heat, and the Jimi Hendrix Experience captured interest of the angry, sometimes violent baby boomers. Noted *Time* in May 1969, "The pop scene has become a roaring, pulsating paradox of sound— the white man singing the black blues."

During the late sixties, some legendary performers who had provided the base for the blues revival started to make some money for their efforts. In late 1968, Mike Bloomfield, the Chicago-born guitarist who had formed the blues-funk unit Electric Flag, convinced Bill Graham to book B. B. King at the Fillmore West. "The last time we played there it was 95 percent black in 1963," said King, who the year before had eked out a living by playing 342 one-night stands. "This time it was 95 percent white. I was shocked. Mike Bloomfield introduced me as the greatest bluesman. I didn't know if I should go out there. When I finally did, they gave me a standing ovation. I wanted to cry. Words can't say how I felt." Added King, commenting on his fans at the Fillmore, "perhaps blues expresses what they can't say."

Young rock-and-rollers also rediscovered guitarist Albert King, the self-proclaimed half-brother of B. B. Albert who had worked as a field hand, a service station attendant, and a bulldozer operator for twenty-five years to support his blues career. During the late 1960s, he at last began to reap rewards for such songs as "Ooh-ee Baby," "Let's Have a Natural Ball," and "Travelin' To California." Growled the six-foot-four-inch, 250-pound King in 1969, "my days of paying dues are over. Now it's my turn to do the collecting." The guitarist spoke for others, such as Muddy Waters, Howlin' Wolf, and John Lee Hooker, who started to be recognized among the rock-and-roll crowd.

HEAVY METAL

Some young blues rockers, led by Led Zeppelin, adopted the electric blues, cranked up the volume, and added a macho stage show for what critics termed heavy metal. Led Zeppelin formed around Jimmy Page, a poor youth from the London working class who had played brilliant session guitar for the Rolling Stones, the Kinks, and The Who before joining the Yardbirds. After the Yardbirds disbanded in June 1968, he enlisted the help of session bassist John Paul Jones, drummer John Bonham, and vocalist Robert Plant, who had earned the moniker "wild man of the blues from the Black Country" for his work with such groups as the Delta Blues Band and the Crawling King Snakes. The foursome toured briefly in Scandinavia as the New Yardbirds before changing their name to Led Zeppelin.

In 1968, Led Zeppelin entered the studio to record their blues-based debut. "I've never been so turned on in my life," recalled Robert Plant of the fifteen-hour recording session. "Although we were all steeped in blues and R & B, we found out in the first hour and a half that we had our own identity." On the album, they unveiled a slashing, amplified blues, including Willie Dixon's "You Shook Me" and "I Can't Quit You Baby," and a reworked version of Howlin' Wolf's "How Many More Years," called "How Many More Times." By early 1969, Led Zeppelin had hit the Top 10 in Britain and the United States with the album, and later in the year hit the top of the charts with their second effort which featured the signature "Whole Lotta Love." The next year, the group topped the charts with *Led Zeppelin 3*, becoming the top rock act in the world.

Black Sabbath played the loud, aggressive blues that characterized heavy metal. Formed in 1967 as Earth by four Birmingham toughs, the band changed its name two years later on the advice of its manager to Black Sabbath and pounded out a hard-driving, militant sound on its 1970 debut. "I don't profess to be a messiah of slum people," insisted vocalist John ("Ozzy") Osbourne, "but I was a back-street kid, and that little demon is still in there, shoving the hot coal in. The aggression I play is the aggression I know. And it's obviously aggression a lot of people have." The group recorded such songs as "War Pigs" and "Iron Man," which embodied the destructive tendencies and the antiwar sentiment of the era.

The band fastened upon a preoccupation with demons and a hellish otherworld that had tormented many Delta bluesmen, such as Robert Johnson, who had recorded "Me and the Devil Blues." They titled their first single "Evil Woman" and followed with "Elec-

Black Sabbath

tric Funeral" and "Sabbath, Bloody Sabbath." "If we come across doomy and evil, it's just the way we feel," contended guitarist Tony Iommi.

Deep Purple turned to heavy metal midway in its history. Funded in 1967 by two London businessmen, the band began to chart with a series of remakes such as "Hush," "Kentucky Woman," and "River Deep, Mountain High." In 1969 they recorded a *Concerto for Group and Orchestra* with the Royal Philharmonic Orchestra. After *Concerto* failed to sell, guitarist Richie Blackmore began to dominate the band, which banged out a series of heavy metal classics such as the 1971 *Fireball* and *Machine Head* and *Made in Japan*, released the next year.

AC/DC brought British blues based metal into the seventies. As with other British metalers, the working-class members of AC/DC owed a musical debt to the electric blues of Chicago. "I started out listening to a lot of early blues people, like B. B. King, Buddy Guy, and Muddy Waters," pointed out the knicker-clad lead guitarist Angus Young. "I liked blues players." After years of playing gigs in their native Australia, the group delivered a deafening, chord-crashing electric blues in *High Voltage*. By the end of the decade, they created the heavy metal classic *Highway to Hell*.

Aerosmith derived their sound from the heavy British blues. In 1970, in New Hampshire, guitarist Joe Perry, bassist Tom Hamilton, and vocalist and then-drummer Steven Tyler formed the group as a power trio. "I think what we wanted to do, without really saying it, was to be the American equivalent of all the great British bands," remembered Hamilton. "Cream, the Yardbirds, Led Zeppelin. They were all so classy and powerful sounding. We couldn't think of an American band like that. We wanted to be the first one." In their first performance at Nipmuc Regional High School in Boston, the band played cover versions of such songs as "Shapes of Things" by the Yardbirds. By the mid-1970s, after constant touring and adding two members, Aerosmith combined the blues-based sound with a pop sensibility to scale the charts with such LPs as *Toys in the Attic*.

WOODSTOCK AND THE END OF AN ERA

The power of the rock generation seemed to reach its zenith at the Woodstock Music and Arts Festival in Bethel, New York, held from August 15 to 17, 1969. During the late sixties, millions of baby boomers gathered at hundreds of rock festivals, the idea for which had originated with the hippies in San Francisco. In January 1967, more than 50,000 attended the Monterey Pop Festival, the first major festival, which brought attention to such performers as Jimi Hendrix, Janis Joplin, and Canned Heat. The next year, youths flocked to the Newport Pop Festival, and the Miami Pop Festival, and in 1969 to the Atlanta Pop Festival and the Atlantic City Pop Festival. From 1967 to the end of the decade, at least 2.5 million people had attended rock festivals throughout the country.

The Woodstock Festival, as with the other rock gatherings, was a well-calculated business venture. John Roberts, a young millionaire who had graduated from the University of Pennsylvania, and Joel Rosenman, a Yale Law School graduate and the son of a prominent Long Island orthodontist, had masterminded the festival. Along with Mike Lang, organizer of the Miami Pops Festival, and Artie Kornfeld, head of Contemporary Products at Capitol Records, they planned the music, the food, the sale of hip souvenirs such as Che Gueverra posters, and the future movie and recording rights to the festival. Although "promoting a celebration of the Aquarian Age, and our patrons fancied themselves as street people and flower children," contended Rosenman, "we were a New York corporation capitalized at $500,000 and accounted for by Brout Issacs and Company, tenth largest body of CPAs in New York City."

Though a business enterprise publicized heavily by the media, Woodstock symbolized the unity of purpose among the swelling ranks of youth who opposed the war in Vietnam and hoped to assert their own power. "Woodstock signified the coming together of all tribes," remarked Carlos Santana, the guitarist, who played a mixture of Latin rhythms and the blues to the 400,000 at the festival.

Jimi Hendrix at Woodstock festival

"It became apparent that there were a lot of people who didn't want to go to Vietnam, who didn't see eye to eye with Nixon and none of that system, you know?"

The music at the festival reflected the antiauthoritarian attitude of late-sixties youth. Though including a motley assortment of sounds from such folk rockers as Melanie to psychedelic bands such as the Grateful Dead and the Jefferson Airplane, Woodstock featured performances by Country Joe and Jimi Hendrix. Dressed in an army fatigue shirt and jeans, Country Joe McDonald took the stage at Woodstock without his band. "I get kind of mystical about my solo performance at Woodstock," remembered McDonald. "I was hanging around, and I was just filling time, singing a few country & western songs and folk songs. Then I did the [anti-Vietnam war] "Feel-Like-I'm-Fixing-To-Die-Rag"—the F-U-C-K cheer — the rest is history. From the first response to 'Give me an *f*', when they all stopped talking and looked at me and yelled, *F,* I knew there was no turning back."

Jimi Hendrix appeared near the end of the festival. Taking the stage with a group of musicians called the Electric Sky Church, he launched into a powerful version of the "Star Spangled Banner" which featured screaming-rockets and exploding-bomb guitar effects and sounded like a heaving, wounded monster about to expire. In his rendition of the national anthem, Hendrix captured the militant outlook sixties youth held toward the government.

The festival at Altamont Speedway near San Francisco, held in

December 1969, diminished the sense of power among the youth that Woodstock had engendered. Drawn by a free concert staged by the Rolling Stones, who wanted to repeat their successful Hyde Park performance, more than 300,000 fans flocked to the site. During the event, hundreds required treatment for drug overdose, including one youth who jumped off a freeway overpass after ingesting some LSD. Horrified spectators watched powerless as the San Francisco contingent of the Hell's Angels motorcycle gang, hired to keep order in exchange for five hundred dollars worth of beer, stabbed to death a black eighteen-year-old from Berkeley, one of four deaths at the concert. In a repeat performance of Altamont a few months later, more than 50,000 youths paid twenty-eight dollars each to attend a "Celebration of Life" on the banks of Louisiana's Atchafalaya River, where the Galloping Gooses motorcycle gang, employed as a security force, chain-whipped concertgoers. Three people died amid the festivities.

During early May 1970, events at Kent State University blunted the resolve of militant sixties youth. After President Richard Nixon had announced that American troops had been sent into Cambodia, students at Kent State University in northeastern Ohio took to the streets. On May 2, they hurled bottles at police cars, smashed store windows, and doused trees with gasoline, setting them on fire. The next day, protesters firebombed the one-story ROTC building on the Kent State campus.

The authorities responded swiftly and decisively to the disruptions. Mayor Leroy Satrom asked Ohio Governor James Rhodes to activate the National Guard. Rhodes, who described the students as "worse than the 'brownshirt' and Communist element . . . the worst type of people that we harbor in America," responded with 900 troops armed with M-1 rifles, submachine guns, and cannisters of tear gas. On the third day of troubles, guardsmen chased a mob of students to a knoll near Taylor Hall. Suddenly, without warning, sixteen National Guardsmen knelt on one knee and leveled their guns at the crowd. Asserted journalism professor Charles Brill, who witnessed the action: "They all waited and they all pointed their rifles at the same time. It looked like a firing squad." The soldiers pumped thirty-five rounds from their M-1 rifles into the protesters standing seventy-five feet away. "It's about time we showed the bastards who's in charge," sneered one guardsman. The gunfire killed four students and wounded ten others. "My God! My God! They're killing us," screamed one Kent State freshman.

The murders at Kent State caused an immediate reaction in colleges and universities across the nation. Students sacked the treasurer's office at the University of South Carolina; a half-million-dollar fire blazed at Colorado State; and 124 students were arrested in a fight with state troopers at the University of Colorado. Protesters occupied the ROTC building at the University of Nebraska; three weeks of rioting ravaged the Berkeley campus; and in rioting at the University of Maryland state troopers injured 138 and arrested 200. Students at the University of Wisconsin, chanting, "We're gonna open up a second front in Madison," took over the Army Mathematics Research Center and were responsible for twenty major firebombings. More than 75,000 students marched on Washington, D.C., gathering in front of the White House, and more than 200 colleges and universities shut down for at least one day, most for the rest of the academic year. In May and June 1970, over 508 protests rocked college campuses.

After initial outbursts of violence, a sense of helplessness enveloped many American youths. Said one youth at the post-Kent State demonstration in Washington, D.C.: "The people here understand that we are surrounded by fully armed troops and that if we start anything, we'd be destroyed." For the first time in a decade, rebellious youths who had hoped for a better world felt that they had reached a dead end.

Shocking news of the deaths of prominent rock figures during the next few months deepened the hopeless mood of rockers. Jimi Hendrix passed away on September 18, 1970, a victim of an overdose of sleeping pills. On September 3, Al Wilson, lead guitarist for Canned Heat, died of a drug overdose. Only a few weeks later, on October 4, at the Landmark Hotel in Hollywood, authorities confirmed the death of Janis Joplin from an overdose of heroin. On July 3, 1971, Jim Morrison of the Doors died of a heart attack in a bathtub in Paris. By the beginning of the 1970s, many youths who only a few years before had vowed to work for sweeping social change, listened to the guns of Kent State and retreated to the cerebral music of jazz-rock and classical-rock and the soft sounds of a folk revival.

11

Aftermath of the Sixties

"These days nobody wants to hear songs that have a message."

vocalist Robert Lamm of the group Chicago

"We know that people and movements are fallible," one college senior from American University told *Time* magazine in the early 1970s. "We're afraid to believe too much in anything or anyone."

In the aftermath of Kent State, most youths in the Woodstock generation agreed with the jaded, critical sentiments expressed by the college senior from American University. Sent to a war in a faraway land and attacked by National Guardsmen at home, they abandoned the hope for a revolution in values and began to turn inward.

Economic conditions caused further concern. From 1969 to 1970 unemployment in the United States increased from 3.5 percent to 6.2 percent. In the same year, the buying power of the dollar declined by nearly 6 percent and the government cut public spending and imposed credit restrictions. Throughout the country, fears of a major recession racked most Americans.

The music reflected a sober, conservative mood as many deserted a hard-driving rock. "The fading out of ear-numbing, mindblowing acid rock," *Time* contended in early 1971, "is related to the softening of the youth revolution. Its decline is variously viewed as a symptom of either progress toward harmony and thoughtfulness or a tragic slide from activist rage to a mode of 'enlightened apathy.' "

Rather than the pounding, loud sounds of psychedelia or the wrenching, angry urban blues, rock became soft, serious, and introspective. Built upon the yen for experimentation fostered during the hippie era, it was fused with more respectable, established musical forms such as jazz, classical, country and folk. From 1970 to 1973, rock-and-roll became an apolitical, intensely personal experience.

MILES AHEAD

Rock-and-roll had always been a union of diverse types of music. At its inception, it had been an amalgam of electric R & B and country, first joined together by Chuck Berry, Elvis and the rockabillies. During the mid-1960s, when Bob Dylan plugged an electric guitar cord into an amplifier, rock merged with folk for what critics called folk rock. Later in the decade, the Beatles and others introduced Indian musical instruments such as the sitar to their music.

Performers during the early 1970s continued to fuse rock with other musical forms such as jazz. Jazz great Miles Davis, who had been present at the inception of bop during the mid-forties, spearheaded the trend. In 1970, Davis blended a raw-edged, slightly dissonant sixties jazz with the electric sound of rock, emerging with *Bitches Brew*. Wrote Ralph Gleason in the liner notes on the album: "This music is new. This music is new music and it hits me like an electric shock and the word 'electric' is interesting because the music is to some degree electric music. . . . Electric music is the music of this culture and in the breaking away (not the breaking down) from previously assumed forms a new kind of music is emerging."

The album included the innovators of the fusion movement: John McLaughlin on guitar, Joe Zawinul's electric piano on some cuts, Chick Corea's electric keyboard on others, and the soprano sax of Wayne Shorter. John McLaughlin, playing with the Graham Bond Organization in the early sixties and later with the Tony Williams Lifetime jazz outfit, went on to form the jazz-rock Mahavishnu Orchestra. Zawinul and Wayne Shorter continued the fusion experiment in Weather Report, and Chick Corea in 1972 brought together Stanley Clarke, Joe Farrell, and Airto Moreira in Return to Forever. These musicians, along with a number of mainstream jazz performers who hoped to make some money with the new style, defined and shaped the sound of the jazz-rock fusion.

Some rock bands grafted a horn section onto their music in the fusion experiment. Organized by Al Kooper, a former member of the Blues Project, Blood, Sweat and Tears played a blues-based music complimented by the horns of such New York jazzmen as trumpeter Randy Brecker on their first LP, the 1968 *Child Is the Father to the Man*. When Kooper quit in 1969 after the album failed to sell, the band recruited vocalist David Clayton-Thomas who added a pop element to the jazz rock for the top-selling *Blood, Sweat and Tears*, which included the music of jazz great Billie Holiday.

The band Chicago also featured a horn section. Formed in 1967 as Big Thing by school friends, guitarist Terry Kath and hornman Walter Parazaider, the band changed its name to Chicago Transit Authority and in 1969 released a political jazz-rock album that included protest chants from the 1968 Democratic National convention. Under the guidance of manager James William Guercio during the early 1970s, the band shortened its name to Chicago, dispensed with radical politics, and fused its sound with pop for a string of hits such as "Saturday in the Park." "These days nobody wants to hear songs that have a message" asserted Robert Lamm by the early 1970s.

Pink Floyd, a sixties British psychedelic band, changed course in the seventies to expand upon fusion's flirtation with electronics. Formed in 1965, the band began by playing R & B music, named after country-blues duo Pink Anderson and Floyd Council. By 1967 Pink Floyd had developed a psychedelic sound, releasing two records in the genre. When vocalist-guitarist Syd Barrett became incapacitated because of an LSD experiment, the group hired guitarist David Gilmore who led the band to a subtle, electronic sound evidenced on a number of soundtracks. By their 1973 masterpiece, *Dark Side of the Moon*, which took nine painstaking months to produce, Pink Floyd had perfected a Wagnerian, electronic sound that provided a backdrop for tales of alienation and paranoia.

CLASSICAL ROCK

Some musicians merged rock with classical music. King Crimson, fueled by the ideas of Robert Fripp, set the stage for classical rock. In early 1969, the band formed around Fripp, who combined classical guitar technique with screaming rock sounds. After backing the Rolling Stones at the Hyde Park Festival before 650,000 people, the group released its debut, *In the Court of the Crimson King*, which neared the top of the British charts and laid the groundwork for classical rock.

Banding together in late 1969 during a chance meeting in San Francisco, former King Crimson guitarist Greg Lake, classically trained pianist Keith Emerson, and drummer Carl Palmer made their debut at the 1970 Isle of Wight Festival. That year they produced their first album, embellished with classical motifs, which reached the Top 10. In 1971, the trio released a live version of Moussorgsky's composition *Pictures at an Exhibition*. In 1974 they

Steve Howe of Yes

recorded *Welcome Back My Friends*, which included "Toccata" by Bach and Aaron Copeland's "Rodeo" and hit the Top 5. According to *Time,* the group used "classical style and technique in much the same way the Stones draw on blues."

Roy Wood also explored the connection between rock and the classics. After leaving The Move in 1971, the guitarist founded the Electric Light Orchestra. The band first released *No Answer,* an album graced with cellos and violins. In 1973 they produced their second effort, which included three former members of the London Symphony Orchestra and yielded its first hit, a richly orchestrated version of Chuck Berry's "Roll Over, Beethoven." "I like the *sound,*" insisted synthesizer player Jeff Lynne. "That's all music is for me. Not for putting a message over."

Yes, a band formed in 1968 during a meeting at a London businessman's drinking club, La Chasse in Soho, featured neoclassical structures and three-part harmonies. After guitarist Steve Howe joined, the group recorded the 1971 *The Yes Album,* their U.S. breakthrough. The same year, after the arrival of classically trained pianist Rick Wakeman, they released the Top-10 *Fragile,* which contained the hit "Roundabout." The group followed with *Closer to the Edge,* consisting of three extended cuts and a four-movement title suite. By 1974, *Time* gushed over "the complex, educated sounds" of groups such as Yes. "Thus do barriers fall," the magazine concluded, "and such often enclosed worlds as rock music get a little sunshine in."

BACK TO THE COUNTRY

Confronted by the harsh, complicated realities of an unwanted war in Vietnam and events at Kent State, some folk rockers began to move toward a storytelling country music which extolled simple living and rural traditions. "Country rock," observed *Time* in 1970, was a "turning back toward easy-rhythmed blues, folk songs and the twangy, lonely lamentations known as country music." The new musical blend, continued *Time*, was a "symptom of a general cultural reaction to the most unsettling decade that the U.S. has yet endured. The yen to escape the corrupt present by returning to the virtuous past—real or imagined—has haunted Americans, never more so than today."

Bob Dylan, the most visible protest singer of the 1960s, led the movement back to the country. In May 1969, Dylan released the country-influenced LP, *Nashville Skyline*, recorded in the country music capitol, which on "Girl From North Country" featured a duet with former rockabilly and country music giant, Johnny Cash. In the same month, Dylan appeared with Cash on a television special filmed at the Grand Ole Opry.

The Band, Dylan's sometime backing group, began to achieve popularity with its country-based rock. Joining rockabilly singer Ronnie Hawkins in the early sixties, guitarist James Robbie Robertson, pianist Richard Manuel, drummer Levon Helm, bassist Rick Danko and organist Garth Hudson by 1964 had formed their own group. Robertson and Helm backed Dylan when he first plugged in an electric guitar and after Dylan's 1965 motorcycle accident the group moved near the reclusive singer in Woodstock, New York.

The Band, as they were now called, recorded their debut at Woodstock in their large, pink-colored house and in 1968 released *Music From Big Pink* which included a number of Dylan songs. The next year, they hit the Top 10 with the heavily country-influenced, self-named LP which included the hit, "Up On Cripple Creek." By late 1970 the group reached the Top 5 with their third album, *Stage Fright*. The Band, wrote *Time*, perfected a rock hybrid that "comes on mainly as country music full of straight lines and sentiment."

Poco offered a similar brand of country rock. In late 1968 when the folk-rock group Buffalo Springfield splintered into the trio Crosby, Stills and Nash and a solo career for Neil Young, Springfield guitarist Richie Furay decided to form a country-rock outfit with his friend Jim Messina. "Richie and I were riding in a cab in Nashville," remembered Messina. "We talked about forming a new band that would be an extension of what we'd been doing with the Springfield, but more country and rock than folk and rock." The duo invited guitarist Rusty Young, bassist Randy Meisner and drummer George Grantham to join Pogo, renamed Poco when the owners of the Pogo comic strip threatened legal action over the use of the name. After two moderately successful efforts, in 1971 the

The Daily *of the University of Washington*

Crosby, Stills, and Nash

group neared the Top 20 with the LP *Deliverin'* which relied heavily on such traditional country instruments as steel guitars, mandolins and dobros.

With the help of Johnny Cash, Kris Kristofferson stepped into the country-rock spotlight at the turn of the decade. After earning a Ph.D. in English literature and serving a stint in the army, in 1965 the songwriter moved to Nashville where he worked as a janitor at CBS Record studios. Four years later Kristofferson dropped in on his idol, Johnny Cash. "One Sunday he landed in my yard in a helicopter and brought me 'Sunday Morning Coming Down,' " remembered Cash. "That's true. He fell out of the helicopter with a beer in one hand and a tape in the other and said, 'By God, I'm gonna get a song to you one way or the other.' I said, 'Well, you just did.' "

Johnny Cash volunteered to allow the brash songwriter to appear the next week at the Newport Folk Festival during his set. At the Festival "when he heard his name over the loudspeaker," recalled Cash, "it stunned him and he just stood there. June [Carter Cash, Johnny's wife] got behind him and put her high heel right on his butt and pushed him out onstage. Next day on the *New York Times* front page: 'Kris Kristofferson Steals Show at Newport.' He was on his way." By the end of the year, the new sensation placed his "Me and Bobby McGee" with country star Roger Miller who scored a hit with the song. In 1971 amid the country-rock boom, Kristofferson approached the Top 20 with his second LP, *The Silver-Tongued Devil and I* and two years later starred with Bob Dylan in the movie, *Pat Garrett and Billy the Kid* which led to a successful career in film.

As Johnny Cash had done for him, Kristofferson helped another country rocker, John Prine. Born in Maywood, Illinois, Prine served a stint in the army and worked in the post office before he turned to music professionally in 1969.

A year after his professional debut, he played the Old Town in Chicago. At that club Prine was discovered by Kris Kristofferson and folk singer Steve Goodman. John Prine sang country-flavored songs with biting, witty and insightful lyrics about the effects of war on a returning Vietnam veteran ("Sam Stone"), the implications of the sexual revolution ("Six O'Clock News"), the loneliness of old age ("Angel from Montgomery") and unthinking patriotism ("Your Flag Decal Won't Get You Into Heaven Anymore"). Commented Kristofferson: "Twenty-four years old and he writes like he's two hundred and twenty." By the end of the late-night performance, Kristofferson felt that watching Prine "must've been like stumbling onto Dylan when he first busted the Village scene." It was "one of those rare, great times when it all seems worth it." In 1971 with the help of Kristofferson, Prine released his first album which crested on the wave of country rock.

SEVENTIES FOLK

The disintegration of the American family, coupled with the decline of political activism, gave rise to a less countrified version of folk music that dealt with the loneliness of the single adult. In the 1970s, as the number of women in the work force doubled, many Americans, especially the baby boomers, began to divorce their partners at an increasing rate. In 1969, only three Americans in 1,000 filed for divorce. Five years later, 4.5 per 1,000 divorced their mates. By the end of the decade, 5.3 Americans in 1,000 ended their marriages, and for every five Americans who married, three divorced.

Many baby boomers began to question the institution of matrimony. In one study conducted during 1971 among college students, more than 34 percent of the respondents believed that marriage was obsolete. Two years later, according to a Rutgers University student survey, 30 percent of the seniors felt that marriage was no longer a viable option.

Getting divorced or no longer entering wedlock, many baby boomers lived the sometimes lonely life of the unmarried adult. By 1978, more than 1.1 million Americans lived in single households, an increase of 117 percent in a decade. To find companionship, they populated singles bars, singles resorts, and singles housing complexes.

In the early 1970s, singer-songwriters sang ballads about the emotional traumas of divorce, lost love, and loneliness in a plaintive, confessional music that had its roots in sixties folk. James Taylor, the prototype of the easygoing seventies folkster, grew up in North Carolina and spent his summers on the exclusive Martha's Vineyard near Boston listening to the records of the Weavers, Woody Guthrie, and Pete Seeger. He began playing with friend Danny Kortchmar as a folk duo, James & Kootch, which won a local hootenanny contest. In 1966, he joined Kortchmar's band, The Flying Machine, which performed in such Greenwich Village coffeehouses as the Night Owl before disbanding a year later. Taylor, exhausted and suffering from a heroin addiction, in 1968 traveled to England, where he recorded his first LP for the Beatle-owned Apple Records. When his vinyl debut failed to chart despite background work by Paul McCartney and George Harrison, the singer returned to the United States.

Taylor rebounded from his setback in 1970. After appearing at the Newport Folk Festival, he landed a contract with Warner Brothers through manager Peter Asher. In early 1970, he recorded the album *Sweet Baby James,* which reached the Top 5 and remained on the charts for more than two years. The singer followed with *Mud Slide Slim and the Blue Horizon*, which neared the top of the charts in the United States and Britain and included the Carole King-written chart-topper, "You've Got A Friend," a soft, reassuring ballad appropriate for the millions of divorced and unmarried baby boomers.

Taylor, as with most of the seventies singer-songwriters, wrote and performed a collection of acoustic confessions. "I wish I weren't so self-centered or self-referred all the time with the stuff I write," he later complained, "but for some reason that's the window I utilize, hopefully in an open-ended way."

Other seventies folk artists, congregating around James Taylor, penned self-revelatory paeans of loneliness and confusion. Carole King, the Brill Building sensation of the early 1960s, became intrigued by the New York folk scene after she divorced her husband-collaborator Gerry Goffin. She backed The Flying Machine in Greenwich Village and in 1968 with Danny Kortchmar formed the short-lived band City.

In 1970, through the help of James Taylor, King again hit the top of the charts. That year she played piano on *Sweet Baby James* and with the encouragement of Taylor released the LP *Writer.* At mid-year, she toured with Taylor to promote the album. In October, with drummer Russ Kunkel, Kortchmar, and Taylor, Carole King began to record the album *Tapestry* which sold more than 15 million copies and included her own version of "You've Got a Friend" which, as with the Taylor rendition, climbed to the top of the charts. She also composed such tales of lost love as "So Far Away" and "It's Too Late."

Carly Simon had an even more intimate relationship with James Taylor. Daughter of Richard L. Simon, cofounder of Simon & Schuster publishers, Carly left the exclusive Sarah Lawrence College to perform and record as a folk duo with her sister, Lucy. In 1967, after the Simon Sisters disbanded, she signed with Bob Dylan's manager Albert Grossman, who hoped to promote her as a female Dylan and recorded four unreleased tracks. Two years later, Carly met Jac Holzman, owner of Elektra Records, who signed her to his label and in 1971 released the singer's solo debut, which reached number 30 on the charts. She recorded her second LP, *Anticipation*, which included the top-selling single of the same name. In 1972, Carly Simon topped the charts with the single "You're So Vain," and the LP *No Secrets*, and on November 3 married James Taylor in her Manhattan apartment. In 1974, the husband-wife team dueted in the Top 5 single "Mockingbird."

Joni Mitchell, collaborating with a number of sixties folksters, strummed to the top of seventies folk. Born Roberta Joan Anderson, she began to play an acoustic folk in her native Calgary, Canada. In 1964, she performed at the Mariposa Folk Festival and the next year, after moving to Toronto, she met and married Chuck Mitchell, who played with her as a folk duo in local coffeehouses. In 1966 Mitchell moved to Detroit, where she became a sensation on the folk scene and began to make appearances in New York City. While in Greenwich Village, Mitchell met such folk artists as Judy Collins, who hit in 1967 with Mitchell's "Both Sides Now."

Mitchell, signed to Reprise Records in 1967, released her debut album, which was produced by ex-Byrd David Crosby and included on guitar Stephen Stills, formerly of the folk-rock band Buffalo Springfield. The next year, she recorded her second LP, *Clouds*, which reached the Top 30 and earned her a Best Folk Performer award.

Mitchell, as with other singer-songwriters of the era, sang about the loneliness of broken relationships. In 1971, enlisting the support of Stephen Stills on bass and James Taylor on guitar, who had asked Mitchell to sing background vocals on "You've Got A Friend," she recorded the album *Blue* which featured such tales of lost love as "The Last Time I Saw Richard," "This Flight Tonight," and the title song. "When I think of Vietnam or Berkeley, I feel so helpless," Mitchell told *Time*. "I just write about what happens to me."

Joni Mitchell helped propel to stardom Crosby, Stills and Nash, two of whom had aided Mitchell on her debut LP. In mid-1968 after the breakup of the folk-rock group, Buffalo Springfield, Stephen Stills began to practice with ex-Byrd David Crosby (a.k.a. David Van Courtland) and Graham Nash, formerly of the Hollies. A year later the folk rockers released a self-titled album which featured a blend of floating harmonies and acoustic guitars. As their album slowly scaled the charts, the group asked ex-Buffalo Springfield guitarist Neil Young to join and in May 1970 released *Deja Vu* which topped the charts and included their best-selling single, Joni Mitchell's "Woodstock." Unlike most other seventies folksters, in 1970 Crosby, Stills, Nash and Young directly confronted the tragedy at Kent State, recording the blistering, electric "Ohio." In late 1970

Photo by Bonnie Lippel, courtesy of Peter Asher Management

Linda Ronstadt

amid a tour, the foursome disbanded due to internal tensions and splintered into four successful solo acts. With the help of Joni Mitchell, David Crosby neared the Top 10 with the album *If I Could Only Remember My Name*. Stephen Stills, studying guitar with Jimi Hendrix, released a blues-drenched solo LP which almost topped the charts, and in 1971 Graham Nash recorded his solo debut. In late 1970, Neil Young released the Top 10 LP *After the Goldrush* and two years later followed with the chart-topper, *Harvest* which featured James Taylor and Linda Ronstadt.

The Arizona-born Linda Ronstadt provided the focal point for several other folksters. In 1964, she moved to Los Angeles to join the folk trio the Stone Poneys. Though selling few copies of their debut, the group scored in 1968 with "A Different Drum" before disbanding.

After a series of unsuccessful solo albums, Ronstadt recruited from the Troubadour folk club in Los Angeles a tour band including Glenn Frey, Bernie Leadon, Randy Meisner, and Don Henley. In 1973, she hired as manager Peter Asher who had advanced the career of James Taylor.

With a new band and manager, the singer released the LP *Don't Cry Now*, which remained on the charts for fifty-six weeks. During the next five years, Ronstadt recorded a number of top-selling albums that combined the sensitive ballads of seventies folk with new renditions of country-based oldies such as the Everly Brothers' "When Will I Be Loved," "I Can't Help If I'm Still in Love with You" by Hank Williams, and Buddy Holly's "It's So Easy" and "That'll Be the Day."

Linda Ronstadt professed jaded, conservative beliefs so prevalent during the early 1970s. She hoped for a "real resurgence of patriotism in this country." After campaigning for liberal candidates, the singer felt that "I really didn't know what I was talking about. Who knows who should be President and if anybody should have an interest in determining those things, shouldn't Standard Oil? I mean, they have more to gain and more to lose. If something terrible happens to Standard Oil, a lot of people will be out of jobs. You can say what you want about big multi-nationals running the country and stuff, but the fact remains that we need that, we need their services, we need jobs from them and they are in a better position to decide what's going to be good for the economic climate of the country and for the rest of the world."

Ronstadt's tour band, splitting from the singer in late 1971, achieved stardom as the Eagles. In 1972, the group recorded their self-named, debut album which neared the Top 20 and included the hits "Take It Easy," "Peaceful Easy Feeling," and "Witchy Woman." Three years later they scored their first million-selling single, "The Best of My Love," which exemplified their trademark soft, country folk rock.

Jackson Browne, writing songs for the Eagles and Linda Ronstadt, epitomized the West Coast tunesmith of the seventies. According to the singer, he was influenced by his sister, who "was two years older than me, and she hung around with these guys who wrote songs and did a lot of civil rights stuff. I started hanging around with them and writing songs when I was 15. We gravitated toward Bob Dylan, Pete Seeger kind of stuff. This is 1964, '65."

Browne, as with the other seventies folksters and Dylan himself, deserted Dylanesque protest for an intensely personal folk. After traveling to New York City, where he wrote songs recorded by the Byrds, he signed with Asylum Records. In 1972, with the help of David Crosby, the singer-songwriter released his first LP which contained the hit "Doctor My Eyes." Later in the year to promote the album, he toured the United States and Europe, supporting Joni Mitchell. As he toured, Browne hit the charts as a composer of the Eagles' hit "Take It Easy." In 1976, after a number of releases, he hit the charts as a solo artist with the emotion-laden LP *The Pretender*, on which one song described his shattered life after the suicide of his wife, Phyllis.

Elton John proved to be the most commercially successful and atypical of the seventies acoustic solo acts. Unlike folksters such as Jackson Browne, John (a.k.a. Reginald Dwight) was raised in England and as a teen joined the blues group Bluesology. In 1967 he auditioned for Liberty Records and, at the suggestion of the label, teamed with songwriter Bernie Taupin. Three years later, Elton released his debut which featured a gospel-influenced piano sound and the sensitive ballads of Taupin. He crafted fifteen gold albums and twenty-three singles, which reached the Top 40. Five of his singles became number 1 hits, and John became the first act since the Beatles to place four albums in the Top 10 simultaneously.

Different from the subdued folksters, Elton John developed a wild stage act that included handstands on the piano and kicking over the piano bench. "I'm pretty much making up for lost time," he told an interviewer. "Not having had a real teenage life, I'm living those 13-to-19 years now. Mentally I may be 28, but somewhere half of me is still 13."

John complimented his antics by extravagent costumes. Many times, he wore sequined, gaudy jumpsuits, platform shoes, and pink boas. He sported his trademark outrageous glasses, owning more than 200 pairs, including mink-lined glasses, diamond-inlaid spectacles, and a pair with fifty-seven tiny light bulbs that spelled ELTON. "I love people who expect me to wear great, feathery costumes—and I do it," mentioned the singer. "It's like an actor getting into his costume for his part. I don't really feel that part until I'm into whatever I'm going to wear." Though singing sensitive ballads on an acoustic instrument during the early seventies, Elton John reflected the excess that characterized the "Me" generation of the mid- and late- 1970s.

12

The Era of Excess

"You can't make a revolution if you have to make a living."

John Sinclair

"It's a very selfish decade," Tom Hayden, the cofounder of the radical Students for a Democratic Society (S.D.S.), complained to *Newsweek* magazine in 1977. "It's all me. People who experienced profound disappointment trying to change the system are jogging and growing vegetables and concentrating on brightening their own corners of the world."

Hayden's observation characterized the new outlook of many former radicals of the 1960s. One winter day in 1973, Rennie Davis, the other cofounder of S.D.S., closed his eyes, saw the bright light of the mythic "third eye" in his forehead, and, as he related, "suddenly I was in a place no words could describe. I felt such a peace—it humbled me and shattered all my assumptions about life." Having experienced transcendental Consciousness Four, he joined the spiritual sect of the guru Maharaj Ji and began selling life insurance for John Hancock in Denver. Four years later, Davis described his life as "light and music and vibration."

Jerry Rubin, the radical Yippie who practiced his guerilla the-

ater of the absurd during the late 1960s, underwent a similar rebirth. In 1970, Rubin began to question his radical beliefs and by
1977 lived in a Manhattan high-rise apartment, feasted on vitamin
pills and health food, jogged regularly, and attended seminars about
money consciousness. He hoped to be "as Establishment as I can
possibly get."

John Sinclair, the head of the White Panther Party who exhorted the audiences at MC5 concerts to join the revolution, became
disillusioned with radical politics after a prison term and parent-
hood. "The fucking left, man, I'm just not interested anymore," Sinclair, dressed in a suit and tie, told *Newsweek*. "You can't make a
revolution if you have to make a living."

The "Me" Decade

An end to the war in Vietnam, disillusionment with politics, and a
sometimes booming economy helped transform radicals of the late
1960s into Yuppies of the 1970s. The war in Vietnam, escalating
steadily throughout the 1960s, ended by the early 1970s. In 1973
the United States signed a formal peace accord with North Vietnam
and ended the draft, leaving behind 56,555 dead American soldiers.
By 1975 the United States had withdrawn all troops and military
advisors from Vietnam and Cambodia, an action that satisfied one
of the last major demands of the college radicals.

As the war in Vietnam came to a close, Richard M. Nixon, who
had first attracted national prominence for his strident, anticom-
munist stance during the McCarthy hearings, was reelected to the
presidency by voters in forty-nine of fifty states. He defeated George
McGovern, the liberal senator and former college professor who had
been championed by radicalized college-age youths. Coupled with an
end to the war, the reelection of Nixon deflated the rage and
blunted the resolve of the college radicals. As Rennie Davis contended, "Suddenly that collective energy was gone. The war was
over and Nixon had just been reelected. People just found themselves living lives—settling in, getting a job because you had to buy
food and pay the rent."

A new crop of college students in the mid-1970s, the last of the
baby-boom generation, focused their energies on immediate, material concerns. The students, a senior from Boston University told
Time in late 1974, were "seeking tangible, not spiritual returns for
their investment in a university." Oriented toward financially re-
warding careers, they began to enroll in business administration
and engineering classes and bypassed the history, English, and philosophy courses so popular only a few years before. "The mood here
is, 'I'm here for me,'" remarked senior Steve Ainsworth, former
editor of the *Daily Bruin* at the University of California at Los

Angeles. *Time* magazine characterized the students as "the Self-Centered Generation."

The baby boomers, preoccupied with themselves, chased the dream of self-perfection. They aimed at "changing one's personality—remaking, remodeling, elevating, and polishing one's very self . . . and observing, studying, and doting on it," wrote Tom Wolfe in his influential essay "The Me Decade." Some made the trek to Big Sur, California, where they paid $200 a week to attend the Esalen Institute which, in the words of Tom Wolfe, promised "lube jobs for the personality." Others flocked to Oscar Ichazo's Arica or Werner Erhard's est sessions to purge themselves through abuse and self-deprivation. A few expelled personal demons and discovered themselves through primal scream therapy. Unlike the hippies, who rapped with friends about changing the social system, the baby-boom generation in the 1970s paid money for encounter sessions that delved into the individual psyches of the participants.

The baby boomers playfully indulged in drugs that the hippies had considered weapons to break down social barriers and to change the social order. "Drugs have become coopted by the consumer society," asserted sixties LSD guru Timothy Leary in 1976. "Drugs are now just another thing people can buy to make themselves feel one way or another."

Though smoking marijuana had been decriminalized in such states as Alaska and Oregon by 1975, baby boomers began to indulge in the more expensive, ego-enhancing cocaine, the drug introduced to the U.S. market in 1886 by John Styth Pemberton, who mixed it with caffeine for a syrup he called coca-cola. As early as 1973, more than 4.8 million Americans had sampled the drug, which *Time* magazine labeled "tyrannical King Coke." "Why the fad?" asked the magazine. "For one thing smoking pot has become commonplace, even passe, and some people look for new thrills. For another, coke is a powerful stimulant that helps the jaded to forget their ennui."

The rock generation continued to engage in open sexual relations during the 1970s. Unlike the hippies, who substituted communal relationships for the nuclear family, many goal-oriented baby boomers escaped grueling workdays through freewheeling sex. Singles, a category that doubled to 1.3 million during the decade, spent $40 billion a year in singles bars, resorts, and housing complexes in an effort to meet ready partners. More than a few married boomers discussed open marriage, engaged in wife swapping, and joined such free-sex clubs as the Sandstone in Los Angeles, which sought the "membership of stable couples, young middle-class sensualists who believed that their personal relationships would be enhanced, rather than shattered, by the elimination of sexual possessiveness."

The baby boomers, raised with such gadgets as the transistor radio, embraced the full array of new consumer products introduced during the 1970s. They bought pleasure boats, hair transplants, facelifts, automatic garage door openers, and hot tubs. The materialistic boomers purchased food processors, air-conditioned cars, snowmobiles, and ten-speed bicycles.

A prospering economy throughout most of the decade allowed the baby boomers to indulge in their excesses. Though the nation experienced a temporary postwar economic downturn at mid-decade and inflation pushed prices higher, the real disposable income of Americans rose 28.5 percent during the 1970s. It allowed many baby boomers, graduating from college and entering the white-collar work force, to satisfy their fantasies. "To the ghetto-inspired pleasure grabbing of the sixties, the multiple drug abuse and the off-the-wall screwing have been added all those refinements that come with maturity and money," observed *Esquire* magazine in 1978.

ROCK OF THE ABSURD

Rock music during the mid- and late-1970s reflected the excessive preoccupation with the individual, which became apparent in a theatrical, glittery, sometimes androgynous heavy-metal rock epitomized by David Bowie. Born David Jones, a teenaged Bowie joined a number of rock outfits, including the King Bees, the Mannish Boys, and The Lower Third, which released unsuccessful singles. In 1966 he changed his name to avoid confusion with Davy Jones of the Monkees and the next year took mime dance lessons. In 1969, amid the furor of the first moon landing, Bowie released "Space Oddity," which hit the Top 5 in Britain.

Bowie began to change his image at the turn of the decade. After backing Marc Bolan, who had begun a glitter-rock craze in England as T-Rex, the singer began to affect an androgynous image, appearing in a dress in public and on the album cover of the LP *The Man Who Sold the World.* In January 1972, Bowie declared his bisexuality to the British music paper the *New Musical Express.*

Expanding on his image, Bowie created the bisexual, space-age, glittery persona of Ziggy Stardust. On August 16, 1972, at the Rainbow Theater in London, he materialized from a cloud of dry ice adorned by a tight-fitting, glimmering jumpsuit, high-topped, sequined hunting boots, and orange-tinted hair. "His eyebrows have vanished, replaced by finely sketched red lines. He's wearing red eyeshadow which makes him look faintly insect-like," added the *New Musical Express.* "The only thing that shocks now is an extreme," explained the singer about his space-age character. "Unless you do that, nobody will pay attention to you. Not for long. You have to hit them on the head."

The shocking image of Ziggy Stardust began to sell. After having only limited success with his previous albums, Bowie sold more than a million copies of *The Rise and Fall of Ziggy Stardust and The Spiders from Mars,* which featured a hard-rocking band anchored by guitarist Mick Ronson. The next year, he hit the Top 10 with the album *Aladdin Sane* and began to chart with such previous LPs as *Hunky Dory.*

The heavy-metal androgyny of Ziggy Stardust gave direction to the careers of other bands such as Mott the Hoople. Begun in 1969 as a hard-rock outfit led by singer Ian Hunter, Mott the Hoople initially released four poor-selling albums, which convinced the group to disband. On the eve of their dissolution in March 1972, they met David Bowie, a longtime fan of the group, who offered them one of his songs, "All The Young Dudes." The band, agreeing to wear nine-inch platform shoes, heavy mascara, and sequined costumes, recorded the song, which hit the charts in both Britain and the United States and became a gay-liberation anthem. "We were considered instant fags," remembered the heterosexual Hunter. "A lot of gays followed us around, especially in America." Mott the

The Daily *of the University of Washington*

Iggy Pop

Hoople, reinforcing its image with such songs as "Sucker" and "One of the Boys," climbed the charts in 1974 with the album *The Hoople* and the next year with *Mott the Hoople—Live.*

Iggy Pop revitalized his career by following the advice of David Bowie. The young Pop, born James Osterberg, traveled from his native Michigan to Chicago, where he played drums for such electric-blues artists as Junior Wells and Buddy Guy. When returning to Ann Arbor in 1967, he formed the Stooges, which debuted at a Halloween party and during the next three years recorded two slashing, hard-driving proto-punk LPs that failed to chart. Disconsolate, Iggy moved to Florida, where he cut lawns for a living. In 1972, on a trip to New York, he met Bowie and manager Tony DeFries, who persuaded him to reform the Stooges under DeFries's management and Bowie's guidance. In April 1973, Iggy and the Stooges released the LP *Raw Power*, which showcased the thrashing guitar of James Williamson and on the cover pictured a shirtless Iggy with bleached-blonde hair, heavy makeup, dark-red lipstick, eyeshadow, and silver-lame, skin-tight studded pants. Though disbanding shortly after the album's release, the Stooges served as a model for late-seventies punk, and Iggy became a collaborator with Bowie, who wrote "Jean Genie" for the singer.

Lou Reed also collaborated with Bowie. After quitting the Velvet Underground in 1970, the New Yorker went into seclusion. In 1972, Reed met Velvet Underground fan David Bowie, who encouraged him to pursue a solo career. He began to perform with bleached-blonde hair, makeup, and black fingernail polish. In April 1973, Reed recorded the Bowie-produced album *Transformer*, which on the cover pictured a prominent New York drag queen and included the song "Walk on the Wild Side," which became Reed's first pop hit.

The New York Dolls adopted the Bowie-defined image of heavy-metal androgyny. Formed in 1971 and fronted by guitarist Johnny Thunders and singer David Johansen, the group began playing locally at such clubs as the Mercer Arts Center. In 1973 they released their first album, which included such thrashing, driving, proto-punk anthems as "Personality Crisis." On the cover, done in gray and shocking pink with the band's name written in lipstick, the group posed with heavy makeup, jewelry, and ruby lipstick. Johansen, a shoulder thrust forward, stared wistfully into the mirror of his powder box. The other group members looked straight ahead, attired in six-inch-heeled boots, skin-tight leather or spandex pants, and provocative blouses.

Kiss tried to outdo the New York Dolls, their cross-town rivals. "In 1972 there was only one impressive band in New York and that was the New York Dolls," remembered Gene Simmons, the former schoolteacher who started Kiss. "I was impressed mostly by their stage presence, and the fact that they didn't look like other American bands." "In the beginning," he added, "we were extremely jealous of the New York Dolls and we were going to do them one better."

To grab attention, the band, according to Simmons, "decided to put on bizarre makeup. I was the bat, without the black lips, wearing a sailor suit. I had no clue. Paul [Stanley] had the rouge and the whiteface, very much like a pretty boy." Like cartoon characters, the face-painted group began to dress in skin-hugging, bejeweled, spandex pants, platform shoes, and black, glittering, leather shirts. Coached by ex–television producer Bill Aucion, Kiss assaulted their audiences with rockets, police lights, snow-machines, smoke bombs, and levitating drum kits. By 1975, when they released the million-selling albums *Dressed to Kill* and *Alive!* the hard-rock band had become one of America's hottest acts.

Alice Cooper delivered overtly sexual, heavy-metal rock theatrics. In 1965, members of a high school track team in Phoenix, Arizona, performed as a band in a skit for a school assembly. They decided to continue after their debut, calling themselves Alice Cooper, a name eventually adopted by the group's leader, Vince Furnier. Traveling to Los Angeles in 1968, the band met Frank Zappa, who recorded the group on the largely unnoticed albums *Pretties for You* and *Easy Action*.

The band began to attract more attention through sensationalist tactics. In 1971 they released the hard-rock LP, *Love It to Death*, which included the hit "Eighteen" and on the cover showed Cooper's thumb thrusting through a three-inch-wide ring. The next year, they hit the Top 25 with the album *Killer*. Having more money and encouraged by manager Shep Gordon, who felt that "people feel threatened by the sexual thing," the group drew an even larger audience through an elaborate, degenerate show that included throwing live chickens into the crowd, axing off the heads of dolls, staging mock executions in fake electric chairs, Alice draping himself with a live boa constrictor, and beating fans over the heads with six-foot-long, inflated phalluses. By 1974, when they released the Top 10 album *Muscle of Love*, the band had become one of the preeminent practitioners of rock theater.

Genesis, merging theater rock with a softer sound, began to sell records in the mid-seventies. Started by high school chums Peter Gabriel, Tony Banks, Michael Rutherford, and Anthony Phillips, the band released a series of unsuccessful albums during the late sixties and early seventies. Helped by the success of Bowie, in 1972 the band hit the charts with *Foxtrot*. On stage, the bizarre Peter Gabriel assumed the personas of strange characters described in the songs through a wild array of props and settings. Shrugged Gabriel: "I just poodle about and put on silly costumes." In the escapist seventies, the make-believe world created by Genesis seemed a perfect diversion. "With the revolt long since gone out of the music," observed *Time*, "what is left is really a new kind of vaudeville or sometimes a freak show."

Alice Cooper

DISCO

Disco epitomized the excesses of the 1970s. It began in New York
City at black, Latin, and gay all-night clubs where disc jockeys
played nonstop dance music with an insistent, thumping beat. Gradually disco incorporated the antiseptic, rock-steady, electronic beat
of such European synthesizer groups as Kraftwerk which, according
to Ralf Hutter who started the group with Florian Schneider, consisted of "industrial music; not so much mental or meditative music,
but rhythmically more primitive."

By the mid-1970s, disco began to appeal to self-obsessed baby boomers who yearned for center stage. "A few years ago, I went into clubs, and I realized people needed mood music," remarked Neil Bogart, then president of Casablanca Records. "They were tired of guitarists playing to their amplifiers. *They* wanted to be the stars."

Disco, unlike most rock-and-roll, allowed the participants to assume primary importance. Not involving musicians standing on stage, it centered upon the audience. "It's like an adult Disney World. We really give people a chance to get off on their fantasies," explained Steve Rubell, co-owner of one of the premier discos, Studio 54 in New York. "I think the theater atmosphere has a lot to do with it. Everybody secretly likes to be on stage and here we give them a huge space to do it all on." Discos should let "everyone feel like a star," echoed Mark Hugo, manager of a Boston disco.

The various elements of the disco culture embodied the narcissistic extravagance of the mid- and late-seventies. Discotheques, *Time* told its readers in 1977, offered "a space-age world of mesmeric lighting and Neroian decor." Studio 54, once the baroque Fortune Gallo Opera House, featured theatrical lighting, flashing strobes, and more than 450 special effects, including plastic snowfalls and eighty-five-foot backdrops. Zorine's in Chicago offered members rooms of mirrors, twisting staircases, balconies, and secret nooks. In Los Angeles, Dillion's boasted four floors, which were monitored on closed-circuit television. Pisces, in Washington, D.C., was distinguished by old movie sets, 1,000-gallon, shark-filled aquariums, and exotic flora.

The dancers reflected glittery opulence and freewheeling sex through their clothing. Men sported gold chains, gold rings, patent leather platform shoes, tight Italian-style pants, and unbuttoned shiny satin shirts. Women wore low-cut, backless, sequined gowns, spiked heels, long gold necklaces, and gold lame gloves. "The new boogie bunch dress up for the ocassion—with shoulders, backs, breasts and midriffs tending to be nearly bare," observed *Time*. In a disco, where the participants became the stars, remarked photographer Francesco Scavullo, "the dress becomes your dancing partner."

The dances, notably Le Freak, exhibited an unrestrained sexuality. The exotic dance consisted of two people spreading their legs, bending their backs backwards, and thrusting their pelvises against each other in time to the music.

The many openly gay disco dancers mirrored the changing attitudes toward homosexuals. In New York City during the 1970s, contended sociologist Richard Peterson, "it's almost obligatory to have a couple of gay friends." Being gay "is not only acceptable, it's even sort of chic."

Disco, first started in gay clubs, provided a focal point for gay liberation. "The music is a symbolic call for gays to come out of the closet and dance with each other," explained Nat Freedland, director of artist relations for Fantasy Records. It allowed gays, who many times owned and served as the disc jockeys and lighting crews of the prominent New York discos, to become highly visible and respected for their creative achievements.

The disco culture involved the use of drugs, especially cocaine. "Drugs?" replied Steve Rubell when asked about drug use at Studio 54. "What can I tell you? We look the other way. Anyway, so many people are taking pills these days how do I know if it's an aspirin or something else?" As one of its special effects, the New York disco displayed a man-in-the-moon with a spoon uplifted to his nose.

The discos, trading in excess, tried to lure celebrities to their doors. Studio 54 hired socialite Carmen D'Alessio to entice her rich and famous friends to the club. "It's all the celebrities," explained Rubell. "You have to have them first. They draw business in." He successfully added Cher, actress Farrah Fawcett, actor Warren Beatty, Christina Onassis, Woody Allen, and David Bowie to the guest list. Pisces in Washington, D.C. attracted such stars as Elizabeth Taylor and actor Gregory Peck. In Los Angeles, Pip's lured actors Paul Newman, Peter Falk, and Tony Curtis and singer Frank Sinatra. In urban discos, baby boomers rubbed shoulders with stars of the entertainment industry.

The star-studded disco became a craze near the end of the decade. In late 1977, Robert Stigwood, owner of RSO records, filmed the movie *Saturday Night Fever*, which showed the transformation of a poor, trouble-ridden, Italian teenager, played by John Travolta, into a white-suited disco star. He constructed the score of the film around songs written and performed by one of his groups, the Bee Gees. By 1978, the record executive had scored a major success with the movie and had sold more than 30 million copies worldwide of the soundtrack.

Discomania spread across the country in the wake of *Saturday Night Fever*. In New York more than 1,000 discos opened their doors for business. The Holiday Inn motel chain added more than thirty-five discos on its premises. A $100,000 disco even opened in the small town of Fennimore, Wisconsin (population: 1,900). High schoolers went to disco proms and disco roller-skating rinks. One disco in Dubuque, Iowa, provided a disco wedding service complete with smoke-machine effects. Throughout the country in 1978, more than 36 million Americans danced on the floors of 20,000 discos.

Records especially made for disco, first popularized in 1975 with "Never Can Say Goodbye" by Gloria Gaynor, began to sell. The acknowledged queen of disco, Donna Summer, hit the charts in 1976 with "Love to Love You Baby," and followed with a series of disco smashes. The Village People, a costumed band of actors and singers portraying stereotypes of the rugged American male, hit the charts in 1978 and 1979 with the million-selling gay anthems "Macho Man," "In the Navy," and "Y.M.C.A." Even such established artists as Rod Stewart and the Rolling Stones released disco-influenced songs. In 1978, according to *Billboard*, more than 20 percent of the were categorized as disco. "Disco will be the major force in the music marketplace for some time," predicted Nat Freedland of Fantasy Records.

By the end of the decade, disco had become a lucrative business. Besides record sales, it involved such products as spandex pants, magazines such as *Discothekin'*, disco dresses slit to expose the thighs, more than 200 disco radio stations from Los Angeles to Miami, and undersized disco purses. Discos such as Studio 54 netted yearly profits of $800,000. "The profits are astronomical," enthused Steve Rubell. "Only the Mafia does better." By 1979 disco, a mirror for the excesses of the rock generation, was a $5 billion dollar industry.

MUSIC FOR MONEY

Many disco owners, such as Steve Rubell, strove to capitalize upon the music. "When you want to win, you want to win," stated Rubell, a former stockbroker. "And that's how it shows—the score—by the financial success."

Other artists, as with the baby boomers for whom they played, performed for money. To Alice Cooper, "the idea all along was to make $1 million. Otherwise the struggle wouldn't have been worth it. . . . I am the most American rock act. I have American ideals. I love money."

To make money, many musicians eagerly embraced the rock business establishment. Gene Simmons of Kiss equated a "successful rock and roll band" with "a well-oiled machine. It's a good business." As Greg Geller, talent scout for Columbia, noted in the mid-1970s: "Now artists are more upfront about admitting that they are interested in selling some records. This is not an ivory tower age: there's some recognition that we're involved in commerce."

For some, the record business paid off. Don McLean, who scored a hit with the song "American Pie," which described the decline of the sixties consciousness, sold 4.5 million singles and 1.8 million albums of "American Pie," netting around $1.1 million in royalties. Along with $460,000 in publishing and writing royalties and $200,000 in foreign sales, the singer-songwriter earned nearly $1.6 million. After giving his manager 10 percent, McLean took to the bank more than $1 million. Peter Frampton, a former Humble Pie guitarist who became one of the most publicized artists of the decade with *Frampton Comes Alive!* grossed $67 million in 1978 on album sales and tours.

Many seventies stars invested their earnings. The Bee Gees, one of the biggest draws of the 1970s, established their own merchandising company, which sold—as Barry Gibb told it—"things like nice T-shirts. We deal in jewelry but only real gold plate. We're doing a little electronic piano with Mattel Toys that'll be available soon." They also marketed "a cute Andy Gibb doll." Alice Cooper financed such films as *Funny Lady* and *Shampoo* for tax shelters and invested in art, antiques, and tax-free municipal bonds. Ted Nugent, the guitarist who scaled the charts during the seventies with a heavy metal sound and neanderthal costumes, owned a mink farm and a trout operation. Said Bob Weed, the Nuge's financial manager, "all of this fits in with Ted's plan for acquiring land. Sure, we're involved in some oil and gas-lease tax shelters, but when I tell him about property, that's something he understands." Rod Stewart, the blues croaker turned disco star, had a similar investment strategy. "I've always said that Rod isn't a rock star. He's a growth industry," remarked Billy Gaff, Stewart's manager. "Rod is essentially very conservative. He doesn't invest in football clubs or crazy movie- or record-financing schemes. The tax shelter scams are all a little scary, so we stick to art and real estate." All told, in 1973 *Forbes* estimated that at least fifty rock superstars earned and invested between $2 and $6 million a year, each musician accumulating from three to seven times more than the highest-paid executive in the United States.

CORPORATE ROCK

The record industry, consolidating into a few major companies, made it possible for rock stars to amass these astronomical sums of money. During the 1950s, American business in general started to consolidate. By 1955, the fifty largest corporations controlled 27 percent of the national market and sold more than $86 billion worth of manufactured goods, a figure equal to more than one-fourth of the Gross National Product. The trend continued in the sixties, until by 1970 the market share of the 600 largest companies increased to 75 percent, and the share held by the top 200 corporations rose to over 60 percent. The 102 giants at the top of this pyramid, holding assets of $1 billion or more, controlled 48 percent of the market and made 53 percent of the profits.

The record industry followed the pattern of consolidation. Including a number of viable independent companies during the 1950s, by 1973 it was almost completely controlled by seven majors—CBS, Capitol, MCA, Polygram, RCA, A & M, and Warner Communications. The top four companies accounted for more than 52 percent of all record and tape sales, and the leading two—CBS and Warner-Elektra/Asylum-Atlantic—sold 38 percent of the total.

These companies, as with other American conglomerates, had interests in fields besides music during the seventies. MCA owned Universal Films, various television stations, Arlington and Mount Vernon cemeteries, a bank in Colorado, and the Spencer Gifts novelty chain. RCA, the twentieth largest corporation in the country, operated NBC television and radio, owned the Hertz Rent-A-Car company, Banquet Foods, the Cushman and Wakefield real estate firm, and Random House and Alfred Knopf publishers. It also served as a prime defense contractor.

These giant corporations built rock-and-roll, which by 1975 accounted for 80 percent of all record sales, into a multi-billion-dollar enterprise. In 1950, record companies sold $189 million of products, increasing their gross revenues five years later to $277 million. By 1971, in the United States alone, the industry sold $1.7 billion in records and tapes. Two years later, it grossed $2 billion, revenues that surpassed the combined gross revenues of Broadway ($36 million), professional sports ($540 million), the film industry ($1.3 billion), and network television ($1 billion). By 1978, the record industry grossed about $4 billion.

Many companies posted healthy profits. In the summer quarter of 1978, MCA made a profit of more than $5.5 million, CBS cleared $48.5 million, and Warner netted $19.8 million. "Records are where the big money is in the entertainment business these days," observed *Forbes* in July 1978.

Profits came from around the world. In 1973, the companies sold $2 billion worth of records and tapes in the United States, a per capita expenditure of $9.70. That same year, they sold more than $555 million worth of records and tapes in Japan, $454 million in West Germany, $441 million in the Soviet Union, $384 million in the United Kingdom, controlled largely by the British Electrical Manufacturing Industries (EMI), and even $16 million in Poland. Per capita expenditures amounted to $7.57 in West Germany, $6.91 in the Netherlands, $7.64 in Sweden, and $5.14 in Japan.

The companies achieved their profits through well-designed marketing plans. They hired agencies such as First Analytic Center, which initially researched possible markets for the LPs. "We always have a war plan on every record," said Jerry Greenberg, president of Atlantic Records. Company executives subsequently aimed an intensive publicity campaign at a specific audience. Stu Ginsberg, head of publicity at RCA, tried "to create a snowball effect. So you arrange live tours in patterned locations so that the radio and press coverage will overlap. You want to come into a city with advance airplay, and you want to leave the city with press and more airplay. It spreads. New York stations spread to New Jersey, and so on." As RSO president Al Coury boasted, "sales like ours don't just happen. We make them happen! And I sell the sizzle." For help on his label, which marketed *Saturday Night Fever,* Coury hired thirty-four promotional men, half of his total staff.

The selling of Sha Na Na, a seventies band of Columbia University students who specialized in fifties rock-and-roll, provided an example of marketing in the seventies. "To build this group," explained the exuberant Neil Bogart of Casablanca Records, "we created a music industry trend. We called it rock 'n' roll revival. With slogans, stickers, buttons, industry and consumer contests, and even black leather motorcycle jackets for our promotion staff, we brought back the fifties. We took an active part in securing bookings for Sha Na Na at rock palaces such as the Fillmore West. We transported the group from coast to coast, making sure they were seen by their audience and their potential record-buying public. We flew radio men, promotion men, and distributors into New York and San Francisco to see the group. . . . Before the album, they had appeared on the 'Merv Griffin Show' and had been the subject of a feature in *Rolling Stone,* all of which led to their being invited to appear at Woodstock. In fact, by the time the Sha Na Na album was released, the Buddah office had taken on the aura of an Orange Julius on Saturday night in Brooklyn." Sha Na Na proved to Bogart that "talent may be compared to commercial products—the cigarette you smoke, the T.V. set you watch or the car you drive. You select that brand of product that you have been convinced is the one you should buy." Added Harry Anger, a senior vice-president for marketing at Polygram: "If pitching is 70 percent of baseball, promotion is 70 percent of the record business."

By the time a label had packaged and marketed an album, shipped it, and paid royalty fees to the artist and the publisher, an album in the seventies cost roughly $1.55. To break even, it had to sell from 200,000 to 300,000 copies. In 1977 alone, more than seventy records sold more than a million copies, fifteen sold more than 3 million units, and a half dozen racked up sales of more than 6 million to produce excessive profits in an excessive age. By the end of the decade, the corporate rock establishment was firmly entrenched. Soon it would be challenged by the rebellious music of a new generation.

Punk Rock and the New Generation

"You don't sing about love to people on the dole."

Johnny Rotten

"Punk is so constipated it should be called hemorrhoid rock," snapped Linda Rondstadt to an interviewer. "All that punk singers can bring to the presentations of their songs is the gesture of sexual obscenity or of impotent rage. There is a lot of caged simian gibber," wrote Anthony Burgess, author of the futuristic *Clockwork Orange*, in a 1977 issue of *Psychology Today*. "British youth, like American and French and Upper Slobovian youth, needs a good kick in the pants and a bit of solid education." *The London Times* declared that "punk rock is the generic term for the latest musical garbage bred by our troubled culture. It features screaming, venomous, threatening rock sounds."

A new generation of rock-and-rollers centered in New York and London inspired this outrage. Most punkers had been born after Elvis had been inducted into the army and, in some cases, after Bob Dylan first began to sing in Greenwich Village. They had been preteens during the Vietnam War and Woodstock, and had few memories of the civil rights movement and the payola scandal. Most punk rockers had been in elementary school when the Beatles disbanded.

Opposed to the excessive, corporate rock of the mid-1970s, they created a minimalistic, angry music that threatened their baby-boom elders, who had begun to listen to more polished music. In 1977 a new generation had arisen to lay claim to a rebellious rock-and-roll heritage.

NEW YORK PUNK

CBGB, a small bar in the Bowery, New York City, served as the birthplace of punk rock. Established in December 1973 by ex-U.S. Marine sergeant Hilly Kristal, the bar first catered to Bowery bums. "When I first opened it as Hilly's on the Bowery," recalled the proprietor, "I ran it for a while as a derelict bar, and bums would be lining up at eight in the morning, when I opened the doors. They would come in and fall on their faces even before they had their first drink." In a few months, Kristal changed the name of his bar to CBGB—OMFUG which stood for "country, bluegrass, blues, and other music for uplifting gourmandizers."

In 1974, such bands as Television, influenced by the New York avant-garde of Andy Warhol and the Velvet Underground, began to play regularly at CBGB. Formed in late 1973, Television originally included bassist Richard Hell (a.k.a. Richard Meyers) who had traveled to New York City to "become a real sophisticated writer," guitarist Richard Lloyd, drummer Billy Ficca, and vocalist-guitarist Tom Verlaine (a.k.a. Tom Miller), who renamed himself after the French symbolist poet. After debuting at the New York Townhouse Theater, the band convinced Andy Warhol associate Terry Ork to back them. Through the efforts of Ork in early 1974, the group landed a permanent job at CBGB.

Terry Ork, persuading his artist friends to hear Television, created an avant-garde scene at CBGB. "He brought in a lot of theatre and poetry people from this area, since he lived around here and knew them all," remembered Hilly Kristal. "It wasn't really so much his bookings, but because he knew so many things about theatre, film, and art, and he knew all those people. He also had the energy and he was very excited about the whole thing, and he excited me about it. I do think it's true, the whole scene wouldn't have happened without him."

The Talking Heads began to play at the burgeoning avant-garde scene. Fellow students at the Rhode Island School of Design, David Byrne, Tina Weymouth, and Chris Franz traveled to New York and in late 1974 began to play with one another as the Talking Heads, a name found in an issue of *TV Guide*. "We started rehearsing our songs, the songs I had written," remembered Byrne. "I was writing these things but I didn't know what they were for. I didn't have any plans to put a band together, but there were the songs." Living in an apartment only a few blocks from CBGB, the

Talking Heads auditioned for Hilly Kristal and in June 1975 began to play at the bar. In 1977, the group invited keyboardist Jerry Harrison to play with them and released their debut album, which included the eccentric minor hit "Psycho Killer." "The Heads were great and Television were great, but on a sort of intellectual level," recalled Kristal. "The Heads were so quirky and weird that they set much of the stylistic tone. Not punk, but a transition period."

Patti Smith helped transform the avant-garde into punk rock. The daughter of a New Jersey factory worker, Smith worked in a factory herself until migrating to New York. Once in town, she began to write a William Burroughs-Arthur Rimbaud style of poetry. In early 1971, Smith read her poetry at St. Mark's Church in New York, backing Andy Warhol-Velvet Underground follower Gerard Malanga. The next year, she regularly read her work at the Mercer Art Center and published two books of poetry, *Witt* and *Seventh Heaven.*

A die-hard fan of Jimi Hendrix and Jim Morrison of the Doors and a former writer for the rock magazine *Creem*, Patti Smith combined her poetry with a rock sound. In 1973 she invited guitarist Lenny Kaye and pianist Richard Sohl to provide an improvisational rock backdrop to her readings. "Of course it was still more of an art thing," Kaye pointed out. "It wasn't even a club circuit. We played with Television." The next year Smith recorded the independently produced single "Hey Joe/Piss Factory," which convinced Sire Records to sign the fledgling group. After club dates on the West Coast, Smith added guitarist Ivan Kral and drummer Jay Dee Daugherty to form the Patti Smith Group. "As soon as we started adding Ivan Kral and then started adding Jay Dee Daugherty, we became more of a rock band," observed Lenny Kaye.

The poetess adopted the vague, populist stance of the sixties. She admired "all the great sixties guys" who "had sort of a political consciousness." With her music, Smith was "determined to make us kids, us fuck-ups, us ones who could never get a degree in college, whatever, have a family, or do regular stuff, prove that there's a place for us."

The Patti Smith Group, signed a few weeks earlier by Arista Records, in early 1975 brought attention to the emerging scene at CBGB during a seven-week stint at the club. "What happened was that as we played there more and more people came down," mentioned Lenny Kaye. "CBGB became not only a place for them to come and check us out, but it sort of got into the New York consciousness." "Patti's stay here was one of the most memorable seven-week periods the club ever had," added Hilly Kristal. "Clive Davis [of Arista Records] came a number of times and a lot of the record people came, but mostly it was newspapers and a lot of people on the periphery of theatre and the arts. Those first dates put us on the map, at least initially."

The Patti Smith Group began to sound less and less arty. On

the 1975 debut, *Horses*, the group combined rock with the avant-garde in such songs as "Gloria" and "Free Money." The follow-up LP, *Radio Ethiopia*, sounded much the same, with hard-driving numbers such as "Pumping (My Heart)" and "Ask the Angels" interspersed with more freewheeling songs. By the 1978 Top-20 release, *Easter*, the band had largely abandoned an improvisational sound for the hard rock of "Space Monkey," "Till Victory," and "Because The Night," co-written with Bruce Springsteen. Smith "was really the first of, I don't like the word, punks," commented Hilly Kristal.

Richard Hell helped to define the emerging punk rock. As a member of Television, Hell created a minimalist, populist image that would characterize punk rock. He cut his hair in a short, spikey style and wore ripped T-shirts. "My look was a sort of a strategy," explained the bassist. "I wanted it to look like do-it-yourself. Everything we were doing at the time had that element, from having ripped up clothes to not knowing how to play instruments. The whole thing was partly a reaction to the hippie stadium music." "I wanted the way we looked to be as expressive as the material on the stage," added Hell. "It was all of a piece. The ripped T-shirts meant that I don't give a fuck about stardom and all that or glamour and going to rock shows to see someone pretend to be

Photo by Roberta Bayley, courtesy of Richard Hell and Sire Records

Richard Hell: king of New York punk and originator of punk fashion perfect. The people wanted to see someone they could identify with. It was saying, 'You could be here, too.' "

Richard Hell also adopted a populist attitude in his songs. In his 1977 album with the Voidoids, he delivered the New York punk anthem, "Blank Generation," a bitter statement of rebellion without a cause. "It's not that I espoused nihilism," Hell told an interviewer. "What I did was describe the way I felt, and hope that by frankly talking this way when everybody was talking about 'love and peace blah blah blah' I could legitimize and somehow make it possible to be proud of not being there, not being passive. What seemed real exciting then [was] everybody coming around to this kind of attitude."

The Ramones added a buzz-saw guitar attack to the populist stance and ripped T-shirt fashion of Richard Hell to complete the transition from the avant-garde to punk rock. Banding together after playing at a private party in late 1974, Johnny Cummings, Dee Dee Colvin, Jeffrey ("Joey") Hyman, and Tommy Erdelyi adopted the surname Ramone. They first performed in public at CBGB, appearing in black leather jackets, black pegged pants, torn jeans, and ripped T-shirts. "We wanted to do punk rock and decided the punks were people from the fifties like Eddie Cochran and Elvis Presley. You would always see them walking around in motorcycle jackets. We thought that was the coolest thing, to have a motorcycle jacket, to really prove you were in the groove."

The Ramones cared little for the artistic avant-garde. On one tour with the Talking Heads, remembered then-manager Danny Fields, "the Ramones hated Europe. They didn't like the idea that people didn't speak English. The Talking Heads adored it. It was really yuppie chic at work. The Ramones were like Archie Bunker at the Vatican. They were not amused. They hated the food and just looked for hamburgers everywhere." On a Talking Head-engineered side trip to Stonehenge during the tour, the Ramones refused to leave the bus. "It's really nothing to see," explained Dee Dee. "It's not like going to see a castle."

The Ramones reflected their uncultivated attitude in a thrashing sound borrowed from the New York Dolls. "What really kicked it off was seeing the New York Dolls in clubs around Manhattan," recalled Dee Dee Ramone. "It was so inspiring to see a bunch of young people playing rock and roll that we wanted to do it too. It took off from there." Unlike the more meandering art groups, the Ramones sped through eight-song, seventeen-minute sets at CBGB, defining the punk sound on their first LP, which featured "Blitzkrieg Bop," "Beat on the Brat," and "Now I Wanna Sniff Some Glue." "For me it was like I was an old car and I was being taken out for a ride at 100 miles an hour," said an excited Norman Mailer after attending a Ramones concert. "I don't know if I'd like it night after night, and I'm not sure it isn't absolutely killing. You've got to be superhuman to play that stuff night after night and not have your senses wiped out."

Joey Ramone: a CBGBs original

The CBGB Rock Festival Showcase Auditions in mid-1975 brought national attention to the emerging punk scene. Featuring the Ramones, the Talking Heads, and Television, the festival attracted writers from *Rolling Stone, The New York Times*, the *Village Voice*, and the British rock papers, *The New Musical Express* and *Melody Maker*. "The coverage of the festival started making things happen," maintained Hilly Kristal. "The record companies started coming down, mainly Sire Records, but also others."

The Ramones brought punk rock to Britain. In early 1976, they released their first album in England which impressed the British critics and gave English punks direction. "I heard the Ramones' first record and I thought that it was fucking brilliant," remembered Billy Idol who started the punk band Generation X. "We got that first record and every song was under two minutes and it was like a revolution!" "We were playing normal speed until we heard the Ramones," added Idol, "and because of them, [we] revved everything up. Everybody did, 'cause the Ramones really had their groove and we were still searching for ours."

On July 4, 1976, the Ramones further influenced British punks. They celebrated the U.S. bicentennial by performing in London at the Roundhouse, which, contended Hilly Kristal, "started the whole thing going. All the other groups saw them and realized they could do it too." "I feel we were responsible for the whole punk revolution," noted Joey Ramone. "We signed to Sire in 1975 and our first album came out in 1976. It came out in England about six months before it came out in America. That's sort of what inspired the English bands to start up. When we first went over there the big thing was pub rock."

THE SEX PISTOLS AND BRITISH PUNK

Unemployed British youths infused New York punk with political meaning. In 1974, the inflation rate in England stood at about 24 percent. A year later, it had climbed three more points. Simultaneously, between 1974 and 1977 the unemployment rate shot up 120 percent and increased by more than 200 percent among the young.

The Sex Pistols embodied the anger of unemployed British youths. The group began to form in 1972, when London schoolmates Paul Cook, Steve Jones, and Wally Nightingale began to play as the Swankers, attracting the attention of Malcolm McLaren, who owned a clothing shop called Too Fast Too Live, Too Young To Die. The next year Glen Matlock, an assistant in McLaren's shop, joined the band.

Malcolm McLaren traveled to New York in early 1975 to manage the New York Dolls. Upon his return six months later, McLaren agreed to manage the Swankers and suggested the group move Jones to guitar and dispense with Nightingale, who appeared too clean-cut. As a lead singer, he proposed Richard Hell, who had begun to play with ex-New York Doll Johnny Thunders in the Heartbreakers during 1975. Confronted with opposition from the group over an American addition to the band, McLaren decided upon Johnny Rotten (a.k.a. John Lydon) who met the group at the manager's shop, renamed Sex, and successfully auditioned by singing along to Alice Cooper's "School's Out," which played on the jukebox. By November 1975 McLaren unveiled the newly formed Sex Pistols at St. Martin's School of Art in London.

The Sex Pistols combined the energy of the New York Dolls and the rebelliousness of New York punk. Playing their instruments with abandon, the group featured a Ramone-like, frenzied, fuzzy, buzz saw guitar attack anchored by guitarist Jones. They taunted, shouted, and spat at the audience, blurring the distinction between the artists and the audience. Band members appeared in ripped, graffitied shirts and pants, black boots, and leather jackets that flashed with metal studs and zippers. Copying Richard Hell, they cut their hair in a short, spikey style. To reinforce their image, the band in February 1977 fired bass player Glen Matlock because he listened to the Beatles and replaced him with Sid Vicious (a.k.a. John Ritchie) who on stage mutilated himself with broken beer bottles.

The rebellious band offered music to a new generation of unemployed post-baby boomers. "The millionaire groups were singing about love and their own hangups," sneered Rotten. "That's stupid. You don't sing about love to people on the dole. We're totally against apathy of any kind. We have got to fight the entire super band system. Groups like The Who and the Stones are revolting. They have nothing to offer the kids anymore."

The Sex Pistols rebelled against other aspects of the establishment, infusing their raucous punk with an anarchistic message. In November 1976 they recorded their first single, "Anarchy in the U.K." which warned of impending chaos in Britain. The band next blasted royalty in "God Save The Queen," releasing the single to coincide with Queen Elizabeth's Silver Jubilee in June. The Sex Pistols followed with other songs such as "Pretty Vacant" and "Holiday in the Sun," which described the hopeless plight of many British youths. "There'll always be something to fight—apathy's the main thing," asserted Rotten. "The Pistols are presenting one alternative to apathy and if you don't like it, that's just too bad. Anarchy is self-rule and that's better than anything else."

An outraged, threatened establishment aimed a barrage of criticism at the anarchistic Sex Pistols, reminiscent of the outcries against Elvis Prelsey in 1956. On April 10, 1976, the British music papcr *Melody Maker* told its readers that "the Sex Pistols do as much for music as World War II did for the cause of peace." Robert Adley, a Conservative member of Parliament, called the group "a bunch of ill-mannered louts, who seem to cause offense wherever they go." One vicar of the Anglican Church, his face muscles tightened and his head raised high, planted himself outside a club where the Sex Pistols were scheduled to play and warned concertgoers: "Keep out of there! They're the devil's children." Almost every local council in Britain banned the Pistols, publications refused to print ads publicizing the band, and in June 1976 after the release of "God

The Sex Pistols

Save The Queen," royalists attacked both Johnny Rotten and Paul Cook with razors, knives, and iron pipes.

The record industry offered little help to the Sex Pistols. EMI first signed the band for a £40,000 advance. After packers in the Hayes record plant refused to handle "Anarchy in the U.K." and after adverse publicity on the BBC-broadcast "Bill Grundy Show," the company criticized the Pistols for "aggressive behavior" and terminated the band's contract. In a ceremony outside Buckingham Palace during March 1977, A & M Records signed the Sex Pistols and, six days later, rescinded the contract. Two months later Virgin Records offered a contract to the band, which had by that time become notorious and released the LP *Never Mind the Bollocks— Here's The Sex Pistols* in England.

Despite opposition, Sex Pistols records topped the charts. "God Save the Queen," even though banned by British radio, sold 150,000 copies in five days and shot to the number-2 spot on the charts. "Pretty Vacant" hit the number-6 slot, and "Holiday in the Sun" reached number 8. In November 1977, the band's first and only studio album, *Never Mind the Bollocks*, topped the British charts.

Other bands such as the Clash, inspired by the Sex Pistols, joined the punk legion. After hearing the Sex Pistols at the 100

Club in London, Joe Strummer quit his pub-rock band, the 101'ers, and joined with guitarists Mick Jones and Keith Levene, bass player Paul Simonon, and drummer Terry Chimes to start the Clash. The group asked Bernie Rhodes, a regular at Malcolm McLaren's boutique, to become manager and first performed in Sheffield in mid-1976, backing the Sex Pistols. In December 1976 they played on the Pistols' "Anarchy in the U.K." tour. The next month, after the departure of Levene and Chimes, the latter replaced by Topper Headon, the Clash signed with CBS worldwide and in April debuted with the single "White Riot." They released their first, self-named LP, which hit the Top 20 and included such punk anthems as "All The Young Punks," "I'm So Bored with the U.S.A.," "Career Opportunities," and "London's Burning." Though disregarded by distributors in the United States, in 1978 the Clash followed with "Give 'Em Enough Rope," which hit the number-2 slot in Britain.

The Damned began their career backing the Sex Pistols. Formed in 1976 by Dave Vanian, Brian James, Captain Sensible, and Rat Scabies, the group first performed at the 100 Club in London, supporting the Pistols and late the next year played on the "Anarchy in the U.K." tour. In March 1977, they released the first British punk album, *Damned, Damned, Damned*, which climbed to number 36 on the English charts.

Siouxie and the Banshees began as part of the Bromley Contingent, a group of fans who religiously followed the Sex Pistols. In September 1976 at the 100 Club Festival headlined by the Pistols, Siouxie Sioux (a.k.a. Susan Dallion), Sid Vicious, Marc Pironi, and Steve Havoc (a.k.a. Steve Severin) jumped on stage and performed an extemporaneous, twenty-minute punk version of "The Lord's Prayer." At the end of the year, Siouxie appeared with the Sex Pistols on the British television show "Today," and late the next year the fledgling band backed Johnny Thunders in concert. In June 1978 the Banshees signed with Polydor Records and in three months released their first single, "Hong Kong Garden," which hit the number-7 spot on the British singles chart. They quickly recorded the LP *The Scream* which by the end of the year climbed into the British Top 15.

Generation X was started by two Bromley Contingent fans, Billy Idol (a.k.a. William Broad) and Tony James. In September 1976 the duo formed the band with Mark Laff on drums and guitarist Bob Andrews and released the single "Your Generation," an answer to The Who's baby-boom anthem "My Generation." Later in the same year, Generation X became the first punk band to perform at the venue, The Roxy, which became a punk hangout. In March 1978 the group released their first LP, which charted at number 29 in Britain.

ROCK AGAINST RACISM

Rock Against Racism united many of the British punk bands in a fight against the racism rampant in Britain. It began after an August 14, 1976 concert in Birmingham at which a drunken Eric Clapton lectured concertgoers about Britain "becoming a black colony within ten years." "Musicians were coming out with the 'Blame the Blacks bit,'" recalled one organizer. "Bowie and Clapton were the last straws—how dare they praise Hitler or want to repatriate the race that had created the music they profitably recycled. We loved music, hated racism and thought it was about time rock and roll paid back some dues." Rock Against Racism, mentioned the organizer, tried to "fight back against the creeping power of racist ideas in popular culture" and attacked the right-wing, neo-Nazi National Front. By April 1978, the coalition had organized fifty-six chapters and attracted more than 80,000 adherents to an Anti-Nazi League Carnival in London headlined by the Clash.

Elvis Costello headed another Rock Against Racism benefit. The son of bandleader Ross McManus, Declan McManus played at local folk clubs under his mother's maiden name, Costello. In 1976 he signed to Stiff Records, owned by Jake Riviera, who suggested that he rename himself Elvis. He released his vinyl debut in April 1977, "Less Than Zero," a song attacking Oswald Mosley, a 1930's British fascist who inspired the National Front. Costello then recorded a ballad, "Alison," which blunted the hard-edged punk sound and became a model for the post-punk new wave. "What I really wanted to do was approach the music with the same attitude, the same attack as punk, without sacrificing all the things I liked about music—like, say, tunes," Elvis remembered. In the summer of 1978, Costello played such songs as "Less Than Zero" at a Rock Against Racism concert in Brixton.

In June 1978 the Clash, the Tom Robinson Band, and Sham 69 played to 50,000 young punks who attended a Rock Against Racism concert. Tom Robinson, who had formed his band in early 1977 and had hit the Top 10 in Britain with "2-4-6-8-Motorway," shouted to the audience that the National Front must be confronted "at school and at work." "If music can erase even a tiny fraction of the prejudice and intolerance in this world, then it's worth trying," he told an interviewer at the time. "Through my lyrics," agreed Morgan Webster of Sham 69, "I want to show the National Front that they're fucking assholes." "We're against fascism and racism," declared Joe Strummer of the Clash. By the end of summer in 1978, more than 250,000 youths had rocked against racism in thirty-six concerts held across England.

THE JAMAICAN CONNECTION: REGGAE AND SKA

Reggae, the music of the downtrodden in Jamaica, was championed by British punks dedicated to racial equality. It was part of the Jamaican Rastifarian religion, which emerged as early as the 1930s, when the rotund American Marcus Garvey urged Jamaican blacks to return to the Ethiopian kingdom of Haile Selassie, considered to be the Lion of Judah. Garvey's back-to-Africa message appealed to the many unemployed Jamaicans, about 35 percent of the working-age population in the sixties, who congregated in the slums of West Kingston.

Trapped in this poverty-stricken situation, many Jamaicans adhered to Rastafarianism's coherent set of beliefs: Selassie became the prophet Prince of God, or Jah, and, after his fall, the martyred King; the Ethiopian colors—black, green, and red—were adopted as the Rasta standard; Jamaicans began to sport a plaited hair style known as dreadlocks; and in the late 1960s reggae, which combined African and indigenous Jamaican rhythms, replaced the westernized calypso to become the music of the countercultural religion. Peter Tosh, one of the fathers of reggae, explained, "Reggae, the word, means 'king's music,' and I play the King's music. The King put many princes on earth, and the music is given to those who praise Him. You have to be spiritually inclined to deal with this kind of talent."

Reggae originated in the slums of the Jamaican capital. "When I came to Kingston at about 16 years of age," Tosh remembered, "I soon realized that nine out of ten singers found themselves in poverty in Trenchtown, the ghetto. It was me, Bob Marley, Bunny Livingstone, Joe Higgs, the Maytals—we'd sit around every night and just sing. At that time, me and Joe Higgs were the only ones who could play the guitar. Finally Joe Higgs helped to get us into the studio with Sir Coxsone Dodd producing, and that was the start of recording for me and Bob and Bunny." In 1964, Tosh and his friends, calling themselves the Wailers, hit the Jamaican charts with the ska-influenced "Simmer Down." Two years later, they recorded another ska song, "Rude Boy," which immortalized the outlaws of Kingston's shantytown and reached the number-1 spot in the former British colony.

Around 1970 the Wailers abandoned the more traditional Jamaican ska for a new music that was rooted in Rastafarianism and became known as reggae. They delivered such songs as "African Herbsman" and "Rasta Revolution." In 1973 the group released the reggae LPs *Catch a Fire* and *Burnin,'* the second including "I Shot the Sheriff," a song ironically covered by Eric Clapton. Two years later the Wailers cut *Natty Dread,* a testament to the Rastafarian culture.

The Wailers, along with other reggae groups, such as Toots and the Maytals, Burning Spear, Black Uhuru, and Steel Pulse, lambasted the racism and the capitalism that Britain had imposed upon their homeland. Burning Spear (a.k.a. Winston Rodney) used the Rastafarian dialect to express his belief the everyone should "be equal or i-qual and get an equal share. An' everyman entitled to dem share an' should get dem share. . . . The work is to bring the whole world together. See. That is naturality. Non-violence, less pollution, more togetherness, more industry, less institution like prisons; more schools, more hospitals. These things come through the music. And the music is those things and those things is the music." Jamaican producer Lee Perry told a reporter that reggae "denounces the very heart of the system on which much of the capitalist world is built." Not just voicing rhetoric, many reggae bands, such as Bob Marley and the Wailers, actively backed the

HORACE - Bass   NEVILLE - Vocals   RODDY - Guitar   BRAD - Drums   TERRY - Vocals   LYNVAL - Guitar   JERRY - Organ

The Specials: two-tone originals

government of socialist prime minister Michael Manley. At one 1976 rally for the Prime Minister, Marley barely escaped an assassination attempt. Other reggae bands such as Steel Pulse, Aswad, and Matumbi, aligning with left-wing British punks, became mainstays on the bills of Rock Against Racism concerts.

Some British youths took ska—the light, happy Jamaican music that predated reggae—and fused it with the radical message and the energy of punk. "We were the first band which wanted to combine punk and reggae because we liked them both," recalled Jerry Dammers of the racially integrated Specials, one of the most influential of the new ska groups. "Both were rebel music," said fellow Special member Horace Panter. In 1979, the band borrowed £700 to record on their own 2-Tone label the Prince Buster ska classic "Al Capone." They followed a few months later with a debut album, produced by Elvis Costello, which cracked the British Top 5.

The Specials recorded the Selector on their 2-Tone label. Living in Coventry as did the Specials, the racially integrated Selector delivered a politically charged version of punk-ska. Featuring the vocals of Pauline Black, the band hit the charts with singles such as "Three Minute Hero."

The English Beat, the other major seventies ska band, produced a similar sound for a similar purpose. Guitarist Dave Wakeling rediscovered ska because "it said what a terrible world this was—with a smile on its face." In 1979 the Birmingham group created its own Go Feet label and released their top-selling debut, which included "Stand Down Margaret," aimed at Prime Minister Margaret Thatcher.

THE INDEPENDENT LABELS

Other independent labels were established to distribute the politicized punk and ska. In 1976, Rough Trade Records began pressing discs. In the words of staffer Allan Sturdy, the label hoped to "provide an alternative to the music establishment so that a record could be available that otherwise wouldn't." It first recorded the debut LP of the politically minded Ulster band, Stiff Little Fingers, which delivered such songs as "Alternative Ulster," "Suspect Device," "Law and Order," "Rough Trade," and "White Noise," which detailed white Britain's racism toward blacks, Pakistanis, and the Irish. The new independent based its operations on cooperation with the musicians, since, as Rough Trade's Howie Klein commented, most "record companies are part of an anti-social movement in Western society, part of the industrial complex that enslaves people." They split profits fifty-fifty between the company and the artist, keeping the prices as low as possible and funneling business profits back into the company. Also, the twenty-five staffers at Rough Trade democratically made decisions about material, rejecting songs that were sexist or racist. "I wouldn't sign a band that was racist or sexist or fascist or anything like that," Klein told a reporter.

The ethic of Rough Trade spread. Factory Records opened a cooperative venture in Manchester, Fast Product did the same in Edinburgh, and Graduate Records was started in Dudley. Although a few independents such as I.R.S., Virgin, and Stiff became small versions of the majors, many followed the example of the humanistic Rough Trade. A spate of independent newspapers and magazines, such as *Damage, Slash, New York Rocker, Vacation, Hot Press, Sounds,* and *Another Room* publicized the independent releases.

Some punk bands, after starting with the independents, signed with major labels for better distribution of their records. Tom Robinson, facing the contradiction between his leftist politics and the money-making goals of his label, asserted that one has "to use the capitalist media to reach the people. And I do feel that pop music is the way to reach people. Ideally, I'd like to be played on AM stations rather than FM stations, rather than the rarified atmosphere. I'd rather be played in taxis, in factories, for housewives working at home." Joe Strummer tried "to do something new, we're trying to be the greatest group in the world, and that also means the biggest. At the same time, we're trying to be radical—I mean, we never want to be *really* respectable—keep punk alive." Added Mick Jones of The Clash: "We realized that if we were a little more subtle, if we branched out a little, we might reach a few more people. We finally saw we had been reaching the same people over and over. This way if more kids started hearing the record, maybe they'd start humming the songs, they'll read the lyrics and learn something from them."

RIGHT-WING REACTION

The National Front attempted to destroy such politicized bands as The Clash. In 1977 the *British Patriot,* the magazine of the National Front, warned its readers that The Clash was "the most left-wing of the contemporary groups." To diffuse their influence, it instructed National Fronters to keep "an eye out for posters that advertise Clash concerts so that they may be removed from walls and boardings and reconsigned to the gutter where they will reach the most appropriate clientele." During their first tour of Great Britain, The Clash met resistance. Police repeatedly stopped their tour bus for little or no excuse, and the band members were arrested and fined for such dire offenses as forgetting to return hotel keys. In the United States, Epic Record executives at first refused to issue the group's debut LP, *The Clash* (EMI: April 1977), branding it "too crude" for American consumption. They put out the album two years later in an altered form.

Other punk bands also met opposition. In July 1978, the National Front burned down two auditoriums used for Rock Against Racism shows. A year later, British police stormed into the Southall Musicians Cooperative—the home of white and black punkers and reggae musicians—and wantonly smashed instruments and sound equipment. Benefit concerts for the Cooperative, organized by The Clash and Pete Townshend of The Who, generated enough money to replace the damaged goods.

Throughout the late seventies, the new Teddy Boys and the skinheads attacked punks in gangland fashion. The two groups of youth, maintained Pete Townshend, were "fascist. They despise everybody who isn't like them. It's a kind of toy fascism, fed by organized fascism; fed by Martin Webster and the National Front." In 1979 these right-wing teens, organizing into the Young National Front, launched a Rock Against Communism movement to counterbalance Rock Against Racism. They also formed rock groups such as Ventz, Column 44, and Tragic Minds to disseminate such songs as "Master Race," "White Power," and "Kill the Reds."

THE DECLINE OF PUNK

Businesses on both sides of the Atlantic undermined punk by selling punk style without its substance. Punks had created a minimalist fashion directly related to their aggressive attitude. "They wear with snarling pride the marks of the downtrodden," wrote Anthony Burgess. "Hair is cropped because long hair holds lice. Clothes are not patched, since patching denotes skill and a seedy desire for respectability; their gaping holes are held together with safety pins." The punks adopted the agitational-propaganda art form of such Russian revolutionaries as Malevich, Tatlin, and Rodchenko, creating posters characterized by sharp, piercing lines against stark backgrounds.

Business capitalized on a copy of punk fashion. As early as June 1977, *Newsweek* observed that "both Saks on Fifth Avenue and Bonwit Teller carry gold safety pins at prices up to $100, and noted British designer Zandra Rhodes recently created a collection of gowns for Bloomingdale's that incorporate stylized rips and glitter-studded safety pins—at $345 to $1,150 a gown." The June 1980 issue of *Mademoiselle* offered its readers the choice between "punk or prep" fashion in a four-page spread. Richard Hell began to lament that "punk was intended to be a whole kind of consciousness. But then it got corrupted into being simply a style or a fad."

Some soft rockers began to take advantage of the punk image. Linda Ronstadt appeared with spiked hair on the pink-and-black album cover of the 1980 LP *Mad Love*, and covered "Alison" and "My Aim Is True" by Elvis Costello. Billy Joel, the piano man who topped the charts in 1977 with *The Stranger*, posed in a leather jacket and a rock in his cocked arm for the cover of his 1980 album *Glass Houses*. Even Cher, the folk-singer-turned-disco-queen, surfaced in full punk regalia as the lead singer of the short-lived punk/heavy metal band Black Rose. In 1979 Sandy Perlman, producer of The Clash's second album, complained that "no one's really very scared of punk, especially the record companies. They've sublimated all the revolutionary tendencies this art is based on."

Punk rock began to disintegrate. By 1978 in New York, the CBGB bands began to compete for record contracts. "The greatest thing about it in the beginning was that there was no pressure," recalled one CBGB regular. "Then, after a while, the record companies started to come in. And then people started to be cutthroat about being seen and stuff like that, and it was not the same."

The more aggressive British punk bands began to abandon the buzz saw guitar sound for different styles of music. In 1979, Tom Robinson confessed to *Melody Maker* that "after two and a half years, [punk] has become a bit tame and predictable. It's time to move on and try something fresh." He opted for the electronic pop of Sector 27. Amid a 1980 European tour, a disgusted Joe Strummer of The Clash complained to the *New Musical Express* that "punk rock has just hit Europe in a big way, but it's totally worthless . . . It's just another fashion. It's become everything it wasn't supposed to be. I was emotionally shattered." The Clash, incorporating Jamaican rhythms into their music as early as 1976 in a remake of Junior Murvin's "Police and Thieves," moved further and further from the boisterous sound of their first album. By the 1980 triple-album *Sandanista* and the 1982 *Combat Rock*, they sounded little like the snarling punks of 1976.

Even the Sex Pistols deserted punk rock. On January 14, 1978, after an American tour, the group was disbanded by Johnny Rotten, who felt that the band had extended rock to its outer limits. "The Pistols finished rock and roll. That was the last rock and roll band. It's all over now," he told an interviewer. "Rock and roll is shit. It's dismal. Granddad danced to it." Paul Cook and Steve Jones played briefly with Johnny Thunders before starting more pop ventures. On February 2, 1979, Sid Vicious, the archetype of the punk image, died from a drug overdose in New York City. Johnny Rotten reclaimed his original surname, Lydon, and started the "anti-rock and roll" band Public Image Ltd. (PiL) with ex-Clash member Keith Levene, novice bass player Jah Woble, and drummer Jim Walker. Unlike the Sex Pistols, PiL produced a dissonant, jagged, electronic sound perfected by the 1979 *Metal Box*. "I've grown very far away from human beings," Lydon told *Trouser Press* magazine. "I like being detached; I don't even like shaking hands. I don't like sweat. I think everyone is ugly. Faces disgust me and feet really make me reek. I think the human body's about one of the most ugly things

John Lydon

ever created." Rather than people, the ex-Pistol found solice in "machines. Lots of buttons on record players. Knobs and gadgets, electrical equipment of any kind."

HARDCORE

A twisted, despair-filled version of punk known as "hardcore" survived in Los Angeles, the smog-filled, fairyland gone sour. Bands such as X fused the hyperactive roar of punk with lyrics that described a society that had degenerated beyond repair. In 1977 the group began performing a rockabilly-tinged punk characterized by the thunderous drumming of Don Bonebrake, the guitar of Billy Zoom, and the lyrics of the husband-wife team of John Doe and Exene Cervenka. On the debut LP, *Los Angeles*, Doe and Cervenka harmonized on such tales of despondency as "Nausea" and "Sex and Dying in High Society." "You'd be on Sunset Strip with people dangerously close to attacking you for money while all these Rolls-Royces were going by," observed Exene about her hometown. "You just feel like everybody's insane. No one really has any values."

Black Flag, the prototypical hardcore band, dwelt upon masochist despair. Formed in 1979, it featured vocalist Henry Rollins shouting over a thrashing, fuzzy, chaotic, guitar-based sound. The group, after establishing its own SST label in 1981, released its first

Black Flag

album, *Damaged,* which included the hardcore anthem, "Rise Above." It followed with a flurry of LPs that contained such morose commentaries as "Depression," "Dead Inside," and "Life of Pain." "Pain is my girlfriend; that's how I see it," explained Rollins. "I feel pain everyday of my life. When you see me perform, it's that pain you're seeing coming out. I put all my emotions, all my feelings, and my body on the line. People hurt me, I hurt myself—mentally, physically."

The Germs exemplified the self-destructive impulse of hardcore punk. The band, first performing at The Whisky in Los Angeles in

Slam Dancer

1977, featured the staccato fuzz guitar of Pat Smear and the barking of Darby Crash. In concert and on their first LP, *(GI)*, they sang such depressing paeans as "Suicide Madness." In 1979, Darby Crash symbolically committed suicide as a tribute to his hero, Sid Vicious.

Many of the mostly male, middle-class fans of hardcore perpetrated violence upon others and themselves. Shaving their heads in military style, they sometimes "trashed" bums for entertainment. "They're all these rich kids and they're spoiled and have all kinds of money from their parents," complained Derf Scratch of the band Fear. "They got into the punk scene and the only way they can prove to themselves and their friends that they're punks is to beat somebody up." At concerts, the hardcore fanatics slammed into each other and at times leapt from the stage onto the mass of slam dancers.

The Dead Kennedys preached leftist politics to hardcore fans. Meeting in San Francisco during 1978, the band merged the thrash sound with lyrics that attacked U.S. imperialism, the moral majority, and the creeping fascism among hardcore youths, who began to wear Nazi armbands. In their first LP, *Fresh Fruit for Rotting Vegetables*, they criticized California Governor Jerry Brown and "zen fascists" in "California uber Alles," blasted U.S. involvement in Southeast Asia in "Holiday in Cambodia," and tackled the issue of poverty in "Let's Lynch the Landlord" and "Kill the Poor." The band continued to deliver such social commentaries as "Terminal Preppie," "Trust Your Mechanic," "Winnebago Warrior," and "Nazi Punks Fuck Off" until they disbanded in 1986 amid a controversy over censorship of the album cover to the LP *Frankenchrist*.

By the early 1980s, hardcore began to fade into a mutant type of heavy metal known as thrash. Inspired by the hard-driving, double-speed metal of such English bands as Motorhead, Diamondhead, and the Tygers of Pan Tang, in 1981 vocalist James Hetfield, guitarist Kirk Hammett, bassist Cliff Burton, and drummer Lars Ulrich began to perform in the Los Angeles area as Metallica. "When we first started doing clubs," remembered Hetfield, "we were doing mostly covers of the new wave of English metal bands, and because nobody had heard these records, all the bangers thought we were doing our own songs."

Metallica began to speed up the already fast tempo of British metal. "When we first started writing our own songs, they weren't very fast at all," admitted Hetfield. "Then we got a few more gigs, and we got a little more pissed off at the crowd and how people weren't appreciating our stuff. So they gradually got faster and faster as we got more aggressive. Instead of going, 'Please like us,' we were like . . . 'AAAHH! Fuck you!'"

The group began to record, first passing a demo tape to a few fans who circulated it around the country. In 1983 they released their first LP, *Kill 'Em All*, on the independent label Megaforce, and followed the next year with *The Lightening*, which sold more than 500,000 copies in six months. In 1985 the band released a collection of socially relevant songs with the LP *Master of Puppets*, which addressed such concerns as cocaine addiction and war and reached number 29 on the U.S. charts without the help of television or radio, which had boycotted most eighties heavy metal. In late 1988, they continued to churn out topical thrash classics with the LP . . . *And Justice for All*.

Other bands joined the thrash metal fold. Dave Mustaine, an original member of Metallica, formed Megadeth, which featured screeching vocals and a hyperspeed guitar attack captured on such albums as the 1985 *Killing Is My Business . . . and Business Is Good!* and the 1986 *Peace Sells . . . but Who's Buying*. In New York City, Anthrax abandoned hardcore for thrash metal and in 1984 released the LP *Fistful of Metal*. By 1984, even Black Flag increasingly drifted toward metal, with the albums *My War* and *Slip It In*. By the mid-1980s, the aggressive, politicized punk had largely disappeared from rock.

The Post-Punk Explosion

Punk, though beginning to disintegrate by 1978, shattered the monopoly of corporate rock. "Imagine in your mind an ELP [Emerson, Lake and Palmer] number," suggested Joe Strummer of The Clash.

"Then imagine punk rock like a blow torch sweeping across it. That to me is what punk rock did."

Punk rock paved the way for other bands that played music to a new post-baby boom generation. "I did it. I did it," boasted Johnny Rotten. "I made doors open, I made it easier for up and coming bands. It was a Rolling Stones type of monopoly of the entire business. Record companies would not sign new acts. I opened that up."

Some post-punk bands such as Joy Division, following the model of Rotten's PiL, delivered a chilling, dissonant, minimalist music. In 1976, friends Peter Hook and Bernard Albrecht decided to form a band. "We were both 21 when we started and had never played an instrument before in our lives. It was straight after seeing the first Sex Pistols gig in Manchester," recalled Hook. "We thought they were so bad, but yet it was so exciting. God! We could have a go at that." A few months later, Hook, Albrecht and their friend Steven Morris met singer Ian Curtis who, according to Hook, "introduced us to Lou Reed and the Velvet Underground, to Iggy Pop and the Stooges, and the Doors."

By mid-1977 the foursome began to produce a droning, Velvet Underground–inspired sound punctuated by Curtis's gloomy lyrics. They called themselves Warsaw and, to avoid confusion with another band, renamed themselves Joy Division after the prostitute wing in a Nazi concentration camp. In June 1979 the band signed with the newly established Factory Records owned by Tony Wilson, who used his life savings to finance the group's first LP, *Unknown Pleasures*. Joy Division hit the Top 20 with the single "Love Will Tear Us Apart" and started to gain critical acclaim before Ian Curtis hanged himself in May 1980 on the eve of an American tour.

The Cure reflected the post-punk pessimism. Formed in 1976, the band debuted with the single "Killing an Arab," inspired by a passage in the Albert Camus novel *The Stranger*. In May 1979 they released their first LP, the pop-oriented *Imaginary Boys* which reached number 44 on the British charts. The band turned to such pessimistic themes as "The Funeral Party" and "The Drowning Man" on the subsequent albums, *17 Seconds* and *Faith*. In 1982, the Cure released the downbeat classic, *Pornography*, which reflected the deep pessimism of some post-punk bands. "I suppose doing an album like *Pornography* and coming to those depths and coming out of it proves that something can come out of nothing," observed songer-lyricist Robert Smith after the band had returned to a pop sound in the mid-1980s.

Some punks such as The Police offered a bright, pop alternative to post-punk depression. In January 1977 Stewart Copeland and Gordon Sumner, nicknamed Sting because he often wore a black-and-yellow jersey, met at a jazz club and began rehearsing with guitarist Henri Padovani. The next month the trio released the punk single "Fall Out," and in March toured with Johnny Thunders and the Heartbreakers. "All I could see in punk was a very direct,

The Cure

simple image of power and energy," recalled Sting, who had been enamored with jazz as a youth. "I could relate to that. I could easily ally myself with that, and forget about changes, chords with flatted fifths, forget all that."

The Police quickly changed musical direction. They replaced Padovani with guitarist Andy Summers and in 1978 released the single, 'Roxanne,' which blended the energy of punk with a reggae-influenced, jazz-tinged sound. "I'm an opportunist," admitted Sting. I saw this vacuum between punk, which was unschooled, and the horrible corporate rock on the other side. I saw this thing in the middle that was clean and simple. That's what 'Roxanne' is; it's so simple and bare. It's not the energy of *Never Mind the Bollocks,* nor is it corporate rock. It's right in between them."

The new pop sound of The Police led to superstardom. The 1978 LP *Outlandos D'Amour,* which contained "Roxanne," hit the Top 10 on the British charts. "Message in a Bottle" and "Walking on the Moon," singles from the band's second album, both topped the

The Police

U.K. charts. In 1980 the LP *Zenyatta Mondatta* hit the top of the British charts and was the group's first Top-10 effort in the United States. The next year, *Ghost in the Machine* climbed to number 2 in America and again topped the charts in England, yielding such hits as "Every Little Thing She Does Is Magic" and "Spirits in the Material World." The album, *Synchronicity*, provided the band with its first number-1 hit on both sides of the Atlantic, making The Police a pop phenomenon. "I don't think pop music is a pejorative term," Sting told an interviewer in 1987. "I want to be proud of being a pop singer when I turn 40."

Billy Idol channeled his punk energy into a spritely pop. After quitting Generation X in 1981, the singer hired ex–Kiss manager Bill Aucoin and recorded such pop songs as "White Wedding," "Hot in the City," and "Love Calling," which fused the persistent beat of punk with snappy melodies. In 1983 he released the Top-10 album,

Rebel Yell, and followed in 1986 with the million-selling *Whiplash Smile.*

Chrissie Hynde hit the charts with a combination of hard-edged punk and soul. After attending Kent State University in Ohio, she journeyed to London, where she modeled, sold leather handbags, and wrote for the rock paper the *New Musical Express.* In 1974, Hynde worked part-time for Malcolm McLaren in his clothing shop, Sex, and two years later unsuccessfully tried to form a band with guitarist Mick Jones, who had just joined The Clash. Hynde then briefly played guitar for the Malcolm McLaren-managed band Masters of the Backside, which eventually became the Damned.

In 1978 Chrissie Hynde formed the Pretenders with bassist Pete Farndon, James Honeyman-Scott on guitar, and Martin Chambers on drums. During the next three years, the band released two top-selling albums, which expanded the sound of punk by infusing it with elements of soul. "I didn't quite fit into the London punk scene because I'd been listening to too many Bobby Womack albums," Hynde insisted.

Adam Ant, born Stuart Goddard, transformed punk energy into pop hits. In 1977, after leaving Hornsey Art College, he formed a punk band named the Ants, which recorded a series of unsuccessful singles. Two years later he hired as manager Malcolm McLaren, who encouraged the Ants to split from Adam and to form Bow Wow Wow with Annabella Lwin.

Adam Ant, deserted by McLaren, began to adopt a different image. He abandoned the ripped T-shirts and safety pins of punk for foppish scarves, embroidered, double-breasted jackets, skin-tight leather pants, and sashes. Enlisting the help of ex-Siouxie and the Banshees guitarist Marco Pirroni, he formed a pop version of the Ants, which featured an upbeat, drum-based sound. From 1980 to 1983, Adam and his Ants hit the charts with the albums *Kings of the Wild Frontier*, *Prince Charming*, and *Friend or Foe*, which were promoted by videos of the photogenic group. In 1985 Adam disbanded the group, deciding to concentrate exclusively on his acting career. Adam Ant had been transformed from an angry punk into a video star who became popular on an American music channel that would change the direction of rock during the early 1980s.

14

I Want My MTV

"Video will be the way to keep time with the future."

"Increasingly, and perhaps irreversibly, audiences for American mainstream music will depend, even insist, on each song being a full audiovisual confrontation," observed *Time* in 1983. "Why should sound alone be enough when sight is only as far away as the TV set or the video machine?" "Video," concluded the magazine, "will be the way to keep time with the future."

MTV, a new music channel established only a year earlier, was the subject of comments by *Time*. During the early 1980s, MTV began to replace radio among a generation of teens, born during the 1960s, who had no personal recollection of Elvis, the Beatles, or Vietnam and sought their own musical identity. It helped create the visual rock of Duran Duran and pop metal and played a major role in mania over Michael Jackson. In the 1980s, MTV designed and delivered rock to the TV generation.

THE VIDEO AGE

Americans of the 1980s became obsessed with a video technology that had first been introduced to the mass market with the television set. They continued to buy television sets until, by the end of the decade, 98.2 percent of all American households had television, most had at least two sets, and 85 percent owned a color TV. At the beginning of the decade, they elected for president Ronald Reagan, who had been a well-known screen actor during the 1940s and gained unparalled popularity while president for his mastery of the video medium.

American consumers bought millions of personal home computers and accompanying TV monitors, which had become more powerful and less expensive during the decade. In 1981 they purchased 1.4 million home computers for $3 billion, an increase of almost 50 percent from the previous year.

Americans also purchased compact video recorder-players, first mass marketed in 1976 by the Victor Co. of Japan (JVC). In 1981, Americans purchased 1.3 units, a 69 percent increase from the previous year. By 1989, more than 97 million Americans owned JVC-manufactured VCRs. At the beginning of the decade they rented 3 million prerecorded movies and bought 15 million blank videotapes as accessories to the machines. Ten years later Americans bought more than 200 million prerecorded tapes and 280 million blank videocassettes yearly.

Overall, Americans spent $9.2 billion on video products in 1981. Four years later they purchased more than $15 billion in video machines and accessories. By the end of the decade, most American consumers had become part of the expanding video culture.

American teenagers who had been raised on television were especially susceptible to the video craze. The post-baby boomers spent from three to four hours a day in front of the television set at home. By the time of high school graduation, they had spent more time watching commercial television than sitting in the classroom. In a 1981 survey among eighth graders, the youths named TV personalities as their top ten role models. The post-baby boomers even stared at television sets in their school rooms which, by the 1980s, became increasingly equipped with instructional TV.

American teenagers of the 1980s, accustomed to the television screen at home and at school, became entranced by video games. They first began to play Space Invaders at the turn of the decade. By 1981 the TV generation dropped more than 25 billion quarters into video game machines at local arcades, which grossed more than the combined television revenues of baseball, football, and basketball and more than the combined income of all the casinos in the country. Teens, mostly male, spent an average of $4.30 a week on coin-operated video games and in 1981 spent the equivalent of 75,000 years playing Pac-Man, Asteroids, Space Invaders, and other video games. One fifteen-year-old in Arlington, Illinois, played the video game, Defender, for sixteen hours and thirty-four minutes on the same quarter before losing his last ship. In 1982, the Atari Corporation, owned by Warner Communications, grossed about $1.3 billion in home video game console and cartridge sales. By that year, more than 8 percent of all households owned home video games.

MTV: ROCK IN THE VIDEO AGE

Warner Communications quickly applied video technology to the pop music field. Aided by the advent of stereo TV and the deregulation of the airwaves which encouraged the growth of cable television, Warner and American Express invested $20 million to launch Music Television (MTV) on August 1, 1981. They broadcast a non-stop format of three-minute video clips of primarily Warner artists initially on 300 cable outlets to 2.5 million homes.

Music Television, headed by twenty-eight-year-old Robert Pittman, targeted its programming to the under twenty-five-year-old generation, which had been neglected by radio. "Where is the Woodstock generation? They're all old and bald," Pittman told *Time*. Recycling the 1960s ad campaign for the once-popular breakfast cereal, "I Want My Maypo," into "I Want My MTV," he stalked the "TV babies," who seldom read newspapers, books, or even the rock press.

THE NEW ROMANTICS

MTV attracted the TV generation with young, visually exciting bands from the dance clubs of England. Started as a reaction to the austerity of punk, English dance clubs such as The Blitz in Covent Garden provided working-class youths with escapist entertainment. "Most kids who actually live there are sick of the street," contended Gary Kemp, the founder and guitarist of Spandau Ballet, a prominent dance club band. "They take it for granted, because that is where they live, and they don't know anything better. . . . They want to be in a club with great lights, and look really good and pick up girls."

As with its American counterpart, English disco focused on a fashion-conscious audience. "Discos are always parties because you have to make your own visual entertainment," commented Kemp. "The most important thing in a club is the people, not the music they listen to. You become the most important person. You become the visual aspect of the evening, rather than the band." Discos, he continued, appealed to "people who like being looked at—that's why dancing is so important, and why people try and beat each other at dancing. It's also why clothes are so important."

Gary Kemp traced the excessive concern over fashion to British culture. "The attitude behind it has always been there; mods, skinheads and the soul kids—just kids who want to dress smart and enjoy themselves," he told *Trouser Press* magazine. "My dad was a Teddy Boy and my older cousin was a mod. I guess it's hereditary."

The music played at the clubs, a combination of the steady disco beat and atmospheric sounds of the electronic synthesizer, originated with such groups as Roxy Music. Formed in early 1971 by singer Brian Ferry and named after the popular chain of Roxy cinemas in England, the band wore stylish, sometimes flamboyant costumes designed by the futuristic Anthony Price. One member of the group, wrote *Music Scene*, "has been seen traveling the Underground wearing heavily applied brown eye shadow, thick mascara, lipstick, black glitter beads, pearly nail varnish, and violent purple streaks in his blonde hair."

Roxy Music, unlike most glam rockers of the 1970s who delivered hard rock, featured the synthesizer of Brian Eno, which added an almost ethereal element to the music. The band released its debut, self-named album in 1972, which reached the Top 10 in Britain and included the smash British single "Virginia Plain." The next year, Roxy Music refined its distinctive style in the album *For Your Pleasure*, which contained such synthesizer-based songs as "Do the Strand," "Editions of You," and "In Every Dream Home a Heartache."

Brian Eno, who shaped the unique Roxy sound, left the group in 1973 to, in his words, "pursue a partially defined direction—probably involving further investigations into bioelectronics, snake guitar, the human voice, and lizard girls." The band replaced him with the teenage multi-instrumentalist Eddie Jobson and began to deliver a quieter, smoother sound that showcased Brian Ferry's vocals. By 1975, just as the band scored its first U.S. hit single, "Love Is The Drug," Roxy Music disbanded.

Ultravox continued the tradition of Roxy Music and became the direct precursor of the New Romantic movement. Brought together in 1976 by John Foxx, who had dabbled in tapes and synthesizers while in school, the extravagantly bedecked band recorded two albums of straightforward rockers punctuated by the violin and keyboards of Billy Currie. In 1978, the band added the synthesizer of Chris Cross and enlisted the help of producer Conny Plank, who had worked with such experimental electronic groups as Can and Kraftwerk. That year, they released the LP *Systems of Romance*, which offered listeners a sparse, crystalline, electronic sound that defined electro-pop, New Romantic music.

When in December 1979 John Foxx left Ultravox, keyboardist Billy Currie joined fashion-conscious Steve Strange, synthesizer player Midge Ure, and members of a group called Magazine to form Visage. As with Ultravox, the band emphasized outrageous fashion. "Fashion," commented Steve Strange, "has been missing from the scene since the early 70s with Bowie and Roxy, so what we're part of is just an upsurge in fashion."

Visage expanded the Ultravox sound, featuring two synthesizers and guitars grounded by a heavy, repetitious drumbeat. "We were trying to get away from the obvious disco sound," explained Strange. "I messed around with synthesizers and found sounds which were really different from the traditional guitar and bass. We wanted to create a danceable beat, I know you can do that with drums and a bass but it was a new sound that we wanted to use."

Gary Numan popularized the sound of electro-pop that Ultravox and Visage had developed. Born Gary Webb in 1958 and taking his pseudonym from the Yellow Pages, Numan first played in the punk-influenced Tubeway Army. He soon abandoned the guitar for the synthesizer, donned futuristic outfits, and on May 4, 1979, released the synthesizer dance number "Are 'Friends' Electric." Two weeks later, Numan and his band, which included Billy Currie, appeared on the British television show, "Top of the Pops," and by the end of July, the single and the album *Replicas* hit the top of the British charts. "Gary Numan just released 'Are 'Friends' Electric' when everyone thought synthesizer bands were just junk or something or that anyone who used a synthesizer was just a bit of a joke," remembered Midge Ure. "At the time it was very unfashionable but six months later because of Gary Numan it became very fashionable to be a synthesizer band."

The ease of mastering the synthesizer contributed to its popularity. "In some ways it's quite strange that synthesizers were so hated in the punk era," remarked Andy McClusky of the successful electro-pop band, Orchestral Manoeuvres in the Dark, which formed in 1980. "They're the ideal punk instrument if you believe in the ethic of 'anybody can do it.' Someone who's been playing synth for 10 minutes can easily sound as good as someone who's been playing for years, provided the ideas are there." "We couldn't hardly play at all then; we can't play very well now," confessed Andy Fletcher in 1982, a year after his all-synthesizer band, Depeche Mode, was formed. "In pop music nowadays you don't need technical ability, you need ideas and the ability to write songs. That's the main thing."

By the beginning of the 1980s, the portable synthesizers had become relatively inexpensive. Unlike the cumbersome, sometimes stationary Moog models of the previous decade, easy-to-handle portables could be purchased for as little as $100 to $300.

The electro-pop sound of the synthesizer, easily attainable and affordable, embodied the digital, push-button orientation of the 1980s. "Not a day goes by when you don't press a button, whether it's for a cup of coffee or to turn on the stereo or video," observed

Courtesy of Cam Garrett/S.C.V.D. Studio

Gary Numan and synthesizer

David Ball of the two-man synthesizer group Soft Cell, which came together in 1981. "People are so surrounded now by electronics, of course there's electronic music."

MTV GOES ELECTRO-POP

MTV, searching for videos of new bands to air on its twenty-four-hour-a-day format, promoted the electro-pop of such fashion-obsessed New Romantics as Duran Duran. Begun in 1978 as a duo and named after a character in the science-fiction movie *Barbarella*, by 1981 the group had become a fivesome that featured an airy-

Duran Duran

sounding synthesizer, the insistent drumbeat of disco, and a pop
sensibility for what keyboard player Nick Rhodes dubbed "entertainment music." The group achieved notoriety with its first, self-
named album and the subsequent *Rio* (1982) through the
imaginative use of videos on MTV. "Videos are incredibly important
for us," asserted Rhodes. "It's a way of expressing a song in visuals.
It gives another dimension." "MTV," added the keyboardist, "was
instrumental in breaking us in America." Norman Sammick, senior
vice-president of Warner Communications put it more succinctly: "I
think Duran Duran owes its life to MTV."

The music channel helped other electro-pop bands such as The
Human League reach the record-buying American public. The
group, formed in Sheffield in 1977, first produced icy, dense electronic music modeled after such European outfits as Kraftwerk, on
the albums *Reproduction* (1979) and *Travelogue* (1980). In 1980,
founder Philip Oakley disbanded The Human League because of its
heavy reliance on taped music during concerts and with Philip
Wright and four new members reformed the band.

The next year, the revamped Human League secured the support of producer Martin Rushent, who infused the band's
synthesizer-based music with a toe-tapping, pop sensibility. "I
wanted to make a pop electronic album," remembered Rushent. "Not
a DAF or a Kraftwerk, but something that was accessible to everybody. The Human League just walked through the door at the right
time." He replaced the traditional keyboard synthesizer with a Ro-

land Microcomposer sequencer, added the flawless beat of the drum machine and in 1982 produced the album *Dare*, which included the singles "Don't You Want Me" and "Love Action (I Believe in Love)." After MTV placed "Don't You Want Me" in heavy rotation, the song became a number-1 single.

MTV lifted other wildly garbed, electro-pop bands to the top of the American charts. Through repeated showings of selected videos, it successfully promoted Spandau Ballet, the London quintet formed in 1980, which hit the charts with "To Cut a Long Story Short"; *Soft Cell,* which scored with a remake of the obscure soul song "Tainted Love"; and *A Flock of Seagulls,* which hit with "Wishing." MTV also marketed Depeche Mode, which had the smash "Just Can't Get Enough"; the Thompson Twins' "In the Name of Love"; and Classix Nouveaux, which recorded such songs as "Guilty" for its first LP in 1981.

MTV refurbished the career of David Bowie, the 1970s icon who had helped lay the groundwork for electro-pop. Bowie, the king of glitter glam rock, who served as a model of fashion for the foppish New Romantics, began to abandon a hard, guitar-based rock sound for the synthesizer around 1976 when he released a collection of techno-pop songs, *Station to Station.* The next year, he began a three-album collaboration with synthesizer wunderkind, Brian Eno, who produced a sometimes-fragile, sometimes-dense synthesizer sound which he had pioneered as a member of Roxy Music. In 1983, at the height of the New Romantic success, the ever-visual Bowie recorded the LP *Let's Dance,* which, with the help of MTV and a world tour, shot to the top of the charts.

The electro-pop sound, largely introduced to America by videos on MTV, swept the United States by 1983. It dominated the charts, filtered into mainstream pop, and captivated the TV generation. The sale of guitars dropped from 1.2 million in 1982 to 875,000 the next year while the sale of synthesizers skyrocketed. MTV, created in the decade of technology, had sold a visually interesting, electro-pop dance music to a generation raised on glitter rock, disco, and television.

The increase in viewers indicated the success of MTV. Initially broadcast to 2.5 million households in late 1981, by 1983 the music channel reached more than 17 million homes on 2,000 cable affiliates. The average MTV viewer was twenty-three-years old and watched the network an hour a day on weekdays and 90 minutes on weekends. "They're watching it," said MTV vice-president Les Garland in early 1983, "not in front of their homework, not as background. They're watching it."

MTV, attracting the under-twenty-five-year-old bracket, appealed to many corporate sponsors who manufactured products for the youth market. "MTV is very attractive," asserted Joseph Ostrow, executive vice-president of the ad agency Young & Rubicam. "It allows you to target very discreetly to a particular segment of the population. For youth-oriented companies that's terrific." "We are a company that believes in specialized entertainment," agreed John Lack, executive vice-president of Warner Amex when his company started the network, "and if you are a Budweiser or Kawasaki motorcycles or Pepsi-Cola, you want our audience." In its first year of operation, MTV convinced more than 100 companies such as Budweiser to spend $1,500 for a thirty-second spot and grossed $20 million. By 1984, revenues had jumped to $73 million.

Music Television provided a needed boost to an American record industry that had peaked in 1978 at gross revenues of roughly $4 billion and then sharply declined the next year. The network created a style of music for a new generation, which radio had neglected. "Groups are chalking up huge sales on songs [through MTV] that have never been played on radio," boasted Les Garland. In 1983, *Billboard* estimated that exposure of primarily new bands on MTV resulted in sales increases of 15 to 20 percent. "We were there for the industry," explained John Lack. "We found we could help a business in trouble and it's worked, and they've responded. Ask anyone at CBS or RCA or Arista."

MTV AND MICHAELMANIA

MTV continued to support the American recording industry by promoting a Motown revival starting in 1983, which followed naturally from electro-pop. Though using new technology, the New Romantics created a discolike dance music that had its foundation in the slick, fashionable Motown. As a youth Steve Strange of Visage "used to go to these Northern soul clubs," which featured Motown-type bands. "Our direction came from the soul/disco/dance side, not rock," agreed Gary Kemp of Spandau Ballet, which abandoned synthesizers for the Motown sound in 1983. The electro-pop band Soft Cell first hit the charts with the soul ballad "Tainted Love," and in 1982 scored with a remake of the Supremes' classic "Where Did Our Love Go?"

As the synthesizer craze began to fade in 1982, MTV capitalized on the renewed interest in Motown by airing videos of former Motown star Michael Jackson. Growing up in Gary, Indiana, during the 1960s, Jackson and his siblings Tito, Jermaine, Jackie, and Marlon practiced songs and dance steps at home. "When I found out that my kids were interested in becoming entertainers, I really went to work with them," recalled father Joe Jackson. "I rehearsed them about three years before I turned them loose. That's practically every day for at least two or three hours. When the other kids would be out on the street playing games, my boys were in the house working—trying to learn how to be something in life."

Under the tutelage of Joe Jackson, the boys entered and won talent contests in Indiana and Illinois and played at such Chicago clubs as the High Chaparral and the Guys and Gals Club. "This was on weekends," remembered the elder Jackson. "I had a Volkswagen bus and I bought a big luggage rack and put it on the top and had everybody on the inside of the bus."

Joe Jackson approached Motown about his family musical act. In 1967, he laughed, "I sent Berry Gordy a tape. They kept it about three months and then sent it back." Two years later, the persistent father convinced Gordy to sign the Jackson 5, who had impressed Diana Ross when she performed on the same bill as the boys in 1968 at a civic "Soul Weekend" in Gary.

Berry Gordy, following his formula for success, began to groom the boys. "We provide total guidance," a Motown vice-president explained to *Time*. "We provide their material, set their basic sound and work out the choreographic routines." The company gave special attention to the ten-year-old Michael, who was taught to mimic James Brown's frenzy and the romantic pleadings of Smokey Robinson. In late 1969, Motown featured Michael on the first Jackson 5 release, "I Want You Back," which by January 1970 hit the number-1 slot on the singles chart and sold more than 2 million copies. "We're labeling it soul-bubblegum," declared Berry Gordy.

The Jackson 5 became the last major recording act signed by Motown. They followed their first hit with thirteen consecutive Top 20 singles, including the number-1 hits "ABC," "The Love You Save," and "I'll Be There." By 1976, when they left Motown, the Jackson 5 had received a commendation from Congress for its "contribution to American youth," served as the characters of a Saturday morning network television cartoon show and had become the most successful black pop vocal group, selling more than 100 million records worldwide.

The Jackson 5, Gordy's crossover dream, appealed to all races, genders, and ages. "The Jackson music," stated Joe Jackson, "is a type of music that the young kids like, and as you know, the older people like, too. It's music to send a message to all the people whether they're black or white. It's music for rejoicing, whether you're black or white. It's for the whole world."

In early 1976, the Jackson 5 left the Motown stable, changed their name to the Jacksons, and signed with Epic. Using the songwriting team of Kenny Gamble and Leon Huff and then writing their own material, the group continued to churn out hits, including "Enjoy Yourself" and "Lovely One."

Michael Jackson enjoyed a successful solo career as well. As the popular lead singer of the Jackson 5 at Motown, in 1971 and 1972 he hit the charts with the Top-10 singles "Got To Be There," a reworking of "Rockin' Robin," and "Ben." In 1978, he played the scarecrow in the movie, *The Wiz*, an all-black version of *The Wizard of Oz* starring Diana Ross. While filming the movie, Jackson met producer Quincy Jones, who arranged the music for the soundtrack. The next year, assisted by Jones, Jackson recorded the album *Off the Wall,* which sold 8 million copies and contained the hit singles "Don't Stop Till You Get Enough," "Rock with You," "Off the Wall," and "She's Out of My Life."

In 1982, Jackson again joined with Quincy Jones and produced the album *Thriller.* Trying to appeal to both black and white audiences, he chose as the first single from the album, "This Girl Is Mine" a duet with former Beatle Paul McCartney, a choice that ensured a wide audience. He then released "Beat It," which included a guitar solo by Eddie Van Halen that assured play on rock radio stations. To further disseminate his product, Jackson filmed slick videos of some songs on the album.

Video provided an ideal medium for Jackson, who had been trained in the Motown school. "Rock videos have transformed the music industry, providing a showcase for Jackson in much the same way as musical comedy did for Fred Astaire in the 1930s," *Maclean's,* the Canadian counterpart to *Time* magazine, told its readers in 1984. "Videos have revived the demand for old fashion entertainment skills, an ideal situation for Jackson who has been perfecting his act from the age of five."

The singer, unlike most other rock acts, had perfected dazzling choreography, which had been first encouraged by Motown. Gene Kelly, the popular dancer of the 1940s, raved about Jackson's "native histrionic wit. He knows when to stop and then flash out like a bolt of lightening." "I think he's terrific," enthused Bob Fosse, the director-choreographer who became known for his work on the movie *Cabaret* and the Broadway smash *Pippin.* "Clean, neat, fast with a sensuality that comes through . . . It's the style. That's what Michael Jackson has." Even Fred Astaire, probably the most well-known dancer in American history, complimented Jackson: "My Lord, he is a wonderful mover."

MTV, criticized for only airing videos of white artists, played the visually stunning, expertly choreographed Jackson videos and helped to create Michaelmania. Though Jackson's records had always sold well, *Thriller* began to sell at an amazing rate after it had been promoted on MTV. At the height of the mania, it sold a million copies every four days. It stayed on the Japanese charts for 65 weeks, sold on the black market in the Soviet Union, and even topped the charts in South Africa. "Jackson, you might say, bridges the apartheid gap," observed one record executive.

Crazed fans around the globe began to snap up Michael Jackson paraphernalia. They bought the standard posters, buttons, and T-shirts, which most rock acts sold by the 1980s. Michael Jackson fanatics also purchased *Thriller* caps, key chains, duffel bags, bubblegum cards, an eleven-inch Michael Jackson doll that could be twisted into the various dance poses of its subject, and replicas of the single, white, sequined glove that Jackson wore onstage. They even bought a video that chronicled the making of the video for the song "Thriller."

When the mania subsided in early 1985, Jackson had achieved singular success. He had released nine of the ten songs on the album as singles that reached the Top 10. The twenty-five-year-old singer had sold 40 million copies of *Thriller* worldwide, topped the U.S. charts in both 1983 and 1984, and won 150 gold and platinum awards worldwide and a record-breaking seven Grammies. "Jackson," asserted *Time* in March 1984, "is the biggest thing since the Beatles. He is the hottest single phenomenon since Elvis Presley."

Michael Jackson, the most important rock star of the early 1980s, epitomized the growing conservatism in America. He did not smoke, drink or take drugs. He even refused to utter the word *funky*, preferring *jelly* instead. A devout adherent to the Jehovah's Witnesses, the singer attended meetings at a Kingdom Hall four times a week and regularly fasted on weekends. "Such pop superstars as Elvis Presley, Bob Dylan or The Beatles have traditionally posed a sexual or political challenge to the status quo," contended *Maclean's* magazine, "but Michael Jackson is by contrast an establishment figure, perfectly in tune with the conservative America of Ronald Reagan." In 1984, Jackson received a public service award from the president.

Jackson amassed a fortune from his success. By the end of 1984, he had earned more than $30 million from the sale of *Thriller* and grossed another $50 million from the burgeoning industry of Michael Jackson products. The singer increased his personal net worth to $75 million in 1985, becoming one of the richest men in America.

THE JACKSON LEGACY

The success of Michael Jackson paved the way for other soul-pop artists, including such British bands as Culture Club, which merged the English concern for fashion with a Motown-influenced sound to climb the charts. Formed in 1981 by singer Boy George (a.k.a. George O'Dowd), bassist Mikey Craig and drummer Jon Moss, the group dressed in outlandish costumes. "I used to dress up from the age of 13 or 14, and George is the same," related Mikey Craig. "Dressing up in different styles and going to the clubs is a big thrill for kids. You follow the fashion changes and get caught up in it."

The extravagantly bedecked, video-ready Culture Club played, in the words of Boy George, "imitation soul." In 1982, they released the soul-pop album *Kissing to Be Clever*, which included the warm, bouncy "Do You Really Want To Hurt Me" and "I'll Tumble 4 Ya," and scaled the charts on the coattails of Jackson's *Thriller*. The next year, the group produced *Colour By Numbers*, which employed signature Motown riffs. " 'Plagiarism' is one of my favorite words," admitted Boy George. "Culture Club is the most sincere form of plagiarism in modern music—we just do it better than most."

The Eurythmics also scored with an updated Motown sound. Formed in 1980 by Dave Stewart and the photogenic, classically trained Annie Lennox, the duo first recorded electronic, experimental music with the unsuccessful album *In the Garden*. During the next two years, they released five singles, which also failed to chart.

Amid Michaelmania in 1983, the twosome earned international acclaim for *Sweet Dreams (Are Made of This)*, which featured the sultry, Motown-influenced vocals of Lennox over the insistent beat of a drum machine. "I identify my vocal style very much with black soul music," explained Lennox at the time. "Not with blues, but with 60s soul. It really struck a chord in me, and I can't get away from that." "What she really loved was Tamla/Motown material," chimed Stewart.

Wham! another sharply dressed duo from Britain, hit the charts with black-inspired dance music. Wham!'s Andrew Ridgeley and George Michael (a.k.a. Giorgios Panayiotou) met as young teens and frequented local clubs, dancing to the soundtrack of *Saturday Night Fever*. In 1982, the two friends formed Wham! and scaled the British charts with a series of singles, including "Young Guns" and "Bad Boys." In 1984, Michael and Ridgeley released a second album, *Make It Big*, which, after being promoted through videos aired on MTV, yielded three number-1 singles: "Wake Me Up Before You Go-Go," "Careless Whisper," and "Everything She Wants." When Wham! disbanded in 1986, George Michael continued to offer spunky, dance hits on the 1988 number-1 album *Faith*. "The big shame about modern black music is that, to a degree, anybody can pick up a machine and make a funk record," noted Michael. "It's a shame I can do it," he joked.

On the other side of the Atlantic, Madonna combined a decadent sex appeal with black dance rhythms to attain stardom. Born of Italian-American parents in Detroit in 1960, Madonna Louise Ciccone won a dance scholarship to the University of Michigan and at seventeen left school to pursue a career as a dancer in New York City. After briefly studying at the Alvin Ailey Dance Theater, she began to dance at local discos, where she cultivated her trademark attire of lacewear and religious-oriented jewelry. Assisted by her boyfriend at the time, disco disc jockey Mark Kamins, Madonna landed a record contract with Sire.

In 1983, Madonna released her first record, which presented the singer's breathy vocals over a disco beat. Propelled by videos of songs on the album that accentuated her sexually aggressive, Marilyn Monroe-like image, she became a minor hit. Two years later, Madonna attained national stardom with *Like A Virgin*, a dance album that included the hook-laden singles "Material Girl," "Like A Virgin," and "Dress You Up" and on its cover pictured Madonna in a flimsy, lace bodice cinched by a belt that carried the inscription "Boy Toy." By 1986, Madonna had sold more than 9 million copies of her first two albums and, based upon her initial exposure through

MTV, snagged a leading role in the feature-length movie *Desperately Seeking Susan.*

The success of Michael Jackson's brand of Motown dance music also helped the careers of black soul-pop performers. "It inspired black artists not to look at themselves in a limited way," noted producer Quincy Jones. "Before Michael, those kinds of sales had never happened for a black artist. Michael did it. He did it for the first time."

Motown artist Lionel Richie first followed Jackson to the top of the charts. In 1968, Richie joined with five other freshmen at the all-black Tuskegee Institute in Tuskegee, Alabama, to form the Commodores, a name randomly picked from the dictionary. Three years later, the band signed with Motown and for two years served as the opening act for the Jackson 5. In 1974, the Commodores recorded their first album, *Machine Gun*, characterized by a raw, sharp-edged sound. After two more albums, Lionel Richie convinced the group to record his softer, soul-pop ballads such as "Three Times a Lady" and "Sail On," which hit the top of the singles chart. In 1982, the Motown performer released his first solo album, which contained the Top-5 single "Truly." In the midst of Michaelmania, he recorded *Can't Slow Down* which, with the help of MTV, hit the top of the charts and transformed Lionel Richie into *Billboard's* Top Artist of 1984.

Two years later, Whitney Houston achieved similar success. The daughter of Cissy Houston, who had anchored the Aretha Franklin backup group the Sweet Inspirations, Whitney began performing professionally with her mother at the age of fifteen. Three years later, she signed with Arista Records which, as Motown had done with its young talent, groomed the young singer. By 1984, Houston had appeared as a model in *Glamour, Cosmopolitan, Seventeen*, and other fashion magazines and had backed dozens of artists in the studio, including Jermaine Jackson on "Take Good Care of My Heart."

In 1986, Houston recorded her first album, which featured upbeat ballads in the Motown tradition. As the first two singles from the LP climbed the chart, she filmed a video of "How Do I Know," which, according to Peter Baron, Arista's associate director of video production and promotion, "helped build her image. She's become a superstar in a year." The singer had five consecutive number-1 singles and sold 14 million copies of the LP, the biggest-selling debut in history. Houston recorded a follow-up, *Whitney*, which shot to the number-1 spot the next year.

Prince grafted rock guitars and overtly sexual lyrics onto a soul-pop sound for an innovative hybrid of the Michael Jackson formula for success. Born in Minneapolis to a bandleader, Prince Rogers Nelson taught himself piano, guitar, and drums by the age of fourteen and began to play a mixture of rock and soul. "I never grew up in one particular culture," Prince related. "I'm not a punk, but I'm not an R & B artist either—because I'm a middle class kid from Minnesota, which is very much white America."

During the late 1970s, Prince met Minneapolis ad man Chris Moon, who suggested sexually explicit lyrics. "It was amazing to see," recalled Moon. "Here was this very quiet kid, but once he'd discovered the notion of sex as a vehicle for his writing, it was as if a door unlocked for him." In 1978, Prince signed with Warner Brothers and recorded *For You*, which included the suggestive "Soft and Wet." He hit the top of the R & B charts with "I Wanna Be Your Lover" in 1979 and the next year recorded the widely covered "When You Were Mine" on the album *Dirty Mind*.

In 1982, Prince recorded the album *1999* and filmed a video of the song "Little Red Corvette," one of the first clips by a black artist aired on the music channel, which lifted the single to the Top 10. Through constant promotion by MTV, Prince sold 14 million copies of the 1984 *Purple Rain*, the soundtrack for the movie of the same name. As with other black and white soul-pop artists in the wake of the Michael Jackson fervor, Prince had attained international stardom through video.

POP GOES THE METAL

MTV ensured its preeminent place among the cable networks during the decade by creating a craze for pop metal bands. As it had done with electro-pop and soul-pop, the music channel delivered a visually exciting, largely inoffensive heavy metal to the post-baby boomers.

Van Halen served as the archetype for the metal bands of the 1980s. Sons of a jazz musician, Alex and Eddie Van Halen grew up in the Netherlands, where they received extensive classical music training. In 1965, they moved with their family to California, where they discovered and began to play rock-and-roll. In 1974 the Van Halen brothers, with bassist Michael Anthony and singer David Lee Roth, formed a band which for three years performed at such Los Angeles bars as Gazzarri's on Sunset Strip.

The members of Van Halen each contributed an element to their unique sound. "I think the only true rocker of the bunch is Al," related guitarist Eddie Van Halen. "He's the only one who listens to AC/DC and all that kind of stuff. Dave will walk in with a disco tape and I'll walk in with my progressive tapes and Mike walks in with his Disneyland stuff." At home, Eddie preferred the "progressive stuff" and "a lot of Chopin, piano. Very little rock and roll."

Unlike the blues-rooted heavy metal artists of the late 1960s and early 1970s, the eclectic Van Halen presented a more polished, smooth sound. The band favored a variety of tempos, rapid-fire guitar solos much shorter than the extended guitar breaks of the original heavy-metal groups, fast-paced, light bass lines, and periodic harmonies that reinforced the hooks in the songs. In addition, Van Halen featured frequent falsetto screams by the photogenic, acrobatic David Lee Roth, who added a wry sense of humor to the lyrics.

In 1976 the band recorded a demo tape financed by Gene Simmons of Kiss, who spotted them at the Starwood club in Los Angeles. A year later, they signed a contract with Warner Brothers and in early 1978 released their first album, which hit the Top 20 and sold more than 2 million copies. Van Halen followed with four Top 10 albums, the last of which, *Diver Down*, reached the number-3 slot in 1982. In 1984, after Eddie received mass notoriety for his guitar work on Michael Jackson's "Beat It," Van Halen released an album that topped the charts when videos of songs from the album received constant play on MTV.

Def Leppard perfected the pop metal that Van Halen had originated. Raised in the factory town of Sheffield in the midlands of England, Joe Elliott, guitarists Steve Clark and Pete Willis and bass player Rick Savage worked in blue-collar jobs before founding the band and drew their initial inspiration from heavy metal of the late 1960s and early 1970s. "In 1971 there were only three bands that mattered," Joe "The Throat" Elliott told an interviewer. "Led Zeppelin, Black Sabbath, and Deep Purple." In 1979 Def Leppard released the Led Zeppelin-sounding, three-track extended-play (EP) record, *Getcha Rocks Off*, which sold 24,000 copies. They followed with the similar-sounding *On Through The Night* (1980) and backed AC/DC on a British tour.

In 1981, the band joined with producer Robert ("Mutt") Lange, who began to smooth the rough edges off Def Leppard. "I heard those vocal harmonies and thought, 'Wow, an English band doing that stuff,' " remembered Lange. "Since they had the looks and they had the riffs I knew that with me as an extra member, so to speak, we could pull the songs together." The group released the Lange-produced album *High and Dry*, which entered the U.S. Top 40.

By 1983, after Phil Collen replaced guitarist Willis, who became disgusted with the more popular direction of the band, Def Leppard had perfected its sound. The band featured tight vocal harmonies and dramatic guitar work accentuated by Lange's production. Joe Elliott called the sound "nice, youthful melodic rock 'n' roll."

The band members penned catchy, unobtrusive lyrics. "Because the whole idea of Def Leppard is escapism," asserted Rick Savage, "we hate singing about unemployment and such, and we hate bands that do sing about it. Everybody knows it's tough. A band can't change anything. Who wants to go to one of our shows to hear how bad life is." "It's all wine, women and song," echoed Joe Elliott. "Nothing annoys me more than records about politics this, Greenpeace that. Someone has to be the opposite, and that's us. All we are is total escapism."

MTV promoted the photogenic, escapist pop metal of Def Leppard through performance videos. Offering heavy rotation to clips of such songs as "Photograph," the music channel broadcast the band to the mass of teens. Coupled with constant touring, it successfully marketed the 1983 album *Pyromania*, which sold more than 9 million copies, of which almost 7 million were purchased in the United States. "1983 was our year," enthused Cliff Burnstein, co-manager of the group.

The music channel also contributed to the success of other pop metal bands, some of which favored the outlandish costumes and antics of 1970s glam rockers. Formed in the late 1970s by singer Dee Snider, Twisted Sister played heavy-metal glam rock around the New York area for six years. After an unsuccessful first LP, in 1983 the band secured a British television appearance that resulted in a contract with Atlantic Records. The next year, Twisted Sister released the album *Stay Hungry*, which, with an accompanying eleven-song music video, scaled the charts. The band, appearing regularly on MTV, continued to chart until it disbanded in 1987.

Motley Crue played a West Coast version of video-ready glam rock. Nikki Sixx (a.k.a. Frank Ferrano) on bass, vocalist Vince Neil, guitarist Mick Mars (a.k.a. Bob Deal), and drummer Tommy Lee began performing together in 1981 around Los Angeles. Setting fire to their extravagant clothing and chainsawing mannequins on stage, the band gained a loyal following for their brand of heavy metal.

The band identified Kiss as its major influence. "When I first saw Kiss I stood in line for six hours at the Paramount Theater in Seattle, Washington," recalled Nikki Sixx. "I was sitting in the front row, and when they took the stage I knew then that I wanted to have a band that was nothing less than what I saw. The theatre bug bit me. Rock 'n' roll from then on had to have an element of theatre to excite me."

In May 1983 after an unsuccessful debut, Motley Crue signed to Elektra Records. Four months later, they released the album *Shout At The Devil*, which through heavy rotation on MTV entered the Top 20. By the end of 1984, the readers of *Hit Parader* and *Circus* magazines voted the band the Rock Act of the Year.

Ratt came from the same Los Angeles heavy metal scene. Put together in 1981 by guitarist Robbin Crosby and singer Stephen Pearcy, the band played its version of pop metal. "We have more melody in our music," noted Crosby as he compared the group to such heavy metal pioneers as Led Zeppelin. "We talk about love and sex and reality and fantasy—just down-to-earth, fun stuff."

The band members affected a glam image to increase their popularity. "When we first got together, we were a real heavy-metal band—black leather, studs, the whole thing," admitted Robbin Crosby. "We showed up at our first gig—and everybody else had the same stuff. Me and Steve were going, 'This is not cool. We've got to do something to get away from this.' " "We started wearing more fashionable clothes," Crosby continued. "Started dressing real sharp. A lot of the metalers said, 'Whoa! These guys are faggots!' But it's more of a mass appeal kind of thing."

The band proved its popular appeal with the help of MTV. In 1983, they released the LP *Out of the Cellar* and filmed corresponding videos. By the next year, they had sold more than 2 million copies of the debut.

MTV, after somewhat ignoring pop metal amid the Michael Jackson mania and its aftermath, began to show clips of such pop metal bands as Bon Jovi during the last part of the decade. Formed in 1983 by singer Jon Bon Jovi and quickly signed to Mercury Records, the band toured extensively to promote its first, self-named LP. Three years later, the group released the album *Slippery When Wet,* and filmed matching videos, which MTV aired ceaselessly. By late 1987, Bon Jovi had sold more than 12 million copies of its second album. "The success of such current hot groups as Bon Jovi," observed *Time* in June 1987, "is largely traceable to the saturation airplay given their videos on MTV."

The success of Bon Jovi opened the doors for other pop metal groups in the late 1980s. "The majors are now going nuts. Everyone's out there trying to sign up a metal band," reported Bob Chiappardi, co-owner of the metal-oriented Concrete Marketing retail firm. The major labels signed such acts as Poison, Winger, White Lion, Tora Tora, Kix, Kingdom Come, and countless others. After a five-year hiatus, Def Leppard topped the charts with the LP *Hysteria*, which sold more than 5 million copies. Bon Jovi, observed *Billboard* columnist Paul Grein, "opened the floodgates the same way Michael Jackson did in 1983 for Prince, Lionel Ritchie and others."

As the decade came to a close, Guns N' Roses stood triumphant at the top of the ever-changing pop-metal heap. Pieced together by William Axl Rose from the remnants of the bands L.A. Guns and Hollywood Rose, the band in 1986 recorded a debut that failed to chart. The next year, amid a tour in which the band backed Motley Crue, Guns N' Roses released the album *Appetite for Destruction,* which slowly climbed the charts. They continued to attract attention to their live performances, which combined the nihilism of the Sex Pistols with dramatic flourishes of Queen through a concert video which MTV began to broadcast. By the end of 1989, amid heavy rotation on the music channel, the band had sold more than 12 million copies of *Appetite for Destruction* and its follow-up album *G N' R Lies*, and had wrenched the pop metal crown from Bon Jovi. As with other pop metalers, Guns N' Roses had achieved superstardom at least partly through the medium of MTV.

The success of pop metal and electro-pop bands and the unparalleled achievements of Michael Jackson and his successors indicated the importance of MTV. "At any one time, 130,000 homes are watching MTV, according to Nielsen," observed Len Epand of Polygram Records. "If the video is in power rotation—15 or 16 plays a week—and that audience tunes in 10 times, that's 1.3 million people hearing the record and deciding whether they like it or not. If they like it, they'll buy it." "There isn't a national radio station. That's where MTV comes in," added Laura Foti, director of marketing for RCA video productions. "That's where they have their power: immediately showing everyone in the country this new band." Joe Jackson, the balding singer who hit the charts in 1979 with *Look Sharp*, complained about the dominance of MTV: "Things which used to count, such as being a good composer, player or singer, are getting lost in the desperate rush to visualize everything. It is now possible to be all of the above and still get nowhere simply by not looking good in a video, or worse still, not making one."

The marketing clout of MTV translated into profits. For the first half of 1984, when the *Thriller* hysteria had abated, MTV registered $8.1 million in profits from sales of $30.3 million. In 1986, after Viacom International purchased the network from Warner Amex, it grossed $111 million and turned a profit of $47 million. Though its ratings began to decline in 1986, MTV tied USA Network and Cable News Network for first place among the cable channels.

MTV, broadcast on more than 5,000 cable outlets to more than 46 million viewers in 1989, had helped define rock-and-roll during the 1980s, especially during the first half of the decade. It had fostered and successfully promoted the electro-pop and pop metal genres and had created a frenzy over Michael Jackson's *Thriller*. To a large extent, the music network had replaced radio as the preeminent trendsetter in rock. As *Billboard* noted in its wrap-up of the decade, "MTV is singularly responsible for one of the most basic changes in the current music fan's vocabulary: Where somebody might have said ten years ago, 'Yeah, I've heard that song,' that same person now might likely say, 'Yeah, I saw that video,' or, even more revealing, 'Yeah, I saw that song.' " In the 1980s, MTV had packaged and delivered rock-and-roll to the TV generation.

15

The Promise of Rock-and-Roll

"In the '80s, which is a barren era, we look back at the '60s as a great reservoir of talent, of high ideals, and of the will and desire to change things."

Bono

"I'm a romantic," Bruce Springsteen confessed to a reporter in 1980. "To me the idea of a romantic is someone who sees the reality, lives the reality every day but knows about the possibilities, too. You can't lose sight of the dreams. That's what great rock is about to me, it makes the dream seem possible." Rock, added Springsteen, is "a promise, an oath."

The romanticism of Bruce Springsteen, rooted in the idealism of the 1960s, became prevalent during the last half of the 1980s. It appealed to baby boomers who had protested for a better world and against the war in Vietnam during the 1960s. The return of a 1960s sensibility led to numerous benefit concerts, which revived the careers of aging rockers and revitalized the rock industry. It also filtered down to the TV generation, which began to listen to the politicized music of U2, new folksters such as Tracy Chapman, and rappers who graphically described inner-city realities. As the 1980s came to an end, two generations embraced a 1960s-inspired, political, rebellious rock that provided a stark contrast to the entertaining, glossy, sexy images on MTV.

The return to 1960s ideals occurred around mid-decade, when the economy started to decline and the social order became increasingly stratified. In 1981 and 1982 after nearly three decades of prosperity in the United States, economic conditions began to worsen as unemployment increased to almost 10 percent. Though expanding at an encouraging 8 percent annual growth rate in the first half of 1984, the U.S. economy again began to falter later in the year. Employment and wage gains slowed, unemployment stood at nearly 8 percent, and personal consumption declined. "The economy," noted one analyst in early 1985, "appeared to be teetering on the brink of a recession, having swung from boom to bust conditions in one quarter."

Economic stratification added to concerns. While indicating an increase in the number of families which earned more than $50,000 a year, a Census Bureau study in 1984 reported that nearly 66 million Americans in 36 million households received government benefits in the third quarter of 1983. Of the total, which represented nearly 30 percent of the United States population, about 42 million Americans received food stamps, welfare, subsidized housing, or Medicaid. From 1980 to 1986 as the number of families which earned more than $50,000 a year increased by nearly 323 percent, the number of families living on less than $2,500 remained constant.

The government benefits provided to the American underclass shrunk during the administration of Ronald Reagan, who believed in the self-help ethic. The Congressional Research Service found that cuts in cash welfare payments during 1981 had forced more than 500,000 people into poverty and had cost $23 billion to families with incomes of less than $10,000.

THE BOSS

Bruce Springsteen, nicknamed the Boss, sang about Americans who had fallen upon hard times. The son of a bus driver, Springsteen grew up in Freehold, New Jersey. At the age of thirteen, he learned guitar which, as with many other rockers, provided Springsteen with solice. "Music saved me," he told an interviewer. "From the beginning, my guitar was something I could go to. If I hadn't found music, I don't know what I would have done."

Springsteen, armed with a guitar, joined a series of bands. In 1966, he passed an audition to become a member of the Castiles, which performed at local clubs, parties, and school dances, recorded two unreleased demos, and within a year played at the Cafe Wha? in New York City. Upon graduation from high school, the New Jersey guitarist worked with the power trio Earth, and in 1969 started Child, later renamed Steel Mill, which traveled to California to play on New Year's Eve at the Esalen Institute. "I've never been out of New Jersey in my life and suddenly I get to Esalen and see all these people in sheets," remembered Springsteen. Disbanding Steel Mill in 1971, he formed the short-lived Dr. Zoom and the Sonic Boom and then the ten-piece Bruce Springsteen Band, which included David Sancious on keyboards, bassist Gary Tallent, Steve Van Zandt on guitar, drummer Vini Lopez, keyboardist Danny Frederici, and Clarence Clemons on saxophone. "I've gone through a million crazy bands with crazy people who did crazy things," the New Jersey rocker told *Time* in 1975.

Working as a solo act by late 1971, the Boss signed a contract with manager Mike Appel, who arranged an audition with Columbia Records talent head, John Hammond. "The kid absolutely knocked me out," recalled Hammond, who had discovered Bob Dylan, Aretha Franklin, and Billie Holiday. "I only hear somebody really good once every ten years, and not only was Bruce the best, he was a lot better than Dylan when I first heard him." Within a week, Hammond had signed Springsteen to his label.

The newly signed Springsteen initially failed to fulfill the expectations of John Hammond. In January 1973, he and a reformed version of the Bruce Springsteen Band released his debut, *Greetings From Asbury Park* which, though touted by Columbia as a masterpiece by the "new Dylan," in the first year sold only 25,000 copies, mostly to fans on the Jersey shore. They toured to promote the album, mismatched as an opening act for the band Chicago. In May 1973, Springsteen made a disastrous appearance at the CBS Records Annual Convention in San Francisco. "It was during a period when he physically looked like Dylan," Hammond told *Time*. "He came on with a chip on his shoulder and played too long. People came to me and said, 'He really can't be that bad, can he, John?'" At the end of the year he and his group, renamed the E Street band after a road in Belmar, New Jersey, released *The Wild, the Innocent and the E Street Shuffle*, which sold only 150,000 copies in nearly a year.

The next year, Springsteen received some encouragement. In April 1974, after watching the guitarist at Charley's, a small bar in Harvard Square, Cambridge, Massachusetts, influential rock journalist Jon Landau wrote: "I saw the rock and roll future and its name is Bruce Springsteen." "At the time," Springsteen told *Newsweek*, "Landau's quote helped reaffirm a belief in myself. The band and I were making $50 a week. It helped me go on. I realized I was getting through to somebody." Within a year, he hired Landau to co-produce his third album, *Born To Run*.

Springsteen displayed his many influences in *Born To Run*. Besides the obvious Dylan elements that surfaced in his rapid-fire lyrics and harmonica playing, he borrowed the dramatic stylings of Roy Orbison, the wails of Little Richard, and the operatic sweep of Phil Spector, which he labeled "the sound of universes colliding." The Boss also adopted the pounding piano of Jerry Lee Lewis, the intensity of R & B exemplified by the honking sax of Clarence

Clemons, and Chuck Berry's chugging guitar sound and his preoccupation with girls and cars. "I was about 24 and I said, 'I don't want to write about girls and cars anymore,'" recalled Springsteen, who cherished his own 1957 yellow Chevy convertible customized with orange flames. "Then I realized, 'Hey! That's what Chuck Berry wrote about!' So it wasn't my idea. It was a genre thing." In one record, Spingsteen had incorporated aspects of the history of rock-and-roll to produce a signature sound.

Executives at Columbia Records, impressed with the test pressing of *Born To Run*, decided to launch an unprecedented promotional campaign to market the record. They spent $40,000 on radio spots in twelve major geographic regions to promote Springsteen's first two albums, which entered the charts in mid-1975. The record businessmen engineered cover stories in both *Time* and *Newsweek* and organized an exclusive performance by Springsteen at The Bottom Line in New York, reserving almost 1,000 of the 4,000 tickets for the press and radio disc jockeys. "It was a very intelligent use of an event," remarked Stan Snadowsky, co-owner of the club. "Columbia got all the right people down there." After releasing *Born To Run* in September 1975, they spent an additional $200,000 to advertise the record in the press and on radio and $50,000 for television spots. "These are very large expenditures for a record company," admitted Bruce Lundvall, then vice-president of Columbia.

The promotional campaign had mixed results. *Born To Run*, though hailed by the critics and reaching the number-3 slot sold less than a million copies in the first year after its release. The title cut from the album peaked at number 23 on the singles chart. *Darkness on the Edge of Town*, Springsteen's next album, released in 1978 after a year-long legal dispute with manager Mike Appel, who had saddled Springsteen with a punitive contract, stalled at number 5 on the charts. A single from the album, "Prove It All Night," failed to crack the Top 30.

After his thirtieth birthday in 1979, Springsteen began to change along with other baby boomers. "I'm a different person now," he told a rock critic in late 1980. "When you're in your 30s or late 30s, the world is different. At least, it looks different."

Springsteen's music reflected his changed attitude. Rather than dealing exclusively with cars, girls, and the concerns of street toughs, his music began to deal with the plight of average Americans trapped by circumstances. The transition started with *Darkness on the Edge of Town*, which in addition to such Beach Boy-type paeans as "Racing in the Street," included such songs as "Factory" that, in the words of the Boss, described "people who are going from nowhere to nowhere." The 1980 double album *The River* continued to combine such car and girl songs as "Cadillac Ranch," "Crush On You," and "You Can Look (But You Better Not Touch)" with the title song, which told the tale of a factory worker who lost both love and his job because of a collapsing economy.

The 1982 stark, acoustic album *Nebraska* completed the transition. It chronicled the alienation of aging baby-boom Americans who had abandoned their sixties idealism. "I think what happened during the seventies was that, first of all, the hustle became legitimized. First through Watergate," Springsteen told *Musician* magazine. "In a funny kind of way, *Born To Run* was a spiritual record in dealing with values. *Nebraska* was about a breakdown of all those values and all those things. It was kind of about a spiritual crisis, in which man is left lost. It's like he has nothing left to tie him to society anymore. He's isolated from the government. Isolated from his job. Isolated from his family."

In 1984, Springsteen fused his vision with the infectious rock-and-roll of the E Street band to create his masterpiece, *Born In The U.S.A.* He sang in "Downbound Train" about the depression of a lumber worker who had lost his job and his wife when hard times hit. In the brooding "My Hometown," the Boss detailed the bleak changes affecting a town located in the depressed heartland of industrial Middle America: "Now main street's whitewashed windows and vacant stores/Seems like there ain't nobody wants to come down there no more/They're closing down the textile mill across the railroad tracks/Foreman says these jobs are going boys and they ain't coming back/to your hometown." Springsteen gave a powerful statement in the title song, wailing about the dead-end fate of a working-class Vietnam veteran ten years after the war. In "Glory Days," he sang about the aimlessness of an ex-high school baseball star and a divorced ex-prom queen.

The album dealt with the loss of innocence experienced by an aging baby–boom generation during the 1970s. "I think *Born In The U.S.A.* kind of casts a suspicious eye on a lot of things. That's the idea. These are not the same people anymore and it's not the same situation," he told *Musician.* "It certainly is not as innocent anymore. But, like I said, it's ten years down the line." "I wanted to make the characters grow up," he continued. "You got to. Everybody has to. It was something I wanted to do right after *Born To Run.* I was thinking about it then. I said, 'Well, how old am I?' I'm this old, so I wanna address that in some fashion. Address it as it is and I didn't see that was done a whole lot [in rock lyrics]."

Despite an unadorned realism, Springsteen sought a renewed commitment to a 1960s social consciousness. He wrote in "No Surrender": "Now young faces grow old/and hearts of fire grow cold/we swore blood brothers against the wind/I'm ready to grow young again." In an interview with *Rolling Stone*, he pledged a return "to the social consciousness that was part of the Sixties" which during the next decade seemed to become "old fashioned."

The Boss backed his words with action. As early as September 23, 1979, on his thirtieth birthday, he had performed at Madison Square Garden in New York City during a concert organized by Musicians United for Safe Energy (MUSE) who protested against

Bruce Springsteen and the E Street Band

the proliferation of hazardous nuclear power plants. A year later he had played six benefit concerts for Vietnam veterans.

Springsteen intensified his benefit appearances on the *Born In The U.S.A.* tour. He plugged and donated $5,000 to Washington Fair Share, which forced the cleanup of an illegal landfill in Washington. "This is 1984 and people seem to be searching for something," he told the sellout crowd at the Tacoma Dome. In Oakland, California, he urged listeners to donate to the Berkeley Emergency Food Project and in New Jersey he donated $10,000 to a soup kitchen. He sent money to unemployed steelworkers, striking copper miners and food banks across the country. In January 1985, he contributed lead vocals to a USA for Africa benefit disc "We Are The World," to help starving, famine-plagued Africans. "One of the things I can do is play benefits and help people out that need help, people that are struggling, you know, trying to get something goin' on their own," he told *Rolling Stone* in December 1984.

Born In The U.S.A., reflecting Springsteen's social consciousness, appealed to many baby boomers who had protested the war in Vietnam and during the 1960s had hoped for a better world. Snapped up by Springsteen fanatics, who on the average were thirty-one years old, it reached the top of the U.S. and British charts and remained there for two years. The LP yielded five Top-10 singles and by the end of the decade sold 11 million copies.

THE BENEFITS

Other benefit concerts such as Band Aid and Live Aid further reawakened interest in a 1960s social consciousness. Started after singer Bob Geldof of the Boomtown Rats saw a report on the Ethiopian famine, Band Aid united a number of English musicians, who recorded the song, "Do They Know It's Christmas," which was featured at an Ethiopian Benefit Concert at Royal Albert Hall in December 1984 and sold 3 million copies. Live Aid, also conceived by Geldof to aid the starving masses in Africa, involved simultaneous, televised concerts on July 13, 1985 at Wembley Stadium in London and at JFK Stadium in Philadelphia. It boasted such sixties rockers as Eric Clapton, Mick Jagger, Neil Young, Pete Townshend, and Paul McCartney. "This concert is the ultimate expression the pop industry can make," stated Bob Geldof. It raised over $69 million, most of which was used to help famine victims.

Other rock-and-rollers, most from the 1960s, organized benefits. The Grateful Dead, having played countless free concerts during their heyday, organized a benefit to protect the world's rain forests. "It's a problem we must address if we wish to have a planet that's capable of supporting life," said the Dead's Bob Weir. Pete Townshend of The Who donated $10,000 to San Francisco's Hearing Education and Awareness for Rockers (HEAR) Foundation, which championed a cause important to rock stars such as Townshend, who had become partially deaf after years of loud rock-and-roll. Peter Gabriel, formerly of Genesis, united with Bruce Springsteen to tour in support of Amnesty International, which sought to free political prisoners around the world. "The great challenge of adulthood is holding on to your idealism after you lose your innocence," Springsteen, who donated more than $200,000 to the charity, told one sellout crowd on the tour.

Steve Van Zandt, nicknamed Little Steven, organized one of the most important benefits of the era. In late 1985, after leaving the E Street band for a solo career, he established Artists United Against Apartheid, which lashed out against the brutal discrimination of blacks in South Africa and, particularly, the $90 million, white-only Bophuthatswana resort, Sun City, which had hosted Rod Stewart, Linda Ronstadt, and Queen. Little Steven planned an album, book, and video to combat apartheid, enlisting the support of such rock stars as Springsteen, Pete Townshend, Ringo Starr of the Beatles, Bob Dylan, Keith Richards of the Rolling Stones, and Lou Reed. Taking the civil rights movement into the international arena, he donated nearly a half-million dollars to causes supporting the antiapartheid struggle.

The Artists United Against Apartheid had a number of lasting effects on rock musicians, including an interest in African pop. Though an essential part of rock since its inception, African music in its contemporary form was incorporated into rock during the 1980s. At the beginning of the decade, David Byrne of the Talking Heads and Brian Eno produced *My Life in the Bush of Ghosts*, an album based upon African rhythms and voodoo tales. The same year, the Talking Heads introduced African elements into their brand of rock on the LP *Remain in Light*, which sold poorly. "We were really intrigued and excited by the formal aspects of African music, recalled Byrne." Two years later Peter Gabriel established the World of Music Arts and Dance (WOMAD) festival in England, which brought together artists from around the world.

The interest in African pop and world music, fostered by the anti-Sun City project, peaked when Paul Simon released the LP *Graceland*. Half of the successful folk-rock duo Simon and Garfunkel and a respected songwriter during the 1970s who had participated in USA for Africa, Simon traveled in late 1984 to South Africa to record with South African musicians. "To go over and play Sun City, it would be exactly like going over to do a concert in Nazi Germany at the height of the holocaust," Simon reasoned. "But what I did was go over and essentially play to the Jews." He hoped the record, featuring the South African choir Ladysmith Black Mambazo, would serve as a "powerful form of politics" that would attract people "to the music, and once they hear what's going on within it, they'd say, 'What? They're doing that to these people.' "

The record met Simon's expectations. In 1985, *Graceland* topped the British charts and climbed to the number-3 slot in the U.S. Contributing to the heightened interest in world music and especially African pop, it provided such African artists as Fela Kuti an international market for their music.

The reawakened social consciousness of the 1960s, embodied in the anti-Sun City project, helped rejuvenate the careers of some aging rock stars. After a string of disappointing albums, Bob Dylan performed at the anti-Sun City benefit, Live Aid, the USA For Africa recording session, and a concert celebrating the first Martin Luther King, Jr. Day in the United States. In 1986, he released a five-record, boxed set of retrospective material, *Biograph*, which reached number 33 on the charts. Two years later, Dylan joined with Tom Petty, Jeff Lynne formerly of the Electric Light Orchestra, Roy Orbison, and George Harrison, who in 1971 had organized one of the first large-scale benefits, the Concert for Bangladesh, which aided famine victims. They released the LP *The Traveling Wilburys*, which hit the top of the charts.

Other baby-boom rockers benefited from a return to the idealism of the 1960s. Lou Reed, the former leader of the Velvet Underground and glam rocker, turned to serious political issues after his participation in Artists United Against Apartheid. "We're in this terrible morass of people absolutely not giving a shit about anybody but themselves," he told *Rolling Stone*. "And a mean-spirited government that is essentially attacking people that can't defend themselves. That's the weakest people—the kids, the sick, the elderly. And I think we should fight back." "The days of me being aloof about certain things are over," Reed added. In 1989 he released the LP *New York*, which detailed the problems in the City and outsold his previous efforts.

Many psychedelic bands received renewed attention. The Grateful Dead, continuing to attract die-hard Deadheads during the 1970s, continued to tour during the eighties. In 1987, the band released their first Top-10 album, *In The Dark*, which included their first hit single, "Touch of Grey." At the end of the decade, the Jefferson Airplane reformed and released an album. Even Blue Cheer, the loud, psychedelic blues outfit, regrouped. "Speaking of '60s artists," *Billboard* informed its readers in a wrap-up of the decade, "one of the more notable trends of the late '80s was the commercial success of many bands that made their commercial debut more than 20 years ago." "And, as the fairy tales say, it seemed that it might be time again for legends," added *Time* with a flourish in late 1989. "Twenty years later there was suddenly on every side the familiar sound of the '60s."

Radio helped promote the rockers of the 1960s. Largely ignoring the TV generation, which preferred the images on MTV, it programmed oldies for the baby-boom generation, which still purchased the greatest number of records and served as the prime target of most advertisers. In 1988 of the roughly 10,000 stations in the country, more than 500 radio stations broadcast oldies exclusively. The next year, contended Ken Barnes, editor of the trade magazine *Radio and Records*, at least 40 percent of all radio programming fell into the "classic rock" or "oldies" categories. In early 1990 oldies mainstay station WCBS-FM grabbed the number-1 spot in the New York market. Radio, observed CBS Records president Al Teller, seemed to be "chasing the yuppie generation to its grave."

THE COMPACT DISC

The compact disc helped revive an interest in classic rock and rescued a troubled music industry. Introduced to the mass market in late 1982, it provided record buyers with a high-quality, digital, durable and long-lasting format. The compact disc, commonly called the CD, contained millions of digitally encoded pits, which held musical information that could be converted into almost noise-free sound through a low-powered laser beam. Less than five inches in diameter, the polycarbonate plastic disc warped only at temperatures over 220 degrees Fahrenheit, could not be scratched like a vinyl record, and produced up to 75 minutes of music with a dynamic range of 90 decibels.

The silver platter quickly became more popular than its vinyl counterpart. During its first two years on the market, the CD appealed primarily to jazz and classical music fans who appreciated its expanded dynamic range. As the price of compact disc players plummetted from about $900 in 1983 to less than $150 in 1987 and as the cost of a compact disc declined from $18 to $12 during the same period, the convenient CD began to sell to the general rock record buyer. In 1985, 16.4 million CDs were purchased worldwide. Three years later, more than 390 million compact discs were sold internationally, which accounted for sales of more than $6 billion, compared to 295 million vinyl LPs sold for $2.8 billion. Cassette tapes, becoming the most popular format for music during the late 1970s and registering even greater sales after the introduction of the portable Walkman cassette player in 1981, outperformed both with sales of more than $6.7 billion for 787 million units sold. In late 1990 the CD even began to outsell the cassette in such retail outlets as Tower Records.

At the end of the decade, many industry executives predicted the demise of the vinyl LP. "I assume the death knell has been sounded, and there's not much we can do about it," mused Joe Smith, president of Capitol Music-EMI. "It's gasping for breath," agreed Russ Solomon, founder and president of the Tower Records chain. "We'd like to hold on, but unfortunately the world is not going that way." "Our little flat friend the record is what drove the business for a long time, but we're going to be out of the business," mentioned Bob Sherwood, senior vice-president of Columbia Records.

Industry predictions began to become reality. In 1989 the Camelot Music chain of 229 stores dropped vinyl albums from its inventory and other retailers such as the 85-store Disc Jockey chain, the 119-store Hastings Books and Records, and the 60-store Music Plus severely limited vinyl selections. The Hauppauge Record Manufacturing plant, pressing more than 100,000 vinyl records a day during the early 1980s, discontinued operations.

The predominance of compact discs over vinyl encouraged many baby boomers to replace their old, scratched LPs with CDs of the same music. "Talk about trends," observed *Billboard* in early 1990, "If the CD did anything in the '80s, it convinced consumers that they needed to buy their favorite albums all over again. Little wonder, therefore, that artists such as the Beatles were charting all over again in the '80s with records they'd recorded 25 years earlier." *Time* magazine called the compact disc the technology "most likely to bring Elvis back to life. With revolutionary speed, music lovers are replacing their favorite old scratched-up 45s and 33s with shiny compact discs."

A slumping U.S. recording industry was revitalized by the geometric growth in sales of compact discs created in part by baby boomers who rebought the music of their youth. After a high point in sales at $4.13 billion in 1978, the U.S. record industry experienced a sharp decline. In 1979 it sold only $3.67 billion in records and tapes despite a high rate of inflation, a downturn that resulted in the loss of 2,500 music-industry jobs. Over the next four years, the industry stabilized and by 1983 reported only $3.81 billion in total sales despite price hikes, MTV, and the phenomenal success of Michael Jackson.

The U.S. record industry experienced a boom after the introduction of the CD, which cost about 90 cents to manufacture, excluding packaging. In 1986 it exceeded its previous record, shipping $4.65 billion of records and tapes. "The rise in profitability," wrote one reporter at the time, "is attributed primarily to the soaring sales of compact discs which carry a retail price of $12 to $20 as opposed to the $8.98 or $9.98 for records and cassettes." A year later, the industry sold $5.57 billion and in 1988 $6.25 billion in records, tapes, and discs. In 1989, the industry registered $6.46 billion in sales of more than 800 million units, bolstered by a 38 percent increase in CD sales compared to the previous year. According to one report, it registered the highest rate of pretax operating income growth in the communications industry, expanding at 26 percent from 1983 to 1987.

The record industry grew at the same pace internationally, dominated by six corporations—Time-Warner (WEA), Sony-CBS, Bertelsmann Music Group (BMG), MCA-Matsushita, N.V. Philips of Holland, and Thorn-EMI(CEMA)—which by 1990 sold more than 93 percent of the records in the United States. After a drastic downturn from 1979 to 1987, by 1988 it sold more than $14 billion and a year later nearly $17 billion in records, tapes, and CDs. Japan, dominated by the CBS/Sony giant, increased sales to $2.4 billion in 1987, a 10 percent gain from the previous year. In West Germany, dominated by BMG which had purchased RCA during the decade, sales skyrocketed to $1.56 billion in 1987 and exceeded $1.82 billion by 1989. "The German music market is in a healthy state of growth and with East Germany opening up, it will develop even more," predicted Manfred Zumkeller, President of the Federation of German Phonographic Industry in early 1990. The United Kingdom, the fourth-largest market in the world, had sales of $1.5 billion the same year.

The increased sales translated into profits. In 1988 Warner Communications, the largest company in the field, posted sales of $2.04 billion and profits of nearly $319 million. The next year after merging with Time Inc., Warner generated music revenues of $2.54 billion and profits of nearly $500 million. In 1987 CBS made $202 million in profits on $1.75 billion in total sales. The next year EMI, the British conglomerate, sold $1.2 billion in products for a profit of $70.3 million. BMG showed remarkable growth, building sales from $663 million in 1986-87 to $1.1 billion in 1989-90 and increasing profits from $56 million in 1987-88 to $85.4 million in 1989-90. "The ultimate shot in the arm the record industry was craving, the CD allowed companies to rake in the bucks on a product that, in some cases, was one step away from actually being deleted," observed *Billboard* in late 1989.

CHILDREN OF THE SIXTIES

A reawakened interest in the sixties spirit, fostered by the CD, shaped a number of new bands, notably U2. Formed in Dublin by schoolmates Bono (Paul Hewson), The Edge (David Evans), Adam Clayton, and Larry Mullen, Jr., the band won a talent contest sponsored by Guinness beer in March 1978. After two years of local gigs, it released its debut single, "11 O'Clock Tick Tock," which failed to chart. The group recorded two albums, *Boy* (1980) and *October* (1981) which attracted critical attention but sold few copies.

U2 began to infuse its music with a political message. In October 1982, during a concert in Belfast, Northern Ireland, Bono introduced the song "Sunday Bloody Sunday," which detailed the historic political troubles in Ireland. A few months later, the band released the LP *War*, which combined rock with the various strands of punk. "Punk had died," recalled The Edge. "We couldn't believe it had happened, and *War* was designed as a knuckle buster in the face of

Photo by David McIntyre, courtesy of D.M.B.B. Entertainment

U2

the new pop." "We loved the Clash's attitude early on and Richard Hell and the Voidoids, the Pistols," continued the guitarist. "We wanted love and anger. We wanted a protest record, but a positive protest record." "It was an unsettled time, a year of conflict," added bassist Adam Clayton. "We focused on that." As a show of support for a sixties-type protest, in July 1984, Bono sang a duet with Bob Dylan on "Blowing In The Wind" at a Dylan concert in Ireland.

The band continued to demonstrate its commitment to the sixties spirit. Though beginning to replace hard-driving guitars with more ethereal sounds engineered by producer Brian Eno, U2 dedicated its 1984 hit "Pride (In the Name of Love)" to Martin Luther King, Jr. It contributed to Band Aid, played in the Live Aid spectacular in Wembley Stadium, appeared on the anti-Sun City project, and performed on Amnesty International's twenty-fifth anniversary tour. In 1986, the band raised funds for the unemployed, performed with Lou Reed in San Francisco for another Amnesty International benefit, and symbolically was joined onstage in Philadelphia by Bruce Springsteen. By 1987, when it hit the top of the charts with its LP *Joshua Tree*, U2 had become a prime example of the renewed interest in a sixties-style protest. As Bono told an interviewer in 1987, "in the '80s, which is a barren era, we look back at the '60s as a great reservoir of talent, of high ideals, and of the will and desire to change things." As with his counterparts in the 1960s, the singer was interested in "a revolution of love. I believe that if you want to start a revolution you better start a revolution in your own home and your own way of relating to the men and women around you."

Midnight Oil, an Australian band formed in 1976 when Jim Moginie, Rob Hirst and Martin Rotsey of the hippie band Farm teamed with law student and singer Peter Garrett, applied sixties ideals to its own country. "I grew up loving people like John Fogerty," remembered drummer Hirst, "people who commented on what America was going through during the Vietnam war. It was rather natural that this band would choose to comment on the country that it knows better than anywhere else." In their first two LPs, the band decried the nuclear arms race and the dominant presence of U.S. military forces in Australia. In the 1986 *Diesel and Dust* which sold 3 million copies, they protested white Australian oppression of the indigenous aborigines, touring the backcountry to demonstrate their support of aboriginal attempts to regain their traditional lands. With the 1990 *Blue Sky Mining*, Midnight Oil told the tale of Wittenoon miners who contracted asbestos-induced cancer on the job during the 1950s and 1960s and who first secured redress from mine operators in 1988. "What Midnight Oil does have is an underlying belief in the human spirit," remarked Peter Garrett who in 1984 ran for the upper house of the Australian Parliament on the Nuclear Disarmament Party ticket and served as the President of the Australian Conservation Foundation.

The sixties spirit also inspired a late 1980s political folk boom led by Tracy Chapman. Born to a poor family in Cleveland, Chapman had always been interested in social issues. "As a child," she told *Rolling Stone*, "I always had a sense of social conditions and political situations. I think it had to do with the fact that my mother was always discussing things with my sister and me—also because I read a lot." While at Tufts University in Medford, Massachusetts, she began performing on the Boston folk club circuit.

One day in 1986, while playing at a Boston coffeehouse called the Cappuccino, Chapman met fellow Tufts student Brian Koppelman, who introduced the protest singer to his father Charles, the head of the largest independent music publishing firm in the world. Within a few months, with the help of the elder Koppelman, she landed a contract at Elektra Records and secured as manager Elliot Roberts, the manager of Bob Dylan. "You don't have to be a genius to see that words are coming back in a large way, that there's more social consciousness in people, and the apathy that there was for years seems to be slowly declining," observed Roberts in late 1988. "These are going to be exciting times, and I see Tracy as someone who will be at the forefront of these times." In 1988, Chapman released her first, self-named album, which hit the top of the charts.

Other women folk singers began to achieve popularity. Discovered in 1986, at the Kerrville Folk Festival in Texas, Michelle Shocked hit the charts in 1988 with her album *Short Sharp Shocked*. A veteran of the Greenwich Village folk scene, Suzanne Vega combined the New York influences of Bob Dylan and Lou Reed to produce the hit "Luka," a song decrying child abuse. By the end of the decade, other folksters, such as the Indigo Girls, who lobbied for Amnesty International and the Coalition for the Homeless, began to attract attention.

THE RAP ATTACK

Rap musicians grappled with the plight of impoverished, victimized black Americans, an issue that defined sixties protest. Though the black middle class increased in numbers as a result of the civil rights movement, African-Americans generally experienced hard times during the eighties. By 1980 over 31 percent of all blacks lived in poverty, nearly three times the proportion of impoverished whites. Six years later 14 percent of all black families earned less than $5,000 a year, compared with 9.6 percent in 1970, and over 30 percent earned less than $10,000 a year.

African-American youths especially confronted grim economic prospects. The percentage of black males under 24 who never held a job increased from 9.9 percent in 1966 to 23.3 percent in 1977. During the economically lean 1980s, young blacks found it increasingly difficult to find work, more than 30 percent of them unemployed in 1987 compared to 15 percent of white teens.

Many of these poor unemployed youths lived in single-parent, single-income households usually headed by a mother. In 1964 roughly 25 percent of all black children lived in female-headed households. Abetted by a welfare system that rewarded fatherless families, in 1980 the number increased to 40 percent. By 1984 the number of female-headed, single-parent black families skyrocketed to more than 50 percent, compared to 14 percent among white families, and perpetuated the economic plight among inner-city blacks.

Having little money, much free time and less parental supervision than children in two-parent families, many inner-city black youths fashioned a distinct lifestyle. To gain an identity, some joined gangs such as the notorious Crips and Bloods gangs in Los Angeles which warred with one another. Others became involved with drugs, especially an inexpensive type of cocaine called crack, sometimes dealing the drug to support their habit. Many passed their time on street corners, developing a language for insiders which included such words and phrases as "chill out" (calm down), "sweat" (hassle), "posse" (gang), "def" (good), and "wack" (bad).

Rap, or hip hop, arose from and helped shape the African-American counterculture of the inner cities, many times decrying inner-city poverty, drugs and gang-inspired violence. The music originated in the ghettos of New York City. As rapper Kurtis Blow explained, rap began during the early 1970s at private inner-city parties that featured disc jockeys as entertainment. "To attract their own followings, some of these DJs would give little raps to let the crowd know who was spinning the records. As time went by, these raps became more elaborate, with the DJ sometimes including a call-and-response 'conversation' with the regulars in the house."

Inner-city disc jockeys began to combine modern technology with rock history. Relying exclusively on the turntable as an instrument, they sampled short segments of rock records by artists as diverse as Paul Simon and Depeche Mode, favoring songs with thumping bass lines. The DJs scratched these records or with a special stylus rotated records back and forth to produce a unique rhythmic pattern and mixed the beat, quickly fading one song into another. They transformed the records by pushing them slower and produced an echo effect by using two turntables in sequence, a technique called needle rocking. Through these methods, DJs wove together intricate polyrhythms into a staccato sound that mimicked the short, abrupt changes of commercial television.

Rappers used the halting, polyrhythmic sound produced by the disc jockeys as a backdrop for rapid-fire rhymes that described life in the inner city. As with the early blues artists and the toasters of Jamaica, many early rappers such as Kool Herc, DJ Hollywood, and Afrika Bambaataa boasted about their physical and mental prowess.

Others decried widespread crime and the use of drugs in their neighborhoods. Still others described the chilling realities of a tough inner-city life, infusing the music with a social message.

Grandmaster Flash (a.k.a. Joseph Saddler), a hip hop pioneer from the Bronx, used rap for social commentary. After experimenting with a number of turntable techniques, disc jockey Flash joined together in 1978 with Cowboy, Kid Creole, Melle Mel (Melvin Glover), Duke Bootee (Ed Fletcher), and Kurtis Blow to form Grandmaster Flash and the Furious Five. The group first recorded on a series of small labels until late 1979 when it signed with the emerging rap label, Sugar Hill which first hit the charts with "Rapper's Delight" by the Sugar Hill Gang. The next year Grandmaster Flash released "Freedom" which attracted a following for the band in New York. They followed the next year with "The Adventures of Grandmaster Flash On The Wheels of Steel" which featured one of the first examples of intricate sampling. In 1982 the group recorded "The Message," a bleak tale of life on the streets, which hit the charts in Britain and the United States. In November 1983, before fracturing into different bands, they produced the anti-cocaine rap anthem "White Lines (Don't Do It)." Rap, asserted Kurtis Blow at the time, is "a way for the people of the ghetto to make themselves heard."

A youth culture began to develop around rappers such as Grandmaster Flash. "Not only did our fans want to talk like we did," remembered Kurtis Blow, "but they dressed like we did, and seemed to be trying to live out the fantasies we were kicking in our raps." Calling themselves b-boys and fly girls, the rap fanatics in the inner cities of New York, Philadelphia, and Baltimore wore heavy gold chains, oversized gold rings, baseball caps with upturned bills, and Adidas tennis shoes. They practiced the inner-city sport of break dancing and sprayed their art on subway trains. By 1984 the b-boys became immortalized in such films as *Breakin'*.

Run-D.M.C. brought inner-city rap to the masses of American teens by combining it with heavy metal. The group banded together in 1982 after graduating from St. Pascal's Catholic School in New York. The next year, disc jockey Jason Mizel and rappers Darryl "D" McDaniels and Joseph "Run" Simmons, the latter who had worked as a disc jockey behind Kurtis Blow, released their first LP, which after fifty-three weeks on the chart became the first rap gold album.

The group followed its initial success with the LP *King of Rock*, which reached number 53 on the charts through the use of the heavy metal–like guitar of Eddie Martinez. "Run-D.M.C. used to rap over rock records a lot," mentioned Jam Master Jay Mizel. "I used to mix rock tunes, and have the guitar come in a little bit, and then play the drum over and over again. *Toys in the Attic*, Aerosmith, that was the best." The band secured airplay on MTV for its videos of "King of Rock" and "You Talk Too Much," two of the first

Run-D.M.C.

rap videos aired on the network. Through its heavy-metal rap, Run-D.M.C. began to appeal to white teens. "Does the band have white crossover fans?" rhetorically asked Bill Adler, who helped manage the group. "I'll tell you, a typical letter we get is from someplace like North Dakota. They say, 'I'll bet I'm the only white person ever to·write you, but I love Run-D.M.C.' All the white people think they're alone, but they're not."

The group increased its white audience. In 1986 it combined the polyrhythms of rap with heavy metal to hit the top of the charts with a remake of Aerosmith's "Walk This Way," which featured Aerosmith's Joe Perry on guitar and Steve Tyler helping with vocals. The band sold over 3 million copies of *Raising Hell*, the album that contained the hit single. By 1987, after the platinum success of Run-D.M.C., MTV jumped on the increasingly popular rap bandwagon by programming the daily show "Yo! MTV Raps," which popularized such guitar-based rap acts as Tone Loc.

The popular Run-D.M.C., delivering such social commentaries as "It's Like That" and "Hard Times," performed at many of the benefits that aided black Africans and Americans. In 1985, they played at the Live Aid benefit. In November of the same year, along with the reigning rock elite and rappers Afrika Bambaataa, Kurtis Blow, Duke Bootee, and Melle Mel, the band contributed to the Artists Against Apartheid benefit. They also appeared in a promo-

Public Enemy

tional video for the Martin Luther King, Jr., national holiday campaign. "I'm a role model for kids, and I go out of my way to give them a positive message," asserted Darryl "D.M.C." McDaniel.

Other groups, such as the militant Public Enemy, rapped about black pride. "Black men and women are treated like bullshit," declared Chuck D (Carlton Ridenhour) of the group during a concert at Riker's Island prison. "You've got to know the rules of the game so we won't be falling into traps and keep coming back to places like these!" "Our goal in life," continued the rapper who started the group while a student at Adelphi University in Long Island, "is to get ourselves out of this mess and be responsible to our sons and daughters so they can lead a better life. . . . My job is to build 5,000 potential black leaders through my means of communication in America. A black leader is just someone who takes responsibility." By the end of the decade, Public Enemy had sold more than 1 million copies of its LP *It Takes a Nation of Millions To Hold Us Back*, a pointed discourse on drugs, inner-city poverty, and black self-determination. They also contributed the song, "Fight the Power" to director Spike Lee's controversial, popular film, *Do the Right Thing* which pictured life in the inner city. In 1990 the group neared the top of the charts with the album, *Fear of a Black Planet*, released by Def Jam Records which was the largest black-owned label since Motown and which was headed by Russell Simmons, brother of Run-D.M.C.'s Joseph Simmons.

In the late 1980s, others used rap to convey a sense of black pride which they termed "Afro-centric." Sir Mix-a-lot reminded listeners about the murder of Huey Newton in "National Anthem," and Big Daddy Kane rapped about black pride in "Young, Gifted and Black" and "Ain't No Stoppin' Us Now." Female rapper Queen Latifah, *Latifah* an Arabic word meaning "delicate and sensitive" and *Queen* added "as a show of pride for ancestors from whom we descended," even dressed in African-style clothing. "Style is Afrocentric," she insisted, "and my style and music are one."

Some rappers such as Queen Latifah, having pride in her race, warned youths against the crippling effects of drugs. "We guide a lot of young kids," explained the female rapper. "When kids constantly hear rappers saying, 'Don't do drugs, don't do drugs,' there's a chance it will sink in." N. W. A. (Niggers with Attitude) provided the same anti-drug message in the explicit "Dopeman."

In 1989, a number of leading rappers joined together in the Stop The Violence Movement (STV). Denouncing the gang warfare on the inner-city streets and at rap concerts, rappers Chuck D. and Flavor Flav of Public Enemy, Just-Ice, Heavy D., Doug E. Fresh, MC Lyte, and others recorded the single "Self-Destruction," which sold a half million copies. "We wanted to reach the kids most affected by black-on-black crime," noted Ann Carli, Jive Records vice-president of artist development who helped organize STV. Perceiving "crime as a result a lot of times of unemployment which can be the result of illiteracy" according to Carli, members of STV donated $500,000 in royalties to the National Urban League, which promised to use the money to combat illiteracy. "Rap records," added Carli, "can be a tool that can be used in education today; young adults will listen to rap and what rap artists have to say."

West Coast rappers used their music for similar purposes. In 1990, organized by former gang member and Grand Jury Records President Michael Conception, such rap performers as Tone Loc, Eazy-E., M. C. Hammer, Ice-T and N. W. A. banded together for the anti-violence rap single and video project, "We're All in the Same Gang." "I hope it generates a lot of money and we can get it to the people who really need it," Conception told *Billboard*. "If anyone can convince the black gangs, it's somebody who was in one."

Hip hoppers in the west addressed other social concerns. From Los Angeles, the Jungle Brothers used a fusion of rap and R & B "as a tool to bring about peace and unity." "We always felt that spreading a message was the way to go," explained the group's Mike G. (a.k.a. Michael Small), a nephew of the legendary New York rapper, Red Alert. In 1990 the group embarked on the "Politics of Nature" tour which included speaking engagements about "the environment and black consciousness."

M. C. Hammer (a.k.a. Stanley Burrell), selling 5 million copies of his album *Please Hammer Don't Hurt 'Em* which blended rap with melodic hooks, tried to serve as a model to the African-American community. He created Bust It Productions which sometimes hired, in his words, blacks "fresh out of prison, and I say that proudly. I want an established business that can employ people from my community, where they can come and get a fair shot." M. C. Hammer also worked with inner-city school children in his hometown of Oakland. "I make an active role model to kids," he explained. "They need people to show them there's another way." As with the sixties-style message of such artists as Bruce Springsteen, rap restated the promise of rock-and-roll as the 1990s unfolded.

BIBLIOGRAPHY

This bibliography consists of the material that I found most useful in the preparation of this book. It does not pretend to be a comprehensive survey of the thousands of books and articles on rock-and-roll, but rather offers the reader a concise guide to rock as social history. The many quotes and statistics used in this book have been gleaned from these materials.

GENERAL

CHAPPLE, STEVE, and REEBEE GAROFALO. *Rock 'n' Roll Is Here to Pay: The History and Politics of the Music Industry.* Chicago: Nelson-Hall, 1977.

CURTIS, JIM. *Rock Eras: Interpretations of Music and Society.* Bowling Green: Bowling Green State Press, 1987.

FONG-TORRES, BEN, ed. *The Rolling Stone Rock and Roll Reader.* New York: Bantam, 1974.

————, ed. *What's That Sound?* New York: Anchor, 1976.

FRITH, SIMON. *Sound Effects—Youth, Leisure and the Politics of Rock.* New York: Pantheon, 1982.

HENDLER, HERB. *Year By Year in the Rock Era.* Westport: Greenwood, 1983.

JONES, LANDON. *Great Expectations: America and the Baby Boom Generation.* New York: Coward, McCann & Geohegan, 1980.

LAZELL, BARRY, ed. *Rock Movers and Shakers.* New York: Billboard, 1989.

LOGAN, NICK, and BOB WOFFINDEN. *The Illustrated Encyclopedia of Rock.* New York: Harmony, 1977.

MARSH, DAVE, and JOHN SWENSON, eds. *The Rolling Stone Record Guide.* New York: Random House, 1979.

MILLER, JIM, ed. *The Rolling Stone Illustrated History of Rock and Roll.* New York: Random House, 1976.

NITE, NORM. *Rock On.* New York: Popular, 1974.

PARELES, JON, and PATRICIA ROMANOWSKI, eds. *The Rolling Stone Encyclopedia of Rock and Roll.* New York: Summit, 1983.

POLLACK, BRUCE. *When the Music Mattered: Rock in the 1960s.* New York: Holt, 1983.

Rolling Stone, editors of. *The Age of Paranoia: How The Sixties Ended.* New York: Pocket, 1972.

———. *The Rolling Stone Interviews.* New York: Paperback, 1971.

———. *The Rolling Stone Interviews.* Vol. 2. New York: Warner, 1973.

ROXON, LILLIAN. *Rock Encyclopedia.* New York: Grosset & Dunlap, 1969.

SHAW, ARNOLD. *The Rock Revolution.* London: Collier, 1969.

STAMBLER, IRWIN. *Encyclopedia of Pop, Rock and Soul.* New York: St. Martin's, 1977.

WIENBERG, MAX. *The Big Beat.* Chicago: Contemporary, 1984

CHAPTER 1: THE BLUES, ROCK 'N' ROLL, AND RACISM

"B.B. King." *Living Blues* (May/June 1988), pp. 10–22.

COHAN, LOU. "Bo Diddley: The Man with the Beat." *Thunder Road* (June 1980), pp. 26–29.

CORRITORE, BOB, BILL FERRIS, and JIM O'NEAL. "Willie Dixon." *Living Blues* (July/August 1988), pp. 16–25 and (September/October 1988), pp. 20–31.

DeCURTIS, ANTHONY. "Living Legends." *Rolling Stone,* September 21, 1989, pp. 89–100.

———. "Willie Dixon and the Wisdom of the Blues." *Rolling Stone,* March 23, 1989, pp. 109–114.

DEZUTTER, HANK. "Willie Dixon." *TWA Ambassador* (July 1980), pp. 39–41.

GOLKIN, PETE. "Blacks, Whites, and the Blues: The Story of Chess." *Living Blues* (September/October 1989), pp. 22–30.

GILLETT, CHARLIE. *Making Tracks.* London: Sunrise/Dutton, 1974.

GURALNICK, PETER. *Feel Like Going Home.* London: Dutton, 1971.

———. *Lost Highways.* New York: Vintage, 1982.

"Howlin' Wolf Interview." *Living Blues* (Spring 1970), pp. 13–17.

"Intermission with Fats." *Living Blues* (November/December 1977), pp. 16–19.

LARNER, JEREMY. "What Do They Get from Rock and Roll?" *Atlantic Monthly* (August 1964), pp 44–49.

O'NEAL JAMES and AMY O'NEAL. "Eddie Boyd Interview." *Living Blues* (November/December 1977), pp. 11–15.

———. "Jimmie Rogers Interview." *Living Blues* (Autumn 1973), pp. 11–20.

———. "Jimmy Reed Interview." *Living Blues* (May/June 1975), pp. 16–37.

———. "John Lee Hooker Interview." *Living Blues* (Autumn 1979), pp. 14–22.

PALMER, ROBERT. *Deep Blues.* New York: Penguin, 1982.

———. "Muddy Waters: The Delta Son Never Sets." *Rolling Stone,* October 5, 1968, pp. 15–17.

PENN, ROBERTA. "Bo Diddley." *The Rocket* (September 1983), p. 19

RESSNER, JEFFREY. "Pat Boone." *Rolling Stone,* April 19, 1990, pp. 89–91.

ROWE, MIKE. *Chicago Blues: The City and the Music.* New York: Da Capo, 1981.

SIDERS, HARVEY. "Talking with a King: B.B. King." *Downbeat,* March 30, 1972, pp. 14–15.

STEARNS, MARSHALL. *The Story of Jazz.* New York: Mentor, 1958.

STUCKEY, FRED. "Chuck Berry: Exclusive." *Guitar Player* (February 1971), pp. 20–23.

SUMLIN, HUBERT. "My Years With Wolf." *Living Blues* (September/October 1989), pp. 10–18.

"Top Ten." *Rolling Stone,* February 13, 1986, p. 37.

"Turkish Tycoons: The Erteguns." *Time,* July 28, 1967, p. 43.

WELDING, PETE. "John Lee Hooker: Me and the Blues." *Downbeat,* October 3, 1968, pp. 15–17.

———. "Muddy Waters — Last King of the South Side?" *Downbeat,* October 8, 1964, pp. 18–19.

WHITE, CHARLES. *The Life and Times of Little Richard.* New York: Harmony, 1984.

CHAPTER 2: ELVIS AND ROCKABILLY

"Beware Elvis Presley." *America,* June 23, 1956, p. 295.

CONDON, E. "What Is an Elvis Presley?" *Cosmopolitan* (December 1956), pp. 54–61.

"A Craze Called Elvis." *Coronet* (September 1956), pp. 153–7.

"Elvis: A Different Kind of Idol." *Life,* August 27, 1956, pp. 101–9.

"Elvis Presley: He Can't Be But He Is." *Look,* August 7, 1956, pp. 82–5.

ESCOTT, COLIN and MARTIN HAWKINS. *Sun Records.* New York: Quick Fox, 1975.

FLANAGAN, BILL. "Johnny Cash, American." *Musician* (May 1988), pp. 97–111.

FRICKE, DAVID. "Ricky Nelson, 1940–85." *Rolling Stone,* February 13, 1986, pp. 16–20.

GOLDBERG, MICHAEL. "The Wisdom of Solomon." *Rolling Stone,* November 22, 1984, pp. 39–40.

GOLDROSEN, JOHN. *Buddy Holly.* New York, Putnam, 1979.

"Great Elvis Presley Industry." *Look,* November 13, 1956, pp. 98–100.

HILBURN, ROBERT. "Invincible Jerry Lee Lewis." Reprinted in the *Seattle Times,* November 29, 1981, p. E14.

HOPKINS, JERRY. *Elvis: A Biography.* New York: Warner, 1971.

House of Representatives, *Congressional Record,* 86th Congress, First Session, March 3, 1959, vol. 105, part 3, p. 3203.

"Howling Hillbilly Success." *Life,* April 30, 1956, p. 64.

ISLER, SCOTT. "The Everly Brothers in Arms." *Musician* (July 1986), pp. 38–48.

KAYE, ELIZABETH. "Sam Phillips Interview." *Rolling Stone,* February 13, 1986, pp. 53–88.

"Lonely and All Shook Up." *Time,* May 27, 1957, p. 101.

MABLEY, JACK. "Radio and Video." *Downbeat,* August 8, 1956.

McGEE, DAVE. "Carl Perkins." *Rolling Stone,* April 19, 1990, pp. 73–77.

PALMER, ROBERT. "Billy Burnette Rekindles the Family Magic." *Rolling Stone,* November 27, 1980, pp. 16–17.

———. *Jerry Lee Lewis Rocks.* New York: Delilah, 1981.

PATOSKI, JOE. "Rock 'n' Roll's Wizard of Oz." *Texas Monthly* (February 1980), pp. 101–4.

POND, STEVE. "Roy Orbison, 1936–1988." *Rolling Stone,* January 26, 1989, pp. 22–33.

"Presley Spells Profit." *Newsweek,* February 18, 1957, p. 84.

"Roll Britannia." *Time,* February 25, 1957, p. 60.

"Rock 'n' Roll Battle." *Collier's,* October 26, 1957, p. 101.

"Rock 'n' Roll Riot." *Time,* May 19, 1958, p. 50.

SWENSON, JOHN. *Bill Haley: The Daddy of Rock and Roll.* New York: Stein and Day, 1984.

CHAPTER 3: DICK CLARK, DON KIRSHNER, AND THE TEEN MARKET

ARONOWITZ, ALFRED. "The Dumb Sound." *Saturday Evening Post,* October 5, 1963, pp. 91–5.

BUNZEL, PETER. "Music Biz Goes Round and Round." *Life,* May 16, 1960, pp. 118–20.

"Challenging the Giants." *Newsweek,* December 23, 1957, p. 70.

CLARK, DICK. *Rock, Rolls, and Remembers.* New York: Popular, 1978.

Girl Groups. (Film.) Steven Alpert, director, MGM, 1983.

Hearings Before the Subcommittee on Communications of the Committee on Interstate and Foreign Commerce: Amendment to the Communications Act of 1934. United States Senate, 85th Congress, Second Session.

"Jockeys on a Rough Ride." *Newsweek,* December 7, 1959, p. 98.

"Jukebox." *Time,* July 27, 1959, p. 33.

"Payola Blues." *Newsweek,* November 30, 1959, p. 94.

"Rock 'n' Roll Rolls On 'n' On." *Life,* December 22, 1958, pp. 37–43.

SCHIPPER, HENRY. "Dick Clark." *Rolling Stone,* April 19, 1990, pp. 67–70.

"St. Joan of the Jukebox." *Time,* March 15, 1963, p. 50.

SPITZ, ROBERT. *The Making of Superstars.* New York: Doubleday, 1978.

"Tall, That's All." *Time,* April 14, 1958, p. 64.

CHAPTER 4: SURFBOARDS AND HOT RODS: CALIFORNIA, HERE WE COME

ALEXANDER, SHANA. "Love Songs to the Carburetor." *Life*, November 6, 1964, p. 33.

BURT, ROB. *Surf City, Drag City*. New York: Blandford, 1986.

LEONARD, GEORGE. "California." *Look*, September 25, 1962, pp. 27–31.

NICOLOSI, VINCE. "Jan and Dean Interview." *Trouser Press Collector's Magazine* (March/April 1980).

"The No. 1 State: Booming, Beautiful California." *Newsweek*, September 10, 1962, pp. 28–38.

"Surf's Up." *Time*, August 9, 1963, p. 49.

"Two 'Empire States'—How They Compare." *U.S. News and World Report*, December 24, 1962, pp. 44–9.

WALTON, SAMUEL. "The Endless Summer of the Beach Boys." *Saturday Evening Post* (October 1976), pp. 52–3.

"A Way of Life." *Life*, September 1, 1961, pp. 47–53.

"What To Know and What To Look For." *Life*, October 19, 1962, pp. 69–70.

WOLFE, TOM. *The Kandy-Colored Tangerine Flake Streamline Baby*. New York: Farrar, Straus & Giroux, 1966.

CHAPTER 5: BOB DYLAN AND THE NEW FRONTIER

"Angry Young Folk Singer." *Life*, April 10, 1964, pp. 109–16.

BLUESTEIN, GENE. "Songs of the Silent Generation." *New Republic*, March 13, 1961, pp. 21–2.

CARMEN, WALT. "The Children of Bobby Dylan." *Life*, November 5, 1965, pp. 43–50.

CHAPLIN, RALPH. *I. W. W. Songs*. (32nd ed.). Chicago: Chaplin, 1968.

"The Faculty." *Time*, June 16, 1961, p. 56.

"The Folk and the Rock." *Newsweek*, September 20, 1965, pp. 88–90.

"Folk Girls." *Time*, June 1, 1962, pp. 39–40.

"Folk Singers and Their Fans." *Look*, August 27, 1963, pp. 49–59.

"Fourth Man Makes the Trio Tick." *Business Week*, February 23, 1963, pp. 56–8.

FRICKE, DAVID. "Roger McGuinn." *Rolling Stone*, August 23, 1990, pp. 107–110.

GLEASON, RALPH. "The Times They Are A 'Changin'." *Ramparts* (April 1965), pp. 36–48.

HENTOFF, NAT. "Profiles." *New Yorker*, October 24, 1964, pp. 64–90.

"Hoots and Hollers on the Campus." *Newsweek,* November 27, 1961, pp. 84–5.

"It's Folksy, It's Delightful, It's a Craze." *Newsweek,* June 6, 1960, pp. 112–13.

"Just Playin' Folks." *Saturday Evening Post,* May 30, 1964, pp. 24–9.

LEONARD, GEORGE. "The Big Change in Teen Listening Habits." *Look,* January 3, 1961, p. 60.

"Let Us Now Praise Little Men." *Time,* May 31, 1964, p. 40.

"Like From Halls of Ivy." *Time,* July 11, 1960, pp. 56–7.

LODER, KURT. "Bob Dylan Interview." *Rolling Stone,* June 21, 1984, pp. 14–24.

O'CONNOR, RORY. "Albert Grossman's Ghost." *Musician* (June 1987), pp. 25–32.

"Real Long Hair." *Newsweek,* July 9, 1962, p. 53.

RODINTZKY, JEROME. *Minstrels of the Dawn.* Chicago: Nelson-Hall, 1976.

SCADUTO, ANTHONY. *Bob Dylan.* New York: New American Library, 1979.

SHELTON, ROBERT. *No Direction Home: The Life and Music of Bob Dylan.* New York: Ballantine, 1986.

"Sybil With a Guitar." *Time,* November 23, 1962, pp. 54–60.

"Take a Boy Like Me." *Time,* March 29, 1963, p. 40.

CHAPTER 6: THE BRITISH INVASION OF AMERICA

"Air Pollution." *Newsweek,* August 16, 1965, p. 76.

"Beatlemania." *Newsweek,* November 18, 1963, p. 104.

Billboard, January 25, 1964.

———, February 15, 1964.

BROWN, MICK. "A Conversation with George Harrison." *Rolling Stone,* April 19, 1979, pp. 71–5.

"Building the Beatle Image." *Saturday Evening Post,* March 21, 1964, p. 36.

BURDON, ERIC. "An Animal Views America." *Ebony* (December 1966), pp. 160–70.

COTT, JONATHAN. "Mick Jagger: The King Bee Talks." *Rolling Stone,* June 29, 1978, p. 45.

Daily Express, May 19, 1964, p. 1.

Daily Mirror, May 18, 1964.

DALTON, DAVID. *The Rolling Stones.* New York: Knopf, 1981.

DAVIES, HUNTER. *The Beatles.* New York: McGraw-Hill, 1968.

"Evolution." *Time,* February 17, 1967, p. 76.

GAMBACCINI, PAUL. "A Conversation with Paul McCartney." *Rolling Stone,* July 12, 1979, pp. 39–46.

GARBARINI, VINCE and JOCK BAIRD. "Has Success Spoiled Paul McCartney?" *Musician.* (February 1985), pp. 58–64.

"George, Paul, Ringo and John: The Beatles in the U.S." *Newsweek,* February 24, 1964, pp. 54–7.

"Interview with John Lennon and Yoko Ono." *Playboy* (January 1981), pp. 75–106.

"Keith Richards Interview." *Playboy* (October 1989), pp. 59–65.

"Letters To the Editor." *Newsweek,* September 13, 1965.

LEWIS, RICHARD WARREN. "When Four Nice Guys Go Ape." *Saturday Evening Post,* January 28, 1967, pp. 24–7.

"Mick Jagger and the Future of Rock." *Newsweek,* January 4, 1971, pp. 44–8.

"Monkee Do." *Time,* November 11, 1966, p. 84.

MURPHY, MARTY. "I Took Paul and Ringo to the Space Needle." *Seattle Times,* February 12, 1984, pp. F1–4.

"New Madness: R & B Quartet Called the Beatles." *Time,* November 13, 1963, p. 64.

New York Times, February 17, 1964, p. 20.

"Pop's Bad Boys." *Newsweek,* November 29, 1965, p. 94.

"The Real John Lennon." *Newsweek,* September 29, 1980, pp. 76–7.

"Rolling Again." *Newsweek,* November 17, 1969, p. 137.

"Romp! Romp!" *Newsweek,* October 24, 1966, p. 102.

SANCHEZ, TONY. *Up and Down with the Rolling Stones.* New York: Morrow, 1979.

SCADUTO, TONY. *Mick Jagger: Everybody's Lucifer.* New York: Berkeley, 1974.

SCHAFFNER, NICHOLAS. *The British Invasion.* New York: McGraw-Hill, 1983.

Washington Post. February 12, 1964.

WENNER, JANN. *Lennon Remembers: The Rolling Stone Interviews.* San Francisco: Rolling Stone, 1971.

CHAPTER 7: MOTOWN: THE SOUND OF INTEGRATION

GEORGE, NELSON. *Where Did Our Love Go? The Rise and Fall of the Motown Sound.* New York: St. Martin's, 1985.

GOLDBERG, MICHAEL. "Berry Gordy." *Rolling Stone,* August 23, 1990, pp. 67–77.

"No Town Like Motown." *Newsweek,* March 27, 1965, p. 92.

"Recorddom's Berry Gordy." *Ebony* (February 1966), pp. 33–9.

"The Supremes Make It Big." *Ebony* (June 1965), pp. 80–4.

TARABORRELLI, RANDY. *Motown.* New York: Doubleday, 1986.

WILSON, MARY. *Dreamgirl: My Life as a Supreme.* New York: St. Martin's, 1986.

CHAPTER 8: ACID ROCK

BROWN, JOE. ed. *The Hippies.* New York: Time, 1967.

FONG-TORRES, BEN. "Love Is Just a Song We Sing." *Rolling Stone,* February 26, 1976, pp. 58–87.

FRICKE, DAVID. "Lou Reed Interview." *Rolling Stone,* May 4, 1989, pp. 37–42.

GLEASON, RALPH. "The Flower Children." *Encyclopedia Britannica Book of the Year 1968.* Chicago: Britannica, 1969, pp. 790–1.

—— *The Jefferson Airplane and the San Francisco Sound.* New York: Ballantine, 1969.

GOLDBERG, MICHAEL. "The San Francisco Sound." *Rolling Stone,* August 23, 1990, pp. 91–6.

GOODMAN, FRED. "Jerry Garcia Interview." *Rolling Stone,* November 30, 1989, pp. 66–74.

GUSTAITIS, RASA. *Turning On.* New York: New American Library, 1969.

HANSEN, JAY. *The Other Guide to San Francisco.* San Francisco: Chronicle, 1980.

"The Hippies." *Time,* July 7, 1967, pp. 18–22.

"Jerry Garcia: In Search of the X Factor." *Musician* (October 1981), pp. 64–73.

JOHNSON, JON. "Janis." *Pulse* (April 1985), p. 23.

KUNEN, JAMES SIMON. *The Strawberry Statement.* New York: Avon, 1970.

"Marty Balin." *Spin* (August 1990), p. 68.

"Open Up, Tune In, Turn On: The Airplane." *Time,* June 23, 1967, p. 53.

PERRY, CHARLES. "From Eternity to Hell." *Rolling Stone,* February 26, 1976, pp. 38–55.

——. *The Haight-Ashbury.* New York: Vintage, 1984.

"The Rock Family." *Life,* September 24, 1971, pp. 46–53.

"Star Plunged from Heights to Depths: Skip Spence." *Seattle Times,* November 1, 1981, p. F12.

SWARTLEY, ARIEL. "Lou Reed Reconsidered." *Mother Jones* (June 1985), pp. 16–19.

"Swimming to the Moon: Jim Morrison." *Time,* November 24, 1967, p. 106.

"This Way to the Egress: The Doors." *Newsweek,* November 6, 1967, p. 101.

"Timothy Leary Interview." *Playboy* (September 1966), pp. 93–112.

WATROUS, PETER. "Touch of Gray Matter." *Musician* (December 1989), pp. 35–45.

WOLFE, BURTON. *The Hippies.* New York: New American Library, 1968.

CHAPTER 9: FIRE FROM THE STREETS

"After the Riots." *Newsweek,* August 21, 1967, pp. 18–19.

"An American Tragedy: 1967." *Newsweek,* August 7, 1967, pp. 18–34.

BROWN, JAMES. *James Brown: The Godfather of Soul.* New York: MacMillan, 1986.

"Cities." *Time,* August 4, 1967, pp. 13–18.

CLEAVER, ELDRIDGE. *Soul On Ice.* New York: Delta, 1968.

ELLISON, MARY. *The Black Experience.* New York: Harper, 1974.

FLEXNER, STUART BERG. *I Hear America Talking.* New York: Van Nostrand, 1976.

GARLAND, PHYL. "Eclipsed Singer Gains New Heights." *Ebony* (October 1967), pp. 47–52.

HIRSHEY, GERRI. *Nowhere To Run: The Story of Soul Music.* New York: Times Books, 1984.

JONES, LEROI. *Blues People.* New York: Morrow, 1963.

"Lady Soul: Singing Like It Is." *Time,* June 28, 1968, pp. 62–66.

LLORENS, DAVID. "Wilson Pickett." *Ebony* (October 1968), pp. 130–35.

"Pop Singers: James Brown." *Time,* April 1, 1966, p. 75.

"The Races: Hot and Cool." *Newsweek,* April 22, 1968, pp. 24–66.

"Rampage and Restraint." *Time,* April 19, 1968, pp. 15–17.

SANDMEL, BEN. "Katie Webster." *Musician.* (April 1990), p. 16.

SANTORO, GENE. "James Brown." *Pulse* (October 1986), pp. 27–31.

SHAW, ARNOLD. *The World of Soul.* New York: Coronet, 1971.

"Singers: Aretha Franklin." *Time,* January 5, 1968, p. 48.

"Take Everything You Need Baby." *Newsweek,* April 15, 1968, pp. 31–34.

CHAPTER 10: MILITANT BLUES ON CAMPUS

"At War With War." *Time,* May 18, 1970, pp. 6–14.

BOOTH, STANLEY. "Bring Billy Gibbons His Burden." *Musician* (September 1988), pp. 70–9.

"Class of '69." *Newsweek,* June 23, 1969, p. 63.

COX, BILLY. "Jimi Hendrix." *Guitar Player* (May 1989), p. 47.

CROWE, CAMERON. "Jimmy Page and Robert Plant Talk." *Rolling Stone,* March 13, 1975, pp. 33–7.

"A Dignified Protest." *Time,* March 29, 1968, p. 56.

FELDER, ROB. "Black Sabbath." *Rolling Stone,* October 19, 1978, p. 28.

GRIFFIN, BRIAN. "AC/DC Classic Big Rock." *Pulse* (August 1985), p. 34.

HENDERSON, DAVID. *Jimi Hendrix: Voodoo Child of the Aquarian Age.* New York: Doubleday, 1978.

"Lean, Clean and Bluesy: John Fogerty." *Time,* June 27, 1969, p. 58.

"Lifting a Siege." *Time,* May 10, 1968, pp. 77–9.

"The Rebellion of the Campus." *Newsweek,* May 18, 1970, pp. 28–33.

"Rebirth of the Blues." *Newsweek,* May 26, 1969, pp. 82–5.

REDDING, NOEL. "Inside the Jimi Hendrix Experience." *Musician* (August 1986), pp. 64–78.

"Rose Petals and Revolution." *Time,* November 28, 1969, p. 90.

ROSENMAN, JOEL, JOHN ROBERTS, and ROBERT PILPEL. *Young Men with Unlimited Capital.* New York: Harcourt Brace Jovanovich, 1974.

SHERIDAN, KEVIN and PETER. "T-Bone Walker: Father of the Blues." *Guitar Player* (March 1977), pp. 22–56.

"Singing Is Better Than Any Dope." *Newsweek,* October 19, 1970, p. 125.

"Voice of Experience: Jimi Hendrix." *Newsweek,* October 9, 1967, pp. 90–92.

WELCH, CHRIS. *Hendrix.* New York: Flash, 1973.

WILD, DAVID. "The Band That Wouldn't Die." *Rolling Stone,* April 5, 1990, pp. 45–8.

"Woodstock Remembered." *Rolling Stone,* August 24, 1989, pp. 61–92.

CHAPTER 11: AFTERMATH OF THE SIXTIES

"Down to Old Dixie and Back." *Time,* January 12, 1970, pp. 42–6.

"ELO: America Sees The Light." *Rolling Stone,* August 24, 1978, p. 12.

"Elton John Interview." *Playboy* (January 1976), pp. 57–70.

"The Girls Letting Go." *Newsweek,* July 14, 1969, pp. 68–71.

HERBST, PETER. "Linda Ronstadt Interview." *Rolling Stone,* October 19, 1978, pp. 57–59.

———. "James Taylor Interview." *Rolling Stone,* September 6, 1979, pp. 38–43.

"James Taylor: One Man's Family of Rock." *Time,* March 1, 1971, p. 45.

"Return to Good-Times Rock." *Time,* June 2, 1975, pp. 59–60.

"Rock and Roll's Leading Lady: Joni Mitchell." *Time,* December 16, 1974, pp. 63–66.

"Rock Goes to College." *Time,* September 23, 1974, pp. 90–91.

ROWLAND, MARK. "Life's Lessons: Jackson Browne and Bonnie Raitt." *Musician* (August 1989), pp. 57–90.

SOOCHER, STAN. "The Poco Reunion." *Musician* (February 1990), pp. 94–98.

"Timothy Leary." *MacLean's,* November 15, 1976, p. 4

VALLELY, JEAN. "Linda Ronstadt Interview." *Playboy* (April 1980), pp. 85–116.

WHITE, TIMOTHY. "Old Wounds, New Bandages: James Taylor on the Mend." *Musician* (April 1988), pp. 70–80.

CHAPTER 12: THE ERA OF EXCESS

BERNSTEIN, PETER. "Growth Rocks the Record Industry." *Fortune,* April 23, 1979, pp. 59–68.

CHRISTOPHER, RITA. "Every Night Fever." *MacLean's,* May 15, 1977, pp. 55–9.

CROWE, CAMERON. "David Bowie Interview." *Playboy* (September 1976), pp. 57–72.

"Disco Takes Over," *Newsweek,* April 2, 1979, pp. 56–64.

GILMORE, MIKAL. "Stan Cornyn." *Rolling Stone,* November 30, 1978, p. 40.

GOLDMAN, ALBERT. "The Disco Style: Love Thyself." *Esquire,* June 20, 1978, pp. 76–8.

"The Gorillas Are Coming." *Forbes,* July 10, 1978, pp. 41–6.

GREENBERG, PETER S. "Rock and Big Bucks." *Playboy* (January 1981), pp. 201–70.

GREENE, BOB. *Billion Dollar Baby.* New York: New American Library, 1974.

"Hotspots of the Urban Night." *Time,* June 27, 1977, pp. 56–7.

ISLER, SCOTT. "Gregg Geller." *Rolling Stone,* February 22, 1979, pp. 28–29.

"The Man Who Sells the Sizzle: Al Coury." *Time,* December 25, 1978, pp. 48–49.

MCCARDELL, CHARLES. "Kraftwerk." *Trouser Press* (November 1981), p. 14.

"Now, The Self-Centered Generation." *Time,* September 23, 1974, pp. 84–5.

"Pop Records: Moguls, Money and Monsters." *Time,* February 12, 1973, pp. 61–63.

POST, HENRY. "Sour Notes on the Hottest Disco." *Esquire,* June 20, 1978, pp. 79–86.

"The Rockers Are Rolling in It." *Forbes,* April 15, 1973, pp. 28–39.

ROSENBLUM, CONSTANCE. "Discomania." *Human Behavior* (November 1978), p. 27.

SWENSON, JOHN. "15 Years of Making Kisstory." *Billboard,* January 21, 1989, p. K5–25.

"Tyrannical King Coke." *Time,* April 16, 1973, pp. 69–70.

"Vaudeville Rock." *Time,* October 30, 1972, p. 81.

"Where Have the Flowers Gone?" *Newsweek,* September 5, 1977, pp. 24–30.

WOLFE, TOM. *Mauve Gloves and Madmen, Clutter and Vine.* New York: McGraw-Hall, 1976.

CHAPTER 13: PUNK ROCK AND THE NEW GENERATION

"Anthems of the Blank Generation." *Time,* July 11, 1977, pp. 46–47.

AZERRAD, MICHAEL. "Searching for the Cure." *Rolling Stone,* September 7, 1989, pp. 47–50.

BURGESS, ANTHONY, and JOHN LOMBARDI. "Plastic Punks." *Psychology Today* (November 1977), pp. 120–26.

CIOE, CRISPIN, and RAFI ZABOR. "The New Reggae." *Musician* (November 1981), pp. 48–50.

"The Clash." *Musician* (May 1981), pp. 45–72.

"Commando Squad Attacks Musicians' Coop." *In These Times,* June 13–19, 1979, p. 20.

CONSIDINE, J.D. "The Police." *Musician* (December 1981), pp. 59–65.

DANCIS, BRUCE. "Artistic Control and Records Too." *In These Times,* June 4–17, 1980, pp. 20–21.

———. "Reggae Today." *In These Times,* October 25–31, 1978, p. 23.

———. "Tom Robinson Talks to ITT." *In These Times,* May 16–22, 1979, p. 24.

DAVIS, JEROME. *Talking Heads.* New York: Vintage, 1986.

DROZDOWSKI, TED. "Full Metal Justice." *Musician* (January 1989), pp. 44–52.

GILMORE, MIKAL. "The Clash: Anger on the Left." *Rolling Stone,* March 8, 1979, p. 22.

———. "The Talking Heads." *Rolling Stone,* November 29, 1979, pp. 23–24.

HALASA, MALV. "The English Beat Can't Stop Dancing," *Rolling Stone,* November 13, 1980, pp. 24–25.

HAMSHER, JANE. "Stiv Bator and the Dead Boys." *Damage* (July 1980), p. 12.

HEY, JOHN D. *Britain in Context.* Blackwell: Oxford, 1979.

HOCHSWENDER, WOODY. "Slam Dancing." *Rolling Stone,* May 14, 1981, pp. 29–32.

HOPKINS, TOM. "Dada's Boys." *MacLeans,* June 13, 1977, p. 42.

ISLER, SCOTT. "Blondie." *Trouser Press* (June 1981), pp. 19–23.

———. "Fear and Loathing on the West Coast." *Trouser Press* (June 1980), pp. 20–23.

KOZAK, ROMAN. *This Ain't No Disco: The Story of CBGB.* Boston: Faber & Faber, 1988.

McCORMICK, MOIRA. "Richard Hell." *Trouser Press* (November 1982), p. 14.

McNEIL, LEGS. "The Devil Finds Work for Idol Hands To Do." *Spin* (September 1990), pp. 29–32.

———. "We're A Happy Family." *Spin* (August 1986), pp. 66–71.

MARCUS, GREIL. "Pete Townshend Interview." *Rolling Stone,* June 26, 1980, pp. 34–39.

———. "Wake Up!" *Rolling Stone,* July 24, 1980, pp. 38–43.

MARSH, DAVE. "It Takes a Lot to Laugh: The Punks." *Rolling Stone,* September 21, 1978, p. 21.

PALMER, ROBERT. "Joy Division." *Musician* (August 1988), pp. 85–88.

"Prep or Punk." *Mademoiselle* (June 1980), pp. 182–84.

"Rock Bottom: Punk Fashions." *Newsweek,* June 20, 1977, pp. 80–81.

Rock on Right." *Billboard,* August 22, 1981, p. 53.

"The Sky Above, the Beat Below." *Time,* April 7, 1980, p. 75.

SOMMER, TOM. "Black Flag." *Trouser Press* (June 1983), pp. 23–24.

———. "Adam Ant." *Trouser Press* (July 1981), p. 13.

STEVENSON, RAY. *Sex Pistols File.* London: Omnibus, 1980.

WATROUS, PETER. "Sting." *Musician* (December 1987), pp. 60–74.

WILD, DAVID. "Elvis Costello Interview." *Rolling Stone,* June 1, 1989, pp. 59–68.

YOUNG, CHARLES M. "Visions of Patti." *Rolling Stone,* July 27, 1978, pp. 51–54.

ZABOR, RAFI. "John Lydon's PiL." *Musician* (November 1984), pp. 42–48.

ZUCKERMAN, ED. "The Rise of Rock Against Racism." *Rolling Stone,* December 14, 1978, pp. 40–41.

CHAPTER 14: I WANT MY MTV

BAROL, BILL. "1989: MTV." *Newsweek,* July 3, 1989, pp. 50–1.

CONNELLY, CHRISTOPHER. "Ratt: Lap Dogs of the Devil?" *Rolling Stone,* December 6, 1984, p. 50.

"The Copycats That Are Chasing Music Television." *Business Week,* September 3, 1984, pp. 57–8.

DEMARTINO, DAVE. "Decalog." *Billboard,* December 23, 1989, pp. D8–12.

DUTKA, ELAINE and WILLIAM TYSON. "MTV Faces a Mid Life Crisis." *Time,* June 29, 1987, p. 67.

"The Eurythmics." *Trouser Press* (October 1983), p. 13.

FARREN, MICK. "Surface Noise." *Trouser Press* (August 1982), p. 46.

FOLTZ, KIM. "Michael Jackson Inc." *Newsweek,* February 27, 1984, pp. 66–7.

GREEN, JIM. "Culture Club Comes Clean." *Trouser Press* (June 1983), pp. 16–18.

"His Highness of Haze: Prince." *Time,* August 6, 1984, p. 62.

"Human League." *Trouser Press* (August 1982), p. 35.

JAFFE, LARRY. "What Hath Video Wrought, Parts I & II." *Pulse* (September 1986), pp. 32–5; (October 1986), pp. 57–9.

JEFFREY, DON. "Growth Levels Projected in Music Video." *Billboard,* June 17, 1989, p. 4.

"JVC Celebrates Shipping 200 Million Units." *Billboard,* January 14, 1989, p. 58.

KAPLAN, PETER. "MTV: 21st Century Box." *Esquire* (March 1983), p. 222.

LEARNER, MICHAEL. "The Heavy Metal Frenzy." *Newsweek,* August 10, 1987, p. 59.

LODER, KURT. "Dress Right." *Rolling Stone,* June 23, 1981, pp. 14–19.

LUPO, JANE. "Spandau Ballet." *Trouser Press* (September 1981), pp. 16–17.

MCDONALD, PATRICK. "Whitney Houston Rocks to the Top." *Seattle Times,* October 4, 1987, p. L1.

MACKAY, GILLIAN. "The New Wizard of Pop." *Maclean's,* July 23, 1984, pp. 38–43.

MILANO, BRETT. "Def Leppard Roars Back." *Pulse* (September 1987), pp. 46–51.

MILLER, JIM. "Britain Rocks America—Again." *Newsweek,* January 23, 1984, pp. 50–7.

PERRY, STEVE. "Prince in the Purple Decade." *Musician* (November 1988), pp. 83–99.

"The Peter Pan of Pop: Michael Jackson." *Newsweek,* January 10, 1983, pp. 52–54.

PORTER, MARTIN and STEVEN SCHWARTZ. "Madonna." *Seattle Times,* April 7, 1985, p. L1.

SALEWICZ, CHRIS. "Kemp: A Revolt into Style." *The Face* (October 1982), pp. 25–26.

"Sing a Song of Seeing." *Time,* December 26, 1983, pp. 54–64.

SWAN, CHRISTOPHER. "Rock Video Quakes." Reprinted in *Seattle Times,* June 2, 1985, p. E1.

TANNENBAUM, ROB. "George Michael: Artist or Airhead?" *Musician* (January 1988), pp. 27–36.

"Top 100." *Rolling Stone,* November 16, 1989, pp. 55–121.

"The Tour, the Money and the Magic." *Newsweek,* July 16, 1984, pp. 64–70.

"Why He's a Thriller." *Time,* March 19, 1984, pp. 54–63.

YOUNG, CHARLES. "Def Leppard Pulls Out of the Fast Lane." *Musician* (December 1987), pp. 76–82.

CHAPTER 15: THE PROMISE OF ROCK-AND-ROLL

AZERRAD, MICHAEL. "Public Enemy." *Rolling Stone,* September 22, 1988, p. 32.

"Bad Rap." *Time,* September 1, 1986, p. 20.

COCKS, JAY. "Roll Them Bones." *Time,* September 4, 1989, pp. 58–62.

"Compact Disc Players." *Consumer Reports* (May 1987), pp. 283–4

DIMARTINO, DAVE and ED CHRISTMAN. "CD Edges Up on Cassette as Top Format." *Billboard,* June 23, 1990, p. 1.

FLIPPO, CHET. "Bruce Springsteen." *Musician* (November 1984), pp. 53–8.

FRICKE, DAVID. "All Star Line-Up for Band-Aid Shows." *Rolling Stone,* July 18/August 1, 1985, p. 17.

———. "Lou Reed: Back on the Streets." *Rolling Stone,* March 9, 1989, p. 26.

———. "Rage and Roll." *Rolling Stone,* June 28, 1990, pp. 49–57.

FUCHS, LAWRENCE. *The American Kaleidoscope.* Hanover: University Press of New England, 1991.

GEORGE, NELSON, SALLY BARNES, SUSAN FLINKER and PATTY ROMANOWSKI. *Fresh: Hip Hop Don't Stop.* New York: Random, 1985.

GRAHAM, BILL. "U2 Give Themselves Away." *Musician* (May 1987), pp. 79–90.

"Grateful Dead Aid Rain Forests." *Rolling Stone,* November 3, 1988, p. 17.

HAMILTON, TISH. "Rap It Up." *Rolling Stone,* July 12–26, 1990, p. 109.

HILBURN, ROBERT. "Bruce Springsteen." *Oregonian,* October 24, 1980, p. G1.

HUNTER, NIGEL. "Key Global Markets Love That CD." *Billboard,* March 11, 1989, p. 1.

HUTCHINSON, JOHN. "Luminous Times: U2." *Musician* (October 1987), pp. 68–78.

LICHTMAN, IRV. "Music Shipments Hit New Mark." *Billboard,* March 18, 1989, p. 1.

LODER, KURT. "Bruce Springsteen Interview." *Rolling Stone,* December 6, 1984, pp. 19–22.

MCADAMS, JANINE. "A Message of Peace Outta Compton." *Billboard,* May 5, 1990, p. 26.

MACDONALD, PATRICK. "Vinyl's Final Days." *Seattle Times,* January 21, 1990, p. L1.

"Making of a Rock Star." *Newsweek,* October 27, 1975, pp. 57–63.

MARSH, DAVE. *Born To Run.* New York: Dell, 1981.

MEHLER, MARK. "Recorded Music Ranks Highest in Growth." *Billboard,* December 10, 1988, p. 75.

NATHAN, DAVID. "Jungle Brothers Bear Civilized Message." *Billboard,* March 3, 1990, p. 30.

———. "Rap." *Billboard,* December 24, 1988, pp. R1–80.

NELSON, PAUL. "Springsteen Fever." *Rolling Stone,* July 13, 1978, p. 13.

PARELES, JON. "RUN-D.M.C." *Rolling Stone,* July 18/August 1, 1985, p. 24.

———. "How Rap Moves To Television's Beat." *New York Times,* January 14, 1990, Section 2, pp. 1–2.

POND, STEVE. "On Her Own Terms: Tracy Chapman." *Rolling Stone,* September 22, 1988, pp. 55–63.

RESSNER, JEFFREY. "Going, Going, Gone?" *Rolling Stone,* April 20, 1989, p. 15.

"Rock's New Sensation." *Time,* October 27, 1975, pp. 48–58.

RUSSELL, LISA. "M.C. Hammer." *People,* June 24, 1990, pp. 59–60.

SPAHR, WOLFGANG. "West German Record Industry." *Billboard,* February 17, 1990, p. 3.

STOUT, GENE. "Rock Radio Drags On." *Seattle Post-Intelligencer,* July 17, 1988, p. F1.

"Technology." *Time,* January 1, 1990, p. 104.

INDEX

T

Talking Heads, 226–27, 229, 275
Tampa Red, 5
Taylor, James, 206
Television (the group), 226
Television:
    impact on rock 'n' roll, 22, 48–50, 96, 104–5, 142, 257–58
Temptations, 142–43
Ten Years After, 187
Them, 127–28
Townshend, Pete, 107, 108, 240, 275
Turner, Ike, 12
Turtles, 101

U

Ultravox, 253–54
U-2, 280

V

Valens, Ritchie, 59
Van Halen, 264–65
Van Zandt, Steve, 275
Velvet Underground, 149–50
Village People, 220

Vincent, Gene, 46
Visage, 254, 258

W

Wailers, 236–37
Waters, Muddy, 1, 6–9, 19–20, 128–29
Weather Report, 200
Wells, Mary, 136
Who, 109–12
Williamson, Sonny Boy II, 11–12
Wilson, Jackie, 135
Winter, Johnny, 188–89
Wolf, Howlin', 9–10
Woodstock festival, 195–96

X

X, 242

Y

Yardbirds, 126
Yes, 202
Young, Neil, 209

Z

ZZ Top, 189